THE COLLECTED POETRY
AND PROSE
of
LAWRENCE FIXEL

The Collected Poetry and Prose

of

Lawrence Fixel

Edited and with an Introduction
by Gerald Fleming

SIXTEEN RIVERS PRESS

Published by Sixteen Rivers Press
P.O. Box 640663
San Francisco, CA 94164-0663
www.sixteenrivers.org

Library of Congress Control Number: 2019956065
ISBN (softcover): 978-1-939639-24-0
ISBN (hardcover): 978-1-939639-23-3

Photos of Lawrence Fixel by Mark Citret,
copyright © Mark Citret 2020

Interior art by Stephanie Sanchez,
copyright © Stephanie Sanchez 2020

Book design by Wayne Smith

We would like to thank the supporters of Sixteen Rivers Press.
Without them, neither the press nor this book would exist.

Contents

from *The Scale of Silence: Parables* (1970)

from *The Edge of Something* (1977)

Through Deserts of Snow (1975) . . . .

The Book of Glimmers (1979)

from *Unlawful Assembly: A Gathering of Poems, 1940–1990* (1994)

Lost Subjects/Found Objects (1998)

from *All This Is Here (2003)*

Time to Destroy/to Discover (1972)

Uncollected Works

Words on Lawrence Fixel

Introduction

A few months after Lawrence Fixel died in 2003, his wife, the psychotherapist Justine Jones Fixel, and I convened a meeting at their home to talk about publishing Fixel's work.

Years earlier, Fixel had asked me to be his literary executor, and, perhaps rashly, I'd agreed. As to what he had in mind for his work after his death, we said we'd talk of it "in good time," but the years passed and we two had plenty of other things to talk about; that "good time" never arrived.

Seated in the Fixel living room in San Francisco, along with Justine Jones Fixel and me, were people who knew him and his work: the writers Carl Rakosi, Morton Marcus, Laura Beausoleil, Edward Mycue, Christina Fisher, Leonard Gardner, Thomas Sanchez, psychologist Robert Cantor, and Anthony Bliss from U.C. Berkeley's Bancroft Library, where the Lawrence Fixel archive resides.

The topics at the meeting were two: what to do and who would do it.

As to the first, there was general agreement that a major edition of this important writer's work be published. But would it be a selected works or a collected? There was no consensus on this, but the trend, given the volume of his writings, drifted toward a selected.

As to who would do it, with the exception of two, each adult in the room was of sound mind and demurred. Christina Fisher, Fixel's assistant at the time, volunteered to help me if I took on the task. Fixel's dear friend Carl Rakosi volunteered to write the introduction.

My vote in the process was for a collected, but a selected seemed more manageable, and, for me, in terms of the scope of the project, a bit of a relief.

The next day, though, Rakosi phoned me.

"Jerry, I've been going through the books, and I urge you to put out a collected—this is consistently astonishing work. I'll start on an introduction soon."

I assured Rakosi that we had plenty of time—I had a book coming out and couldn't start on the project for at least a year.

I was 56 at the time, so can't blame it on my youth that I assured a man of 99 that he had plenty of time, but I think those who knew Rakosi might forgive my failing; he was blade-sharp, energetic, and mobile. When he died nine months later at the age of 100, his friends were shocked: there was the sense that he'd live forever, bright spirit that he was.

That introduction never got written.

The writer Lawrence Fixel was born in Brooklyn on January 7, 1917, to Max and Frieda Fixel, Jewish immigrants with "decidedly socialist leanings."[1] Soon after Fixel's birth, the family moved to White Plains, New York, where Fixel's father ran a store that sold sporting goods, toys, and bicycles. Fixel worked in that store as a young man, and he also took jobs caddying at the local golf course and selling in a shoe store.

His attempt to start a socialist club at his White Plains high school fell flat, as people familiar with Westchester County's wealth at the time might imagine. Here is Fixel's comment on the political leanings of one of his fellow students:

> I do recall a conversation with someone to whom I mentioned some Socialist ideas and his response: "But I'm a Republican." I questioned him further, asking why he felt this way. "My father is a Republican, and so is my father's father."

After high school, stymied by his milieu, Fixel went out on his own and moved to Manhattan. Encouraged by an English teacher in White Plains, he had literary ambition along with political zeal. Of this trajectory of his life, Fixel says:

> I have first to . . . make a distinction between what happens on the scale of "me and my lifetime" and on the broader scale of what was happening in the world—the personal life placed in the historical context of such matters as the Depression, the rise of Fascism, and the approaching war.
>
>   War then appears as a common denominator: born during the First World War, participating in the Second World War, and with the Cold War that followed, permeated with the apparent "imminence" of a possible Third World War. More than this being Jewish at the time of Nazism and the Holocaust made me aware of living through a period when the "unthinkable" and the "unspeakable" were among the major events of the time.

Given that backdrop and what was to come, New York City was a fit for him. In the mid-thirties, political ferment was everywhere, and at the age of nineteen, he was keen to take part in it:

> It was exciting even if sometimes mystifying. All kinds of things were happening: the Proletarian Theater, the emergence of Clifford Odets as a playwright. Besides the theater, dance and the performing arts, there was the ferment among writers and artists. WPA [Works Progress Administration] artists for the first time were being commissioned to do public murals . . . note that the government, even in the midst of the Depression, thought it was worthwhile to subsidize these things—along with building roads and bridges and public buildings and so on. It was all part of this ferment and emergence.

The young Fixel spent much time in Union Square listening to soap box orators (both leftist and rightist) and widened his discovery of poetry; he was energized by the work of Auden, MacNeice, Spender, C. Day Lewis, and of e. e. cummings, who lived near him. He became friends and chess mates with the poet Kenneth Fearing, founder of *Partisan Review*, and Fearing's wife Rachel Meltzer. Spending time with the Fearings helped embolden his emergence as a poet. (Decades later, Fixel discovered that his friend Rakosi was an old friend of Fearing's as well.)

During these years, Fixel came in contact with Isidor Schneider, a writer closely associated with the Communist magazine *The New Masses*. Schneider told Fixel about the Federal Writers' Project, a WPA program established by President Roosevelt in 1935. He applied and was told that in order to join he must first be on Home Relief, the welfare program in place at that time. Easily qualifying for that program, he became one of the FWP's youngest members.

The Federal Writers' Project was a dynamic enterprise, varied in its undertakings. Fixel was assigned to a group run by black writers—Richard Wright and Ralph Ellison among them—and was tasked, as part of a New York City Guide project, to write about New York church architecture: Harlem's churches in particular.

The Writers' Project group was close-knit and valued solidarity, holding regular rent parties to help each other out (one of which, attended by Fixel, featured Leadbelly as entertainer).

He remembers the Project's dynamism:

> It also served an educational purpose—at one time there was a series of lectures; one was given by Thomas Mann, another by Alfred Adler. The format was lecture and discussion. The political thing was that we were involved in the issues of preserving and extending the Federal Arts programs along

with the larger issues: War and Peace and Fascism. We marched in the May Day Parade. The writers' contingent carried pens—pens that were made of heavy cardboard, painted black, outlined with gold leaf, with a stick to hold [them] in place. We would raise and lower [them]—hoist these pens . . . while we were chanting . . . "Wages Up! Prices Down! Make New York a Union Town!". . . I don't know how big that contingent was . . . maybe seventy-five . . . but identified with the whole labor movement.

Also during these years (1935–38), Fixel became focused, as many leftist, politically active Americans were, on the atrocities of the Spanish Civil War. He went to the Civilian War Effort office and volunteered to be an ambulance driver, but was told that the quota had already been met. (Anyone who remembers Fixel's reputation as a driver might breathe a retrospective sigh of relief at this.)

After his time in the Federal Writers' Project, he lived in at least six different places (including a three-dollar-a-night room without windows; a fifth-floor walk-up in Greenwich Village where he had a wounded Spanish Civil War survivor as a roommate; and the Chelsea Hotel, which charged $4.50 a week in the years before its owners went bankrupt in 1939).

Rather than remain in New York and attend college (aside from ever-present financial issues bearing on that, he was an adamant autodidact, content to let his own interest guide his studies), Fixel launched off on a hitchhiking/train-hopping tour westward through the American South. During his travels he kept a journal, *Journey South*, a young man's rather Whitmanesque celebration/inquiry into the idea of America—its diversities and unities. In one late entry from 1940, he writes:

> It takes not one year but many years, not one place but many places, not one person but many persons—to know this America.
>
> But more than that it takes a way of knowing. It takes a lot of asking— the manufacturer as well as the prostitute.
>
> And asking of oneself as well.
>
> I went the hard way over four thousand miles in the past year. I stood under sun on hot roads waiting.
>
> Most of the people I spoke to were waiting also—for answers to their lives. And as they waited the face of the land changed. The coasts pushed together, the boundaries moved. There was a stirring among the people, asking where do we go from here? Some said, what does it matter, let's go.
>
> America, my land, my people . . .
>
> So the quick-talking New York mechanic went to the slow-speaking states, so the farm boys came to build bombers in Los Angeles. So the Texas

lads found other Texas lads when they came to Detroit. Some brought their girlfriends. Some brought their wives.

America, my land, my people . . .

The writer arrived in Los Angeles at the beginning of a decade that would soon see the bombing of Pearl Harbor (a place few on the mainland had heard of at the time; Hawaii itself was a distant idea), the country's entry into World War II, and the ultimate unleashing of the atom bomb.

Before departing for the journey south he'd left the writings he'd done in New York City in the custody of a trusted friend. The friend disappeared, and with him, Fixel's earliest work.

Fixel found a place in the Echo Park neighborhood of Los Angeles, first living in a shack behind the home of Clara and Ed Robbin, whose previous tenant in the shack had been Woody Guthrie. (Robbin subsequently wrote a memoir of his time with Guthrie, *Woody Guthrie and Me: An Intimate Reminiscence.*) Fixel later rented a furnished room in the home of Carl and Gerda Lerner, who themselves were influential: Carl a respected film editor (*Twelve Angry Men*, others), and Gerda an author and early feminist historian (*The Creation of Patriarchy*, others). The Lerners, committed Communists at the time, were later blacklisted during the McCarthy scourge and left Los Angeles for New York.

In Los Angeles Fixel found employment as an office worker for a steel and iron broker, then worked for a firm that sold and repaired manikins; all the while he continued to write.

The war broke out. He volunteered for the Merchant Marine, was immediately put on a freighter that set sail for six months, stopping at ports along the western coast of South America, then was transferred to another ship for another six months in ports including Australia, India, through the Suez Canal to Algeria, then to New York, where he sailed on a converted Liberty Ship transporting Canadian troops to Europe. His ship arrived in France two days after D-Day, June 8, 1944.

His commitment completed, Fixel returned to Los Angeles, where he married Alexa Rifkin that same year. He and Alexa had a daughter, Kate, born in 1944. The marriage lasted only four years, and the couple divorced in 1948.

Fixel missed his connection to writers and fellow poets in New York. He had only a few poet-compatriots in Los Angeles, but among them was Tom McGrath, who not only influenced him in his writing, but also helped him publish in literary magazines.

Newly divorced, Fixel moved to San Francisco, where he met Justine Jones. The two married in 1952, and that city became Fixel's home for the next five decades, the place where his writing and his connection to the literary scene flourished.

He and Justine moved into a house on Willard Street, at the top of San Francisco's Mount Parnassus—a curiosity not lost on him. Ruth Witt-Diamant, the founder and then-director of San Francisco State's highly respected Poetry Center, lived a few doors away, and a friendship developed and deepened. Within Witt-Diamant's poetry coterie, the Fixels became dear friends with George and Mary Oppen, who lived on lower Polk Street, and with Carl Rakosi and (later) his partner Marilyn Kane, who lived close by on 17th Avenue. Fixel and his wife eventually developed a wide web of friendships with poets young, old, local, national, and international, including Édouard Roditi, the Franco-American surrealist poet.

The Witt-Diamant/Fixel-Willard Street soiree and party scene drew many poets, some visiting from out of town, including Marianne Moore, Dylan Thomas, Theodore Roethke, W. H. Auden, Langston Hughes, Allen Tate, and William Carlos Williams.

Friends and relatives tell of long nights in the Fixel home with compatriots and Fixel's sister Pearl, a committed Communist and member of the California Labor Chorus who once sang with Paul Robeson at a campaign rally for Henry Wallace. (Pearl and her husband, family lore goes, smuggled Communist leader Archie Brown, wanted by the FBI for his political activities, in the trunk of their car from Chicago to San Francisco.) The Fixel home was a lively one, with friends dropping in freely and staying for passionate, thoughtful conversation.

In the late sixties, Fixel began a monthly writing critique group at his place on Willard. He was a kind, welcoming man with a solidity about him that other writers trusted, confident that their work would be respected in a group that followed the rules he insisted on.

Over a period of years, many writers attended, with the group ultimately moving to William Dickey's home on Liberty Street in San Francisco. Those attending either regularly or occasionally over the years included Ruth Witt-Diamant, Shirley Kaufman, George Keithley, Raymond and Maryann Carver, Jack Gilbert, Morton Marcus, Laura Ulewicz, James Schevill, Edward Mycue, Linda Gregg, Harold Norse, Susan McDonald, Josephine Miles, Robert Bly, Charles Simic, Honor Johnson, Wayne Johnson, Mark Linenthal, Frances Jaffer, Adrianne Marcus, William Dickey, Gina Berriault, Leonard Gardner, Ann Stanford, James Tate, Frances Mayes, Lennart Bruce, Sonya Bruce, Rosalie Moore, Kathleen Fraser, and Nanos Valaoritis.

Eventually, though, an incident occurred in the group that caused Fixel to disband it. He wouldn't talk about it subsequently, but it was clear that someone had broken with the protocol of civility he'd established. He called it "a personality conflict" caused by "irreconcilable differences" among two or three members. I've heard rumors of the precipitating incident, but could never get Fixel to delve into it. He was a "gentle warrior," as his friends called him, who avoided conflict of any sort. The incident grieved him, and it grieved him to end the group after five robust years.

The San Francisco decades were rich for Fixel, for though he was not "famous," the local (and, for him, widening) literary world suited him. Respected by his peers, he published steadily in avant-garde and mainstream journals, and his relatively low profile (see "The Smile at the Foot of the Ladder") gave him *time*: time to read, time to be at his desk writing/revising his deeply philosophical and allegorical prose poems, parables, and poetry, and—not least—time to engage in his beloved correspondence. He became a partner with Dennis Koran and Edward Mycue in Panjandrum Press, an avant-garde poetry publisher in San Francisco. His work with Panjandrum further widened his connection with the literary world.

Among the Lawrence Fixel papers at U.C. Berkeley's Bancroft Library are letters, both incoming and outgoing (he usually made carbon copies of his own typewritten correspondence) with more than a hundred writers, either occasional or frequent. Many notable writers are included in those cataloged boxes, including Andrei Codrescu, Jack Gilbert, Michael Heller, Raymond Carver, Jack Marshall, Mary Randall, George Oppen, Laura Ulewicz, and others. His correspondence with the seminal prose poet Russell Edson was prolific, and the letters between Cid Corman in Japan and Fixel comprise perhaps the thickest folder in the collection. A selected edition of the letters themselves would make for fine reading.

Fixel's publishing career took off slowly. He worried that his lack of formal education (he never formally attended university) would keep him on the periphery, an outsider in the literary world, but this was not the case. Though many of his narratives may contain "outsider" motifs, the literary camaraderie he found in San Francisco propelled him forward in his work.

It was an effort for him to take time away from that work to send writing out to magazines, but he did, and by the mid-sixties his poetry was appearing regularly. During those years he began teaching humanities and poetics part-time at the University of California San Francisco medical school campus, and at the same time became associated with the larger-than-life George Hitchcock and his magazine *kayak*, which published many writers whose work still resonates today. Hitchcock published Fixel's *The Scale of Silence*, a collection of his parables, in 1970, and his list of publications grew from that date: books, chapbooks, and magazine publications in England, France, and the United States. Raymond Carver nominated his chapbook *Through Deserts of Snow* (included in the present collection), published by Capra Press, for a Pushcart Prize.

A bibliography of Fixel's publications can be seen at the back of this book. To the end of his life he continued publishing in progressive/experimental magazines, his work often sought by editors decades younger than he. The last part of this book includes "Words on Lawrence Fixel," short essays by writers and editors about him and his writing. They help to sketch out the complex portrait that was Lawrence Fixel and his far-reaching body of work.

As editor, it's not my role to engage in an extensive analysis of Fixel's work, but I will offer a few thoughts on its orientation and scope for readers new to him.

Any collection of American prose poetry and parables would be incomplete without the work of Lawrence Fixel. He was one of the first sustained practitioners of the prose poem and the parable in the country. (Regarding the parable, see Fixel's own definition of it in his foreword to *Truth, War, and the Dream-Game.*)

His early work did include poetry in verse. In that realm, though rarely employing rhyme (distinguishing himself from many of his generation), his work was controlled, measured, and stylistically conservative. He experimented in the use of "projective verse," or composition by "field"—certainly influenced by Charles Olson, but also by Robert Duncan, whom he knew and with whom he studied. In some instances (see "Time to Destroy/to Discover") Fixel blew his own field wide open, taking all the space he could get to make his poems, contracting his earlier lyricism into Olsonian breath-units.

This was an exception in his verse, though, and when reading Fixel's lineated poems one can almost feel the poet wanting to break into a more discursive prose field, where his essential questions could be given room to be expressed without the compression that a tightened, postmodern poetics requires.

The prose poem does not have a long history as a legitimate literary form in this country. Though introduced in France more than 150 years ago and regarded as a valid form on the continent ever since, it wasn't until the publication of Michael Benedikt's (now, sadly, out of print) *The Prose Poem: An International Anthology* (1976) that the form was seriously considered in the United States. (And even then, it was not widely appreciated for decades. A dozen years ago at a book fair, I approached an editor at the table of a well-known university press and asked if they'd be open to considering a book of prose poems. He raised a single eyebrow most dramatically and said, faux-generously, "Well, I *suppose* we would . . ." Things have changed since then.)

Fixel was compelled by a European aesthetic, and, not surprisingly, drawn to Kafka, studying Kafka deeply. He was also drawn to philosophers, Hegel among them, and his attention to both literature and philosophy informs both his prose poems and parables. It's easy to see Hegel's dialectic in Fixel's work, as well as the concept of thesis/antithesis/synthesis, as Christina Fisher suggests in her essay on Fixel in this book. (The dialectic is an essential element of much writing in this volume; the reader may often feel as if a voice from "the other side" is present below the text, almost sub rosa.)

One insight into the working of Fixel's mind might be found in a reproduction of Pieter Bruegel the Elder's *The Peasant and the Nest Robber*, which the writer kept on a bulletin board in his study. It was one of his favorite paintings. In it, the large figure of a peasant points to a man perched in a tree, robbing a bird's nest of its eggs. It's been called among the most difficult of Bruegel's paintings to interpret. Some have said that the painting is the depiction of an old Dutch proverb: "He who knows where the nest is has the knowledge; he who robs it has the nest." Fixel had another, concomitant interpretation. The main figure appears to be unconsciously stepping into a creek as he focuses on the man in the tree. In an interview, Fixel speculated that the painting might also be called *The Next Step?*— depicting "someone who is oblivious and doesn't know where his next step is going to lead him, which is right into the drink." This sense of *threshold* and *boundary*—the presence of something about to happen that might not be the predicted outcome—is central to this writer's work.

A reader expecting speed and rhetorical pyrotechnics will be disappointed here, instead finding careful craftsmanship approaching (often elliptically) the struggles inherent in the state of being human. What *won't* be found are easy answers, bromides, or nostrums. Fixel adamantly regards the reader as equal partner/equal struggler in our stupidities and contradictions—equal, intelligent participants—as if to say that we're playwrights and actors and audience at once, seeking coherence and meaning while rarely finding a scintilla of either, but recognizing paradox and contradiction and leaving the theater being forced to think again about what we were once certain of. (The poet Jack Marshall, at a celebration for Fixel's eightieth birthday, offered the ancient quote, "There is no answer. Seek it lovingly," as an insight into Fixel and his lifelong work.)

Which doesn't mean he was nihilist. Surely at least partly because he was alienated by the treatment of American Communists at mid-century, he didn't vote—a fact that infuriated his wife, Justine—but nonetheless possessed an adamant optimism, a belief in the power of Enlightenment-engendered logic, an abiding hope that the rational would one day prevail.

This optimism can be seen readily in his prose poems and parables, as can what one might call a visionary template. He did not write "political" poems— polemics so obvious in their intent that they're dead as soon as they hit the page. But he wrote many poems with a political overlay that transcends national boundaries and governmental systems, as if he were writing from an Everyman point of view. A new reader might find strange, at first, his apparently random capitalizations— the Zoo, the Circus, the General, the Caretaker, to use some examples of apparent orthographic eccentricities, but they aren't at all random, for the names and roles in society are symbolic for Fixel of "stock" players in the milieu in which we continue to stew.

Fixel was a careful writer and a habitual reviser. Often he'd return to work that he had "completed" thirty years earlier to revise it radically while retaining its characteristic steadiness, solidity, deep intelligence, and gentle voice—a voice worth returning to again and again.

Lawrence Fixel's *Truth, War, and the Dream-Game: Selected Prose Poems and Parables* (Coffee House Books: Minneapolis, 1991) begins the present collection. That book included both newly published poems/parables and work from earlier collections. I regarded poems/parables appearing in *Truth, War* that had also appeared in earlier books as primary texts, as Fixel had the opportunity to revise them, and he preferred the newer versions—therefore I didn't reprint the same poems from their original volumes. For that reason, some of the succeeding volumes might seem thin; in fact, they included many pieces appearing in *Truth, War.*

The selections are not arranged chronologically, but in a way that seemed to make for the most fluid reading of the Fixel oeuvre. I found that although decades might have passed between particular books, the author's voice remained remarkably consistent. Included toward the end of this collection are writings, published in various magazines, that never made it into books. I found them almost uniformly excellent, no matter their date.

While this book comprises almost all of Fixel's published work, much other material exists. His *Book of Glimmers* in its published version holds only a fraction of the "glimmers" Fixel wrote. ("An endless supply of lenses," the writer once called them.) About a thousand more single-spaced, typed-on-onion-skin pages of these writings exist and can be found, along with the rest of the Fixel archive, at University of California Berkeley's Bancroft Library. I made an attempt to select and "curate" a few hundred more pages of these, apportioning parts to various poets I admired and asking them to select sections worthy of publication, but I found their tastes so varied that the compilation had a disunified feeling, and I abandoned the project. Such would need to be a more long-term, singular effort. His unpublished novel "Journey for a Witness," written during his years in Rome, also is not included here. Thousands of pages of notebooks, many including original prose and poetry, exist as well. It's my hope that I haven't missed any published work that appeared in magazines, but that remains possible; his career was long, and his publications wide.

Fixel's copious correspondence with other writers itself could fill more volumes. The letters between him and Cid Corman referred to earlier, for example, or between him and Russell Edson, are worth study. Most of Fixel's own letters are typed, single-spaced, and carbon-copied. (Fixel used to say that the biographical details of his life were not as important as the time he spent "in the company of writers," both in person and in these prolonged correspondences.)

This unpublished body of work might someday engage a future scholar with an eye toward publication. Those interested in such a project should feel free to contact me at geraldfleming@gmail.com. If for reasons of incapacity or mortality I'm no longer able to do so in person, I hereby grant permission. I ask only that you do a good job, a careful job.

Many of Fixel's books, though similar in their habits of paragraphing, were laid out slightly differently from the way they are here. I came to realize that this was more a matter of publishers' predilections than Fixel's. I've standardized them here.

The author's use of ellipses was prolific, but not profligate. They had meaning: not simply a denotation of continuation or something "missing," but either a suggestion of irresolution or a different kind of continuation: that of the human condition; therefore I've left them intact. (Often ellipses are used to open a piece of writing, as if Fixel wanted the reader to enter rather a liminal state before entering the piece itself: a sense of unsure footing necessary to countenance so much of his work.)

Grammatical errors or misspellings/nonstandard/inconsistent spellings not caught by earlier editors have been corrected. And in cases where Fixel dated his work, those dates were left in. Some pieces are "double dated," Fixel's way of telling the reader the date of the original and that of the revision.

I would like to thank Christina Fisher for her great help and collaboration in the early stages of this project, and for her words on Fixel, Sharon Coleman for— among other things—offering manifold insight and encouragement as well as her own essay, Mark Citret for his photos, Stephanie Sanchez for the use of her exquisite paintings, Kate Fitch Frankel Nikolenko, Joshua Frankel, and Wendy Berkelman for helping with biographical information, Ed Mycue for support, encouragement, critical information, and his essay/riff on Justine Jones Fixel—so important a partner in Fixel's life. I thank Peter Money not only for his words on Fixel but also for the important biographical details available in his Gale Research interview, upon which I depended; thanks to Peter Johnson, David Lazar, and Donald Soucy for their own words on Fixel. To Molly Giles, Sharon Olson, Stephen Vincent, Helen Wickes, Ellery Akers, Judith Serin, Frances Mayes, Thomas Sanchez, Jack Marshall, Cole Swensen, Michael Heller, Michel Delville, Joyce Jenkins, and Richard Silberg, thank you for your various kindnesses. Naomi Schwartz's support was abiding and essential, and I grieve that she did not live to see this this book published. Thanks to Carolyn Miller, Steve Gilmartin, and Wayne Smith for their fine work on the book. I thank my wife, Gerry, for tolerating my years of distraction. Thanks to Stephen

Black and Bonnie Bearden at UC Berkeley's Bancroft Library. Finally, deep thanks to Sixteen Rivers Press of San Francisco not only for their patience, but also for having faith in this complex project.

—*Gerald Fleming*
2020

---

[1] This and other quotes herein are from Peter Money's interview with Fixel, found in the Gale Contemporary Authors Autobiography series, Volume 28, pp. 135–66. I am grateful to Peter Money for this source.

In View of This It Begins

To begin at the beginning. For whatever it is, however it turns out. An offering of some kind. A contribution to be made. A niche to be filled—or is it "a need." (How often the two are confused!) For now though, this is premature. All one has to think about here are the words, the sentences. And of course what they are about, where they might be leading...

And so it is that the writer remembers that he is also a reader. That he wishes for the reader what he wishes for himself as a reader. That his attention is not a small, unimportant thing: to be played with in some game which is more self-display than meaning, more momentary than memorable. That which appears and disappears, leaving no "afterglow," no invitation or urgency for return . . .

I stand and walk toward the shelf. What I'm looking for is somewhere in the lower left-hand corner. I anticipate some difficulty, a bit of a search. But no, I extend my hand, and it is the right thing—that feeling of being guided which has happened so many times before. It has a brown cover, angels astride the globe, and various other mysterious objects. I open the magazine, and read these words on the inside page: "Once there was a man whose grandmother was a powerful magician." The magazine is *kayak No. 11*; the publication date is 1967. 1 read my own name in the table of contents, and turn to the page indicated.

PROCESS: I have this to bring into being—this that does not yet exist. As I give the work form, it acquires presence as itself. The work completed, released, then becomes available for its own subsequent history. Thus it embodies, anticipates, and shapes the future. More difficult to express, to believe, is that it does the same with the past: it changes our view of what was there; it activates and animates what was rigid and consigned.

—

This from a piece called: *Soundings*, the first of a series of conceptual, aphoristic texts. That led to the publication of *The Book of Glimmers* (Cloud Marauder, Berkeley, copublished by Menard Press, London, 1979). A beginning that led to a series of beginnings. And which I now refer to in this month of February, in this year of 1995. Words of this kind, searching and learning, to start the day, to ask impossible questions of the night.

—L. F.

Truth, War, and the Dream-Game: Selected Prose Poems and Parables, 1966–1990

(1991)

*Arrangements such as the layout of a city or building, a set of
tools, a display of merchandise, the verbal exposition of facts or
ideas . . . are called orderly when an observer or listener
can grasp the overall structure.*

—Rudolf Arnheim

*Meaning then is an indication of something beyond mere
existence, either an end and aim, or the notion of form. . . .
Any action, design, quest, or search carries meaning as purpose,
any work of art is meaning as form.*

—Erich Kahier

*All these parables really set out to say merely that the
incomprehensible is incomprehensible, and we know that
already. But the cares we have to struggle with every day:
that is a different matter.*

—Franz Kafka

for Justine: this time with time as measure

Foreword to Truth, War, and the Dream-Game

Written over a long period of time, the three texts included here—*Tracking Stations, Chance Scripts, Structural Pursuits*—involve both retrospect and prospect. That is, they are part of a still-evolving effort. The primary text, *Tracking Stations*, completed in 1981, was offered for publication by itself. I have left it here unchanged as an example of "making a case" for what a specific genre, the parable, has to offer.

I realized then that the ancient parable, as a brief narrative, sometimes with an explicit moral, sometimes as riddle or enigma, still provoked controversy: in the conflicting interpretations of readers, critics, scholars. But in contrast to a living form, it might be considered vestigial, an anachronism. The modern parable, still not widely known, was assigned largely to the seminal examples of Kafka and Borges and their penetrating, often devastating illumination of a world split between psyche, spirit, and material concerns. At present, however, an increasing number of writers are finding in the parable a flexible, versatile instrument especially suited to convey the distilled essences of a fragmented world.

For my own part, I felt the challenge of finding other realms for subject and theme: for instance, the more neglected immediate issues of politics and war, religious cults, terrorism, etc. At the same time, I felt the need to articulate a particular view. I found this in the observation that both the ancient and modern parable often involved the overthrow of an expectation: the reversal of some deep-grounded assumption or explicit belief. Examples of this could be found not only in Kafka and Borges, but in Jesus, Kierkegaard, and Brecht. Even further, the continuum could be extended to Heraclitus, to the Midrash, to the Zen koan, the Sufi story. Over this whole panorama, paradox is a key element, opposing the identity of opposites to any commonsense, linear, or literal view. Specifically, I found a particular use of metaphor as analog: juxtaposing actual, virtual, and fictional worlds, transposing and connecting the different scales, planes, and dimensions of reality.

At this point it may be useful to offer some minimum distinction between prose poem and parable. As I see it, the parable is required to be *about something*—something that connects with, even though it conflicts with, our sense of the world. Thus it challenges our assumptions while, paradoxically, it evokes some feeling of universality. The prose poem, characteristically, as its name implies, is viewed from its ambiguous location somewhere between poetry and prose. Thus it tends to be lyrical, subjective, impressionistic. Based more on self-expression than the combination of concept and metaphor offered by the parable, it can provide a counterpoint of *possibility* to balance the parable's greater concern with *necessity.*

There is more to be said about the passage from *Tracking Stations* to *Truth, War, and the Dream-Game.* In brief, I continued writing, exploring, until the boundaries between "prose poem" and "parable" shifted and narrowed. Again, in retrospect, this appears mainly as a shift in emphasis from "content" to "form." Specifically, it involved more latitude for a free play of the mind: for impulse to have an equal share with intention. This, I suggest, is indicated by the very titles of the more recent work: *Chance Scripts* and *Structural Pursuits*. It is hoped that, while each piece is a discrete entity, the reader can envision further: behind this a shared, perceivable world.

There are some other considerations that I have left for the afterword. These concern the possibility of readings and rereadings based more on thematic content. The last point here is that words on a page need to be released and renewed in the reader's mind. Released to acquire—whatever thought or feeling they may evoke—their own subsequent history. So that a work of words may join the play of mind—join in a kind of dance, where meanings remain to be dreamed upon, not finally determined.

—L. F.
March 1991

Tracking Stations:
New & Selected Parables, 1966–1981

PART ONE: THE FLIGHT/THE QUEST

We live in a time when flight and quest bear the closest resemblance.

—

No longer objects of compassion, they seem to have reached—and settled into—some realm we are not permitted to enter.

Flight Patterns

Between the void and the sheer event.
                    —Paul Valéry

1.
It is said, of the millions who undertake the journey, that the greatest number are lost somewhere along the way. To prove this, evidence is produced, statistics gathered, witnesses summoned. There are even films of the long, straggling procession, which presumably reveal the fate of the missing. Yet it appears no one—ourselves included—is deterred by this, for it is equally intolerable to remain where we are.

2.
. . . Word continues to arrive from monitors at the highly equipped tracking stations. They report a whole series of unexplained dots and dashes on the flickering screens. Even the most experienced observers—using the most advanced techniques—concede that the habitual flight patterns can no longer be interpreted. . . .

3.
I have seen some of the incoming messages. They bear such strange notations as "missing in action," "dead on arrival," etc. With so many different languages, from such different worlds, the gap between what is transmitted and received continues to widen.

4.
I have resolved not to be upset by any of this. To limit myself to what can be verified by sensory evidence. One thing is clear: whether we travel the direct route of desire, or detours of illusion, we still miss connection. Something is *there*—ahead of or behind us—and we are drawn in that direction. For a time we seem to have arrived. . . . But as the wind changes, the mist descends, we can no longer tell where we are.

5.
Let us suppose, for instance, that you have been where I have been. We meet one afternoon in a village in a neighboring country. . . . Joining the crowd in the plaza, we observe the stately walk of the costumed women. Moving on, we notice in contrast the immobility of the vendors: the heavy bodies squatting beside the earthen jars.

6.
Is the scene familiar? Then let memory take a further step: to that moment when armed men in gray uniforms appear. . . . Suddenly we feel a sharp intersection of

competing gestures, of inviting and disturbing fragrances. Someone drops petals in front of the candle-lit altar; someone else throws poisoned meat to the hungry dogs. . . . Speaking of this later, disturbed by our fragmented impressions, the question arises: What name can we give to this land?

7.

We may of course continue the search, each producing letters, photographs, documents. Or simply recognize that, between any two witnesses, we can expect these differences. Each might then retreat into a private retrospect. . . . But what if we decide to give up these wanderings, returning to this body, this present time? It may then occur to us that what signifies this world is nothing else but the current of our feeling. And as for the flesh that dissolves, disappears, who can say it will not appear again? If not in this form, this familiar image, then perhaps as an *intention* that moves through silence and the quickening wind.

1978/1979

Above It All

Destiny, if you thought I had the potential for departure,
you should have given me wings.

—Pierre Reverdy

If God intended us to fly . . . The proverb becomes a cliché, a joke, then disappears. But not entirely. With our desire to ascend, to sail through the air, comes also a sense of transgression. We go so far, so fast, carried along by sheer momentum. Then suddenly something happens to remind us that—unlike cloud, bird or star —here we are intruders.

Remember the tale of "The Horse with One Wing"? For those who don't, it goes like this: Once there was a band of wild horses who roamed freely in open space. Then came settlers who captured and tamed them. Still later came those whose secret intention was to turn them into food for domestic pets. . . . One day, as the story goes, one of the horses noticed a small wing growing out of his side. He would run with the others, then find a place alone. There he began leaping, dreaming of flight. When the band was reduced to a few survivors, he knew it was time. He ran to the edge of a nearby cliff. . . .

Intolerable alternatives—are there no others? It would seem that there are those who still persist in their search. Even now someone is at work in a garage, a small shed, to find a solution. Not far from where we live, there is one almost ready. Some morning soon, a figure will appear on a roof, waiting to lift off. Not an apparition, I assure you, but someone like ourselves . . .

I write this as testimony, this fifteenth day of April, 1980. The same calendar tells me also: *born this day in 1452, Leonardo da Vinci.*

Give Up, Give Up

As Kafka tells it: a man wandering in a strange city notices a policeman standing nearby. He hesitates, then decides to approach and ask directions. . . . Stopping here, we might expect a familiar response, appropriate to the ordinary situation. This is quickly shattered, however, by the extraordinary reply: "Give up. Give up."

In the absence of further details in the original, I have invented some that would soften the impact, make the reply sound less absolute. I have even written a story that—however intended at the time—now appears as a kind of response. . . .

➤

. . . *Stephen X.* has escaped from a prisoner of war camp. He wanders through a procession of deserting soldiers, refugees in a nation falling apart, close to revolution. . . . When the policeman approaches, he has to choose whether to remain or to run. Deciding to stay, his mind forms a desperate strategy: "To reach the man beneath the uniform, I would speak of his own family, loved ones, their need for peace and survival." In my story then, the appeal is successful: the policeman responds, directing him to a place where he finds food and shelter.

➤

If the reference to the "fiction" is not enough, I offer something from my own experience. It was many years ago; I was then perhaps twenty or twenty-one, hitch-hiking through the southern part of this country. It was my very first journey; I still pictured myself as an unarmed "wanderer" in a hostile world. . . . When the man in uniform came toward me, I remembered stories of vagrants being jailed, sentenced to hard labor. So that when he spoke, I could hardly hear what he was saying. When I was able to sort it out, I finally realized the kind intention. . . .

➤

Kindness or cruelty—so far I have looked at it only from one side. The picture changes when I also recognize in *myself* the one who wears the uniform. And in this role I have to ask, have to remember: what has been my response? For reasons I cannot now pretend to understand, I have at times turned away with indifference and cruelty.

So that there remains—as in a disturbing, recurring dream—the image of one who continues to wear the disordered clothes of the wanderer. The one who must wait, without protection and without certainty, for the figure coming toward him: *so do ye unto me.*

1979

Destruction of the Temple

*Finally, because of its situation at the center of the cosmos, the temple or the sacred
city is always the meeting point of the three cosmic regions: heaven, earth, hell.*

—Mircea Eliade

1.

First the incident on the airstrip, then the even more shocking news: the "slaughter" of
nearly a thousand men, women, and children. What is still not certain, as I write this,
is whether murder or suicide is involved. Like everyone else, I wonder how it started,
why it ended this way. But even to begin to understand, one would need to know
who these people were, what they were searching for. Also it seems, something to help
explain the extraordinary power and magnetism of their leader.

2.

As the days go by, there is talk about *The Temple* as an unfortunate attempt by those
without power and influence to create a community outside the laws that bind us
together. Inevitably, the words *utopia* and *paradise* are heard, sounding strange in
this secular, cynical time. I am reminded of certain dark events, centuries ago, when
groups of *heretics* went to their deaths. Am I wrong in recalling that, through periods
of persecution and torture, the victims experienced a kind of *ecstasy?*

3.

. . . All this passes through my mind as I read the letters of Q. and N., which arrived
today. They write from different parts of the world, offering sympathy along with
their views on what has happened. What remains in my mind are their notions that
The Temple, like any other structure, is subject to decay and dissolution. For any
form to contain a substance, it must be flexible enough to withstand the pull of con-
flicting desires. At other times I might be grateful for the metaphysical speculation,
the extravagant mind-play. This time, however, I feel their elegant reasoning as an
intrusion—as if upon a simple private grief of my own. . . .

4.

. . . I have started daily walks in the neighborhood, feeling it better to be outside—
away from the enclosed space of walls and mirrors. Occasionally I stop in where
coffee and wine are served, taking the opportunity for brief, casual conversation.
While the subject is not mentioned directly, it is clear the fate of *The Temple* is on
everyone's mind. . . .

5.

I still do not feel ready to respond to Q. and N. But I am spending more time at home, doing the usual chores, reading and writing in my notebook. Yesterday I made the following entry: *Each time we search for light, a greater darkness enters.* I started to cross this out, then decided to leave it in; later I added: *What can we do without the visible Heaven, the tangible Hell?*

6.

The bodies have arrived in metal coffins. We're told that, after a while, those that can be identified will be shipped to their *city of origin.* (Curious that the word *home* is not used in these accounts.) Besides the walks, I have been taking buses and streetcars to unfamiliar sections of the city. And writing in my notebook: *The world wavers in my sight. It grows harder to tell who or what we are.*

7.

Some days ago I finally wrote—just brief notes—to Q. and N. I merely thanked them for their letters, said I was well, promised to write again when I had time and energy. Even this much was a great effort, since I felt absent, encased in silence. I have made no plans, beyond routine things that have to be done, for today, tomorrow or the following days. I will continue writing here—not with hope of understanding or release—but only as long as I recognize my own voice. . . .

1978/1979

The Departure/The Return

Zero, as he has chosen to be called, signals his comrades and moves up the steps to enter the plane. He is a robust man, tall and with a thick black moustache. At the moment, with success of the operation almost assured, his whole being expresses exultation. . . . This takes place after he and a dozen followers—using numbers instead of names—enter the government palace and, with perfect timing, emerge with the "emblems" of power. The quality and rank of the hostages—an Archbishop, a General, two Ambassadors—indicates what they have achieved. . . . In a short while, the plane takes off. Nervous moments follow as government planes appear, but as these veer off, without further pursuit, confidence and exhilaration return. The flight continues without incident; less than an hour later—securing asylum in a neighboring country—they make a safe landing.

At the palace, the besieged Dictator is being interviewed. Facing the "eyes and ears of the world," he declares it is better to suffer this momentary humiliation than the loss of so many lives. (Whether he actually says "innocent" lives is not clear from the translation.) He also lets it be known that, in making this decision, he has been guided by the traditional values of Family and Religion. (Curiously, his voice and manner express the same sense of exultation shown by his opponent.)

As the news broadcast shifts to another subject, the Poet presses a button that blanks the screen. All this, he tells himself, has happened over and over again. The names and titles of the rulers change, but for the *ruled*, the round of days remains the same. . . . Some time later, still unable to return to more immediate concerns, he drifts into reverie. . . . What emerges is a figure on a platform facing a huge crowd. On the very streets now being besieged, there stands the indigenous Poet—(Brother? Comrade?)—returned from long exile. . . . Something must have happened *there and then* that cannot be forgotten. Suddenly, he experiences, as if in a real present, in his own flesh, the expectancy of the crowd. He stands beside them as Rubén Dario begins reciting "The Motives of the Wolf."

1979/1981

The Refugees/The Pilgrims

1.

Seated at the table, we look for what we remember: the gentle enthusiast, at home on his own small plot of ground. Also for the changes, in the intervening years, since he started working with the dispossessed. We notice then that his speech is softer, slower, that his hands more often gesture uncertainty. We try to imagine that part of his life: visiting refugee camps, disaster areas, talking to officials unable, unwilling to listen. . . .

2.

This is T.'s report: You see the ordinary life—which at one moment seems unalterable—thrown into turmoil, beyond intention and control. For instance, on a given day, a small boat leaves the mainland. It is poorly equipped, with an inexperienced crew. On board are dozens, even hundreds, with just the few belongings they can carry. We call them "refugees"—not exiles or outcasts—to indicate the lack of choice. . . . On another day, we receive word: a plane has crashed; there are so many victims, so many survivors. In this case, the passengers were "pilgrims" on their way from another continent to visit the sacred shrines. . . .

3.

He goes on: Between the plane that crashes and the boat sunk by gunfire or swamped by the tides, there is some connection. But what is it? We think of refugees as homeless, dispossessed. And pilgrims as on a journey, on their way somewhere, devoted and highly motivated. Yet they both seem dislocated, and in some sense interchangeable. . . .

4.

Why is T. telling us this? Is there something he wants to reconcile in himself, a feeling of being dispersed, becoming part of the endless stream of the wanderers, the uprooted? Before this, we recall, he told us anecdotes, stories that illustrated problems related to solutions. This time, however, the tone is uneasy, the voice of an inward questioning. . . .

5.

With dinner finished, we sit facing the lights of the familiar city. T. looks at his watch, mentions the hour of the departing plane. We are used to these short visits, knowing that he goes when he has to, wherever he is summoned. . . . Time for one more account, though, of that part of the world where everything, a whole nation, can be overturned: "They closed the borders, sealed the cities. Yet one group who got away—not believing what they were told—demanded to be sent back. We helped them, since this is what they wanted. They went back across—about fifty of them—and vanished. . . ."

6.

Twilight around us; the sky thick with clouds. T. seems already on his way, gone somewhere beyond us. . . . I wonder now what T. has failed to tell us. *The refugees.* *The pilgrims.* His example of those who travel by boat, by plane, leaves something out. . . . I think of the solitary figures, walking across the dry land. I see them bent and bony, leaning on a stick—going nowhere. Visible only to the barking dogs, in the most remote villages. What can we say about these—immemorial wanderers— for whom we have no name?

7.

We say goodbye, watch him turn and wave before entering the waiting taxi. We close the door, return to the table as night comes on. It has not yet come through to us (the thought arrives later, just before sleep) that we live in a time when flight and quest bear the closest resemblance.

1978

The Base Camp

I have seen their attention wander, their eyes looking toward the door, when the survivors speak. And it would be foolish, a waste of time, to try to change this. What I write here then is for myself, for those who care to remember. . . . There is no flag, no plaque, nothing left to mark the place. Yet it is *there*, as real, as tangible as the mountain itself. For without that what would I be—what would *we* have been?

I have been told it is best to remain silent. To let the others, those who come after, have their say. Well, then, listen to their voices: *Whatever it was, it is gone. With our new strength, improved equipment, we have moved the Base Camp farther than they ever dreamed possible.* . . . I recognize the tone, the self-assured authority. But then I remember: the tents lashed against the wind, the sky blurred and gray, the unknown towering over us. . . . How closely we worked together, moved together, as if gathered under a single name. How vivid those moments, whether climbing or staying behind . . . *Staying behind*: when and how did that become a choice? What was it like then, waving goodbye to the few who insisted on that final, vertical assault— and were never seen again?

◆

. . . Feeling anchored, at peace, in this warm, familiar room. Sifting through those lost days and hours, there is nothing I can retrieve or rearrange. Whatever has to be confronted, now or later, will not change the outcome. Surely it is enough to have shared those hazards, gone that far. I need not recognize the one who never wanted to leave, to step outside the safety of this room.

1981

Absent Without Leave

They have not, as of this writing, been in attendance. And from all indications, they do not plan to attend. This, in spite of the various inducements, prizes still being offered. On rare occasions, however, one stands before us: the dark face impenetrable, the words openly or implicitly accusing. . . . And after the departure, what are we left with? The sense of yet another world, closing in on itself, shut off from sight. Inevitably, we are reminded of our own presences and absences, of the distance between desire and fulfillment. Yet how to compare this with their struggle to achieve *visibility*?

◆

All this, I realize now, is somewhat misleading. It does not take into account how incredibly much the world has changed. For as it now appears, it is the *invisible* who are less vulnerable, less easily targeted. No longer objects of compassion, they seem to have reached—and settled into—some realm we are not permitted to enter. And where we still wait to be invited . . . But the invitation does not arrive. And when we open our passports, stare at the photos, we suddenly notice: *Not valid for travel in* . . . We remember something peculiar about the signs at the various terminals. There was always one that pointed toward "access," while another, just beside it, seemed to indicate "refuge." With this in mind, we begin to wonder whether there is a travel agent—one with more knowledge, more influence—who could arrange . . .

1981

The Crossing

1.

It is twilight when we reach the border. (Late summer: our first crossing.) The long line of cars. The slow inching forward. Ahead, dark-faced men in creased uniforms. Stepping out of the glass-enclosed booths, they reach for and examine the folded papers, then gesture this way, that way. We cannot tell what it means, but it seems that some will go through at once while others have further questions to answer. We take it for granted that we will be among the latter. . . .

And so it turns out. We are directed to a low building off to the side. There we enter a small, square room: plain wooden benches, watermarked walls, the faces of those who wait to learn which way they are going.

Asking the questions, the bored official scratches his neck, waves at the flies that circle the document in his hand. Finally he nods, goes to the typewriter. Placing the forms before us, he indicates where to sign. Holding the pen, our hands are wet; our fingers tremble.

But we are not through yet. Outside, another one goes through our boxes and suit-cases. (Is there something whose presence we cannot explain?) He walks away. We wait, still unaware of what has been decided. The man returns, places a small disk on the windshield. And as we remain motionless, he shrugs, points toward the road that lies ahead.

2.

We are disobeying the injunction not to travel at night. Of course it has all been explained: the condition of the road, what has happened to other travelers, etc. Thus we are reminded the journey is our own choice, our own responsibility.

All of this comes to mind as the light slowly disappears. What matters now is this nar-row strip of black asphalt; our purpose and presence centered on the turning blades, the revolving wheels. We soon notice and are disturbed by the absence of the white line. And there is no space beside the road if we should have to stop. In the swelling dark-ness, we sense the solid pavement falling away—a weightless descent into nothingness.

. . . Lights in the distance. After what seems like a long interval, they remain the same size and in the same position. At last, the lights of cars coming toward us. (Will there be some notice, sign of recognition?) Nothing happens. The space widens, darkens as they go past. And it appears as though we are going toward what they are in flight from.

. . . Remembering the warning, we watch for the appearance of animals. And from time to time, they materialize: white shapes with burning underwater eyes. We are not prepared, though, for the walkers: tattered clothing, bare legs, some kind of weight on their backs. They straighten and stiffen under the headlights.

3.
The air thickens. A long time since we have exchanged a word. Yellow knives slash the fabric of night. All the signs of impending storm—yet here we cannot tell. The dry tongue searches the dry mouth. Clothing sticks to the skin. . . . Now we are in it, but there is no name or precedent. (Knives and drums warring in the sky— but no downpour follows.) It is as though, having strayed into some off-limits area, we are being tested, forced to validate our presence. (Borders within and borders beyond.) But not knowing the purpose, what is expected, one can only hold tight to the wheel, continue staring through the windshield. . . .

4.
All this is behind us; we have indeed passed through the interminable night. Whatever it was that threatened, whatever related the shapes outside and those in our minds, the "attack" went no further than this. (The swarm of insects, the gray bird that splashed against the windshield.) Perhaps, then, this is the nature of the test: to withstand the assault on our senses, to contain and integrate what is there and what we are forced to imagine.

. . . Crossing the dry river bed, seeing the first volcano, the first convoluted growth of jungle. With night turning into day, we found ourselves involved in some vast metamorphosis, with that whole panorama—animals, plants, the earth itself— moving into light. What does it mean: this sense of passage from one state of being to another?

5.
Entering the town, we make inquiries. After a few wrong turns, we locate the narrow, tree-lined street. We drive carefully across the brown cobblestones—trying also to limit our anticipation—and at last come to the house.

A servant answers the bell. We are led to the back of the house, and then into the garden. A few minutes later, the woman—whom we have not seen for years—

appears. She stands there for a moment, among the flowers, the fruit trees, the bright-colored birds. Then with a smile, her arms extended, she comes toward us.

6.

In spite of the welcome, the warm exchange, it soon becomes clear that we live in different worlds. We have passed through the long night and emerged, but still our identity depends on where we have come from. But she has made another commitment: to these orange flowers, these green and yellow birds. And to these dark-faced people. She seems ready to share not only their songs, but their diseases. (Waking to find rats streaming across the floor. Being operated upon by the local doctor—the surgery performed on a plain wooden table.)

And so we leave the following day. For her, the encounter could be no more than an interlude. For she has crossed over—to the other side of things. She may at times look back—but only to see how far she has come. Our presence, any protection we might offer, is no longer relevant.

7.

We go further into the dry, spiked landscape. There are mountains and valleys; the climb is slow, prolonged; the descent is swift, perilous. At last on level ground, we pass abandoned cars, rusted machinery. Several times we notice the heavy birds circling above a dark mound, a weighted presence in the dust-filled air.

Stopping at a small village to slake our thirst, we move through a row of hooded, sweat-stained faces. We discover the focus of their attention—a smudged notice tacked to the wall: news of an ambush, a flood, other disasters—and recall the gray bird that found death on our windshield, other things that filled the sky that deep, wet night.

8.

We reach our destination: a village in the mountains recommended by our friend. In contrast to the landscape we have passed through, there is a lake and tall, sheltering trees. The nights are cool. We find several here who speak our language. (None of them has "crossed over.") After a few days, we decide to remain. In the time that follows, we take short trips into the surrounding countryside. Occasionally, we attend a party or a picnic. We grow accustomed to the faces, the weather. We live through various illnesses.

There are nights when we cannot sleep, mornings when we wake to the shriek of a slaughtered pig. And always those dark brown things that crawl through the cracks in the tiled floor—sickness and death in their sting.

And there are also festivals.

—

Reading the above, it is clear that not enough has been said about those moments that immediately precede the crossing. For so much then seems to weigh in the balance: all we leave behind, whatever we are going toward. We already sense what is on the other side: a place where expectations are irrelevant and have no connection with reality.

—

It is this that echoes again on another continent, perhaps a decade later. (Can it be that long?) Once more we approach the border. Surely this time, considering all we have lived through . . . We hand the green-uniformed guard our passports. He turns the pages, compares the small, glossy square with eyes, mouth, color of hair. We notice the thick leather belt, brass buckle, polished boots. (Will he be the one to discover who and what we are?) The white-gloved hand waves us on. . . .

—

It is possible, of course, that we have missed something. That we have not yet learned to make the crossing as it should be made. (Consider those who cross not once, but twice during a single day.) We are not, after all, smugglers, nor have we ever been in the pay of a hostile power.

Yet we cannot help wondering: Was it ever possible for us to be at home with those bright-colored birds, those rich, pure flowers? To understand those voices that cried so hard and sang so loud—in one strange language after another?

1966/1970

Leaving the City

Time to get out of the city! With all that's been happening, it's no surprise to be hearing this again. The only difference this time is being told it's not necessary to travel a great distance. A day's drive, they say, is far enough. We can head north along the coastal road to where the population thins out. (In the few far-between towns, there are often only a few hundred inhabitants.)

And what do I think about all this? It's hard to leave friends, treasured objects, the charm and excitement of the city. And for some it may prove impossible. For those able to make the choice, I recommend a location near where a river enters the sea. (About a hundred miles north, there are a number of such places.)

The suggestion is made because on days when the coast is bleak and fog-covered it is often clear just a few miles inland. The places I have in mind are easily accessible, with paths to follow, beaches to rest and picnic on. One can lie on the warm sand, listen to the wind in the dry stiff grass. One note of warning, however: be alert to what happens in the sky. The presence of certain birds, the portent of a wandering cloud, needs to be kept in mind.

For the fact is, having lived so long in the city, we may have some difficulty separating promise from menace. And because of this we may fail, at some essential moment, to distinguish the Vulture—the dreadful image—from the majestic circling of the unimprisoned Hawk. . . .

1979

PART TWO: THE WATCHERS/THE WATCHED

We have learned then to be careful, to examine the faces, listen for a word, an accent that does not belong here.

◆

Trying to decipher what moves faster than the eye, the mind.

The Invaders

1.

There was a time when they appeared at a distance: poised on the hill in perfect ranks, armored, helmeted, spears glinting in the sun. Everyone considered then what it meant to be besieged. No one considered himself especially vulnerable, singled out by fate. Those legions were sent where the land was green, the vaults and coffers filled, jewels and women ripe for the plucking.

But as I say, that was a long time ago. We still wonder at the recollection: how simple it all was! For since then we have seen worlds falling—sometimes by assault, sometimes for no apparent reason. And the common view today is that the enemy has moved within the gates, taken up permanent residence among us. We have learned to be careful, to examine the faces, listen for a word, an accent that does not belong here. We have of course no idea where they might have come from, what their intentions are. But it is felt they could be walking among us—the disguises subtle, not easily pierced.

2.

. . . Moving from one room to the next in this small apartment, I keep turning up evidences of one or another unexplained presence. Just this morning, for instance, I opened the closet door: hanging there were suits, jackets, shirts—different styles, sizes, and colors. I had no idea where they came from, whom they belonged to.

And the same thing a couple of days ago when I looked into the kitchen cupboard. Filling the shelves was a fantastic variety of herbs and spices. As I read the exotic labels, I was struck by the irony: I do my own cooking, prepare only the simplest meal. . . . Why not throw out all this stuff? So says the naïve voice that always seeks an easy solution. But a moment's thought reveals the complications inherent in the real situation. To mention just one: the different views at different times. Thus I have to admit this is only clear to me—as right now—when I can see it with my own eyes.

For at other times, I could be standing at that same closet door, hand on the glass knob, and everything would appear in order. I could reach in, take out one of the shirts, put it on, and only later, while passing the mirror, become aware this was obviously not mine. (Never would I have purchased these garish stripes, this fancy silken material!)

3.

Why persist in these fantasies and self-deceptions? I know perfectly well there are no strange garments, exotic foods. I must stop playing these silly games—or risk never coming to grips with the real situation. To set the record straight: I have, it seems, invented these "appearances" and "disappearances": there are no "uninvited guests." And my reasons for this elaborate charade? Perhaps simply because it is more interesting to have all this going on. And I suppose it also helps to account for what is a genuine difficulty in maintaining my own presence, keeping things in order. (In a time like this, occasional "absences without leave" become necessary.)

Once this is admitted, it becomes possible to describe the experience: (1) I am standing right here, speaking in my own voice; (2) for no apparent reason I begin to "drift off"; (3) I find myself "somewhere else," listening, watching what is going on. To borrow a familiar image: writing the play, watching the play, performing the different parts, all at the same time.

It is only when I question or reject the whole process—usually on the grounds that it's too far removed from the rational view—that "the others" make their appearance. Clearly, this happens because it is preferable to credit them with a separate existence, rather than regard the self as so many fragments. (Our number-one article of faith: the whole greater than the parts.)

Looked at in this way, it all becomes harmless enough. I need not consider myself an exception: no one can be "himself" all the time. I have only to stop this insistence on living *my own* life, speaking with *my own* voice. The advantages should be obvious: the increased mobility, wider range of roles. I am wherever and however I appear. (Even in that silken, striped shirt!) And thus say goodbye to that fear of invasion, of displacement.

4.

None of this will do. These rational explanations all come to the same thing: by providing names and labels, they tend to make it all sound harmless, unimportant. All the torment, the sense of crisis disappears. What we have been subject to then becomes the result of some error, some defect of vision. So that one need only make an appointment with the nearest eye doctor, take the tests, find the proper lenses. One can then go forth upon these streets, between familiar walls, and find everything in place. No more blurring, no more distortions . . .

5.

I seem to be back where I started. But with this difference: I have finally realized this must be happening all over the city. So there may be an obligation to share what I have discovered. It seems important then that I speak out, not remain silent. This would be with the greatest reluctance, since mine is not the temperament that seeks confrontation. Instead, my natural tendency is to breathe the air of the present—whatever it may be—and to avoid public pronouncements. Yet one does not always have a free choice in these matters. . . .

6.

I wonder if, after all, some kind of compromise can be worked out. Is there some way of calling them to account, setting limits, clarifying where each properly belongs? But how does one get into a position where the authority to settle these matters can be invoked? The minimum requirement would seem to be that kind of presence and appearance that "the others" would be forced to recognize.

It would be simpler, of course, if one could honestly speak of and believe in the existence of "the enemy." We could rely then on the military metaphors: strategy, tactics, logistics, etc. The struggle would end in either victory or defeat; we would then be forced to arrange a truce, cease fire, draw up some sort of treaty. As it is, we continue to flounder, unable to resolve anything.

7.

To be silent—or to speak out? I would be willing to take a stand, but I know how easily my words could be distorted. At a time when public statements are suspect, it seems clear that anyone who steps forward will be subject to rigorous scrutiny.

Perhaps when the atmosphere is more favorable, certain steps might be taken. For instance, it might be of some value to reinstate the frontiers. After careful screening and selection, guards placed at all the known entrances. Of course, the gates would have to be locked, and an especially strict vigil kept on dark nights. We do not want to be unduly harsh in these matters, yet in order to maintain peace and stability . . .

1967/1970

The Situation Room

1.
We sit facing rows of brilliant machines, trying to decipher what moves faster than the eye, the mind. Our fingers, agile from long practice, reach for the buttons, the small switches. A series of intermittent dots, broken lines, flash across the molded screens. . . . This, we are told, is an exercise, a low-level alert. Another name for it is "the game," in which we simulate what has so far been called unthinkable. In this room, we are fairly low in the chain of command; we do not make decisions. Instead we separate "possible" from "probable," so those above us can select or discard. . . .

2.
With all our training, it is still hard to accept: the games are over. We learn this when the light above the metal door turns red. Our attention now is centered on a huge electric map, which pulses and glows, articulating the target areas. . . . *Calls coming in*: rumors that we are, or are not, going to land in the desert. Outside, I suppose there is still day and night, regular breathing, personal concerns. . . .

3.
Staring at a trajectory of swirling lines that streak across the map. A voice within says: *time to forget before and after*. Armed men are already on their way, moving toward the zero boundary. Men in jumpsuits, faces and hands smeared, are prepared for the leap, the dark visitation. . . .

4.
On the desert the night has almost ended. Whirling blades create a hover motion; in a slow wobble, the craft descends. . . . And we who are waiting, watching, *what* are we? An inner voice responds that we are what we worship. When the news comes of the colliding machines, the failure of the mission, we tell ourselves: we must build new and better altars. . . .

1980

The Retreat of the Leaders

With the whole world looking on, there are limits as to what can be achieved. For whatever takes place in public view becomes, inevitably, a performance. Yet there are grounds for believing that, while staying out of sight and in close contact, something can be accomplished.

Here, the setting and atmosphere at Camp David can play a decisive role. Within the confines of this historic retreat, our leaders may reflect, not only on immediate concerns, but on the surrounding environment. On their walks, whether conferring or relaxing, they may observe the testimony of trees, plants, and animals—direct evidence of what is endangered. And with the presence of these more profound influences as incisive reminders, we may breathe easier. For we too have walked along similar paths, shared the feeling of an enduring order. . . . *Retreat*: the word itself echoes. We recall those who went into the forest, not only to meditate and reflect, but to live. And at times in areas where life could only be sustained with berries, herbs, edible plants . . .

I have to record now—while hoping it is temporary—a feeling of disappointment. This follows our leaders' much-publicized excursion to the nearby Gettysburg battlefield. News photographs show the three of them on the summit of the historic hill, looking out across the scene of conflict. It was just here, we remember, that the Gray charged the Blue, and the nation wavered, almost split apart. (*Retreat*: an order given by a commander, usually in the face of a dangerous or hopeless situation.)

What happened at that moment when they stood—larger than life, if we believe it—above the visible, contained space of a miniature war? Were they frightened, or exhilarated, by the limited scale of destruction—the heritage of battles where the dead still had names and could be counted?

Whatever the answers, we cannot help wondering what makes them appear so content, even pleased, posing beside the polished barrel of an antique cannon.

(*Retreat*: going to the edge, then pulling back, after a brief glimpse of the Abyss.)

1978

The Leopards/The Temple

Leopards break into the temple and drink to the dregs what is in the sacrificial pitchers; this is repeated over and over again; finally it can be calculated in advance, and it becomes part of the ceremony.

—Franz Kafka

1.

Not knowing the language of the original, I stare at the words, which by now have an aura of autonomous existence. What can I add that will not disturb their equilibrium? But I must not attach too much importance to my own reading. These fragments, after all, have a way of *floating* through our history: Archilochus, Heraclitus, etc. Century after century the hand, the eye, examines them, finds something interesting, intriguing, then sets them aside, turns toward something else.

2.

How poorly I read; how seldom I see beyond the surface! I remember the sociological rendering, which once seemed essential. The Leopards, I thought, are at first viewed as fearsome invaders. But then it is realized that—as fear can be mastered by desire—their return can be manipulated. Measures are then taken to convert their rage into useful energy, bringing it into service of the Establishment. . . . Of course, this appears now as simplistic—a small first step toward unraveling. . . .

3.

Before going on, I need to express thanks to a number of friends, particularly to J., to P., to R. With their patient help, I have begun to sense the myriad possibilities within and beyond the words. One direct result is that I have looked closely at the word *pitchers*, separating it from the word *sacrificial*. Thus I have been able to ask the necessary questions: (1) What are the pitchers *made of*—glass, pottery, silver? (2) What do the pitchers *contain*—blood, water, wine?

4.

Do the Leopards in fact *break into* the Temple? This would imply the doors are locked and guarded. Yet more likely the doors are open; the Leopards *wander in*, are as astonished, as bewildered as the Congregation. As for their return—"over and over again"—how is this credible? (Unless induced by bribery, false promises, other forms of duplicity.) Note too how the original departure, as well as the dramatic entrance, is left as ambiguity. Is it going too far to suggest the subliminal effect is, finally, to change "ceremony" into "performance"?

5.

We may have to abandon this line of inquiry. Our scholars, priests, and clerks, ingenious as ever, can undoubtedly make all this believable. Of greater concern is the continuing triumph of the strategy by which we subdue and obliterate the wild. For by now, with our advanced technique, it is not necessary to use "real" Leopards. (For that matter, the Temple itself may just as well be simulated.) Is it any wonder then that—whatever we desire or fear—we can no longer tell whether a Leopard, a Unicorn, or the neighbor's child is even now standing before the door?

1978

Trading with the Enemy

There are subjects not to be talked about, secrets not to be told. In the outer world, we hear of spies, double agents, a whole collection of shadowy figures who commit intrigue and, at times, violent acts. In the personal realm, however, the secrets are more tenuous, elusive, affecting only a few. Looking closer, the picture changes. True, what is at stake here is often only an image, an idea of the self. But still, for the individual—as for the government—there is a sense of humiliation, betrayal. . . .

—

. . . Sorting out the damage from the last visit. Determined next time to take action, to make sure the *enemy* is barred, kept at a distance. But is this really possible? Experience shows that the determined "other," after some delay, can always gain entrance. But this suggests we are dealing with an intruder. More likely, we know, that it is someone we have invited, been especially close to. . . . How does it start? In obvious ways: a random encounter, a phone call, a letter. In a short while, not knowing exactly how it happened, there is an involvement. It seems then we have only to travel that short distance between desire and fulfillment. It is only later, in retrospect, that the mirrors, even the walls, tell a different story. . . .

—

The one we have invited, cared for. Yes, now I remember. I was at home that afternoon, listening to some music, feeling quite relaxed. When the bell rang I walked slowly— with no apprehension—toward the door. *Do you remember?* Remember that, even though the visit violated our agreement, I greeted you warmly? Said nothing that could have given offense. Yet in a few moments, you stood there shouting. . . . I ask now: Isn't there some way to avoid this? To find out, in advance, what has to be negotiated? For it is clear that, without compromise, there can be no reconciliation. Think about those things you could give up and still be . . . On my part, I assure you, I would be more than willing to . . .

1980/1981

Caesar's Thumb

. . . Still pouring into the Stadium, leaving hardly room to stand. In a short while, Caesar is to make an entrance, here at this festival, the games that honor the Gods. To some he may appear no different, no greater than the Senators who surround him. But for us, even at this distance, a special aura will radiate his presence. Arms extended, we await that moment when Caesar stands there. It is then that our combined voices will break loose, reach toward the sky. For with that shout, we are embraced, included within the whole known world. . . .

The picture fades—that is the scene, the particular image. But desire, stronger than memory, moves us to fill the empty space. We dream other occasions—with horses, bulls, flashing capes—the combatants elaborately costumed or naked to the waist under an intense white light. Or we gather under some emblem or banner to ask forgiveness, to exorcise the violent impulse. . . . Yesterday Caesar, the Pope, the General, the President. And tomorrow? Our need for spectacles, for embodiment, takes many forms. Sometimes we yearn for a single figure who connects an enclosed Earth, a limitless Heaven. At other times we turn toward some less imposing, less obvious power symbol. Recently, for instance, a short, squat religious leader, an overweight adolescent with vacuous eyes . . . Well, says the cynical voice, the Stadium is *there*, it has to be filled somehow. . . .

Standing before the full-length mirror, I rehearse the gestures. First the welcome: turning this way and that so all may feel included. Then calming them down, orchestrating the emotion. The idea is to sense what is *out there*—and just at the right moment, letting it enter a little at a time, before sending it out again. . . . I raise my right arm, waiting for the impulse to decide which way the thumb goes. My arm stiffens; even in this empty rehearsal, I cannot complete the turn. . . . Whatever happens, the outcome must not be traced here, but to the general movement, the anonymous voices in the crowd. So that I cannot be blamed for either punishment or reward—not even if neutrality is called "abandonment," given the name, the image of indifference.

1980

The Contest

1.
It is fortunate there is a deadline. Otherwise, where would it end? Looking around the crowded room—clerks carrying sacks and boxes, sorters busy at the metal tables—I wonder how much longer we can handle the deluge of entries.

For days now I've been sitting here, examining the glossy prints—a few in color, but mostly black and white—trying to find some basis for a choice. We have been told only to look for something *memorable*. Yet is this part of the intention? I am reminded this is a competition: with entries offered to gain the prizes.

I stretch, shift my position, lean back in the chair. Images of the day, the season, the year, the decade—the hurried view of a succession of moments? Clouds, trees, shadows, traffic, the faces of children. Out of all this to select eight or ten whose force and value cannot be denied. . . . The stack beside me glitters; a pile of discards reflects from the floor. Once more I try to separate what seems posed, artful, labored, from what respects the eye. But there it is: once more my attention goes to what needs to be excluded. No wonder I have so little to show . . .

2.
How does one get into a situation like this? In the usual manner, I suppose: there is work to be done, an opening occurs, a name is mentioned. There is an initial interview—a Secretary, an Assistant—and if all goes well, personal contact with the Director. And if it gets this far and the contract is signed, then it is obvious no mistake has been or could have been made. Perhaps that is why no one has interfered or objected.

3.
It is typical that, having reached this conclusion, within the hour a note should arrive from the Director. He wants to know—as I might have guessed—what is holding up my selections. And concludes with the polite question: Would I mind stopping by to let him know how things are going? Somehow, for the moment, I feel more relieved than upset. There is plenty of time before the deadline. And looking around, I imagine that none of my colleagues are in better shape: a huge pile of discards surrounds each of them as well.

I start to reach into the nearest stack, but instead open the drawer and remove—is this all?—two that I have set aside: a woman seated in a chair by an open window, a man leaning against a streetlight. . . . I was sure there was at least one more—yes, that one of the ship going down. I search through the pile on the table, sift through what has landed on the floor. Only then does it occur to me: it was in yesterday's batch. So of course it is too late: by now it has gone down the chute to be chopped or burned with the rest of the excess paper.

I close my eyes. There was the prow sticking up out of the water, gulls circling, a slash of moonlight. It brings back various ships on various seas, and that time when, close to the shoreline, the waters turned red. . . . I open my eyes: this kind of drifting can be dangerous. Perhaps I should resign. I should have realized that to dream and to act are opposites. Even more confusing when to act means to choose, to judge the value of another's dream.

4.

Waiting to enter the Director's office, I reread and study the note. It is on good paper, with neat margins, and the words are printed. It is disappointing not to have a sample of his handwriting, yet the small letters, the light blue ink must mean something. . . . The buzzing sound is repeated several times before the Secretary emerges, announces a delay. I relive the moments just before, passing through the Judging Room. For the first time, I felt the presence of the others in a special way. A kind of complicity in that slight turn of the head, eyes raised and quickly lowered . . . Can the chooser tell when he is chosen? I see now that my presence here is nothing but an embarrassment for the Director. Efforts of the kind I exert—or fail to exert—are precisely what interferes with the best intentioned of projects.

5.

. . . Good to be once more in motion, taking steps on stone, on grass-covered ground. Pleased my vision has not been affected, that I can look at what is here without having to judge, to evaluate, part of that whole mechanism that offers rewards—or confirms obscurity. Pleased, too, the Director accepted my resignation in good grace, so that my failure here will not stand in the way of future employment in some other, more congenial capacity.

6.

Seated at my own desk, I open the large yellow envelope. (How was I able to get past the guards with so little effort?) This is what I have taken with me, a last-minute impulse, after leaving the Director's office: a small collection of images that represent a curved span of years. . . . The handle of a plow surrounded by a vast expanse of sand. A woman's name lettered across the side of a tank. A dark, plumed shape darting through the air. The pockmarked sphere itself, turning in wild, blue space. . . I squeeze the envelope into an already overcrowded drawer, and, closing it, make the usual resolve to some day organize its scattered contents. . . . What I need to know is that I have been where I have been. I could look inside, take out the personal albums—and beyond these, letters, folders, schedules. But what would that prove? That I have set foot in the river, swimming sometimes with the current, sometimes against, other times floating easily in the sun . . . I am not sure whether to laugh or to weep. Images of burning buildings, of snow, of waters on the rampage. Then suddenly in the center of a peaceful town, the stone steps of a Courthouse . . . No need to ask who sits there, or in what capacity. Consider instead those darting figures ready with shutter and lens: future contestants.

What prizes then for the eye behind the eye? What rewards for the quick fingers— bent just that much—that unite memory, as evidence, with precise and unfailing judgment?

1980

The Cage: The Performance

Sharing the common darkness, we wait for the figure clothed in light to appear. We have seen M. many times before: the incredible body moving through space, presenting a world we imagine but can never express. With affection and admiration, we recall his performance as Clown, as Tramp, as Lover, bringing a kind of delight we thought lost, reserved for children. . . . But tonight, mixed with our anticipation, there is also a certain uneasiness. This centers on a work being premiered, with the disturbing title *The Cage Inside the Courtroom*. The program refers to it as an update of an earlier piece, using images from recent political events. . . .

◂

Watching the lithe body, with its stark counterpoint of black tights and whiteface makeup, we do indeed begin to feel the enclosed, stifling space of the Courtroom. Without props and without words, the scene starts to emerge: the uniformed men on guard, the terrified spectators, the machine-like exchanges between Prosecutor, Judge, Lawyers for the Defense. And finally the Defendants pacing the floor of the Cage: the curious gestures of those who are both threatened and threatening . . . With the performance reaching its climax, we have a sense of the Defendants *clawing* at the bars. But then, very subtly, we are shown the other side of this—as though the "clawing" is being replaced by "stroking." The Cage then appears as not only a prison within a prison, but also as "home" or even "nest." And it is as though, with this shift from outrage to languid unconcern, the verdict has already been rendered.

◂

As it turns out, we may have somewhat misinterpreted M.'s intention. For what is going on now, with the Defendants having subsided, the Cage itself fading into the background, suggests more of a game than a shrill reality. What we sense now is the Magician at work, letting us know this too can be dissolved, made to disappear, but strangely also—how to say this?—a kind of pedantic Lecturer sketching and erasing on the invisible blackboard a series of indecipherable equations.

◂

The faces in the lobby tell more than the applause. Leaving the theater, they seem more perturbed than pleased. As though with all the admiration for M.'s consummate skill, there is also a certain resentment. With this response, we should not be surprised if this too—like the earlier version—is dropped from the repertoire.

For as a shrewd judge of what will and will not "play," M. knows there is no substitute—no matter how interesting or daring the experiment—for material that can "captivate" an audience. Even in a medium that, presumably, extends beyond the barriers of language.

1978

The Actor: Farewell & Return

—for George Hitchcock

1.
Waiting for the applause, for a moment he feels nothing is going to happen, that a wall of silence is about to descend. He tries to shrug it off as the vague residue from some untraceable dream. . . . As the sound reaches him he exhales, relaxes. Then starts the practiced bow: to the left, the right, the center . . It is time, he thinks, to say goodbye. Goodbye to all this light and noise. But he is not yet ready to make the necessary move. Something needs to be solved, to be remembered. But what is there, beyond the recited words, the costumed character? He breathes deeply, shakes loose from the reverie, and at last in motion, begins the practiced exit. Slowly then, with every nuance of that borrowed authority, he makes his way offstage.

2.
In this cooler, darker place—hanging ropes and stored scenery—he leans against a curved façade and waits. The sound is less than desired, but more than feared. With an unconscious motion, he raises his arm, holds the watch close to his ear. Someone approaches, whispers a few words, walks away. The applause begins to fade; it is the difference between enthusiasm—lightly motivated—and passion. It seems that is indeed all—all there is going to be. . . .

3.
In the dressing room, rows of short-stemmed bulbs frame the mirror. For a while, he sits there staring at the glass. Then he dips his fingers into the open jar and rubs the thick cream over his face and neck. Wiping it off, he squints and scowls, makes faces at his changing face. With a sudden motion, he stands, sheds the rest of the costume: the brocade, the sash, the satin-edged pants. At the moment of nakedness, there is first a feeling of relief then—in quick succession—chills, panic, and a feeling of confidence. . . .

4.
Approaching the door that leads to the street, he stops, unable to continue. He feels the pull, the pressure of unfinished business. He turns, retracing his steps, back toward the stage. . . . All at once he is there, feeling awkward, strange, in his street clothes, alone in that huge, empty space. Why has he come back? His hands and lips begin to move. . . .

5.

. . . Now that it is being said, he can express regret for past performances—on stage and off—that evoked facile loves and naïve hates. (While under the mask or make-up, the feeling of nausea was barely held in check.) Well, now that he is leaving, he confirms that none of this was meant to be taken too seriously. For the fact is that, moving out into the formless world, he has no magic or arms with which to defend himself. Instead, where his presence *as himself* is required, he faces predicaments for which there is no plotted outcome.

6.

The dark, the single light dissolve; the theater warms to his gestures, his soundless words. He stands for another moment, testing the air, waiting for the voice: *Speak, speak now, but only as yourself.* . . . He is left with this and nothing but this. And so he says aloud: *As you are, I am myself.* . . . And with this there appears row after row of flowering faces. Here, there, everywhere, bringing the gift of their responding hands . . . At last he turns, moves off the stage. Nothing can stop him now. Carried along on this warm current, he can go forth upon those anonymous streets, taking with him those lively, lovely hours of pretense.

7.

Let us assume then that he finds as much to dream about in this ordinary, actual world. That here too entrance and exit can be as easily arranged as where whispered cues underline the action . . . Move then where he moves; stand where you can see his many selves joining hands, forming a lively, colorful throng. Who are those prancing figures dressed in velvet, striped silks, wearing painted masks? We can guess or imagine according to our fancy. For as we watch, it seems their antics— *vivre* and *survivre*—could indeed transform the very air.

1973/1980

The Trouble with Winds

The winds arrive; the winds descend. At first we feel grateful, released from the oppressive, stagnant air. It is only later, as we observe the direction and the greater force, that we become concerned. . . . This, then, is how it might happen: a day or two of advance notice, to which some respond. But thousands, hundreds of thousands, are too preoccupied (and with what?) to pay attention. For these, even a hurricane, an earthquake, is somehow to be lived through, evidence of a will or pattern beyond their control.

◆

I have been watching, listening to the news. A month ago, winds twisted through the Midwest, leaving whole sections of cities as scattered debris. More recently, a hurricane swept across the peaceful, musical islands south of here. . . . Once more the images of dazed survivors: an old man wandering among the remnants of a house, a child holding a headless doll, a cat crouched inside a bathtub . . .

◆

If we could trust the instruments, the experts, we could still carry on the ordinary business of living. We could continue using our voices, the known words, to verify our existence. Instead, we have begun listening for a "voice" within the wind. Various governments have even installed huge metallic "ears" in strategic places. . . . Can these ever bring the message—if not redemption, then at least some possible reprieve? Or when finally heard and deciphered, will it be nothing more than the report of worlds shattered and renewed—aeons before our earth was formed?

1980

PART THREE: THE CODES/THE SIGNALS

What then is this: some magic in the gesture, in these particular hats? Is the nod, the slight bow, a sign of mutual recognition—of a secret brotherhood?

Forgotten also those fantasies of the knock as "signal" to the one inside: lover, confederate, secret agent—

The Hat, The Indian, The Lizard

Neither an Australian bushman nor an ancient Greek could be expected to realize that the lifting of a hat is not only a practical event . . . but also a sign of politeness.

—Erwin Panofsky

1.

An Indian stands watching as two men, moving toward each other, raise their hats, nod, and go their separate ways. The hat, he thinks, is to cover the head, protect it from sun and wind. What then is this: some magic in the gesture, in these particular hats? Is the nod, the slight bow, a sign of mutual recognition—of a secret brotherhood?

2.

An Artist is in his studio painting the portrait of an Indian. The Indian is in formal dress: jacket, pants edged with black satin, a white silk shirt with ruffles and pleats. Completing the outfit, the hat is of a kind once worn by bankers and presidents. . . .

3.

This painting is now finished. I have just received notice it is for sale. At the price asked, I can recommend its purchase: in years to come, it is bound to increase in value. I should mention, however, that it is not a "pretty picture." For one thing, the Indian appears more confused than noble. Also that, for reasons beyond me, the Artist has draped a fierce-looking lizard across the Indian's shoulders.

4.

Can we come back now to the original situation? Only this time, to clarify matters, let us stand on the street. Witness now the exchange as two or more—man, woman, or child—approach. Notice that, even without hats, there is some gestural wave or nod. . . . Is this too familiar, too trivial for comment? Note what it signifies: no harm offered, no fear evoked.

5.

For contrast, we might recall the scene from a recent film: twilight on a deserted beach; from behind a cluster of rocks a shadowy figure emerges. . . . No need to fill in the details; we have imagined this or some variation a thousand times. That is, we have felt the one coming toward us as the source of mistrust and danger. So that even without the hat, the Indian, or the lizard, we still need some icon or amulet to protect us from the other.

I have tried ending the parable here. But private memory wants to add something to social memory. I move past a series of barriers, retrieve the title of a long-forgotten poem: "The Survivors: A Legend." The West as dream, as myth, as lost reality. A few lines return: "Beside the painted bodies of the slain / Dust rises where the lizard's quick tail / Scatters the loose pebbles."

The primitive, someone says, is never far away. No matter how often we change our icons, our styles of clothing.

1980

The Given Day

—for Édouard Roditi

1.
We choose the time—or the time chooses us. Whichever way it is, encounters, events only signify in retrospect. While it happens, things simply follow one another: the faces, the names, the places drifting past. . . . The first day of W.'s last visit. Thinking of it now, it centers on that silly errand to City Hall. Imagine, the new rules require a Visitor's Permit, which for some reason is available only at the Tax Collector's office.

2.
Early afternoon, a bright, warm day. Approaching the building, we are both in a good mood, though irritated at having to waste time in this way. . . . We enter, moving past the security guards, the metal detectors. Crossing the stone floor, we pass a row of tables covered with booklets of various sizes and colors. This turns out to be part of a temporary exhibit: *Keeping Your City Beautiful.* Walking past we are each handed a blue plastic bag—a trash bag!—which we fold and stuff into our pockets. . . . W. has never been here before. When we come to the open space and the wide stone staircase, he stops and looks around. I think he's going to comment, but he just shakes his head, shrugs, and we move on.

3.
. . . I fill out the form, pay for the permit. We are ready to leave, when I notice a familiar face. I introduce A. to W. "What are you doing these days?" "Well, I've just published a book." "I have, too." We write the titles on scraps of paper. As A. leaves, I glance at the title: *Morality and Existence.* I wonder how to reconcile this with his offhanded reference to "some real estate venture," which he's just offered to account for his presence here. . . .

4.
. . . Crossing the street, W. notices the sign outside the Museum: Art and Geometry. I'm not very interested, but W., as a sculptor, architect, recognizes some of the names. . . . We spend an hour or so going from room to room. Occasionally, W. stops and makes a brief comment. . . . Leaving, I notice he seems depressed. When I ask, he says it's been happening on all his recent visits to museums and galleries. He explains it's not what's being shown, but the feeling of a kind of "packaging" that includes everything. . . .

5.

We sit silently, driving through traffic. I recall our first meeting—on a day not unlike this—on a street in Rome. We were standing beside a fountain, looking at the gleaming statuary. . . . There is a sense of convergence when he speaks: "In time, that staircase will take on a patina too."

6.

The staircase, the pseudo-classical interior. What makes the connection—the recent shooting there, the dim echoes of a falling Caesar? Whatever it is, my mind travels from the staircase to the corridor beyond, to that afternoon when the Mayor invites the distraught man into his office, then stops as the shots ring out—echoing and reechoing across the polished stone. . . .

1981

The Career of Hands

Seated at the desk, I wait with hands poised above the keys. Usually I get a signal, a clue on how to proceed. This time, however, only some vague suggestions, impossible to follow. My choice then to lower the hands and make contact is arbitrary, without direction. But for a while, just the sight of letters becoming words is reassuring. . . .

◄

. . . Under a shaped beam of light, I see the bench, the polished, curved wood of the piano. The stage is immense; the audience a silent, weighted mass. Coming forward, I resist the impulse toward panic and flight. Since I am here, I tell myself, my destination is also my destiny. Yet I cannot be sure whether I am worthy of the instrument, or whether I can perform the prescribed music. . . .

◄

. . . As I enter the crowded chapel, heads are turning, being raised toward the huge panorama on the ceiling. Bending back to look there, I find the familiar images of God and Adam somehow distorted, out of focus. . . . I turn then toward the walls, the curved arches that support the ceiling. What of the mason, the laborer, who put the stones in place? No clue as to what brings the urgent question. No possible answer. Above us the extended arms, the groping fingers continue to miss connection. . . .

1979

A Simple, Factual Report

1.

A curious item arrives in the mail. At first sight it appears a routine announcement: some poets giving a reading. But then I notice, below the names, a printed diagram. With this is a set of instructions—for some sort of computer—on how to deal with the human voice. If a "wrong" procedure is followed, the voice will be disregarded. If correct, the message will be received; then and only then will the proper circuits be activated.

2.

A man with no voice is seated on the brown couch in our living room. He makes himself heard by a device—fitted into the palm of his hand—placed flat against his throat. At first, the sound is unclear, the words barely recognizable, but then, listening closely, we are able to follow. . . . He is saying that the device was originally developed for use in animated films, to simulate speech for the "talking" creatures. He has been using it for the past few years, following an operation during which his larynx was removed. . . .

3.

He places before us a small collection of carved wooden dance masks. Their history, the myths, the symbols, are unknown to us. And for him, as a dealer in art objects, they are primarily items for sale. . . .

4.

What I am writing here is a factual report. Nothing is being added to color or intensify what happened. Why then the sense of struggle, of conflict, of fear? As if there were something forbidden about the mask—these particular masks. Vaguely we recall myths of spirits summoned and dismissed, of protection and exorcism.

5.

Disturbing echoes—yet we still insist on the need for fiction, for ritual. This, while it appears certain that the voice which struggles with emotion, with meaning, is now obsolete. Already available is a wide selection of devices, all of which are better suited for the transfer of information. Becoming more and more efficient, they are able to not only record what we say, but keep what we remember in a safe, warm place.

1980

Reading the Text

From our part of the world, the effort to separate the sacred from the profane seems to require an elaborate system of taboos and prohibitions. Yet from the perspective of the *Mudra-Shad*—a copy has recently, after much delay and involved effort, come into my possession—these restrictions are irrelevant, even absurd. For as I read the Text, what comes across is a tolerance for whatever happens, for all human actions. This derives from a view of phenomena within some vast cyclical scheme of things. And while this may appear to Western eyes as random, chaotic, the Text itself offers evidence of design and pattern emerging *naturally*, according to the scale and time frame.

Thus, instead of the complicated structure of logic and reason, we are invited to partake of a universal vision. Central to this is the premise that, while what we do or fail to do may *irritate* the gods, it does not call forth rage or vengeance. What we call "sin" is there regarded more as a matter of intrusion—in an area and at a time disturbing to the gods, busy with their own concerns.

◆

So far, we are still reading—in line with our traditions, our inheritance—with expectations of punishment and reward, following the metaphor of "rise and fall." And while seeking, I might add, not merely equilibrium, but something more extravagant. I refer of course to our numerous myths of death and resurrection.

What the *Mudra-Shad* offers, however, is in the more modest realm of transformation. This means putting aside our yearning for an accessible heaven, in favor of a "renewal" in which another, but still earthly form is assumed. . . . An equally important difference, revealed as I turn the pages, is how the metaphor of Water takes over the role we ascribe to images of Light. So that where we refer to "radiance" as reflections of Supreme Being, the Text speaks of a "current" within the flow of things.

◆

How curious then—and how confusing!—to turn from this to the "dry world" of our own sacred texts: dust returns to dust. Or when we read the words of one of our poets: "fear death by water." This in contrast to the opening lines of Book One: "In water we began. In water we continue." *Remarkable* when we consider these lines were composed by monks dwelling for centuries in almost total isolation—a few thousand feet below the peak of an almost inaccessible mountain!

◆

Further comment at this time seems needless. The *Mudra-Shad* is a text no scholar or generation of scholars can adequately render or transcribe. Like any eternal work, it appears differently in different times and places. . . . With all this said, I regret that, due to the enormous labor, the difficulty of transportation, it is impossible to tell when additional copies will be available.

1978/1979

The Master

Of course the birth took place. For those whose interest centers on this, there are documents, witnesses, and so forth. I have held in my own hands volumes in which the circumstances are described—and in such fashion as to convince all but the most biased and self-seeking. One such volume I recall with a thick blue binding, on good paper, and with a number of clear, detailed photographs. Others I have looked at appear well researched, comprehensive in their presentation of the facts.

But I learned long ago that the real interest of all these scholars, critics, commentators was in something beside the facts. This happened when I first came across the phrase "born of the cruelest of fathers." The writer's name, understandably, has been forgotten, but the sentimental and misguided intention—which put me on guard for what followed—has remained. For it was the starting point for a whole school of would-be analysts, making careers out of what their probing fingers pulled apart.

I will not put either that life or those words under that harsh, searing light, but will repeat what is beyond dispute, that the birth took place. And add a few words, not to explain anything, but to express my feeling about a presence that changed the course of my existence.

I am sometimes asked to comment on how it is that this terrible gift and burden appears so incredibly close to our own time. And yet, as one considers it, it could not have happened any sooner. One realizes that somehow it had to be in just that country, and after those particular wars. One cannot help thinking of those tidal waves that, in their own time, reach the intended shore. Or to change the figure, of molecules already in the air, seeking the body they have to enter. Whether others would go quite that far, I cannot tell. But there should be little disagreement on the force and significance of his presence. I have to call it a great "dividing line"—one of the greatest. Let those who would dispute this only look at their morning paper; let them take the shortest walk on our endangered streets. That is where they may test the clear-sightedness of his prophecy—on those destroyed faces, in the vague eyes of wandering, mindless children.

I am tempted to say the obvious: *his children*. For who else understood so well the role of corridors, of endless desks placed side by side? But it would not be accurate to present the prophecy that flowed through him as if it were, literally, the work of his hands. It was rather what he saw and felt and lived with—if we understand this in the proper way and in the proper dimension—as far as our own limited minds can reach.

—

With these few glimpses of what lies beyond, I am content now to take my place among his readers. His words are by now preserved in countless editions. Let those who read make of them what they can. They have the printed pages; they can use his name wherever and however they choose. What is missing, of course, is his voice. That was available for only a short time, and for those few to whom he gave so generously of his unique spirit. *His voice.* Those seated beside him at the same table . . . The words go on; they flow through his silence. That silence which was his last considered choice. For wasn't it enough for them to know that he had been there; could they not have pooled their memories of his presence? But this was not to be. The hand of one closest and most trusted sifted through his papers; fingers tightened on sheets covered with black ink.

We have read those words—read and recited over and over again—and understood nothing. The experts still express astonishment that he could speak of the Garden as if he had been there in person. Some of them even revel in the opaque, counting the tiny prisms made with the points of their pens. They cannot grasp what goes deeper than their lives. Not a choice for darkness but for the earliest light: *before the forest awakens, before the intruder arrives.*

1970

The Sacrifice

He is there with a number of others—all of them articulate, concerned with words—trying to decide what can be said, what can be heard as intended. Their voices join, separate, dispute. He wonders, as always, where the voices come from, go to after leaving this privileged space.

Only recently he has had to record the impact of another death. This particular one, skilled in the manipulation of images, has died after an incredibly prolonged ordeal. . . . As the voices continue, he recalls the published account of his friend's death: with sight gone, with speech gone, there was still a choice for life. It was only when the man's *hearing* started to fade that the choice for death was made. He wonders then at the cost, the value of speech. Words as urgent and terrible as *knife, gun, axe*. Words to suggest the flesh deprived, destroyed . . . It occurs to him that, over and over again, the sacrifice has been made. But the lesson—whatever it is—is quickly forgotten. For the strange part is that before the sacrifice, an offering must be made. And while sometimes this is acceptable—victim and martyr honored, later even worshiped—at other times it has been ignored, refused. More than this, if certain accounts are believed, it has been laughed at, ridiculed.

Someone beside him asks for his response to the words that have just been read aloud. He pauses for a moment, then answers with words appropriate to the question.

1978

Protective Measures

We humans are held together by signals which move back and forth across our body, just as an army is held together by its messengers.

—J. McKim Malville

Almost a year has passed since our last meeting. And we still think of G.—whenever we do—in her role as teacher, rather than friend. For the fact is we are too busy, too concerned with immediate tasks to observe the obligations of friendship. And no regrets about this. Where nothing more is asked, or promised, no harm is done. Difficult enough to maintain ties with those close at hand, without expending energy on those far away. (C. lives in another country, returns here once or twice a year.)

How long must one live to apprehend the truth of things? Not just these things, but *any* things. For as I think of G., I wonder what we have in common. During her absence, for instance, what does memory visualize? No more than a vague image— the energetic, the "life-affirming"—a metaphor instead of a person. In this respect, she does come to mind more than the other distant ones. This happens when we perform the exercises—or lessons, as C. prefers we call them. And especially when we recite the simple phrases—"chest buoyant, fill the space with your breathing"— she spoke while her skillful, healing fingers probed.

I am still withholding something, offering less than the truth. For I have not yet admitted that these lessons stir resentment, the sense of participating in an absurd activity. What are we doing, I wonder, giving our bodies so much attention? As much or more than we used to reserve for a book, a painting, a piece of music. There is nothing, after all, the least enthralling in the simple process: taking in and expel-ling air. And if our bodies suffer, even disintegrate from the absence of this constant scrutiny, it will be because we are directed elsewhere.

1979

The Shrinking City

It is time to acknowledge openly what has already been verified by a number of independent sources: *our city is shrinking!* And this in spite of all efforts, especially in the past year, to further various "expansion" programs. These include raising the permissible height for new structures, as well as extending the city limits. . . . As for the reaction of our citizens, it is varied. Some still insist nothing has changed. Confronted with the evidence, they claim that it is our perception that has some-how been altered. Some have even suggested a temporary affliction, to be corrected by the compulsory wearing of special magnifying glasses.

All this brings us to a difficult point: is the same thing happening to us, the inhab-itants? I refer now to my own experience: earlier this year I had already noticed the smaller size of the house, the furniture. One day, returning from work, I had to squeeze through the door. The next day, to my surprise, I was able to enter without difficulty. I decided to check my appearance in the full-length mirror in our bed-room: *there was no change!* It was only later that it occurred to me: of course, the mirror itself was now reduced. . . . This morning on my way downtown, I recalled the old saying, "Never a disaster but someone benefits." Yet as I thought of it, who could that possibly be? An obscure item in the morning paper caught my attention: model makers, toy stores selling miniature houses, doll furniture report that busi-ness has never been better. . . .

1980

The Knock

Kings do not touch doors.

    —Francis Ponge

1.

Thinking of what I am about to write, it is already clear how much has changed. That is, having settled into the role of the one whose door is knocked upon (clumsy as that sounds), I have forgotten those times when I stood outside, waiting for someone to respond. Forgotten also those fantasies of the knock as "signal" to the one inside: lover, confederate, secret agent—all actors in the drama of my younger days . . .

2.

Hearing it now, in this present time, I listen for a sound that signifies. Is it a demand or, more moderately phrased, more of an inquiry? Obvious that the light tap, compared to the urgent pounding, sets up a different expectation. Also that each caller has the choice of whether to knock or ring the bell. Some constant visitors—as I recall—make the same choice each time, but others, for no apparent reason, alternate between one and the other.

3.

The door is our front door, which opens on the street. Those who live at some height, whose doors open onto other doors, must have a different perspective. The image there is of numbered rooms along a narrow corridor, as in an apartment house or hotel. . . . Does anyone come knocking there? I imagine that the sound is becoming rare. Callers use bell or buzzer, are scrutinized upon a glass screen, or through a slotted opening. . . .

4.

The intersection then of a need and a fear. We live in a time, a place, where each encounter is valued or rejected as it relates to one or to the other. With this in mind, the parameters of "good news" and "bad news" can be guessed, seen as predetermined. And if this sounds vague, listen to the voice of another time: *Where I grew, up, the doors were always left unlocked.* . . .

5.

Memory provides the counterpoint. Leads to another house, another street. To the child who, not long ago, came calling here. As I come to the door, see him standing there, I anticipate the words: *Do you have any cookies?* I open the door wider; he follows me into the kitchen. I reach for the container, lift the lid. . . .

6.

The view of the child, of the *as-yet-unrealized*, remains one of a continuing world, with all its difficulties, dangers. And of a door that can still provide a positive entrance. . . The knock rather than the bell? It could be that. For however uncertain or preemptory, it proposes a sound unmediated, unchanged by connecting wires. The contact between flesh and wood may also, on some subliminal level, evoke a body as fragile, as endangered as our own.

◆

There is a different way to treat this subject. One I would rather not think about, try to remember. It concerns knocking on a wall instead of a door. The sound there would be tentative, holding off desperation. Repeated a second, a third time, there would be more and more urgency. . . . When the response comes—the sound that tells us we are not alone—it would begin again. This time with a careful phrasing, the controlled waiting, and then the slow deciphering of a message we have never heard before.

1981

PART FOUR: THE MYTHS/THE EMBLEMS

From here we may begin the decisive voyage: setting sail toward what is surely there.

—

We still need this bright emblem to fill the dark moments of our empty, aimless days.

The Fifth Room

1.

For years we have heard there is such a place—in fact, there always has been. And I have been content to leave it at that: as an open possibility. After all, I am not one of those active seekers who, when the news reaches them, decide this is what they have been waiting for. Who prepares then for an arduous journey—ready for any sacrifice. But of course, if there is something at hand and the opportunity presents itself . . .

2.

At the invitation of a friend who works at the Museum, I arrive there early one foggy morning. As arranged, we descend to the basement, enter an area of packing boxes and dusty display cases. From one of these we remove a heavy leather-bound portfolio. Inside are drawings of hooded monks, grotesque birds of prey. Moving across the black and white tiles of an immense room is a weird procession of chained animals, prancing Gypsies, crippled children . . .

3.

Months later, I return for the widely publicized show: *Forbidden Objects: The Underside of the Ancient World.* At first, it seems nothing more than what is advertised: instruments of torture, crude weapons, erotic art, etc. But as I drift through the eager crowds, the recognition comes. Could this be it, I wonder, could this be the *Fifth Room*? Yet why now, why here, is it being displayed openly?

4.

The show has closed after only a few days. For the first time in memory, the Authorities have found it necessary to issue a statement. It seems that, due to conditions in the countries of origin, the objects will have to be returned. A brief news report, however, reveals that the leaders of certain sects are claiming their most important shrines have been violated.

5.

In the last few days, we have been inundated by competing voices. Some say that action, protest, is called for. Others that this is futile, absurd: the exhibit was only a semblance of the "true space"—a harmless deception. Yet the clamor continues, with the argument that any display profanes what must, by its very nature, remain sacred and invisible.

6.

. . . Feeling more at peace now, having realized that all this will be resolved at some future time. It is for the others—those who come after—to decide. In this way Thought merges into Dream, raising Spirit beyond present boundaries to a wider horizon. . . .

7.

Are we in fact enclosed in a long, dark corridor? Or is there space, enduring space, beyond this? Surely this is the true question of the Fifth Room. For what is a place— or rather, what makes it for us *the* place? With so much pathos, so much longing, the names resound: Jerusalem, Alexandria, Athens, Byzantium. . . .

8.

It has come to me at last: it is not, as we were taught, some green paradise or moldy prison. But wherever we may approach and dream upon the visible shore . . . From here we may begin the decisive voyage: setting sail toward what is surely there. . . .

1980

The Message/The Messenger

It has been told so well, so definitively, that many of us still sit by our windows, waiting for a Messenger who never arrives. From this it is clear that Kafka, as teller of the tale, has indeed outdone himself. For his own "message," far from being lost or dissipated, continues in our consciousness. And to such an extent that the symbols by which he resonates that remote imperial world carry forward into our own frenetic age. Thus, we have not yet been able to admit that the King no longer dies—or if he does, no one pays attention to his dying words. The sad fact is that the King's death has become a statistic: as quickly, easily forgotten as any other.

How then explain the persistence of Kafka's "An Imperial Message"? Is it simply nostalgia for a time when, it seems, a few word could explain and resolve matters of the highest urgency? I believe it is more than this. For we have now available to us—by instant transmission—news of anything that happens anywhere. Speakers and listeners have become close as brothers, as lovers even, across the vast spaces of our planet. Yet through this enormous outpouring of speech and noise, data and opinion, we feel further apart than ever before.

It is clear that as long as we remain passively at the window, we only perpetuate the legend of the Castle, the stalwart, futile Messenger. It might be said, then, it is time we found another location. Not an easy choice to make, since it requires we leave this entrancing view, so close to the seething life of the streets. Besides, such a move, while it might benefit some, leaves out of consideration those who continue to dream of the dead King. I know of one, for instance, who dreamed only recently the King was still alive. They met in a garden and, for an hour or two, strolled hand in hand among the lush plants and graceful flowers.

Also to be considered is that—in Kafka's version—the Messenger is signified with the symbol of the highest authority—nothing less than the Sun itself!—glittering on his chest. And while we have no solid evidence for a witnessing of this triumphant image, it connects with countless examples from religion and mythology. (I should note: both those that encourage us and those that warn us not to dream this far.)

It seems certain then—even without the Messenger, or even the King—we still need this bright emblem to fill the dark moments of our empty, aimless days.

1978

Angel in the Freezer

One room in our house has a wall almost completely covered with painted wooden dance masks. I need not say, since it is outside the purpose of this narrative, how all these were acquired. But in order to not create a mystery, some were purchased years ago on our travels, some from a dealer only recently. Of the latter, two were obtained at a greatly reduced price: an Angel and a Devil. The dealer offered these for less because the wood was infested with tiny worms. I remember how we hesitated, wondering whether to accept his assurance that the problem was easily solved: a few days in the freezer and . . .

◆

I have just been looking at the recently published *Book of Masks*. I am disappointed that, while several others are pictured there—the open-mouthed Jaguar, the woman's head surrounded by snakes—there is no representation of our Angel, our Devil. I will try then to give some sense of their appearance. The Devil is pink and brown, somewhat demonic, though not enough to inspire any real fear. The Angel, whom we have placed in the far corner, is more imaginative and surprising. The figure is definitely male, with a thick black moustache. The face suggests a peasant prototype, like those that appeared so dramatically in Eisenstein's *Thunder over Mexico*.

◆

Why am I telling this? Is it the "symbolic evidence" implied by the display of our very own Angel and Devil? This does seem to have awakened old feelings about dealers and collectors. Not only the greed, self-indulgence, but the offense committed by placing the sacred object in profane hands. I know, of course, that is not quite the case here: it is likely that whatever we own was never intended for any more than the marketplace. . . . Thinking it over, it occurs to me that something else is involved. Freezing the Angel, the Devil, saves them from the garbage can. And yet, and yet, if this was their destiny, how did we dare to interfere?

1980/1981

Reading Borges

For years 1 avoided reading him. Then one day, at the urging of friends, I read a few of the parables, the shorter "fictions." I saw at once how one could become intrigued with that intricate vision, but also how easily admiration could lead to imitation. For even if controlled, there was still the dazzling example of "a world which somehow we are permitted to enter" ("Borges: The Strategy of Emergence," Jean Perrier, *The Enigma Review*, Fall 1972). Perrier's phrase underlines the danger. Especially the word *somehow*, with its suggestion of an "entrance" into another realm—without knowing how we got there, how to manage the passage, the return . . .

—

I have put aside the books, but the words, the images continue to resonate. If Borges is right, the Labyrinth is not myth or metaphor, but inescapable fact— even the central fact of our existence. The case appears at its strongest in the story of Pierre Menard, referred to as the "contemporary author" of another version of *Don Quixote*. (Somehow identical with the original!) As one tries to penetrate the intention here, what emerges is the view that—at some other level of awareness— individual creation is, at the same time, the property of the whole species. For as we look in that direction, who appears but Quixote himself: eyes glazed, the elongated, disarrayed figure crossing an endless plain. But notice also: the same Quixote we always expect to see! One cannot help wondering: if we could somehow erase the expectation, what then would appear? Perhaps a Quixote who is both *everyman*— forever subject to fantasy and illusion—and the *very man* whom Borges describes as "always unique, always unfathomable."

—

. . . It begins to appear that all this merely scratches the surface. Coming back to the same story, observe how, just as Menard replaces Cervantes, he is in turn replaced by none other than "Borges" himself, who may very well be—we are led to believe— merely another version of the original Borges who set all this in motion. What then are we left with? More confused than ever, our minds turn back to the mythology (history?) of the Labyrinth itself. We summon the figures, repeat the names: Daedalus, Minos, Ariadne, Theseus, and of course the Minotaur. . . . But this too, we realize, has to be abandoned. For what Borges has done is to locate his central metaphor not in this remote world but in a structure that is almost too familiar: the Library!

. . . Moving past those endless shelves, we follow a *fragrance*, as it were, that both invites and repels. Taking another look at Perrier's commentary, I find this phrase:

"Borges sees through the one who is seeing through." Somehow, this is both comforting and disturbing. On the one hand, it makes clear our need to be recognized as more than image. But on the other, it brings into view the self-conscious architect who presents this sense of confinement. So that with all our admiration for the constructed Library/House, the soothing overtones of Shelter/Sanctuary, there is still the sinister paradox: Prison/Labyrinth. . . . We return then for assurance to our own travels, in and through our dreams. Moving through memory, silence, and reflection, we amplify a certain scene. Fixing the time and place, we select a certain summer, bending to our purpose the uncertain light: staring through the train window, heading north that year . . . *Suddenly the Caribou, appearing in that untouched elsewhere, beyond dream and remembrance, as we rounded the turn . . .*

1980

The Choice

1.
After all these years, the same room, same furniture. He stands holding back a corner of the drape, peering down at the quiet street. I wait for him to speak, knowing he will without turning, without raising his voice. *You have a choice*, he says.

So that too has not changed: the dry tone, the slight accent. I remember how it used to bother me: Christ, are we going through *that* again?

He moves away from the window, goes over to stand beside the bookcase. He pulls out a thick volume, holds it close to his face. What is it going to be this time? Buddha, Maya, Tetragrammaton, Mazda—something about the Quest, legendary figures rising out of the sea? He puts it back without saying a word, sits down in the faded pink chair. Again, I anticipate the gestures, as he takes out that old brass key, begins turning it this way, that way.

2.
How long has it been? It doesn't matter, I suppose, except for the expense. A brief glimpse of a procession of mornings: my voice, his voice, the silences . . . I feel the present silence gathering: could easily become one of those prolonged ones. And so I speak, as much for the sound: You think I'm ready? *I think it's possible.* How can I tell? *You can't tell—in advance.*

We talk this way, I suppose, having gone over the same ground so many times. I am to understand, for instance, that the "in advance" refers to the need for discovery, but there are "no guarantees, no immunity"—whether going this way, that way, or standing still. (All I can make of this, in terms of choice, is that it seems to exclude retreat.)

And what will tell the others? He shrugs, puts the key back in his pocket. *You'll find something.* But it will be difficult, I insist. *Yes, it will.* His voice sounds far away; he seems eclipsed by the objects in the room.

3.
He has become more voluble, more animated. As though, having said this, something has been released. He is telling some tale about a man with a cart: there are the cows whose color changes, now black, now white, now something in between; the man's encounters with the people who live on the mountain; the adventures that

come with the slow, difficult descent. . . . I can already tell how this one is going to end: the man returns to the marketplace (by this time, almost thirty years have passed) and, unrecognized, takes his place among the friends of his youth. All is as it was, except that now he sees them differently: the butcher, the potter, the wine seller, the rug maker, all clothed in radiance.

But as he talks, something else is going on. My mind travels a different route—this way, that way, with no stages, no direction, no view that puts it all in place. Everything seems here and there, arbitrary, interchangeable.

I try to work it out: what do I mean by "there"? I mean meadows, hawks, shepherds, temples. And what do I mean by "here": lost streets, crippled dogs, store windows and newspapers, tabletops guaranteed not to burn, etc. And it is with these my days are filled. So that while it may be valuable to have that "panoramic" view, it is the immediate with which l have to deal. . . .

He gets up, starts pacing the floor. Clearly he is disappointed at my lack of response. (I'm surprised how tall he is—never realize it until he stands, begins that back and forth motion.) Finally he returns to the window, continues in that low voice, again as if speaking to himself. And I listen in the same way, attention fading in and out, coming back, hearing it chime in my head.

4.

It is almost time to leave. My mind is filled with echoes and images: persons, places, remembered, forgotten. I regret not being able to accept the myth; certainly it would make everything easier. But it is the surface appearances—no matter how shifting or transient—with which I am most familiar. And at last this seems to reach him; for after another brief exchange, we are again mired in silence. . . .

Images of childhood; the usual inflated fears, the distortions associated with those dark places. All this, sharply intersected by equally vivid images of old age: at eighty, his leg turned black, gangrened; he began regularly to wet the bed; one day he bit an attendant . . . Something begins to emerge: The Family Portrait. Look this way, toward the crawling child. Look that way, toward the crushed skin, the infected bone. Somehow, this is what his words have evoked. It's hard to tell, though, if there's any connection.

5.

Is it possible a week has gone by? The usual absurd question. He looks at me expectantly. I plunge right in (to hell with those silences!) and make my report: dreams, streets, the office, the bed, etc. He listens, nods, waits for me to finish.

He reaches into his pocket, and it occurs to me it's rather soon for turning the brass key. But I look up startled as I realize it's a nail file. (And he actually begins filing his nails!) Our eyes meet for only a second—long enough to establish the transgression—and it is back in his pocket. He is again attentive and concerned. After the initial irritation, I'm prepared to dismiss it as a momentary distraction. And yet his next response, when it comes, makes me wonder. . . .

I can't imagine what brought this on, but he has started talking about himself, some recent events in his own life: his daughter's wedding, his wife's collection of seashells, plans for remodeling his house. . . . I suppose this sort of reversal does happen, yet it's extremely uncomfortable, being thrust this way into the role of listener. And if it had to happen, I cannot understand the choice of these trivial details. . . .

So we have lost it then—is that what it means? Yet I had felt we were at last coming close to what had to be said. I remember particularly the phrase "the grace of affliction." The way he stopped then, took a deep breath—as though having tried to say too much. For a moment then, there was a tone I'd never heard before, and the glance that asked an urgent question. All I can make of it now was that some kind of "commitment" was called for: by its very nature not to be named. Something I had to give up, without asking anything in return.

6.

We are back now exchanging words. And I find that I am missing the old silences. Is it possible that I have got it all wrong? That I have understood nothing about the climbing of the mountain, the return to the marketplace?

Yet I still feel that, in my case, this is not intended. In spite of everything, I seem to belong with those who are bound—over and over again—to make the small mistake. The journey then remains, as before, from here to there, without intentions and without reasons.

As far as the brass key is concerned, there are doors *not* to be opened. Not only then is it difficult climbing those rocks and gullies, but even those few stairs above and below the present level of my existence. I realize that I may never reach what lies scattered in the attic, stored in those cold cellars.

Yet aside from this, I am willing to let the light fall in whatever direction; spaces open and close where they can and have to; entrance and departure take place with neither sign nor announcement.

1970

The Loaves/The Fishes

1.

It's like a fish, he said, *a fish you're trying to fashion.* The voice on the phone said, *A fish?* Then after a pause added, *Trying to fashion?* It had slipped out; he tried again: *Not the real thing, but a semblance. As if you're working with clay, with dough.* Later in the conversation, he heard himself saying, *Make up some small individual loaves. . . .*

2.

Hours later, while shuffling papers on his desk, it suddenly struck him: the loaves, the fishes. What could he have had in mind? The words had come out while speaking of language, trying to say how one sought form and expression. It was a reminder, perhaps, from some unlighted, ungovernable source of a realm beyond intention. All very well, he thought, but then wondered what brought the metaphor of feeding—even feeding the multitude?

3.

He went through the day—another unremarkable day—before the thought returned. It came back as he recalled the party on the terrace. . . . It was years before, in another country. A dinner served at twilight, in the presence of diving birds and gleaming statuary. The enormous fish was carried in on a silver platter. Carrot slices for eyes. The image focused to include cucumber wedges for scales, wavering lines of mayonnaise to represent the sea . . . *Do we eat the words?* A mocking voice answered him, *In the beginning there was a loaf, a fish.*

4.

That night, in dream, he crossed the desert and reached the sea. On the shore, he came upon a small group of kneeling figures. Coming closer. he remained standing, wondering what it was that kept him apart. Under the bright sun and searing wind—as the stained robe stuck to his skin—he felt the hand that cooled and sustained them.

1979

The Dark Pattern

The shroud bears a dark pattern that appears to resemble a crucified man.

1.
What to make of this? A piece of cloth bearing an imprint, an image. Something to be stared at, fingered in the mind. A brief note from Q., which enclosed the clipping, suggested we might go there and see for ourselves. But that would imply a certain readiness, a certain predisposition. To go there properly—considering the hardships, the expense—wouldn't that mean to enroll in a kind of pilgrimage?

2.
Q.'s note has started a series of reflections. The obvious thing is that a man lives, a man dies. Of this life—no matter how short or long, fulfilled or meaningless—there are tangible and intangible reminders. The intangible emerge and recede in the flow of memory; the tangible, as valued objects, are stored in a safe place. Safe, that is, for as much as a lifetime. But after this, their fate is questionable. We see them vanish in flood and fire—by the hands of thieves, under the boots of a pillaging army.

3.
But what if it is more than a man—more than a King, or the greatest of men? The flesh that was, we mean to say, has had its corporeal existence, has been incarnated with the divine. Is it appropriate, here also, to be concerned with tangible reminders?

4.
Consider the fragment of bone from the *sacred body*—this Saint's toe, that Saint's finger—which draws throngs of the curious, the faithful to certain cathedrals, certain shrines. Note that the relics are kept in vessels, often crusted with jewels, wrapped in gold cloth—whereas the authentic thing, it seems, would signify its own presence. Consider also the anonymous tin paintings—done within the past century—nailed to the outside walls: the reverence of the poor. This in contrast to the image that acquires value because of the *image maker*: the skilled craftsman, the great artist.

5.
Faith, said Paul in his *Letter to the Hebrews*, is without eyes. Is this view to be considered hopelessly antiquated?

6.

A long letter from Q. He says now that I've been taking the whole matter "too seriously." He quotes a recent book that claims, "Christ was one of a number, prevalent at the time, of magicians or mountebanks." Q.'s comment is that, while the tricks or miracles of the others died with them, Christ managed to perpetuate himself in a "marvelous, post-existence illusion."

7.

The news item in today's paper quotes two scientists with competing methods who have offered to analyze a tiny segment of the shroud. One of them is quoted as saying: *if these were rocks being carbon dated, wouldn't we be pleased at the addition to our knowledge?* Why then feel so dubious, so uneasy about submitting a single thread to his laboratory?

8.

A man lives, a man dies. But that is not the end of it. There is need to solve the dark pattern, transform it into a source of light. The mind wants to finger what the hands cannot touch. So we summon that length of linen: soft, simple, stark enough to wrap the body.

But with that commitment to the tangible, we provide an opening for those marvelous instruments: letting *them* decide what is authentic. . . . Isn't it strange, though— and even Q. with his "penetrating" insights has failed to note this—that the test would be conducted in the same laboratory where the atom was shattered? That the same technicians could be called on to verify the power of spirit—that otherwise we would always remain in doubt, not knowing which way to turn?

1978/1979

The Return of Sadhu

Sadhu, as he now calls himself, sits on a grass mat in a corner of the hut. Time for his rice and tea. I place cup and bowl beside him and wait for a word—a word that has yet to be spoken. He sips the tea, utters the fragment of a smile. Light touches the face and shoulders; the frail body is almost translucent. . . . I step outside, inhale the spiced air, the odors of morning. Beside me the familiar noises of the village—dogs barking, children playing—suggest a space confined, yet somehow limitless.

◆

. . . Several months now since his return. More than a decade, I recall, from the day he disappeared. Not entirely gone from our lives, however. For besides memory and anecdote, there were the constant rumors. This or that traveler, passing through, saying they had seen or heard of him. These encounters, though, always in some remote area, under dubious circumstances . . .

. . . Who could forget the day of return? After raining all morning, around noon it suddenly cleared. I noticed the excited movement, the busy voices, the sudden rush of children drawn to that one place. . . . He has been with us ever since, a declining but still vibrant presence. We are so pleased to have him back, even with his new name, the enigma of what must have been an incredible journey. . . . Honored that having traveled so far, endured so much, he has chosen to live out his last days with us. . . . I have been particularly impressed by the spontaneous gathering, each evening, in front of his hut. It is then that he emerges, waves, smiles. He moves among us—venerable yet sprightly—touching and letting himself be touched. The gesture is playful and lighthearted on both sides. The touch I imagine is to prepare himself—and us as well?—not only for the coming absence, but surely also for the next return.

1980

Say We Are Going

Ah, here it is at last: the distinguished thing!
　　　　　　　　—Henry James

Really my dear it is nothing, nothing at all.
　　　　　　　　—Italo Svevo

Say it is going to happen—as with these two—in a civilized manner. One has had this illness for some time and there is no remedy. One grows weaker, more confused. . . . The scene focuses on flowers in a blue vase. These are at first changed every day. Then, for reasons only too plain, every other day. In the last stages, the flowers remain until the petals are crimped and curdled. And so with the faces of the visitors: the expressions there too seem to shrink and wither, until signs of boredom transform the mask. . . . Forgive the hackneyed scenario. You may discard it, substitute something else from your own imagination. I would ask though that one version—on the grounds of personal distaste—be excluded. I refer to the scene in a novel (not by either of these writers) in which an old man falls, striking his head on the sidewalk. The psychologists will have no trouble with this: *the head is very important to you.* Yes, and it bothers me now because I have not said what I started to say: my love for both Svevo and James, encompassing the great differences between them. They both understood so much, wrote so well. . . .

1979/1980

The News from Dronesville

It may be only a habit of mind, an immemorial longing. But we invoke its exis-
tence as part of our own, as real as anywhere, anytime. By this process then—part
memory, part invention—we construct the streets, the buildings. The Town, we tell
ourselves, is now ready to be entered. The name, the location are not important; we
need only be sure it's small enough, remote enough, to exist somewhere between
sleeping and waking. . . .

—

. . . Children playing on the grass, old men and women seated on warped wooden
benches. Entering at the town square, we stroll through the small park which serves
as focus, as center. . . . A warm day, almost without wind. Moving through the scene,
we have for once the advantage of invisibility. Perceiving without being perceived,
we could take our place beside any of these. We could be holding that newspaper,
staring at the sun, or chasing that pink balloon. Part of whatever it is that intensifies
the light, the shadows, the greenness of the grass . . . For a moment, though, our
mood changes as we view the discordant alternatives: the hurrying, not-seeing faces
of the nine-to-five world. . . . The brief shadow disappears. We return to the scene as
it was, as we want it to be. We feel confident enough now to even improve things.
Our first choice is to add a statue: some benefactor or minor hero, the inscribed
name suitably obscure. And next to it perhaps—why not?—a bronze cannon with
intricate decorations . . .

—

. . . Yes, we have chosen well, avoiding the temptation to convert peace into som-
nolence. We retain here the emanation, the fragrance of a world that reconciles the
best of dream and waking. It can do no harm, in any case, to call attention to this
neglected realm. For it is just here, where we assumed there was nothing more to
learn, that we suddenly encounter the most appealing . . .

1980/1981

The Trial of Two Cities

1.

The argument went on for so long, reached such intensity, we feared it might erupt into open, armed conflict. Yet how could this happen? The Visible City had the arms, the resources, the technology. In the usual terms—logistics, strategy, fire power—it could achieve victory within hours. The Invisible City, considering its traditions, the very premise of its existence, might not even call for resistance.

I refer now to reports of a secret meeting in the Visible City of the responsible military and civil leaders. If my sources are correct, the possibility of an attack was discussed but quickly rejected. This on the grounds that the basic documents upon which it was founded expressly forbid such action. Especially telling were the phrase "We, the People" and the accompanying words "One nation under God . . ."

2.

A few days later, two proposals were offered. One was for a public referendum, with a ballot that listed a series of alternatives: toward unity or toward an ordered, defined separation. The other was for an appeal to the Circle of Judges who had jurisdiction, at least nominally, over both Cities. Finally it was decided to combine both the appeal and the referendum. (The vote alone could be construed as merely an expression of public opinion.)

3.

And this is how it stands today: the Circle of Judges has agreed to hear the case. Depositions are being taken, briefs prepared, the whole machinery has been set in motion. One positive result is that there is less fear, less talk about armed conflict. . . . Later news indicates, however, it may well be years before a decision is reached. One reason for the delay, it appears, is that public pressure is being exerted on the judges to disclose their places of residence. According to polls released a few days ago, a majority believe this would affect their decision. . . . One of the judges has just decided to disqualify himself. The thought that others might follow his example has given rise to further uneasiness—and as of this writing, we remain suspended between impossible alternatives.

1980/1981

More Than a Thing

—for David Gascoyne

1.

There was not enough to describe, to record. There was just the moment when, responding to her call, he entered and saw the spidery *thing* scoot across the pillow. He remembered making some kind of motion, then hearing her say: *It has as much right to be here as we have.* Was that in response to his gesture, or a message to herself? He had said something, then returned to the other room; as he stood beside the window, the sky and water claimed his attention. . . .

2.

They were in the house beside the sea. It was after a day spent walking on the beach, watching the boats move past the stone jetty. . . . They had returned in late afternoon. The wind had come up—not cold enough for a fire, but making it right for a drink, for the tape playing Vivaldi. . . .

3.

What after all was this "it"? Was his gesture, seen through her eyes, one that invited defense of the fragile *thing*? To make it more real, he could summon the image, even make a drawing, but that would be using the lines, the paper itself, as a substitute reality. . . .

4.

. . . Something moved beyond the window. It was a doe standing there head raised, neck arched, immobile. He was ready to turn, to call the woman, when a second doe appeared. He wondered then: Who are the witnesses, the intruders? Again, the slightest gesture could be interpreted as a threat. Yet if he remained silent, they might miss the unique moment, the moment come alive with their sharing. . . .

1981

Chance Scripts:
Selected Prose Poems, 1970–1987

The Concert Hall/The Big Tent/The Pasture

Music is perpetual, and only the hearing is intermittent. . . .

—Thoreau

1.

Consider this a farewell to you, my audience. Sending you this message, I set aside the musical skills I have developed slowly, painfully over the years. Some of you may regard this use of words, instead of music, as a sad mistake. That you will have to determine for yourselves. I know, however, that if I had attempted to reach you in the cloistered, enclosed space of the concert hall, it would have been perceived as an intrusion, a violation. Imagine the scene: the orchestra has just concluded its tuning up; there are a few moments of awkward silence; the heavy, dark curtain parts; and the composer, steps forth and begins what—incredibly—sounds like a lecture. . . .

2.

. . . I am standing in an open field preaching to the cows. The cows, the trees, the grass, the birds are too busy with the light, the wind, to be even called indifferent. . . . Nothing good, you say, can come of this. It is time to leave the scene, to exit in a graceful, dignified silence. Well, you are probably right—at least in the rational, logical world. I ask, though: what alternatives are there? My friends have by now all taken their places inside either the Concert Hall or the Big Tent. When I was younger, I did briefly appear in the Big Tent. The gaiety, the exuberance was appealing. But I soon learned I had none of the temperament, the personality of the performer. Now only the performers are in demand, and to follow their example, I would have to follow in their footsteps. . . .

3.

And to follow their example, I would have to follow in their footsteps. . . . The words repeat, this time with a different sound. As I hear it now, this would mean to exchange the sense of failure with an equally ambiguous, equally depressing notion of success. For what do the success seekers bring to their chosen art, and what do they take away? Whatever it is or was, something is lost in the process. What poured forth as original, undeniable impulse is now arranged to meet an established taste or longing. After a while, there is something even the most accomplished virtuoso, playing the prescribed music, can no longer call forth. If you have guessed that this has happened to me, you are probably right. You may then be more sympathetic to my decision to move offstage and take my place, unobtrusively, among you in the audience. . . .

4.

. . . What is to come of this, this period of prolonged listening? I cannot as yet be sure of what I hear, but strangely there is a greater clarity in what I see. I hope I will not be ridiculed for this, but at the moment what I perceive is a "thread" of sound. But where the thread might be leading, I cannot tell. So far it just seems to go on unwinding, drifting through the air. . . . Is the end result of all this intense listening to be nothing more than what the ancients already knew? *Not the play or the players—but the played upon?* For was it not the word itself, the word as music, of which the Psalmist sang: "I will incline mine ear to a parable: I will open my dark saying upon the harp." *Upon the harp*, I hear myself echoing, *upon the wind*.

1981/1986

Goodbye to a Village

1.

I had thought to remain here, without interference, as long as I wanted to. But the arrival of the letter—with its vague suggestion I might be needed elsewhere—has put this into question. While telling myself not to be upset, I have begun a kind of reprise, to consider not only what brought me here but what has kept me here. . . . Going back to first impressions: the view of winding streets, red-tiled roofs, the village itself surrounded by small, friendly hills. For once, I felt I had arrived where there was no split between being and belonging. Almost from the start, I noticed a quick, easy acceptance by those who were born and would die here. . . .

2.

My stay here may indeed be drawing to a close. I should have known this even without the letter. Signs of this now whenever I appear on the street. Where before there were special greetings, now there is a slight, embarrassed smile, a quick departure. I connect this somehow with the recent arrival of a small group—with whom I share the same language—whose presence has yet to be defined. It has even occurred to me that they may remain, as replacements, after I have gone. I have noticed already that their presence has brought something alien to the spirit of the village. So far there is no direct evidence, but I have begun to look at their faces, listen to their voices, with ever closer scrutiny. . . .

3.

A sudden disturbing thought: Couldn't the same suspicion have greeted me on my arrival? For who knows what brings one to these remote places and how one is perceived by the inhabitants? It is hard to tell, even for oneself, whether one is in search of or in flight from something. All the visible signs, and my own feeling, suggested I had come to the right place. But I was especially careful to avoid any self-deception. After all, I was among people for whom betrayal was almost a daily occurrence. I realized I would have to earn their trust, not seek their gratitude. . . . How different it seems for the recent arrivals! Already there are expressions of discontent, of having come here too late, or to the wrong place. . . .

4.

Does it make any difference whether I stay or go? The inhabitants continue with their lives, performing their simple tasks, as they always have. Still I find it hard to avoid the question: *But for how much longer?* As for the recent arrivals, what is this village to them? Perhaps no more than just another part of their floating world, to be talked about, written about, and then abandoned. One can almost predict the course of their disenchantment, followed by the withdrawal, the whispers: *Not here: This is not the place.*

5.

I realize now I should be grateful for the opportunity presented by the letter. For the chance to leave before the rumors start that there is another village—closer to the forest, the jungle—where the "real people" may be found. My mind turns toward what stirred me so deeply when I arrived. The women in the marketplace, kneeling among the shawls and pottery, or offering for sale those incredible blue and orange-colored mushrooms. The woodcutters at first light, setting off for the tree-lined hills, the donkeys alongside, their lifelong companions. The small boys carrying, strapped to their backs, unknown burdens, whatever anyone paid them to carry . . .

6.

And what to say to these burdened children? I could tell them about the letter: "They wrote to me and said it was time. . . ." But what would that sound like to those who have never been taught to read? They would have to imagine a voice that comes from elsewhere and gives orders that are to be followed. But these are the children who are born and die here, without ever having known any *elsewhere*!

And is there anything to tell the recent arrivals? I could try saying, *Mira, no mas.* "Just look, that's all." But that, I suppose, is what they cannot do. For even the sight of those faces, those ancient time-haunted eyes, and their illusions, their personal quests and adventures, might come to an abrupt and intolerable end.

1970/1986

Limbo

Once more I have written a book. With what in mind and at what effort, I do not intend to say. I acknowledge though that I have thought and rethought, written and rewritten, calling upon all I know and can imagine. And the result is—something the world has surely the greatest need of—another book. But even as I write this, I recognize the poor attempt at humor. For it is not "another," it is this book—or even, so help me, *the book*.

What is still difficult to admit, now that it is out there, is that it is now in the hands of *strangers*. But that may give the wrong impression, for it has not yet found a publisher. And as things stand, it may never be published. What then do I mean by saying it is "out there"? It seems obvious: out of my hands and into "theirs."

. . . I see now what I have retreated from, what I have avoided saying. It means what it has always meant, though unacknowledged, unstated: it is *I* who have been placed in the hands of strangers. And the terrible thing is that I alone have made this choice, have sought this result, have persisted through endless hours, painful choices, all in order to . . .

1981/1986

The Book/The Mailing

. . . At last the day comes when I appear, nervous but in good spirits, at the book-binder's. As he hands me the wrapped parcel, he advises me not to look inside, but to take it at once to the post office. Time was when I could not have done this, could not have trusted myself that much. But now I feel more in charge, prepared to handle the doubts, the longing for just one more look. . . . Very well, then: the book is not only written, but printed and bound. After the long struggle with words, sentences, chapters, I can begin to live again as others live. No detours, I tell myself, straight to the post office . . . Arriving there, I go to the nearest window. Standing behind it is an attractive young woman in a dark blue cotton smock. As she asks the contents, I tell her it is a book. Of course, she says, and you must be the author. When I nod agreement, she is pleased, excited. She calls over a few of her coworkers. *Good luck*, they say, *all the best for you and your book*. . . . I leave in the best of moods. I have done what I set out to do. I am wise enough now to know that the story is like all other stories: someone is falling in love, someone is dying, someone is being born. . . .

. . . Does it matter that the book was lost in transit? That someone planted a bomb in the mailbox, and all that was left was a few charred fragments? Some of you may think that was a terrible outcome. But you would be wrong. For the fact is, as we both know, it was lost the moment it left the hands of the author. . . .

1970/1986

The Error Catastrophe

. . . F.'s return is unexpected. He phones one morning, having just arrived from the East Coast. In spite of my resolve not to permit any more unscheduled visits, I agree to see him. . . . A half hour later, he is at the door. Not much change since his last visit, about two years ago. He is still shy, almost inarticulate, except on the subject of his work. But since he is the only scientist I've known for a long period of time, I still find this interesting. (As much of it, at least, as I can understand.) His news is that he has been working on some compounds that may have an analog in nature. I sense his excitement, even though these exist at present only in the laboratory. He is confident, in his quiet way, that his results will be verified, duplicated. (Later in the day, after his departure, it occurs to me that his compounds are, and may remain, genuine enigmas. Reflecting further, I attempt an aphorism: *The incomparable is also the impenetrable.*)

. . . I have been trying, in exchange, to tell him something of what I'm working on. For it seems necessary to preserve the semblance of a dialogue, even though our words may falter at the edge of contrasting worlds. My writing too, I say, seeks some kind of analog in nature. Feeling somewhat reckless, I venture that there is a metaphor that makes relations apparent, but also metaphor as analog that transcends scale. Something in these words (I'm not sure what) suggests what he calls "the error catastrophe." It sounds very strange—as though nature has calculated in advance how to profit from its own mistakes. Those scientists, he says, who subscribe to this view even call themselves "catastrophists." I get the strange feeling that confirmation of this belief among them would be important, no matter what it includes.

. . . Our words move back and forth from one world to another. Through it all, the word *analog* serves as a bridge, a point of reference. As I keep trying to translate his experience into familiar terms, I suddenly remember René Daumal's book, *Mount Analogue*. I tell him briefly about the quest, about the travelers climbing a symbolic mountain. His response startles me: "I'll be leaving here in the morning. Going to do some hiking." And he names a nearby mountain. In a sense that finishes the conversation, for although I repeat the name of the book, I'm sure he will never read it. . . .

I keep trying, after he leaves, to remember more of what the book contains. And trying to connect it with his pursuit of those peculiar compounds. (Which presumably have been there all along, waiting to be discovered and named.) I feel somewhat resentful, as if I had failed to say what most needed saying: that his empirical search is just as saturated with illusion as anything encountered by Daumal's nebulous group of travelers on their own basically unbelievable mountain.

1981/1986

The Candidate/The Canceled Child

1.

Let it be known: no matter what the inducements, I am not a candidate. Those who are—their names are known to you—have worked hard and long to get their names in lights, their faces on the screen. And by offering their faces, their names for public inspection, they may fill a need, provide some essential service. I don't happen to believe this, but on rare occasions it might be the case. . . .

2.

What brings this to mind is a recent conversation with an editor of a small, new publishing firm. We were meeting for the first time, talking generally about writers whom we both knew. I noticed a large manuscript displayed prominently on his desk. As he followed my glance, he reached over and handed it to me. When I indicated that the name was unfamiliar, he said it was the work of a talented young poet who had suicided a month before, at the age of twenty-five. I thought at first that some real question was involved—something for me to understand or comment on—but as I handed it back, he said, "This is going to be a valuable property."

3.

What did I start to say? Something about personal politics in the literary scene, and the curious resemblance—as the microcosm to the macrocosm—it has to politics on the grand scale. At least that's what I had in mind. Yes, I know now: the Candidates—the self-advancers—were to be the target. But surely that is too obvious for comment. More important is what happened to C., dead at twenty-five: *canceled.* For if we are to really consider this, we may find the prototype within a long tradition.

There is something to be said for the intensity of the short life. And there is some peculiar connection with the intensity that the Candidate seeks and generates. As if there might be some failed or dead artist buried deep within them. Next time you find yourself standing close to one of them, try looking closely, notice what is missing from his eyes. . . .

1981/1986

Framis: More or Less Himself

1.

Those who have heard of him—one time or another, one country or another—will have doubts about what follows. They may call this a biased, personal report, and frankly so it is. I start with a statement you may accept or reject: Framis can appear anywhere, anytime. Need I add: in one of his many aspects? It is not merely a question of disguise or costume, but that his *being* and his *seeming* are in fact inseparable. This I have come to believe is his greatest strength, the source of his most lasting appeal. For he does not, as those we see every day, derive from a cluster of fictions. It would be more correct to describe him as a natural force, a kind of weather. . . . I might go on in this vein, using various metaphors, making all sorts of claims. But this would only underline my belief that Framis cannot be contained or defined within the usual boundaries. . . .

2.

Framis was, Framis is, Framis will be. I say this as quietly, as gently as the words permit. Others of course might not be so circumspect. In the present climate, with its ambiguous longing for both the exalted and the debased, one can imagine Framis as Saint, as Sinner, within a scenario that places him one moment in the public eye, the next in some elusive, subterranean existence. Some kind of cosmic traveler, moving not merely across the earth, but in some grander, wider space. So that wherever he goes, whenever he returns, he stretches our tolerance for the incredible. . . .

3.

. . . I have been asked once more to confirm the rumors of Framis's impending return. I can only say that, sooner or later, in one form or another, he will reappear. Whether this will satisfy our most urgent need, that is another matter. For it is possible that instead of rejoicing, we may feel let down or angry. We may witness, then, what we are not prepared to accept or approve. I have in mind certain occasions when he transformed a whole array of props, which he first summoned, then made disappear. As I recall, these included a large tub of wet cement, a dangling rope, a plaster tree—along with various other insidious and anxious objects. There are those who, on the basis of this, predict that, in his next "materialization," he may feel inclined to do away with such items as a dressmaker's dummy, an enormous pincushion, a fur-lined teacup. Items that have for so long dominated the symbolic landscape of our time.

4.

And now to conclude, I offer a few key words essential to understanding what Framis is really about: *dream* and *redeem*, *resist* and *exist*. Words I have heard him say not once but many times. But one must not be surprised if he follows these serious, almost programmatic words with some incredible gesture. Like pulling a hair from his beard and handing it to you: "Here, use this for a filament." And be ready if, a moment later, his physical being begins to contract—growing smaller and smaller until there is nothing, absolutely nothing, left but an aura, a charged space. . . .

1982/1985

The Lost Parable

We show ourselves at our best, or worst, in how we feel about what we have lost.

—R. W. Wainwright

1.

It is no longer possible to think of the text as misplaced or missing. Too much time has passed for that. I have to admit the loss and, as so often before, put it out of mind. And yet, and yet . . . Mind has so many recesses and residues, who can tell what may yet slip through in an unexpected, unguarded moment? And even if it is beyond any literal retrieval, it may still find some other existence. I mean, aside from the physical text, that it may be constelled in one mind or another, where its "home" is memory . . . This is no vain hope, for there are indeed those whose memory can be called upon. As it happens, I asked one recently if she remembered that afternoon—about a year ago—when I had read the parable to a group of mutual friends. She answered, "But of course: it was at Bill's house. You read the one about the forest." She supplied a few references that coincided, rather closely, with my own memory. Then she added, to my surprise, that she had talked with a few of the others, and they had agreed it was one of my best pieces of writing.

2.

It is this, I now realize, that I find so depressing. It is hard to deal with the thought that I have been unable to equal these lost words. But what I have written since has lacked some quality I find hard to define. I cannot make the comparison, for all I remember is a small part of the content: a small group of adult students has signed up for a tour of an area designated as wilderness. The "tour" has included lectures and seminars on survival: the search for edible plants, construction of emergency shelters, what to do upon losing a sense of direction, how to deal with predatory animals, etc. All this I can recognize as proposed by the rational, conscious mind. What was strange (how did I come to write this?) was a group activity called *Hunt the Abandoned Child*. This was not merely a game but a climax of the survival tests. I recall also that there was available, for those who remained for the whole course, several units of school credit. But of course, this was optional. . . .

3.

Why does it sound so like a dream? Yet I remember having worked hard and long on the writing. In any case, there was the reading before the group. The comments, I recall, were certainly favorable, if less than ecstatic. It is only now that I hear this unqualified praise. . . . This should be enough, I realize, to make me suspicious. But

I have to stop thinking entirely about these missing pages and show, instead, the confidence and strength of mind to move past this latest disappointment. As with all that is gone and "forgotten," there will be compensation in having conceived the work, given it existence. As for what may happen now, there is an impetus, a residue that lives on. I believe what I have to believe: that it will make its presence felt—perhaps just at that moment when I face the blank page that waits to be inscribed. . . .

1981/1986

Second to the Wolf

. . . He heads north until he reaches a place with a name: Glacier Bay. That is, it has a name, is marked on his map. Beyond that there is nothing: no dwellings, no inhabitants. But this is where he has planned to pitch his tent. It is still daylight, late afternoon. As he unpacks his gear, prepares to build a fire, a wolf appears. . . . Listening to him tell this, we sense his excitement. The year before, we recall, it was sighting an eagle that climaxed the trip. In other years (each year at this time he heads north, to the same general area), there was an encounter with a bear. Another time he came upon an old Indian camp that apparently no one before him had come across. . . . We begin to wonder: Why the wolf? The story, in fact, has no climax: just the wolf standing there, for a long time, watching him, then taking off through the woods. . . . He has presented it, though, as a culmination of past experiences. Which only begins to make sense when he tells us this was his last trip. He says that it ended *perfectly*: at last the one thing that was missing . . . his joy and our resentment. We who have never even dreamed of this kind of adventure. Who have always required the known in the known circumstance: the house, the street, the city, the voice that speaks directly to us. . . . Now his voice changes from exultation to something vague, uncertain, as he says: *No more . . . can't keep it up . . .* The conversation ends with his saying he'll see us next year. The promise has the sound of resignation: going *south*, where we live, is evidently a poor alternative. It is clear then, in spite of the long friendship, what we really are to him: *second to the wolf.*

1981/1986

No Time for Gestures

When we die, we don't leave the world—rather it leaves us.
—Edvard Munch

It has happened so often that the idea is ingrained. Our journeys have been of limited duration, to a known destination. And each departure has been followed by a return. At some point, however, we start to think about, even prepare for, a departure that is without return. It is then that we find ourselves—like actors learning a new part—rehearsing certain gestures. We wonder then: which is the most appealing, the most appropriate? Lacking an audience and not trusting the verdict of the mirrors, we cannot tell which to choose. We continue setting the scene, summoning various colors and textures, trying to decide about music and speech, makeup and costume. . . . Someone is sure to ask at this point: does it have to be so theatrical? We do not respond but go on arranging the decor, the lights, the shadows. As if we could indeed enhance those last moments with an aura, a special intensity. But the rational mind, breaking in on this complicated reverie, tells us that *this* departure is not what we perform—but what is performed upon us.

All this could be written by anyone—with just an adequate imagination—in touch with their deepest fears and longings. What cannot be written, planned for, is what happens to come our way. As for instance this letter from a friend who quotes these words of Edvard Munch. Now it has come to my attention, I have still to think more and longer of what it means. If I read it right, there is no time for gestures. For it is not departure that we face, but an abrupt, unprecedented abandonment. . . .

1982/1986

A Picture in the Voice?

Where there is something to draw, there is something to draw upon. Are these words his own, or has he read them somewhere? Following the thought, he is not sure what it means. Perhaps that only what can be seen (perceived?) can be expressed. If nothing more is involved, it is too literal, too familiar. He is ready to let it go, turn his attention elsewhere. But there is a sudden feeling of uneasiness. As though what the mind has rescued from the void amounts only to this: no picture, nothing, no idea. So that the effort to put picture into words—or words into picture—is inherently a waste of time. . . .

He stands in front of a mirror. What he sees reminds him only vaguely of what he used to see. For the aging face tells a different story. One that even now is being written on his flesh. He walks away, walks through the rooms that remind him of his life. On one wall is a photograph of his younger self; on another wall, from about the same period, is a pencil drawing, a portrait, done by a friend. Something to draw upon—*or something that defeats time and memory?* On other walls, pictures, various objects, masks, spread across where and what he has been. His presence, his being here, is linked with all this. The next step, he tells himself, is to decipher, to remember what all this means. But if this were possible, something else would be missing. *If only there were a voice in the picture—or a picture in the voice?*

At the threshold of nonsense and silence, he chooses silence.

1982/1986

The Feathers of My Wife

. . . Once more we are walking on the beach. As so often before, I see her hesitate, stop, and search the sand. *What is it this time?* I see only sand—no pebbles, no shells, nothing. I walk on, certain she will follow in a moment. But then I too stop, turn and look back. She bends down, picks up a small gray feather. *A feather?* While I wait, she gathers a few more. There is about her an air of discovery, something in the way she holds them. . . . The sea calm; fishing boats anchored in the bay. One of the good days, I think, one of *our* better days. For a few moments she remains beside me, walking at the same pace. But she says nothing; her eyes continue probing the sand.

. . . I recall times we walked on other beaches, along this same coastline, or earlier, in other countries. Even then, I realize, we seldom walked side by side. Either I would lag behind, stopping to light my pipe, or she would be picking up this and that, accumulating her "treasures." I think of the crowded shelves at home: boxes crammed with pebbles, tinted glass, dried, brittle miniature crabs. . . .

The true distance, I think, is in the seeing. Our view of things, like our footsteps, never quite matched. The tinted glass, the shells, the pebbles—*and now the feathers?* What she saw in and through these things, I have yet to discover. For what I saw— what I see now—is the usual intersection of beach, sea, and sky. Children playing in the sand, seagulls diving, dogs running toward the water. What is there to add; what is there to take away? What has escaped me, what has escaped her, that this is not enough?

1983/1986

Between Worlds

An interview with M. in the morning paper. Now seventy, he has just published his twentieth book, a memoir of his early years. The photograph shows him much the same as when I last saw him, ten or twelve years ago. I remember how I kept urging friends to read him as one of the most neglected of our novelists. How remote it seems now, thinking of all those "vanished worlds." Still I am touched by M.'s reference to "memory and emotion" as essential to the imagination. This while one wonders if there are any serious readers left . . .

A letter just received from a young writer. He insists on the need for "new vantage points." He says there must be alternatives to the established forms: different words for a different time. I place the letter beside the interview. The two voices resonate a dilemma. I wonder if these split allegiances are inevitable, or can somehow be reconciled. . . .

All this has had more impact than I expected. I have been trying now to write things that reflect these different ways of seeing. The result is confusion, close to chaos. For if M.'s "memory and emotion" is set aside, what is left may be mere information, mechanical noise. While the other view, which seeks surprise, discovery, may achieve only the brief span of novelty . . . It has occurred to me, in the last few days, there is within us—beyond the level of "citizen," of "artist"—two distinct creatures. One sets off to join the thirsty herd, in search of nourishment at the waterhole. The other, with the same features and form, moves slowly, inexorably in the direction of the darkening hills. . . .

1981/1986

The Agony of Crevices

For those who have not heard the sound—imagine twilight in one of those bleak, shattered places—I assure you it can be both painful and puzzling. There is a sense of vanished worlds, brought closer as one thinks of the ravaged, the unavenged, the homeless dead. . . . A few days ago I was reading the report of an obscure archaeologist, written early in the century. What struck me was a brief reference to "a peculiar *humming noise*, apparently issuing forth from between the stones." Still trying to absorb this, I read further: "Strange to be hearing this—since it was on the evening of the very day we had decided to abandon the site."

—

The space between? Cries and whispers of the abandoned—heard just when their story was about to be told? It seems quite fanciful, yet I wonder: We know about those vast trenches where victims of plague, war, genocide are buried, but what of those small fissures between earth and stone? Who knows what worlds of betrayal, of chilling, dreadful secrets might be hidden there? So far, this is beyond the range of even our most advanced, most delicate instruments. But some day we may hear and be able to decipher the message. And trace that *humming noise* back to those torn from life, voicing in strange syllables their abandonment and neglect. Then we will know what is concealed within the agony of crevices. The question then will be: how to respond to their fractured voices, in chorus with the impatient cry of the as yet unborn?

1978/1986

One Vote for the Vulture

. . . He had written of the growing feeling of menace in the city, the alternative of moving to the country. But had added a kind of symbolic warning: "Those who consider this, however, should know that the vulture, the dreadful image, is sometimes mistaken for the hawk, the symbol of freedom."

But reading this, she found it hard to accept. The hawk, she said, had nothing to do with freedom. Witness the field mouse plucked from the grass, the tiny cries unheard by an indifferent, amoral sky. On the other hand, she thought that one might respect, if not admire, the essential role of the vulture: "Without him the landscape would be littered with half-digested, torn-apart creatures. . . ."

It comes to mind for both of them, while walking on the beach, at the sight of the torn body of a baby seal. They stand for a moment, looking up at the birds circling, looking down at the flies on the wet gray flesh. Ahead of them is a stone jetty marking the end of the beach. They set off in that direction, slowly and in silence. They watch a few fishing boats heading out toward the open sea. . . . He looks up, scanning the clear sky; the vultures are now out of sight. He extends his hand; their fingers close. For a while they walk this way; then as they turn toward home, their fingers loosen. They move farther and farther apart. . . .

1981/1986

A Stone Taking Notes

Somewhere among us a stone is taking notes.
                    —Charles Simic

1.
Surely not your ordinary stone: something that appears in the field of vision, that you glance at and turn away from. The poet calls it "a stone," but bestows upon it a special, unique status. What goes through the mind, if we decide to honor the poet's imagination, may be something like this: can a mere stone be so endowed, transformed, elevated? Doesn't this usurp the role of listener: our role? And note that the poet doesn't stop there: he implies that the stone is positioned somewhere out of sight. *Somewhere?* The location is left vague enough to suggest a disturbing mystery. For while the next words—*among us*—apparently shorten the distance, it remains remote and hidden. As for the concluding words—*taking notes*—surely this augments our uneasiness, plays upon the surface of our always latent paranoia. . . .

2.
Assume this is indeed a stone set apart from all others, from any we have noticed or studied. Try then to visualize color, shape, size—even adding distinctive marks and scratches. Enough to make it identifiable. Does this mean we can convert *any* apparently anonymous object into an efficient "machine"—or even a piece of art? A thought I find both intriguing and depressing. For it opens the possibility that the designated object may have or acquire personality, judgment, will—even desire. (A stone's "desire" is a subject we may speculate upon freely—for who could prove us wrong?) And since we have gone this far, say that a stone's most profound, most secret desire is to discard its anonymity, to be emblemized: *Rosetta, Sphinx, Pyramid, Cleopatra's Needle*, etc. We may add to this list others that, for one reason or another, have achieved their own eternal name.

3.
At this point someone *among us* (!) is sure to claim we are better off without emblems. But someone else, more experienced, wiser, is likely to reply: *without emblems there can be no legends. Without legends, we can have no heroes. Without heroes, all that is menacing, inaccessible must remain that way. . . . Out of reach those distant ice fields and moon fields, never to know the sound of live footsteps and answering voices . . .* But then suddenly it occurs to us: if a stone can take notes, why not also record, store, transmit? Imagine retrieving the sound of vanished worlds: dinosaurs mating, the great cry of perishing populations before the flood, the fire, the erupting volcano.

. . . A stone that survives, tells this much, yet leaves some part of its secret coded message intact, some faint signal, not quite decipherable, that might signify another chance, another dawn for consciousness.

1982/1986

How Tall Was Toulouse-Lautrec?

The film presents the life. Costume and decor, choreography and spectacle offer entertainment as evidence. The paintings, the posters dissolve; what remains is a vague memory of a few staged scenes. One is of the actor, absurdly dressed in black and white formal clothes. We see him bowing, tipping the stovepipe hat. But this only reminds us: it is the *actor*, not the artist, who claims our sympathy, touches our sense of pathos and distress. Another scene: interview with his mother in the elegant, high-ceilinged room. Close-up of the mother's face: the absence of any real suffering. A dialogue between strangers. Sense of tradition and privilege enforcing a politeness—a conspiracy to pretend—that obscures everything.

━

Toulouse-Lautrec in the café with the cancan dancers. The faces, the figures remind us of what—somewhere else—is real art. The posters come to mind at the same moment that they appear on the screen. They appear now, in close-up, faded and peeling from the wall, in the relentless rain. . . . The scene shifts to the warm, dry rooms of the whorehouse, where he relaxes in the profusion of ample, perfumed flesh. Here he is known and welcome, in this refuge from loneliness and isolation. The women carry on a bantering conversation, while he sits propped, doll-like, on the edge of the bed. . . . *How tall was Toulouse-Lautrec?* The absurd question enters the mind from some unlikely source. *Tall, dark, and handsome.* What brings the cliché, the stereotype? Something in us that equates endurance and pain with the romantic hero. In any case, the absurd image drives out the real biography of the real man. But in a few minutes, the counterimage returns: the bulging back, the too-large head, the withered legs. Not a freak in this version, but a creature at home in a world he has created for himself. *At home?* We are more inclined to place him—the man, not the actor—among those on whom life has played its cruel joke. Is there a kinship with all of those, or some of those? Is there for him, *for them*, some "compensation" that might sustain the soul—beyond neglect and ridicule?

━

About that kinship: imagine the spirit of the dead artist entering a procession of the freaks and dispossessed. Think of them as having departed, bound for some other realm, not available to the more normal dead. . . . See them arriving in some undefined elsewhere, where their bruised and trampled souls may find refuge. . . . Imagination will not take us all the way, but permits us to approach the threshold, the boundary. From there, night after night, we may hear sounds of music, of rejoicing. Enough to suggest that Giant and Dwarf have found not only solace, but at last fulfillment of their dearest, wildest dreams.

1981/1986

Among Other Things

The freedom of each word, punctuated by an obscurity.
—André du Bouchet

1.
Silence prints upon the page. Black letters assemble into a pattern; one by one the words, the sentences form. We follow across and down the page; we enter into and depart from a series of realities. We observe here turning into there, then into now, there and then into elsewhere. All at once a particular place and time emerges, seeks its specific image, its undeniable name. Event follows event, encounter follows encounter. From all this, something we have come to think of as "the real subject" has begun to emerge. . . .

2.
I have written your name and placed it somewhere. More precious when the scrap of paper is apparently lost and then by accident found again. . . . Holding it in my hand, I notice that the letters are small, the handwriting almost indecipherable. What is missing, of course, is your face, your voice. . . . As I recall it now, I saw your face, that first time, without hearing your voice. You were standing on a red-tiled floor in a small alcove beside a row of white candles. I watched from a distance as you leaned forward and blew them out one by one. It was too soon to come forward, to announce myself. It occurred to me then: for every being born, endowed with a name, there is another who remains unsignified, at home in the dark.

3.
So at times the lost one is retrieved, identified. The dialogue that began so suddenly—and stopped without apparent reason— begins again. Begins where it left off: with your passionate references to the living beast. The beast, you said, may be perceived in different ways. As the target, to be approached with our sharpest, deadliest weapons. But also as the object of worship, to be garlanded with flowers, paraded in ritual procession . . . I believe you went on like this for some time. Finally I had heard enough. What has all this, I asked, to do with men, with the rulers of men? We both know that the statue may be toppled, the monument destroyed by the raging crowd. The King may be deposed, exiled to a bleak, distant island. . . .

4.
Suppose then that we arranged to meet on that same island. Suppose even that we were to send word to the King that we would like to be invited for lunch or for tea.

Awaiting his response, we could spend time on the beach. We could talk of this and that, pretend that we understand each other. Whether the invitation comes or not, we could agree to meet again—perhaps the following year. We could even send word to our closest friends: come and join us where the sky is lettered, where the late glow is Byzantine.

5.

. . . Already you have begun drifting off, returning to the wind and fog of memory. Are you going then—once more to assume your true reality in the realm of *back there and then?* It brings to mind one of your previous incarnations and disappearances. The last words you said were "If only the world was a brighter place." I watched you then turn silently toward the shadows on the wall. And I thought: if only we could go back to that morning in the Cathedral, when we followed the monks in their trailing robes. . . . Dear friend, don't you see that even now, at the very moment of your departure, there is some other vague figure coming toward us. Notice the grave courtesy of his silent, almost imperceptible greeting. And if either of us were to ask him "Will it be any different next time we meet?"—surely we both know the answer.

1973/1986

Question of a Shovel:
Notes Toward—and Away from—the Writing of a Poem

Deeper than the summer
The shovel breaks,
Deeper than the cry
In another dream

　　—Yves Bonnefoy

There is no way to read about people who lived a million years ago.
We must find their bones.

　　　　　　　　　　　　　—Kamoya Kimeu

Deeper in our lives, in our minds
Than any song, than any pictures

　　—George Oppen

1.

Two items in the morning paper, juxtaposed, bring forth the thought, present a challenge. The first is of an unnamed city official reacting to new rumors of a long-delayed building project: "I'll believe it when I see the shovel." The second is the story of Kamoya Kimeu, the fossil hunter, the man from Kenya. Turning from one to the other, I sense opposing views of reality. The city official seems to be saying: *Wait for the tangible reality; the rest is conversation.* While the fossil hunter, already renowned for his discoveries, reminds us of what takes place in the mind as one reaches the source . . . *Whatever comes to mind, comes to eye, comes to hand.* I have written this somewhere, and wonder now if it is true. I summon the image of the clenched hands, the weathered wood, the stained blade. With a little further effort, I picture the body twisting, the blade thrust toward the ground. . . . I recall the recent digging in the vacant lot across the street. The scene shifts to another place, another time: a desert in Africa, a mountain in Brazil. . . . I sense the questions forming—questions I do not feel prepared to answer. A number of literary allusions come to mind; none are adequate to the real act in a real landscape. Not words, but experience, must tell the tale. And I have held and used a shovel so seldom that . . .

2.

. . . Shovel lying flat on the ground. Who left it there, for what reason? It belongs in the potting shed, with the other tools, found there when we moved into the house. Strange that, in all these years, I have never questioned their presence. I assumed they were left there by the former owner for work in the garden. . . . *There was that other garden, where we entered going past the iron gates: tropical flowers, the perfumed air in a secluded place above the drowned city. . . . That other garden, the high-walled garden where the children were playing. Gunfire in the distance. The children led away, never to return . . .*

3.

The mind moves abruptly from *garden* to *trench*. And not just a small, shallow trench, but something wider, deeper that extends somewhere out of sight. Something to stand up in or crouch down inside while exploding objects fall from the sky . . . So after all these years, I have come to the question of the shovel. To wonder how this simple tool has retained its integrity, its basic shape through all the wars, the disasters, the tedious, painful attempts to rebuild, to restore . . . What occurs to me is that the shovel is in the shoveling (as the hammer is in the hammering). The unexpected words restate the question: Who is shoveling and for what reason? Shovels raised and lowered. Shovels digging a trench, a tunnel—but also sifting through debris, through mounds of garbage . . . *What can be retrieved, what can be redeemed?* Something forms at the edge of perception. It may be a dream, a film, a memory. Suddenly there is a city, many cities; at their outer limits, in the early-morning light, crowds gather. Bent bodies cluster around piles of rubbish; busy hands scrounge and forage for something to use, to repair, to sell. For a chair, a table, a blanket, a child's toy—whatever can be carried off to the squatter's shack, the tarpaper shelter . . .

4.

But it is too hard to dwell on this. The mind seeks alleviation: something more tolerable, more pleasant. I look beyond the cities, beyond the hills, to the shore of a calm blue sea. Inevitably, as I sift through the familiar images, there is a child playing in the sand. As remembered, almost as ordered, he holds a toy shovel, moves dirt into and out of a toy pail. After a while, he throws the shovel aside, begins scooping and shaping the moist sand. He has something in mind—whatever it is, it confirms an element in the child's world, bringing a smile of recognition and pleasure. . . . Perhaps it is not too different from those who are digging for shards and artifacts, when they find fragments that connect a missing part of their world. Among them I place now the man whose picture is in the morning paper: the fossil hunter, the man from Kenya: "There is no way to read about people who lived a million years ago. We must find their bones."

5.

And when we find their bones: will it tell us about ourselves as well? Will it be something we need to know, or prefer not to know? Will there be a small hole in the skull—

made, we guess, by some vengeful instrument—a hole that narrows the distance between then and now? We have come this far with an image of a thing. But no single idea, no single image. For we have encountered along the way conflicting images: the shovel as toy, tool, weapon. For each one who thinks of uncovering new life, new growth, there are many who think only: it throws dirt on your face. We cannot choose among them, for none of them are wrong. We can only wonder at what sight or sound comes through our voices. Still unsure of what it is we have to tell, we feel a poem stirring, seeking a space not occupied by story and photograph. . . .

6.
Between shadow and stone
      between the hand that searches
      and the hand that is sought
let the shovel decide—
While Kamoya Kimeu having located the skull of a man
a million years old   probes now for the fingers—
Let the shovel decide   how far the blade goes in
between the delicate layers
      before the form emerges
that tells us what we were and are—
Let earth itself be witness
      to the mingled grass and blood
      as the red and green we live with
      the brown we have yet to imagine.

Life & Death of a Guide

Man's natural situation is to be disoriented and lost.
> —José Ortega y Gasset

You can't get there from here.
> —Yankee proverb

Say that we are in fact here. That we have a legitimate desire, a sensible purpose in wanting to be there. It appears that we may begin to plan and prepare for departure. But as we look into the matter, we discover it is not that simple. For the "there" we have in mind appears in different places on different maps. A growing number of uncertainties stand in the way: besides the exact route, the availability of food and lodging, there is the unpredictable weather. All this combines to make us realize that its accurate name is *elsewhere*.

It is then that we are put to the test. Our need for and love of adventure is balanced against our instinct for self-preservation. And if these were the only alternatives, we might find ourselves stalemated, mired in a dilemma. But fortunately there is still the option of hiring a guide. Not the guide who only knows the trails in familiar places, but one who has himself survived passage through *terra incognita*.

I want to make it clear now that I am not recommending myself. I have been asked at different times to join a party of explorers—and once even to lead an expedition. I realized early that I had neither the temperament nor the stamina for such under-takings. I have on occasion, on request, offered a few words of "guidance," but that is all. Aside from this, especially in these latter years, I have not thought of going anywhere. I feel now that it is enough to be what one already is. Being here, then, has replaced the desire for going or getting somewhere. As for a voyage or journey to *elsewhere,* there is one that may require no effort or plan. Love is a companion that takes us to the boundary, but there is no guide across the threshold. . . . I begin to hear rumors that I can only identify as coming from the dead, the unborn. But it would be foolish, and premature, to repeat them.

1986

Say He Arrives There

Whether the image arrives or is somehow summoned, it is hard to tell. What appears, though, is the figure of a man, hunched over, staring out across an immense, empty stadium. He is seated in a lower tier, somehow near the center; around him the deserted rows suggest an eerie, almost grotesque absence. Who is he? What brings him here? No clue in his appearance: an unlikely combination of introspection and anonymity. He could be a former athlete coming back for one more view of the playing fields, dreaming of past glories. Or a discharged employee—a groundskeeper?—returning out of habit, having nowhere else to go. He could also be—are there any limits?—a confused sports fan, appearing on the wrong day, having forgotten to check the schedule. . . .

—

. . . As to what brings me here, I cannot be sure. There is an impulse to go where one is not expected, where one does not belong. One has had this feeling before, but this time it is stronger than any restraints: the desire to experience, in isolation, what attracts and motivates the passionate multitude. For what surrounds me here is the shared reality of witnesses to a contest that is part game, part war. This is what excites the crowd, allowing them to identify with those who perform the alternating roles of hero and victim. In this arena, physical encounters, given the status of events, are offered as the food of memory, the feast of legend.

. . . I feel impelled to rise now, to salute those enactments of triumph and disaster, those ghostly banners and emblems unfurled by the shifting wind. I turn and look above, below, all around me, wondering how to signify my presence.

And then I understand what I have to do: I bring my hands together in a slow, rhythmic applause. A few moments later, I feel ready to begin my speech. . . . It is hard to believe what I am hearing: a small but sympathetic response. It comes from one section, then another: voices sounding through their own silence, their own invisibility. I take my place with those who have yet to be heard, to be recognized.

1986

The Door to Have

When I saw that door, in that house, I knew I had to have it.
—Georgia O'Keeffe

Remember that she chose an austere landscape. That she lived in it and created—among other things—paintings of flowers. Nothing like the still lifes we had seen before, but the single flower, augmented, magnified. In pursuit of that vision—so we imagine—she placed next to the flower, a skull, a sky suffused with strong, clear light. . . .

But we are getting away from *that door*, and what it might have signified. Assume then that it kept in what she needed to enclose; kept out confusion, distraction; helped her to focus what she faced day after day: sun, sand, stone. Shadows spreading as she returned to the focus of arrival and departure. Waiting for her—as she touched the hard, cool knob—was the threshold to inner space, refreshing as water in an earthen jar. The door she had to have: the precise marker in all that vast and void-like uncertainty . . .

But how could she have known that? Intuition we know can be correlative of will and desire, can offer its growing forms as deliberate as evidence. What is less obvious, harder to decipher, is how these forms flowered and danced in her mind. For something like this set in motion an intricate transaction between eye, mind, and hand—opened the way between paint and brush and canvas. The door, after all, did open and close; space within walls merged with space within herself. . . .

. . . Walking past the paintings, we arrive at a world not seen before. Not sure yet what we are looking at, looking for. No single name, here or elsewhere, contains the whole array of thought and feeling. And yet there is the sense of something solid and self-sustaining. The knob itself is cool to the touch. . . .

The Door to Have (2)

Facing the desert on a copper morning
the sun factored her skin and mind:
imprint of the primary line waiting to find
its further life in paint—insistent questions
kept her returning to a dark still space
where whitewashed walls waited to be filled. . . .

In retrospect we wonder how she survived
the light that swam through shadow: to create
the flower more predator than prey—something there
frightens even while it reassures: refraction
of will and desire upon the hard-edged door
closing upon the space that framed her eye and mind. . . .

It was important to know she could step inside
and be there at the exact meridian to calculate
the orbit of earthly terrors: self-scaled delights—
measure her mood and motive with the dry clear
transit of the desert night: guess how the fragrant stars
told her where landscape ended: where the worlds conjoined.

1986/1987

The Trouble with Keys

It was not that long ago that we read the story of the man waiting to be admitted by the Doorkeeper. The lesson of it was so powerful, so clear that it dominated our imagination. It was not that we were denied access, but our own passivity, our lack of self-esteem kept us outside. . . . How much has changed since then! One hardly ever hears now about the Door as an obstacle, a barrier. The Doorkeeper himself has, as it were, completely disappeared, forced perhaps to seek other employment, the occupation itself become anachronistic, obsolete. If we still have a problem with access, it is that with everything apparently available, we no longer know where to turn. . . .

I seem to have overstated the case. We still have a problem with access, but this appears now in a different light. It is no longer a problem with doors, but a problem with keys. I refer first to the common experience of misplacing and losing keys. Inquiry at various Lost and Found Departments reveals that of all the articles we deal with every day, it is the key that is lost most often. . . .

. . . Perhaps I cannot explain this after all. There is so much more to be considered than I realized. For one thing, it is not merely a matter of losing, but also of finding keys. This became clear to me the other day when, sorting through our collection, I found dozens of keys of various shapes and sizes that we had somehow accumulated. Some were rusty, tarnished, of different shapes than those now commonly used. Where were the doors to which they were originally fashioned? We thought of previous dwellings, here and in other houses, other cities, other countries. Even if a few might fit those doors that were part of our lifetime, our occupancy, there were others that belonged to another time, perhaps another century. . . .

. . . So we have come to this place and stand once more before the entrance. How can we tell what has brought us here, and if this is where we belong? *We have found the keys. But the doors are missing . . .*

1986

Truth, War, and the Dream-Game

God sees the truth, but waits.

        —Tolstoy

There is something intriguing, but annoying, about this. Perhaps the sense of cosmic hesitation—even indifference. The closer we look, the more massive the ambiguity. The truth, we know, is so elusive, so *wayward* that it hardly deserves the name. Anything more is reserved for that rare state we call "revelation." (Approach this domain quietly; speak of it with a whisper.) As for the notion that the source of revelation is Himself seeking revelation—isn't that wildly improbable?

What then is He waiting for? Our understanding is that truth, at this level, requires that perfect vision which is part of His very being—yet so remote from ours. To deny this, placing the mask of dream upon the face of truth, is illusion and madness. But our dream, our madness, is not ours alone. It is more of a dream within a dream, with the Ultimate Dreamer as the One who is also being dreamed. . . .

All this is prelude to a recent dream of mine. Unfortunately the greater part disappeared shortly after I opened my eyes. What remains is this fragment: a group of men, seated at a long, narrow table, are waiting for God to make His presence known. Some are playing cards; some are studying large military maps spread out before them. I sense that these are not live figures, but spirits who have "passed over." I understand too that, in life, these were all top-ranking diplomats and generals.

After a while, most of them move to one end of the table—leaving just a few card players—and begin an animated discussion of various battles and campaigns of the Second World War. As they argue back and forth, it seems they are trying to work out a single, believable "story" to tell Him. . . . I find myself growing rather impatient, annoyed by His absence. Then suddenly it occurs to me: this meeting is taking place inside God's mind—*and nowhere else!* Yet the participants—used to power and command in their earthly existence—are performing as if nothing has changed. They seem assured that, when He does arrive, it is their efficiency, not their guilt, that is to be considered. For surely He knows that they were only following orders. . . .

As I tell it now, the dream seems more "political" than what I remember. For at the time of dreaming, what they said, or left unsaid, had lost its urgency. As if the war were only abstract, theoretical, and besides, too long ago, too far away. Their talk of troops, victories, defeats, logistics almost an escape from boredom, a form of entertainment. What puzzled me more was the intensity and concentration of the card players, who remained apart from all this. . . .

Before this leaves the mind altogether, there is something else I need to remember. (I tell this with some reluctance but feel it has to be said.) More important, in some curious way, was the sense that the dead, when they reach their destination, bring along the same identity. That they retain some distinct features of what had been their individual consciousness. I found this so surprising, so *reassuring,* that I could put aside even the questions of collective guilt and divine irresponsibility.

As for the question I started with—*what then is He waiting for?*—that too appears in a different light. It seems now that it is *not* for the truth, which in any case He can perceive in an infinite number of ways. I feel it is more to the point to consider the "game playing" that centers around His presence or absence—even to ask if He needs to be taken seriously. It is as if He has located Himself inside a theater of His own design and choosing. And what He is waiting for is for the curtain to come down. Whether this is for the end of the play, or for some next act, we cannot tell. If there is indeed a *next act,* will He offer us one that is better performed—or at least less threatening?

1987

The Place/The Name/The Child

Get there if you can and see the land you once were proud to own.

—W. H. Auden

1.

Childhood: *another country*. She remembers the extraordinary size of an ordinary summer—the extended days dissolving into nights without number: a time without boundaries—and how suddenly it ended one morning with her mother's voice saying, "Time for school." All the strangeness of leaving the house—breaking one connection, as it were, before making another—and walking toward the school. The incredible distance that stretched out before her, block after block . . . But when she returns as an adult, walks those few blocks—so ordinary and compact—she wonders: How could it be? The question brings other reminders of her changed size and status. There was the drawing she did one day in class: her parents seated at a round table, not looking at each other. On the back of the drawing—on an impulse—she had scribbled these words: "When we grow bigger, adults grow smaller."

2.

So we join other minds, in reverie, in the *community of memory*. Not in the search for what is lost, irretrievable, but to perceive, to validate, that earlier being. For the child, become *children*, surpasses the mode of specific circumstance. The question comes again: How could it be? Asking now what separates, or unites, one life and another. Asking also who it is that answers to a particular name in a particular place and time. We sift through words and images: the sense of this, the color, the sound of that. Existence layers the real and mythical city. Main Street is interspersed with Byzantium and Bethlehem—we dwell there for a moment, with the thought of that luminous star.

3.

The voice that asks about this is joined now by a responding voice. Searching through dream and memory, the voices begin a dialogue of inner and outer worlds, of presence and absence. . . .

—I wonder about that "luminous star." About the birth that takes place at the dying of the year. One can't help thinking of a child in winter: all those myths of renewal: the death that leads to resurrection. . . .

—What brings those myths into being? Perhaps that other view of winter: as a place, a time where snow covers everything. We glimpse a vague figure wandering through a vast, empty landscape. Appearance—and then disappearance—and that is all. There is no monument, no amulet, to discover or recover.

—No monument, no amulet, no name. Between monument and amulet, there is some difference of size and status. But the death of a child, or a king, makes no difference. The winds blow across sand and snow, across a timeless, spaceless space. . . .

—And for this we invent and imagine, making the myths more attractive and more complicated. But isn't this to obscure what we already know: that we implant, impose the name upon the place, merge one with the other, for the mind to make real? For the child that was to become *the person:* as having been, as going to be, remembered?

—To become the person is one thing: the one who is and is not. The one who does and is done to. Or as it appears in retrospect: the one who fails to do what has to be done.

—Perhaps that is how it appears on the scale of "me and my lifetime." But when we look across the river, toward the nearby mountain, our vision changes. For there, all evidence of erosion and attrition is part of natural process. We arrive and depart, however, not as tree and stone, but under flexible schedules that we call "generations." What we add then, under the aegis of desire and longing, is that enlarged sense of being: the child as ancestor. The going to be again of what was: the beginning of dream without end . . .

1987

Structural Pursuits:

Prose Poems and Parables, 1987-1990

The Photographers

1.

The photographers have come and gone. And with their departure, the house has begun to return to its familiar, comfortable state. Now, once again, I tell myself, a wall is just a wall, a mirror just a mirror. No longer do I have to fend off the reflections of objects that somehow have acquired eyes—and not merely a placid gaze, but a kind of inquisitorial look. Yes, it is almost possible now to sit down somewhere, free of the sensation of being constantly under scrutiny. My situation here as tenant, as inhabitant, seems about to resume. For the shape, color, and form of things in their natural state, as themselves, has started to return. . . .

2.

What am I trying to describe—or to avoid describing? It suddenly occurs to me that all this has the sound of a survivor: someone who wanders about the scene after a disaster. I understand this is an exaggeration. For in fact nothing has been broken, and by the usual standards, one could reasonably say "no harm done." More to the point, I realize now, is to ask what the photographers have done. The question is surely premature, since I have not yet seen the pictures. And perhaps there may be other, more pointed questions when they have become available. Of course this assumes that their promises will be kept, and the delivery made on schedule. But even if my suspicions are unfounded, and the photographs reach here after a reasonable interval, I would still wonder about the packaging, and whether they will have fulfilled their obligations as to size and quantity. . . .

3.

. . . I have still not been able to face "the other, more pointed questions." I must do so now: Why did I agree to this in the first place? But even before that: How did they hear of me, and why was I selected? And why was it necessary to send four photographers—all of them young and energetic—instead of one? Some of this I can answer: my name and address can be easily obtained. And when they called, they made it clear that I was one of several chosen, with the simple qualification expressed in the name of their project: *An Old Man in an Old House*. I went through a whole range of emotions when I heard this. And when I finally responded, it was hard to recognize the sound of my own voice: "Sure, why not?"

4.

. . . The pictures have finally arrived. They are indeed well packaged, and in the size and quantity specified. I cannot say that this is not what I expected, since I had no real idea what to expect. It is understandable, is it not, that I looked first for the portrait that would reveal this old man in this old house. Well, it turned out there was only one of me, seated at my desk. Aside from this, there are several dozen posed arrangements of miscellaneous objects—mostly photographs of masks. And what is surprising, even startling, about this is that each of them—all four of these young enterprising photographers—has been photographed beside the masks, their own faces hidden, turned away from the light. . . .

1989/1990

Words Out of Reach

It is easier to include the universe in a word than in a sentence.

—Marcel Havrenne

1.

. . . As for instance now, with the sense of something close, but just out of reach, that might bring a clearer, brighter view of things. This has come with the sudden aware-ness of a few words—as yet with no apparent connection—hovering as it were just at the edge of consciousness. *Place, name, remember.* After several efforts to combine them in a way that makes sense, I come up with this: "It was the name of a place one would have to remember." I recognize at once that this is far from satisfactory. I run through a series of variations, all equally ordinary, all leading nowhere. . . .

2.

. . . Still reluctant to let go, still getting nowhere. All I can do now is open the mind to other possibilities—whether they relate to this or not. What is going on here? I can't seem to distinguish between articulation and communication. If I were only trying to articulate, I believe I could sooner or later find the appropriate words. These words could be arranged as I saw fit to please the audience of my mind. But to communicate, I have to consider the presence, the needs of the Other. . . . Just as I begin to reflect on this, three other words, uninvited, make a sudden appearance: *child, water, wind.* It is already clear that this can only complicate matters.

3.

Where do the words come from, and where do they go? The voice of the child. There is a place in the mind, I say, and that is where the words appear and disappear. It is a place that has no name—although we call it "memory," or sometimes "dream." Something comes into us, and later out of us, in ways we cannot guess or foretell. There are times when we assemble all the words into one word: *love.* And as long as the feeling lasts, we say and are ready to believe: love is the water and the wind in which the syllables and letters form and take shape. Love is the face that has nothing to show, nothing to tell. It is the "no-word" sounding soundlessly with the "no-voice" that the mind has learned to trust and believe in. . . .

Whether or not the child is still here, still listening, we cannot tell. But the no-voice is still present, carrying on its incessant, urgent whispering in the mind. What its voiceless urging implies, surely, is the death of words—somehow similar to the death of snow on black asphalt. This love then—of which and for which there is no utterance—offers only the nourishment of loss. For even if it could speak, it would possess the shortest, bleakest vocabulary: *hello, goodbye.*

We learn then that what is said between these two words is only of minor importance. It is even possible that one is implicit in the other, so we are really left with the single word: *goodbye.*

Goodbye to a place. Goodbye to a name. Goodbye to remember. This is the nature of one, of many, of all uncertain things. Now if only we could see the face of the child, anticipate the direction of the wind, locate a source for the clear water of the soul . . .

1987/1989

Kafka's Bridge

1.

We cannot tell, of course, just how this happened. But we can imagine that the image must have appeared to him at a moment of great intensity. That it came with a sudden rush of feeling—one of surprising directness and clarity—although with much yet to be defined. Perhaps for a while then it was still that familiar object enclosed in its own space: that taut swaying structure he had seen many times before, both in actual form and in dream. But then, as he looked closer, there was much that puzzled him as to the true nature of its existence. It appeared then, in spite of its bulk and material force, as a more ambiguous structure: a monument to human longing, to the restless desire for passage across divided shores. . . .

Thus as the bridge augmented, magnified, he began to compare his being *here* with its being *there*. The sound of the wind, the fragrance of the sea air entered the realm where dream and memory coincide. He began to feel what it would be like to hang suspended, totally exposed to the caprice of weather. As though its "body" had become his body. And he could watch the dark-winged birds diving past, pausing at the top of the taut, swaying steel cables and towers. . . . As he plunged further into this transformed state, the wind played upon the surface of his skin, forcing him to feel its impact, to become part of its steel and wind-tuned song. . . .

2.

Let us admit now what we must admit—that the reader may well perceive this as fantasy, wondering how the present writer could allow *his* imagination to go this far. I can only say in response: How else could Kafka have written his famous story of the bridge that "awoke" one day and saw itself as imprisoned, condemned to carry the weight of human longing and restlessness?

How else could he have intuited that bizarre transformation: the tremors, the spasms, the uncoiling of that vast structure, that monument to human ingenuity and desire? Above all, how was he able, with passion and convincing detail, to bring us to that climactic moment when it began trembling with its newfound intimations of "consciousness"? Then started that fatal turn, twisting loose from its foundations, making that enormous, grinding effort *to look back upon itself.* . . .

3.

For years now I have planned to reread the story. But each time persuaded myself to be content with the version imprinted in my memory. It was better, I thought, to leave it there. Better to consider now what happens *in real life*, where for any number of reasons, one bridge after another has come crashing down. For I recall, as we all do, how after each of these disasters a parade of experts appear, all offering rational explanations. How from then on the air is filled with their absurd, ambiguous testimony. And of course nothing is accomplished. . . .

I suppose that we could end here, on this skeptical, despairing note. But the story of our own bridge, which only recently survived a major earthquake, sustaining only minor damage, may offer a more hopeful example. For after many years of neglect, of taking its existence for granted, we have at last been sensible enough to begin correlating its existence with our own. We have instituted a celebration of the anniversary of its completion, honoring the workers and engineers who sacrificed so much to bring it into being. And just this year—as an example of civic pride—we have garlanded its towers with hundreds of small, friendly lights. Thus we have taken steps to ensure its appeal, not only in the present, but for years to come. We can only hope that our example will be noticed, and that similar steps will be taken—before it is too late—in other parts of the country. . . .

1988/1990

The Bridge to Dream/to Remember

1.

For years we lived with both bridges in place, satisfied that this arrangement offered an adequate choice of direction. The names alone, it seemed, served to clarify our intentions whenever we set forth on our various journeys. If asked about this, we might have replied: our need now is to cross *The Bridge to Dream*. Or with equal certainty: *The Bridge to Remember*.

Only a few of these journeys (do we need to explain?) have turned out well. In retrospect, we have made the wrong choice over and over again. And with each of these mistakes, concluded that going the other way would have made more sense . . . It is only recently that it has occurred to some of us that we need another alternative. Some of our leading citizens and lawmakers, acting from a variety of motives, are suggesting now that a third bridge must be constructed. A few speculative drawings have even appeared in the daily press; these purport to show it is entirely possible to connect this with the two already in use. . . .

2.

The Remember/Dream Commission, as it is popularly called, has had its first meeting. As many of us have expected, the advocates and opponents are sticking to their already announced allegiances. The arguments offered are almost impossible to follow. Instead of dealing with practical matters—the cost of such an enterprise, how it would deal with the worsening traffic situation— there is much concern with the "symbolism" of a third bridge. Much talk about an appropriate name: how could it be reconciled with the metaphoric content of *Dream* and *Remember*? No wonder our citizens are confused. For all this is creating a situation where one part of the population may well consider the two bridges already in place as separate, hostile entities: mutually exclusive and forever apart. . . .

3.

A bridge to dream. A bridge to remember. We name them separately when we need the separation. We name them together when these names appear as aspects of each other. But somewhere else—in another part of the mind—possibility beckons and necessity urges yet another (still unnamed) alternative. And still no one has suggested, as of this writing, that the structural engineer, the traffic expert sit down with the poet, the psychologist, the metaphysician and try to find out what this obsession with motion is all about. For according to the last figures, more than 25 million of our citizens move in any given year. And to accommodate the extravagant illusion that a better life can be found elsewhere, more highways, bridges are constantly being suggested. . . . If we were really to dream, really to remember, wouldn't this begin to subside? For if we began to confront what sends us forth on these endless forays and excursions, wouldn't it become plain what we have wasted and destroyed in the process?

But as things stand now, we continually retrace our departures and entrances, turning and returning across the same roadways, not willing or not able to name a single belief or allegiance to what was once—in some dream, some lost memory, the promise of arrival. . . .

1987/1990

The Awakening

—for Zdena

. . . *Does it happen this way?* The question startles her. It comes, in a moment of reverie, after the more urgent questions have apparently been dealt with. Questions that have centered on the ending of one phase of her life and the beginning of another. She wonders if the difference now is that those others were concerned with getting ready to move, with the uncertainties of new circumstance. Facing a threshold that both beckoned and repelled . . . It takes her a while to realize that what she is perceiving is not a further difficulty, but a convergence, on the plane of being, within herself. . . . She feels ready to accept this, even though there is no single defining image. She recalls and reaches for a photograph—taken some time ago—that she has felt was most herself. She holds it up toward the mirror. . . . No, she tells herself, without photograph, without mirror. She is surprised then at the sudden sound of her voice, speaking her name. At first what it summons is the child—those mysterious encounters and events—and then the woman. And through all of this, the changing outlines of form and figure. Then later the name takes its place among the nameless, the unnamed. Takes its place in a world of things, a world of people . . .

◆

. . . She understood that this was an "awakening." A departure from how she had seen herself, how others had seen her. So perhaps a different name was needed, one that would reflect this new state of being. Perhaps some name taken from nature. *Cloud. Bird. Tree. Spring.* She smiled at the extravagance of this, and just for a moment, it seemed the photograph and the mirror were smiling back. . . . She felt fully awake now. More awake, more alert than ever before. *So this is what it's like,* she thought. *This is what I've become.* And then, quite unexpectedly: *this is what* we *have become.* She heard herself speaking aloud again, alternating her given name with the name taken from nature. She could not be sure at this moment—and perhaps from now on—who the speaker was and what the listener might be hearing. . . .

1990

Portrait of the Man: As Novelist

. . . Suddenly he was famous. It was not what he intended, worked for, thought about—but there it was. He had written and published a novel; a lot of copies had been sold. He had been photographed and interviewed and invited to parties. Many parties. As he sifted through the events that led up to this, he recalled a specific morning when something—a kind of story—had appeared in his mind. It dealt with people he had seen only briefly and had not until then considered writing about. But that morning their voices, their faces entered the room. And when they remained, became more and more prominent, more *real*, he knew that these uninvited guests would not leave. . . .

◆

. . . The day arrived when his phone stopped ringing. There were no more photographs, no more interviews, no more parties. The room where he worked each day seemed emptier. The days were much too long; the nights opened into a space, a time that excluded him. It was time, he thought, to write another book. He set to work devising a plot, inventing characters—all the while missing the ease, the flow of the first book. Finally, he was able to put words on paper, to write pages and chapters, until it all came together. . . . When the book came out, there were reviews, a few photographs, even a few interviews. But there were no parties. He reread the reviews for a clue. One in particular caught his attention: the letdown experienced here was part of a "second-book syndrome."

◆

. . . This remained in his mind in the months that followed. He wrote now from habit, from the knowledge that he had the discipline to see it through to the end. He was able then to write this third book with no great effort. And after a suitable interval, to bring a fourth book to completion. He was by then no longer surprised or disappointed that there were no more photographs, interviews, or parties. . . . He was, however, somewhat surprised when one morning the uninvited guests of his first book appeared. He offered them something to eat and to drink. They seemed indifferent, remote. He knew then that this time they would leave of their own accord—at a moment and for reasons of their own choosing. . . .

1988/1990

More About Stones

—for Bob Arnold

1.

Facing the stone-covered hill, there is an echo, a reverberation, that reaches into some unfilled corner of his mind. Curious that it suggests both a presence and an absence—unconnected with this landscape or any particular memory. Perhaps it is something more inherent, innate, carried over from a time when the stones were simply there. A time when the stones were used for protection against the wind or an advancing enemy . . .

He walks a few steps, looks at the trees, the sky. Almost lost in the reverie, he cannot be sure that what he sees next is real or imagined. At a distance, in the uncertain light, is a group of vague, shuffling figures. As they move closer, he notices they are wearing a kind of peasant clothing, costumes that belong to another place and time. . . . He stands apart, watching them, as they take out and unfold crude burlap sacks and begin gathering the stones. There is no apparent difference between what they pick up and place inside the sacks and what they scrutinize and throw back upon the ground. . . .

After a while, on a signal from one of the men, they stop and gather in a circle. They begin an animated discussion in a language he has never heard before. One after another they reach into the sacks, take out a few stones, hold them up to the light. They seem to be responding to a challenge, as though their choices must be justified to each other and to their leader. . . .

2.

. . . He stands alone in a darkened room. A stone glows on the table in front of him. He picks it up, raises it to his mouth. He blows upon it, warming it with his breath. Was it a weapon or a tool? He looks for clues that might define the difference. It seems shaped beyond what was needed for any particular use. Whoever did this, he thinks, was motivated by some obscure intuition. Perhaps a notion that the extra shaping might add something—something to please and surprise—each time one picked it up. He returns the stone to the surface of the table. The unknown maker—a figure he cannot summon or define—beckons to him across the centuries. . . .

3.

The stones are fitted, set into a wall. Those who walk by the wall a thousand years later wonder at the seamless joining. How did those builders, with only the crudest tools, carry out their task? Strange that this thought comes to him one afternoon in a museum. He is looking at a collection of stones placed in haphazard fashion on the museum floor. There is a title for this "work." The card on the wall gives the name, the name of the artist, the date of completion. . . . But why are the stones *here*, and not in the earth where they belong? He enacts a scene where the artist is asked the same question. The artist hesitates, shrugs, then responds, "I've wondered about that too."

4.
A stone is a stone. It is not, in itself, a sign or signifier. Bereft of any elevated status—as monument, amulet, or emblem—it retains its "stoneness." What is our difficulty in accepting this? Is it some need to fill those unfilled corners of the mind? To perceive it as this stone—or even *our* stone? As though to place upon it the burden of the story of who and what we are.

That we may appear to be more than the sum of our appearances and disappearances. That the scale of our small lives may be decisively altered by incising upon its surface the enduring name. And if that is asking too much, perhaps just a few distinctive markings to indicate it has passed into and through our hands . . .

. . . We have come back then—have we not?—to that stone-covered hill, to those vague, shuffling figures whose reality we can neither dispose of nor verify. Come back then by some curious, circuitous route to that nameless, unmarked hill—where we always need protection against a stronger wind, an advancing, ever more ambiguous enemy . . .

1987/1990

Wind, Says the Voice

1.

Wind: the bone-flutes of memory. Here on a cliff overlooking the northern sea, we stare at the darkening sky, the churning water. Birds circle and descend. Water cutting into rock, a dark line wavers, widens across a strip of yellow sand . . . What are we looking at, what confronts us here? The chill we feel is more than what plays upon the flesh. Something of dream, the untraceable reminder, the return of something lost. Perhaps the overthrow of yesterday . . . Yesterday when, a few miles inland, we watched a placid duet of clouds and sky, the rise of unknown birds above the winding river. And on that leisurely, peaceful walk, we passed a whole series of neat, compassionate gardens. . . .

. . . Here now the errant wind disturbs, altering the scale of our perceptions, bringing unwelcome reminders that make us guess and fear. . . . And so the scene shatters; the fragments that emerge appear on a different plane, across a world of time. . . . A procession of dark figures moves across the sand. (Who are they? Where have they come from?) The answer comes across a great distance, traversing a memory, an inheritance longer, deeper than our own. It tells us these are the Trojan women searching the stained, littered beaches—among the bodies broken and becalmed—for the face that only yesterday lighted their waking eyes. . . .

Wind, says the voice. It is not their loss that concerns you. You have no friends, no relatives among the slain. No mothers, no daughters among the keening women. No friends to console you—to compose elegies (and eulogies) for the grieving— among those who so quietly, gracefully finger their guitars. We see you instead conspiring with fire, and while we watch this churning water, you make furnaces of our trees. . . . Are you then, as some have said, the one who batters and erodes our monuments, the force that scatters the syllables of our broken, rootless words?

2.

Wind, have you returned to another time, another setting? I hear through the swaying branches morning being drummed out of season. Is this then your other face, which brings to an end your little lyric dance among the leaves? How is it we are still— after all these years—so full of plans and expectations? Still placing so much trust in insulated wiring, in copper pipes installed in our houses? Perhaps we should move to the plains, where the grotesque, shattered fences point toward a deadpan sky. Landscape of dead automobiles, of stained, disconnected bathtubs, of ripped, water-soaked mattresses . . .

Wandering through those twisted spaces, a bewildered child sifts through the debris for a cat, a doll, a soft companion for his broken sleep. . . . Wind, we place all this before you, inviting inspection of spaces you have swirled through, callous, undeniable. Isn't it time and more than time to withhold this fury and vengeance? Let us be sensible, set aside our differences, and begin to negotiate some sort of treaty. On our part we agree to your right to appear and disappear without prior notice. We ask in turn that you consider our joint status in regard to all living things. So let us clarify our standing here among sheep and elephants and dancing bears. . . .

. . . Invader of caves, inspirer of eyes staring into craters, we offer you these mounds opening into air, this horn of plenty, the ghosts of these dead automobiles. Leave us the spirit and souls of those who have strayed into the nameless spaces of dry canyons—where at night they form the outlines of shapes we remember under the full moon. Help us to bring them back from their secret homes, where they have taken up residence among coyotes and timberwolves. We realize there is no use sending out searching parties, but perhaps with your help we can. . . .

1979/1990

The Jugglers

We live in a time of surprising, even heroic transformations. Heroic at times, but absurd at others. I still remember, for instance, when the Myshkin brothers earned their living in the most ordinary way: as handymen or doing rough carpentry. Who could have imagined that, only a few years later, they would appear onstage, billed as The Amazing Myshkins. It started, so I'm told, one afternoon when, becoming totally bored with the routine of work, they started a game of catch with their tools.

I have it on good authority that one or the other of them then began juggling his screwdrivers and pliers. Some time later they worked out some routines and began inviting a few friends to witness and even join in the fun. One of these friends, it turned out, was performing as a clown in a local nightclub. He invited them to join him onstage one evening. . . .

◆

They were an immediate hit. The sight of hammers, screwdrivers, files, even small saws flying through the air entranced audiences. At some point they introduced a variation in their performance, stepping down from the stage and performing in the aisles. They also began recruiting members of the audience to stand between them (those brave or foolish enough to participate) while the tools passed back and forth. I'm also told that, later on, they refined this part of the act by limiting the choice of objects to hammers and sickles. But whether this was pure symbolism or meant to be a special challenge to their dexterity, I could never be sure. . . .

◆

Success, it seems, is no cure for boredom. For a while yes, but given the restless spirit, that too begins to pall. I think what happened was this: they began to miss the genuine work with tools, perhaps some pride of craftsmanship. Back in their workshop, one of them reached into the bin where they stored scraps of wood. He nailed together a few pieces, and saw that it formed the letter A. His brother then nailed together the letter Z. One nodded to the other; they gestured back and forth in wordless understanding. Another enterprise, profitable or not, but surely pleasurable, was under way.

◆

I never had time to attend any of their performances. But those who did said it was great fun. The sight of those letters flying through the air was even more enjoyable than the screwdrivers and pliers. . . . The act came to an end, I understand, one evening in a crowded nightclub when they tried to get the whole alphabet in the air at the same time. Some of the letters struck some of the patrons; others crashed into the huge mirror at the back of the bar. . . .

I heard nothing further about them for some time. Then from someone close to them—one of the few they continued to permit access to their workshop—came this news: they had resumed work on the letters. But now they were working only with choice, expensive woods. They were experimenting with different wood stains and an array of waxes—sending for materials that can only be obtained in certain tropical forests, in certain remote parts of the world. . . .

1990

The Poet Digs a Hole

. . . He stands in an open field, shovel in hand, staring at the ground. He turns, raises his head, as some small dark birds descend toward a nearby tree. His attention lingers there, and beyond them toward the motion of some drifting clouds. He waits a few moments longer, then returns to his shoveling. . . . *What has brought him here?* Whatever it is, we are intrigued by his dedication to this simple, purely physical task. Watching as he bends and scoops, it occurs to us that, with this much effort, he must have more in mind than an ordinary hole. We imagine a prolonged period of meditation, reflection before making the choice of location. We even envision an earlier scene: at the hardware store, he questions the owner as to the merits of the various shovels offered for sale.

◆

. . . Still no clue as to what has brought him here. We concede, though, that whatever a poet digs may be considered a "poetic" hole. That is, one shaped and formed in response to some complicated intention, the eventual form of which is not immediately apparent . . . We were about to say more, but the thought is interrupted by the arrival of a group who position themselves nearby. We can hear enough of their voices to identify them as critics and theorists. This is confirmed by occasional words—*metaphoric, metonymic, opacity, transparency*—that fill the air with a strange, disembodied sound. . . .

◆

. . . He continues raising and lowering the shovel with a rapid concentrated motion—but then more slowly, with frequent pauses, staring at the trees, the birds, the sky . . . We are startled by the sudden motion as he lets the shovel fall, jumps down into the hole. He walks back and forth, testing the ground. It seems he has found the ground too soft, too damp. He climbs out, picks up the shovel, begins refilling the hole. . . .

◆

. . . A minor disappointment or a major setback? A momentary impulse or part of some enduring passion? We cannot even begin to answer these questions. We do not even know whether this hole—poetic or ordinary—was meant to build upon, or to bury something in. And if the latter, was it to contain a treasure, or to hide a guilty secret? Whatever the case, the poet has again undertaken a project involving intense labor, leading to another absurd outcome. And not only the labor, but the purchase of a shovel—when his imagination could have invented one. One that could be lying on the ground next to *a red wheel barrow glazed with rain water beside the white chickens.*

. . . As an alternative, he might have moved closer to the watchful group of critics and theorists. Close enough to hear what they were saying and perhaps to follow their advice. He might then, however, have moved to another location—and begun the same process over again. . . . But perhaps the thought of this is too much, and we may be ready now to turn our attention elsewhere. . . . Let us leave it then for some future archaeologist puzzling over a series of holes apparently started and then abandoned—with not a single artifact in sight.

1988/1990

The Cheering Section

. . . Yes, it is unlikely. But say it is autumn—with all its sounds, smells, colors—and we have come here in real time, in the real world. Our presence then is evidence, as physical as the striped clothing on the striped field. (Not memory, not dream.) And we are not merely present in the flesh, but just here, in this row of seats among these noisy, absorbed partisans. So much a clear and conscious choice that we can offer allegiance to the locals, deny affection to the visitors . . . Voices getting louder by the moment. If we add our own or withhold them, will it make any difference? But what happens to the one voice when it is absorbed, totaled into thousands, into millions?

. . . Breathe quickly now, breathe heavily. Watch the locals, appropriately clad in red and white, leap into the air, clasp each other in triumph. And since we have become partisans and believers—we are of them, as they are of us—why not do the same? *But what of the losers?* Of course, we do not have to think of them, not even glance in their direction. And yet, isn't this the moment when we can most afford to be generous? Still, we may live better without these reminders: how they sit in the hollowed space, sprawled on the narrow benches, slumped and dejected. . . .

—

. . . Yes, I have written these words. Words that only touch the surface, presenting a world in which there are only partisans and believers. But where are the specific emotions, anything as personal, as inevitable as rage and delight? Emotions we were bound to express as children—not as opposing choices, but brought together: *the outrage of delight.* Nothing here either about the nature of the contest. How precisely it defines the separation, and the coming together, of the "not yet" and the "no longer." So that this little play of winners and losers is surrogate to our dreams of defeat, and defeat of our dreams . . . But hold on—what's going on there?—that group of children on the playing field. Are they locals or visitors? Without uniforms it's impossible to tell. All we can cheer now is the season itself. . . .

1988/1990

Who Waits for Whom?

. . . A brief response to what perhaps does not need to be taken seriously. What may be considered no more than a minor provocation. Well, no need for long-winded introductions. The plain fact is that a curious document has recently come into my possession. As to the source, how it got here, I am not permitted to say. I can reveal that it is evidently a response to my essay "Who Waits for Whom?" (*The Enigma Review*, vol. 1, no. 4, 1986). An essay in which I put forth the view that not all of us are waiting for His return, that for a good many this would be either undesirable or impossible.

. . . Now comes this document which presents evidence—some of it with that surface gloss that makes it appear convincing—that our own waiting is a minor matter, hardly measurable on the cosmic scale. The writer of this piece (using a pseudonym) argues that it is His waiting, through countless aeons, that has created a being for whom the term "infinite patience" has almost a literal meaning. So that when we ask, What is *He* waiting for? we are coming closer to the true state of things.

The question is relevant *because* it is unanswerable—for its suggestion that it is not for us but for Him to answer. That answer, when it comes, will be an *event* originating and contained within the bounds of His boundless mind. And therefore not available to our own limited understanding. What we can, however, reasonably assume is that the nature of His being is what He both is and is going to be. So that all the arguments over His reported "death" are both exaggerated and premature. We have only to put aside the story of Genesis—as it has been read and commented upon—and convert it to its true meaning. For according to this view, Genesis was nothing more than an alteration of circumstance, a clue to the emergence of a Guiding Force. All that He has been—it is at last clear—is almost nothing compared to what *He has yet to be*. With that recognition—when it finally occurs—we may then at last set foot upon a stage whereon is performed a grander, as-yet-undreamed-of destiny. . . .

1990

The Universal Delivery Service

1.

The question of how things get from here to there—which is taken so much for granted—has puzzled me for years. It may be my natural pessimism, but it still surprises me that a letter arrives where intended. The same with packages, parcels, foodstuffs, artworks, furniture, etc. This in a world where, as seasoned observers agree, chaos and even apocalypse are never far away. Still, I admit a kind of order—at least on this level—does persist. My view of all this, in any case, is soon bound to be altered, as I have recently been offered a position within the Service. I have accepted this, as a kind of experiment, with the understanding that I may leave at any time. . . .

2.

. . . I am pleased of course to have an office of my own. But on entering, I see there is not much reason for rejoicing. For one thing, the room is small, the furniture nondescript, the windows smudged. Also, it is located in an unused part of the building, which seems to be an old warehouse. The only signs of activity are the unmarked trucks that, about once an hour, appear at the loading dock. Men in dark uniforms load and unload boxes; this is done quickly, almost mechanically, with gestures instead of speech. As far as I can see through the filthy glass, the boxes are of a uniform size and shape, with no apparent difference between those delivered and those taken away. . . .

3.

I have been here over a week. The telephone was installed several days ago, but so far there have been no calls. I have kept busy arranging and rearranging an assortment of catalogues of various kinds of equipment and machinery. Aside from the trucks, the only contact with the outside world is the mail. Each day, as I open the door, I find a dozen or more envelopes littering the floor. These invariably have printed messages on the cover: *Please fill out and return. Last chance. Opportunity of a lifetime.* I have delayed opening any of these, since none are addressed to me, until I receive further instructions. . . .

4.

This morning an unsigned note arrived. (At last, something with my name on the envelope!) The brief typed message is that all mail received so far—and until further notice—is to be marked *Please forward as instructed.* There is no indication, however, as to where any of this is to be sent. I can only assume that, sooner or later, the information will arrive. . . . A few days later, a second envelope arrives. I open it and read the brief message: *Please disregard previous notice. Material in your office is now subject to revised procedure. In a few days, everything will be picked up and turned over to the Central Office. You will then be assigned to different duties.*

5.

. . . Sitting here in the empty office, ready to gather my few belongings and leave. Everything else left with the truck an hour ago. I tried to engage the driver in conversation, but his replies were brief and noncommittal. One thing, though, caught my attention: when I mentioned that I was awaiting reassignment, he responded, "The U.D.S. goes anywhere and everywhere." I suddenly realized that this included me as well. I told him this would be difficult for me, as I had obligations here. He shrugged and said, "As far as the U.D.S. is concerned, space is no barrier, time is no obstacle."

6.

. . . I see now that I will have to resign. I realize this means I can no longer observe the workings of "the system" from the inside. Still, I have learned much in a short time, even though in a larger sense my experiment must be considered a failure. Perhaps if I could have entered at a level more consonant with my abilities, more could have been accomplished and learned. I might have had more opportunity for contact with the shadowy figures who design policies and procedures. . . . As it is, the question remains: Is there indeed a delivery system that can go "anywhere and everywhere"? Deep inside me I find this, curiously, both reassuring and frightening. I suppose this reaction may be due to the belief—instilled at an early age—that borders and boundaries are not only necessary but may at times even be considered as sacred. . . .

1987/1990

The Fourth Step

So much has been written about the first three that my reference to a "fourth step" may not be taken seriously. While prepared for the rejection, I offer this as a possibility. But first, let me honor the courage and perseverance of those who have "stayed the course," and have accepted their new state of being. What seems to have happened is that even the most strongly convinced have acknowledged the stirrings of a new wave of confusion and discontent. We have the testimony of those who gave evidence as to the validity of their transformation, but now admit the continuing erosion of their created self.

One of them, I recall, made quite a point of this at a gathering that I happened to attend. He said in a loud voice and with a sweeping gesture that included all around him: "But of course we have all invented ourselves." The problem now, he went on, was to find the way back to who we were *originally*, at the beginning of our lives. It was in that split between the original and the created self that we now experienced a kind of fragmentation. "Taking those three steps," he said, "was a wonderful, challenging experience. The trouble was it was just not enough—not enough to last."

◆

It was this encounter, and later a number of others, that led me to the notion of a fourth step. For those unacquainted with the theory, the ritual that led to "The Three Steps to Self-Awareness," I will summarize them briefly: Step One is *ordeal*; Step Two is *pilgrimage*; Step Three is *transformation*. At this point, I want to be careful not to overstate the case. There must have been quite a large number for whom this was enough. They had embarked upon a journey into their own interiors. And they had discovered capacities and qualities beyond expectation and dream. For a while then, as I've already indicated, they could experience the satisfied passion of the completed journey.

◆

I hope I have not relied too heavily on a too-familiar metaphor. But I find the reference to "journey" to be the simplest, most useful expression here. So once more, there was the realization—sooner and more intensely among those with a greater sensibility—that with all their journeying, they had not arrived at "the place." I will add now that it is time to change *they* to *we*. For we, too, have come to a place we have been permitted to glimpse but not to enter. Have come to a door that might open with a spoken word. But the word does not come to our lips. . . .

◄

. . . For the longest time, we could only stand there staring, waiting. And then somehow we felt a curious sensation that words were already inscribed on that door which we had to decipher. We could not be sure, but it was as if, after a while, letters appeared and formed these words: *For Saints and Martyrs Only.* Considering who and what we are, perhaps the word can now be named: *redemption.* The word that contains and modifies all those other words. The word that is still whispered, pronounced only in private. How much longer, we wonder, will this continue? Perhaps until we are aware of and prepared to take the Fourth Step. It seems obvious now that this must indeed be the case. And yet when we think of how difficult it has been to have come this far, think of how many of the brightest and the best have fallen along the way . . .

1988/1990

Next Is This

. . . So much talk about "the word." What it is, what it ought to be, how it should be used, etc. And of course this includes the "right" word in the right place, the right time. But when a word suggests itself—comes forward and asks to be recognized—how can I prove it meets these requirements? I can only say that it is here and insists on being named. As in the present moment I reply to this insistence and type the letters: *n-e-x-t*. Staring at this I'm suddenly reminded of a line I once wrote: "We are left then with a choice between silence and nonsense." I seem prepared to take the risk and make the choice. For it occurs to me that the sense of it may be present to all kinds of people in all kinds of situations. It may be a poet who thinks of it, or a scientist, a barber, a fruit vendor. And if this is a desired moment, we may say to ourselves, *at last, at last*. And if we are facing what we have feared, sought to avoid, then we may wait and urgently hope someone else will step forward.

◆

. . . So it is when we feel stymied, suspended between an intractable "not yet" and, after a barely noticeable interval, the dismal announcement of a "no longer." What then have we missed? What failure of attention has caused us to turn away at just that moment which was to be completely ours? I refer to the arrival of just that "next" which was to be genuinely new—rather than more of the same. It is just then, I suppose, that we fall back upon the trite images spawned by tiresome references to faith and luck. This in spite of our long experience that there can be no anticipation without apprehension. And it is at this very moment that "the unprecedented" comes into view. . . .

◆

We may be brought then to consider what happens in nature. As the poet/naturalist reminds us, there may yet appear *forms that break step with knowing*. A fish that flies, a bird that swims. Whatever exotic beings are still coming ashore, their shapes and colors as yet undetermined, unimagined. But even within this present time, studying the motion of a single wave, we have something to learn. We can watch it being formed, rising, poised at its apex, then released for its sudden descent. . . . What this one wave engenders—with the sun, the light, the wind as variables—can be as new as *never before*, as ancient as *always was*. . . .

◆

This ends for now my reflection on the word *next*. Before putting these words on paper, I assure you, I had no idea how they would come out. It is only now that it occurs to me: *rhymes with text.* As if to say: whatever appears here has its own reason for being. If we can accept this, we can look beyond the familiar, beyond the need for context. I like to think that we can venture this far, in this simple way, beyond restricted space. And having established a sense of confidence that we can survive even without an "event horizon," why not be prepared to welcome the *as yet unrealized?*

1987/1990

Afterword to *Truth, War, and the Dream-Game*

Once we leave behind the residues of either/or, and for or against, we enter a different, more pluralistic realm. This may be apparent with no more than a closer look at the book's title. Words like *truth* and *war* may suggests a whole range of meanings even within the mind of a single reader. As for *dream-game*, where there are no fully realized associations, a greater effort may be called for. Significant clues are part of the dream-game, but its rules and procedures, its invisible, unsettling influence, may be even more difficult to trace.

The first grouping is of those pieces that deal with the theme of what we have come to call "Spirituality"—not confined to any one religion, nor to religion itself.

(from *Tracking Stations*)
"Destruction of the Temple"; "The Refugees/The Pilgrims";
"The Leopards/The Temple"; "Reading the Text";
"The Message/The Messenger"; "The Choice";
"The Loaves/The Fishes"; "The Dark Pattern";
"The Return of Sadhu"; "The Choice"

On Politics, War, and the Effects of War:
 (from *Tracking Stations*)
"Flight Patterns"; "The Departure/The Return";
"The Refugees/The Pilgrims"; "The Situation Room";
"The Retreat of the Leaders"; "The Given Day";
"The Trial of Two Cities"
 (from *Chance Scripts*)
"Truth, War, and the Dream-Game"

On Man, Woman, and Child:
(from *Tracking Stations*)
"Give Up, Give Up"; "Absent Without Leave";
"Trading with the Enemy"; "The Actor: Farewell & Return";
"The Master"; "Protective Measures"; "More Than a Thing"
(from *Chance Scripts*)
"The Candidate/The Canceled Child"; "The Feathers of My Wife";
"One Vote for the Vulture"
(from *Structural Pursuits*)
"The Photographers"; "The Awakening"; "Portrait of the Man: As Novelist"

On Language, Writing, and the Writer:
(from *Tracking Stations*)
"The Sacrifice"; "Reading Borges"
(from *Chance Scripts*)
"The Lost Parable"; "Between Worlds"
(from *Structural Pursuits*)
"Portrait of the Man: As Novelist"; "The Jugglers";
"The Poet Digs a Hole"; "Next Is This"

On the City as Concept and Metaphor:
(from *Tracking Stations*)
"Leaving the City"; "The Given Day"; "The Shrinking City";
"The News from Dronesville"; "The Trial of Two Cities"

All this is offered to focus, but not to limit, the reader's own exploration. In addition to the cross-referencing already indicated by these groupings, there can be a briefer alternative: that of pairing. That is, between two pieces that especially reflect upon each other. Examples of this: "The Cage: The Performance" along with "The Actor: Farewell & Return"; "A Stone Taking Notes" and "More About Stones"; "Say We Are Going" and "No Time for Gestures"; "The Door to Have" and either "The Knock" or "The Trouble with Keys"; "The Contest" and "The Photographers." A special case is the linking of "The Door to Have" with "Question of a Shovel"—the only two pieces in the book that end with a poem.

—*L. F.*
March 1991

from

The Scale of Silence: Parables

(1970)

The scale creates the phenomenon.
—Mircea Eliade

The Garden

1.

The flies were not here yesterday. But neither was that brown splashed on the grass. What else may be noticed with the same air of surprise? The flowers, stones, the vine all in place—perhaps a bit brighter, more vivid than usual.

I turn to look at the weathered table, the abandoned chairs. A scattering of plums from the one tree that still bears fruit. Those I pick up are gouged and porous. Only on the tree do they ripen properly. Yet even there the birds feed on them, the pierced skins subject to infection and decay.

So the lessons are learned; one is informed of things about which action may be taken. What is more worthy of attention? Perhaps something in the light that, at this moment, needs further study. Not only the vividness, but the stirring of the unseen—the pervasive underside that has never yet emerged.

2.

I have come to this place, to this same light that is now to be questioned. Looking back, I would have to add: across great distances. But that is not my present concern. For the moment I do not care to add or to subtract anything. I suspend and put aside the sense of loss, of deprivation. My eyes measure the space; I look farther, to the neighbors on both sides, to the row upon row of houses.

I sit down at the bench beside the table. What comes to mind are all the things that have to be done. The weeds to be pulled; those dry places the water has not reached.

I search the pitted leaves, the broken branch, the decayed fruit. I notice that nameless bush, untended, growing across the walk. Left alone, it might grow to fantastic proportions—perhaps entirely out of hand, covering the whole front wall.

I recall suddenly the story of a canyon, the mining town built along its slopes. A period of great activity, of machinery and imported populations; of fortunes made and lives destroyed. But then the minerals under the earth gave out; one by one the houses were abandoned. Finally the houses decayed and were torn down. A few years later the grass returned, covered the slopes; wildflowers and bushes sprang up everywhere.

3.

Purple and orange flowers, gray and red stones. Besides what is planted and grows of its own accord, objects put there to decorate the ground. I notice the bleached cow skull, the duck fashioned in clay, painted black. When the mind is put to work, one finds an event, an occasion, to account for their presence.

At first I recall nothing of the skull, just something I picked up somewhere on my travels. But then the dry, flat landscape returns: wind blowing the fine brown dust. . . . On the way to the border, after six months in that country. Many hours on the road; that white spot looming in the mind. (Some fears to be met; some to be avoided—which is this?) This time, the hand forced to answer the challenge—to reach down and pry loose *one thing* from the vast and drifting sand.

As for the clay duck, I recall at once the cluttered house and yard. There it was among the live dogs and children, goats and chickens. Left there by the potter, among a pile of the unfinished, the broken, the rejected. That wiry, brown-faced man smiled when I pointed to the object of my affection. Whatever I wanted to give would be enough.

Whatever I gave was returned in other ways. The cool glass of wine; the sound of their voices; the sight of them seated around the table. For that was the work-shop—from the youngest to the white-haired man, there was work for their hands. But the potter alone put on the finishing touches: drew the clown's face, eyes of the painted birds.

4.

These are reminders: there are other dimensions to the seeing. Part of the view here is that of being touched in ways beyond recollection. I have put my hands to many things—and for various reasons withdrawn them. It is hard to say what is given and taken away. But with these plants and flowers, a few days without water, the signs of infection ignored, and there is death.

I reach for the hose, determined not to miss anything, to make up for any recent neglect. I loose the fine spray upon what manifests the intention to grow. And with the drops gathered on the leaves, the blades of grass, once more slip out of the present. . . .

It was in another country, another time. The boy on a bicycle riding past the garden wall. He parks the bicycle against a tree and climbs over. He knows the family who lives there; the girl and her brothers are his friends. He spends the afternoon visiting, playing tennis, telling stories of school.

Usually he rides home after these visits; but this time on impulse he heads for that part of the city where lights and noise beguile and threaten. He walks past where the men are talking; the name reaches his ears. He buys a newspaper; but the words merely flicker on the page. . . . I do not want to finish the story. It is nothing that happened to me, neither fantasy nor dream. Yet I know that the boy and the garden survived. While the family who lived there were taken away and destroyed.

I turn off the water, let the green hose fall upon the ground. The clouds move across the flat sky, a movement I have seen many times before. Of all that is here, I look closely at the pitted leaves. There is a sharp-edged balance between what grows, what is eaten and cut down.

I have often missed what is in front of me; looked away at the wrong time. But now I have kept staring until the light has told me something: there are lines that reach across—from the potter to the boy on the bicycle. And I am ready now to go inside.

The Prisoner

1.

I am making every effort to avoid the fiasco of last year. With the return still some weeks off, I am going through the house, checking everything in sight. As it appears now, there is not much more to be done. I have no intention though of letting up, growing lax through over-confidence. I know only too well how important details can be overlooked.

So this time I intend to search every corner, even those places completely out of sight. For it is necessary to look beyond appearances, to sense a totality that includes every object in every room. And even then to remain alert—for what may be picked up by the careless hand, put down somewhere beyond recall.

I have learned not to be surprised that this often happens prior to the Caretaker's periodic visits—or worse, the annual arrival of the Master himself. I recall walking a few steps behind the Caretaker, while he peered over thick glasses, stopped to make notations on the form sheet attached to the clipboard. At those times I have been almost ready to ascribe a spirit of waywardness, even malevolence, to the objects entrusted to my care.

2.

Once more up and down the stairs, poking in drawers and closets, making sure things are where they belong. This time I have tested the lamps, checked the wiring, traced the pipes to their source. And I have furthered and perfected various arrangements: the books, for instance, not only according to subject and author, but with concern that they present perfect rows. Outside, I have watered the garden with care for the exact amount required by the various plants and flowers. I have trimmed the hedges, gathered the dead leaves, swept the walks in front and back. As it stands now—to anticipate any possible criticism—there is only one thing. In the last few days, certain smudged spots on the windows: a kind of film that resists my best efforts. And, curiously, this has appeared also—almost identical—on glass pitchers and water glasses. Having done all I can, however, I do not intend to become upset over what, in any case, could only be a minor infraction.

3.

The weeks of preparation are almost over. At this point, whatever happens, it is hard to feel there will be any major surprises. I have often wondered how it might be to be informed of the actual date of arrival. But clearly this is not in the scheme of things. And while I cannot say I am reconciled, there is no longer the same apprehension. In those first years I experienced the full range of fear and trembling. But most of that has worn away; the days are fairly calm and stable. It is in the nights then—particularly at this time—that there is difficulty. As the time approaches, I find myself lying awake for longer and longer periods. Until, as happened a few nights ago, I reach the stage of watching the morning light arrive. As it turns out, that is usually the signal that the time has come. . . .

4.

I don't quite know what to make of it: the Caretaker came and was gone within an hour. He arrived without form sheet and clipboard, dressed as if going to a party. Instead of the usual meticulous examination and scrutiny, there was a glance here, a glance there, and repeated consulting of the watch. He did stop several times; but not in the usual places for the usual reasons. As I recall, he paused before the wooden Madonna, the straw Christ, and the display of cloth dolls. And each time I noticed he touched and shifted something! A few inches to the left or right, back and forward. But he said nothing, voiced no criticism.

Thinking it over, it occurs to me that there is one possible explanation for this eccentric behavior—nothing to do with procedure, maintenance, or with arrangements for the arrival of the Master. It could only have been an expression of *personal* taste, a feeling for those objects that came from within.

5.

For the past hour or so I have been pacing the floor. The wire in my hand arrived this morning. I hold the yellow paper with the black spaced words: open and close, smooth and crumple. I am sure there is no precedent—none at all. *Choose.* Meaning that I can choose the time of arrival. And that is not all. There is also the phrase: *for services rendered.* And I find that almost equally disturbing. . . .

It has just occurred to me that I might get some idea if I could pretend *to be* the Caretaker. At once, I step out into the street, approach the house, ring the doorbell. Entering, I nod a curt silent greeting, begin looking around.

I notice first the sensation of being watched. Some kind of inner critic's eye judging the performance. Finally though, I seem to have the walk, the gestures. At last I am ready to try the voice: "After all, it's not a mausoleum." But the tone is not quite right; I try and try again. . . .

I see that this is all quite useless, nothing more than a waste of time. Even if I were to rehearse each gesture, the performance would not improve. It is too much, is it not, to think of oneself on both sides of the door?

6.

Being back at the hotel has its advantages. The brief vacation while the Master moves into the house is for me usually a good time. Whatever could be done has been done; I can no longer worry about the consequences. One thing is still on my mind: in respect to the wire, it would have been easy to have made a wrong move. In that kind of situation, all one has to go on is a certain instinct, an intuition. One learns then, as it were, after the event. . . .

Staring out the window, as now, I can be sure that several of those shady, shambling figures will be gathered at the corner. It seems that all kinds of transactions, perhaps of the kind one used to call evil, are taking place. But there is something—how to say it?—clear and energetic and vital about their movements. At least that is how it appears at this height, from the context of my own circumstances. . . .

7.

Before I have a chance to examine my feelings on being back in the house, there is the matter of a second telegram. Opening it with some irritation, I crumple and carry it to the nearest wastebasket. It seems I am to have an *assistant*! No name, no sex is mentioned; time of arrival is given, request for room on upper floor to be assigned. I recall the phrase from the previous wire: *for services rendered*. It would be nice to know, would it not, whether to consider this reward or punishment?

8.

Waiting for the assistant to arrive. The idea of a female seems unlikely; I have therefore worked out my attitude toward *him*. For there is no need to wait to form a judgment. No, this one will arrive, bright and energetic, begin making himself at home. Within a short time, he will begin taking over some essential duties. Soon, he will make suggestions, offer ideas for better ways of doing things. Before long I expect to be accommodating myself to the uninvited presence, to the changes.

And I cannot help asking: as I did before to the Caretaker, to the elaborate needs of the Master himself? But I perceive that here something else is involved. For I shall then be listening to the voice from *below*, as before I attended those that came from above.

Let it be clear I am still grateful for the Master, that I do not regret having entered his service. I still regard it as the deepest cure for the strongest illusion. But as to the nature of obedience, of moving and being moved, I seem to be nearing the end of a long deception.

The Examination

1.

The chairs not quite as remembered, but basically the same design: two curved boards at the back, the metal frame, the writing space on the right-hand side. I notice the neutral color, the high gloss of the varnish. I sit facing the empty blackboard, waiting for the signal to begin.

In a few moments we are to open the printed forms, answer what we can in the allotted time. I wonder what it is that has brought us here; how it is we have agreed to appear, to submit to these questions. I turn to see if the faces offer any clue. No sign that anyone else is having similar doubts.

The curved boards press against my back. How is it these chairs are still made in the same way, the same size? As though entering here, we are expected to shrink, to fit that childhood situation of being tested and examined. But again that is perhaps just my way of seeing.

I find myself settling into the chair, becoming more used to it. One should be more adaptable, shaping body and mind to the contours, the present circumstance. Thus there are times to stand tall; and others, as now, to adjust to the crouched position.

I wonder if I have prepared properly, whether the questions are the same for all. As I understand it, we are only required to fill in the empty spaces, put checks in the squares, circle the proper numbers and words. We are not then to be graded, marked up or down, for the proper intention, the facile expression. While this leaves room for both guess and knowledge, the judgment will be objective. When it is over, we can all be measured by the published scores.

There is then in this case—as perhaps in not many others—a clear connection between one's choices and the outcome. It does not seem one is ever permitted to ask for anything more.

2.

There goes the buzzer. The others have already opened the wide, stiff sheets. I can feel the intense concentration, and I seem to hear the slight movements, even the whisper of voices reading the printed words.

Above and beyond—if I am not mistaken—the noise of a fan, a buzzing sound from the blue-white tubes suspended from the ceiling.

With the pages spread before me, I wait for the words to assume some sort of coherence. To overcome this initial blurring, I carefully wipe and rub the lens of my glasses. Now the letters and numbers are clear and in place, I begin to see what it is I have to deal with.

The first view is reassuring. The questions seem straightforward, none of that tricky wording one might expect. The choices are few and sharply limited. No reason then to spin things out, to sound impressive or seek complications. Holding to this, and with eyes and mind kept from wandering, I should have the whole thing finished within a couple of hours.

It occurs to me, even in this short time, it would not be a bad idea to check on how the body performs. Perhaps three or four deep breaths between each set of questions; feet flat on the floor, back straight against the back of the chair. The left foot—which sometimes gives trouble—moved enough to prevent numbness.

3.

How long since I have been a room of this kind, listening to pens scratching on the page? But this is not what I am here for—the mind must not be permitted to wander. For it is clear that once *these* questions begin, those on the page blur and disappear. Nothing is more enticing, disturbing than that backward look, that swarm of possibilities. . . .

What is it that is out of place? The feeling is vague, yet perhaps not to be ignored. I look around for something tangible to confirm or deny this slight unease.

I return to the printed form, make a few marks upon the page. The buzzing sound from the blue-white tubes attracts my attention; looking up, I notice the veil of air near the ceiling. I trace it to the black metal vent in the corner, a few inches lower down. Back to the page; no problem here. But as this is the last in the series, I take the deep breath—hold it a bit longer than usual.

I am pleased now to go along with the words, to fill in the squares and spaces. The echoes have stopped; no more drifting toward the past. And as for that trickle of air, there is nothing out of order. To confirm this, notice that no one is looking in that direction. On the contrary, nothing but serious and absorbed faces, the concentration appropriate to what has to be done.

4.

How is it that, put to so many tests, I have never been in the position of giving one? Over the years I have suffered through one and another with the feeling of being put through some sort of obstacle course. And who is it that stands there, stopwatch in hand, ready to make the final click?

But I recognize that it is just these absurd images—tortured climbers and lung-bursting runners—that do not belong here. If they have any place at all, it can only be where they do not interfere with the matter at hand.

. . . I detect signs of growing unease. Is it the smoke coming through the vent? One scratches his nose, picks at the corners of his mouth; another presses knuckles against her forehead. I notice bodies shifting, shoes scraping.

The room seems somewhat darker. Perhaps the glass tubes are not giving off as much light. I seem to have read somewhere that even the best generators do not always perform at top level.

5.

It is entirely possible that smoking is permitted in the next room. It could be something in the pipes, or a fan blowing the wrong way. Perhaps this is why so few have glanced toward the ceiling, even turned their heads.

I must remember we are all here for a serious purpose. The added income—and the prestige—is a very real thing. Therefore the emphasis, the concentration on getting the job done. What is going on in the next room, or in the past, or on the outside, is nothing more than a distraction.

If anything were seriously wrong, an alarm would already have sounded. Note that everything has been prepared with the utmost efficiency. Even the small things: the papers placed neatly on the writing surfaces, and in the text itself, not a single misspelled or ambiguous word.

6.

I wonder where the idea has come from. For the first time it has occurred to me that I do not have to remain. After all my present position, while low on the scale, need not be considered degrading. And what is there on the outside I have not faced before? Days of panic and laughter. No more than this.

I press my weight on the polished surface, feel the slow rising. I wait for the heads to turn, for the piercing glances to penetrate. The familiar numbness in the left foot engages my attention. I take one step; the weight holds, the knee performs.

A few more steps and the numbness recedes. I am actually in motion; I shall reach the door, and from there begin the long walk through the corridors. As to what happens then I cannot tell. It may not be possible to leave through the door that I entered. In that case I shall look for some other way to reach the outside.

The Circus/The Zoo

1.

Well, another winter. We go around doing the routine things, playing cards, killing time. A few talk wistfully about next year: things will surely improve; by spring we should be on the road again. There have been other years when things have seemed to touch bottom; it is a fact that, one way and another, we made it through another season.

It has been helpful, in times like these, to observe the reactions of Gilda, the Bearded Lady, and Bozo, the most experienced of our clowns. Before anyone else they seem to know what's going on, which direction things are moving. This year I've noticed how withdrawn they both are. Gilda seems fatigued and silent, not at all her usual rasping and abrasive self. As for Bozo, outside of mealtimes, he hardly leaves the trailer. Passing by, several times I've heard the sound of a typewriter. Gilda says she thinks he's writing his memoirs. I wonder if this could be true, and what it means.

2.

The last few days have been warmer; the wind has died down. It is too early to think of spring, yet surely the worst is behind us. We are still inclined to be cautious, not to expect too much, but I notice face and eyes have lost that dazed, dull look; there is more movement and color.

But with this also begin the jealousies and strife, the usual stirrings of vanity and ambition. One thing that has struck me, more than ever, is how this is picked up and reflected by the animals. In the dejected time, that same flatness could be found in all the cages. Now there is the sense of a greater alertness, of wider and more frequent changes of mood. I've noticed for instance how the Lion, the Elephant, the Tiger, seem to move from apathy to apprehension. And at the same time, rather curious, they seem more responsive to each other. As though for the first time aware of a common bond—would it be too much to say an awareness, a resentment, of their dependent condition?

. . . Cleaning the empty cages this afternoon, it occurred to me that my own closest relationship is not with either animals or men. Filling the galvanized bucket, dumping the stained, crushed straw, pushing the long-handled broom, I felt a definite kinship with the tools of my trade. As though with the bucket free of dents and rust, the bristles strong and resistant, I can do what has to be done.

3.

The Bearded Lady invited me in this morning. I watched Gilda dealing the cards, studying the printed charts. This went on for about half an hour. Finally, she pounded her fist on the table. Nothing she could say on the basis of such confused and conflicting reports. She would have to make further calculations, review each of the signs. I was foolish enough to ask about vibrations. "Hell, there aren't any." I've never seen her so disgusted, so unsure of herself.

About an hour later though, things began to stir; for a moment all the counters on the board pointed in the same direction. She murmured to herself for a while, then stood and went to the window. I heard her voice, quite distant, directed toward the glass. "There may be a journey." She turned and faced me; she looked upset, agitated. "That is, to another country."

Before I left, she made me promise not to repeat this to anyone. Closing the door to the trailer, I wondered about both the original reading and the abrupt change in the signs. For the first time I missed that surge of confidence that had followed her previous pronouncements.

4.

A few days later, without my saying anything, the rumor was already making the rounds that we were going to another country. Details are vague, and perhaps one shouldn't pay attention. Yet I find myself wanting to believe, wishing it were true. Until now I had prided myself on a refusal to panic, a quiet belief in some sort of solution. (Even after that long series of contract cancellations.) I had even told Bozo that soon there would be a new crop of children, for whom his performances would be an exciting experience.

Meeting him this afternoon, he recalled the statement. I couldn't tell what mood he was in, until he commented: "Forget the whole thing. There are no more children." And when I started to reply, he added: "For you it's no problem. You can always clean cages in the Zoo."

Of course I was offended at first. After all these years my attachment to the Circus is a deep and genuine one—even if my own work never comes to the attention of the public. I understand what it means to put on these shows, traveling through inclement weather, facing audiences often bored and hostile.

Yet later that same day, finishing up my tasks, I began to look at the matter in a different light. If the change had to be made, did I have what it takes to begin a new career? I know nothing of Zoos, of what the work might involve; yet the people are there, the animals are there. Would it make that much difference? Perhaps one must learn to adapt—not to be stuck with the notion that one has a special life, a career that contains and defines one's identity.

5.

Leaving the tent after lunch, there was the notice stuck to the canvas. It is signed by the Director: nothing has been decided yet, but negotiations are under way. Definite word should come through within a few weeks. One thing caught my attention: *for an indefinite stay*. No explanation for the use of the phrase.

What then to make of this? I've been watching the others, listening to the loud, eager voices. All sorts of speculations and fantasies have been let loose. (The announcement failed to mention what country or countries were involved.) It's clear that all this noise and confusion is to cover the anxiety. At times like these I wish I could speak directly to the Lion, the Elephant, with their deep, experienced eyes.

The vagueness of it continues to bother me. Not that one place or another makes that much difference. No, I am just deeply puzzled over the whole transaction. I have begun to wonder what kind of country this is, prepared to give up its last remaining Circus. And on the other side: who are they that seem never to have had one of their own?

6.

Of course I should have known: the announcement has been posted. I tried to get there as soon as I could, but by the time I finished breakfast and the necessary chores, a crowd was gathered in front. I saw Bozo and the Bearded Lady at a distance, but as I looked toward them, their heads turned in the other direction.

I walked away a few moments later, having exchanged a few words with other members of the clean-up crew. The phrases danced in my mind; and I began at once to prepare speeches of farewell. Walking through the grounds, I repeated the words, *for an indefinite stay*. And then with a dry taste in my mouth, *only essential personnel . . .*

7.

It is fortunate that I have had the chance to speak at some length with Bozo before having to say goodbye. While occupied with his own situation, he took the time to discuss the realities of what I was leaving, and what I might have to face. What especially impressed me was his utter frankness, even to the extent of comparing his situation with mine. First, he wanted me to know that he had no illusions about things being better where they were going. He saw that his was probably a dying art, and that while the audience might still laugh at the pratfalls, there was not much chance the fine points would be appreciated.

As for what I might expect at the Zoo, I could still feel that I was doing something worthwhile. And if there was not the excitement, the sense of sharing I was used to, I could still find other possibilities—the joys and pleasures of daily life. But it was just as I was about to leave that he said the really significant thing. He was packing, putting away his makeup kit, when he said:

"One never knows what is required in any situation. But only a few things call for that full measure of devotion. I cannot say I was especially chosen, but I understood when I started here, I would try to give whatever was asked."

He closed and locked the case, put it to one side. I thought then that, no matter how difficult, I would ask the question: "And if nothing is asked?"

But just then the door opened; and the room filled with visitors and well-wishers, all talking at once.

8.

I have just finished the first week. It is not as bad as I imagined. The roughest part was filling out the forms, being photographed, fingerprinted, issued a card of identity. I have determined not to make any premature judgment. My fellow workers have been courteous and helpful; the daily crowds are pleasant and undemanding. As for the animals, I find the variety rather confusing; I am still, as it were, learning the species, not yet able to consider any of them as individuals.

It has just occurred to me that I, too, have moved to another country. Although I live and work well within the zone of the safe, the familiar. Still it is a kind of exile from what I have known: that closely bound family of outcasts, looked upon with so much desire and suspicion.

Only this morning I recalled again that last conversation. I can still hear Bozo saying that I must do what I can—even if it is only to make the cages habitable. Even here between one species and another, certain gestures will be made, recognitions passed back and forth. Whenever it is possible then, I will try to make some appropriate response.

The Travel Agent

1.

I'm pleased you decided to enter. I noticed you standing in front of the window—eyes fixed on the posters—four or five days, isn't it? Let me give you these folders; look them over, take your time. Just let me know if you have any questions. . . .

You've traveled before, I presume. I would guess you're old enough to have been a few places, seen a few things. But of course age is not the determining factor. Not these days. Now it's go where you want, when you want—but that doesn't make it any easier. On the contrary, there are too many choices, too many decisions.

Yes, it is rather quiet. A month ago you hardly could get through the door. They come in droves, wanting to be taken care of all at once. Not all of them going somewhere. Some are just asking questions—a way of passing the time. For those who are serious, we stand ready of course to assist in making arrangements.

No, it's not all routine. Something new keeps turning up. Recently, for some reason, a special interest in volcanoes. Now I say: if it's volcanoes, let it be volcanoes. If it goes on, next year we may even arrange a Volcano Tour.

Of course then there are the silent ones. They come slouching in, hair over their eyes. They won't say what they have in mind; go through a whole ritual of furtive looks, whispered asides. When they finally come out with it, it's some place vaguely heard of—a name they can't even pronounce—almost impossible to get to.

There usually is such a place. Finally it turns up on one of our detailed maps. But it's quite a job, first of all to find it and then to figure out the connections. When I try to explain there may be difficulties, it seems I must be putting obstacles in their way.

Sometimes I'm tempted to just sell tickets—let it go at that. But I feel an obligation to make facts known. That means on occasion saying things people don't want to hear. It's all very well to make plans, have expectations. But let the wind shift, the fog drift in, a good storm start, and you see what happens: the road blocked, the airport hidden, the train delayed.

Of course there is a lot of routine. Most people only plan to go those short, safe distances. But even there you can't be sure. . . . Well, take a recent example. This was one of the timid ones. All he had in mind was a small hotel, modest accommodations, trees, a lake, that sort of thing. A quiet place for a quiet man.

What happened? I suggest such a place, make arrangements, and off he goes. A week later he calls. His room has been ransacked. The cook has had a stroke. His mail has been mysteriously misplaced. And so on. Now, this is a place of which I have personal knowledge. I had already looked the man over, decided this is one to be careful with. I've been in this business long enough to spot the potential victim. But as you see . . .

I see that you seem to favor the islands. Well, I was noticing how you've arranged the folders. You placed mountains on one side, deserts on the other, islands in the center. That usually suggests the preference. No, I'm not trying to read your mind. Or to direct your attention, force any choice. After all, it's taken a week for you to get inside the door. . . .

2.

Sorry about what happened. Something I seldom do. No, of course there's no obligation. Here are the folders; take your time. You *are* interested in the islands? I won't say another word until you come up with a specific question.

Good weather, white beaches, not crowded? That's possible—I mean it's still possible. A few years ago of course it would have been much easier. Yes, but those people have their own boats—which makes for a different situation. For one thing, they can sleep on the boats; they can get in and out of the more remote islands without any trouble. No, I didn't see the film. The actual location? I wouldn't be able to say.

Now that you mention it, I recall another film made several years ago. One of those same islands, I'm sure. Yes, now I remember. Man on trial for his life. Few days before the murder stopped in at travel agency, asked about round the world cruise. With him was a very lovely, expensive-looking young woman. I forgot to mention the victim was an old lady; he was included in the will. That part is rather trite. What I found interesting was that they put the travel agent on the stand. Something you seldom see. Usually we're part of the background, while the hero or antihero is off on his great journey or mission or quest—whatever it is.

Certainly you can take the folders with you. We have extra copies, most of them anyway. If you wish to return them, of course we'd be glad to have them back. That's entirely up to you; whenever you care to make a decision . . .

3.

Something interesting? Yes, I've had quite a time with a certain young man. This one kept showing up here for about a week. Actually almost two weeks. The first week staring in the window. Then coming back with another question—set of questions—each time. Whether he heard the answers I couldn't say.

Well, at first the usual things. But then it got more complicated. What's on the other side of the mountain? Where does that river begin; where does it end? You've run into it before, I suppose. No, as a matter of fact it started with the islands. That's the trouble these days: too many choices, too many decisions. And the more you're told, the less there is to discover.

Of course I tried. But what do you make of this? The last time he dropped the folders on the table, started to walk away. I wish I could remember what he said—

what was the phrase? Out of sight, out of mind—but still *there*. Did I know of any such place? I started to ask him to clarify, to be a bit more specific—but before I could say anything, out he went.

So you were up at the cabin. How was the lake and the fishing? I haven't decided yet where I'm going. Not very far, I'm sure. The lake is all right, but the days get too soft, too lazy. For me, a lot depends on the wind. When it's heavy it seems oppressive; when it stops the flies come and settle in—flies and mosquitoes—and that spoils everything.

The Portrait

1.

Photographs posted on the wall, a drawing table facing the window, a desk and two chairs placed near the center of the room. On the desk, neatly arranged, pencils, crayons, sticks of charcoal. With the board braced on his lap, he waits for my statement. (What kind of marks will the yellow pencil trace on the tacked sheet?)

With a few variations, a few omissions, I repeat what I told the officer earlier: walking along the dark, wet street, the blow on the back of the head, the blurred view of the man in the white suit. Not much more I can say—no matter how often the scene is replayed. For what my eyes opened on was less than visible, less than credible: the figure jogging along with that easy motion—not that of a man who expects to be pursued. And then that brief glimpse of the chalky face under the streetlight, just before he turned the corner . . .

2.

The hand that holds the pencil has made a few tentative motions. But as though directed by my voice, stops and starts with the sound. He looks up when I fail to respond to a question, yet is obviously not concerned or involved. He waits to confirm that I have nothing more to say, shrugs, lights a cigarette; his eyes return to the unformed face. The pencil resumes its motion—I can tell from the way it moves when the lines are light, heavy, wavy, straight. Black lines on white paper. He reaches for a pink eraser, shakes his head as he corrects the "mistake." (At this point, without my voice to guide him, he is on his own.) His fingernails scratch the sheet as he dusts off the grains. Hard lines, soft lines . . .

He raises the board, studies the features, holding it close to his face as though it is a text with fine print to be deciphered. With some reluctance, he finally turns it around, offers it for my inspection.

I look at the *facsimile* of a face—for that is what he has drawn. What is missing—how to say it?—is the sense of its being *inhabited*. Mister Mister, whose eyes and mouth have nothing to say. (And yet this is an absurd judgment, for on the basis of the available "information," what else could it be?)

My first impulse is to say nothing; yet I cannot let it go at that. The problem is to control my voice, to keep out anything that suggests anger and disturbance. Choosing my words carefully, I merely refer to what seems to be missing.

A slight lift of the eyebrows. Again the fingernails tap the sheet, brush away a few grains. A pause, and the yellow pencil is put down beside the pink eraser. The voice thickens as he asks for additional details, something specific. And just at this point, all at once, something breaks loose inside. I find myself responding as if to a "challenge"; in a tumble of words I issue directions: the cheeks higher, the nose longer, the lips thinner. (How easy it is, after all, to slip from memory to invention!)

He reaches for the eraser, makes a few flicking motions. He picks up the pencil, studies the point, discards it in favor of another. For a while he seems busy, almost absorbed. My eyes roam the walls of this crowded office: all those glossy, anonymous photographs, those pale, lifeless drawings. (Which of them identified, convicted?)

When he turns it toward me again, I feel the clash of opposites: it is and is not the same face. All at once, something close to panic. Do I want to see, to know any more than this? I wait, then look again. Not at all what I thought, but out of another place, another time . . . I do not quite understand what is happening, but those earlier feelings—his boredom and my confusion—seem completely gone. Instead, we seem to be involved in some joint project, some kind of compact we have entered into.

3.

As I wait for the bus, my attention remains on what is going on around me: the street, the store windows. I am sure now that I did what had to be done; at any rate, it is unlikely that anything more will come of it. Of course there were certain minor discrepancies between what I told him and the officer who interviewed me earlier. But this can be easily explained in that the "artist" is able to stir memory, focus and clarify certain details. No point then looking further, trying to define the precise nature of the transaction . . . And yet one thing makes me wonder: going out the door, that absurd impulse to ask—as if there were no rules, as if he were a free agent—whether I might have a copy . . .

4.

Retrieving the newspaper from the front porch, it occurs to me that even this minor event might be reported. . . . I find it in a lower corner on an inside page: the face small and dark, the text brief and factual. I read it quickly, scanning the lines, then fold it and put it away; I go on then with my usual morning routine.

The story of course gives no indication how these things happen. One goes along in the familiar way, doing what has to be done, staying close to the same people, the same streets, the same hours. But at the first small departure, here comes this sharp intersection, bringing a different order of things.

It is not really unexpected, for it is not difficult these days to fall into the roles of victim and witness. What surprises though is when, as here, the two are so neatly joined. Still no need to treat a mere incident as some kind of cataclysm. (It was only a glancing blow, and I have not missed the few dollars taken from my wallet.)

And yet, and yet . . . Can one go on in the same way—as though nothing has happened? For it is significant that at least part of the unseen has become visible:

that face by skillful questioning drawn out of the recesses. (The officer, higher paid, with all of his authority, could not even get close to the source.)

I have at this point to restrain myself from going to the wastebasket, retrieving the paper from among cigarette butts and assorted debris. Instead, I move into the kitchen, pour coffee out of the glass jar. . . .

We started (did we not?) with confusion, suspicion, and fear on my part, and he had that bored expression, certain this would be something he'd heard many times before. How then were we disengaged from these positions—working through a complicated set of feelings in such a short time, making possible that brief but intense collaboration?

So many words. And perhaps all this was to avoid what has to be said: that face, exposed to the light, has become public property. . . .

from

The Edge of Something

(1977)

We move between the need for discovery on one hand, and equilibrium and stability on the other.

◆

The problems of this world are potentially solvable. It is when we approach the higher, darker mysteries that we experience difficulty.

—Ortega y Gasset

The Edge of Something

1.

There was a moment when, nearing the end of the beach, neither of the two men was aware of the distance between them. It was Gerson who noticed first that Evers was no longer at his side. He turned and saw him, a few feet away, standing with his back to the water: head raised, eyes scanning the white cells that segmented the mountain. The hunched, bony figure appeared against sea and sky, part of the empty space that surrounded him. At the sight, a quick ripple of cold crossed Gerson's flesh—the wind, he told himself, a slight shift in temperature. And yet they stood under the sun, exceptional for this time of year. . . .

The day before at almost the same hour, driving down from Rome, the wind was a constant presence. At one point, perhaps halfway, the sky had turned from gray to black, unleashing one of those abrupt, startling Mediterranean rainstorms. Peering through the drenched windshield, Gerson had asked himself why, with so many bright days to choose from, Evers had to pick this one. He knew of course that the choice was limited: the place in Porto-Vecchio already rented, someone waiting to move into the Rome apartment. But the irritation remained—prolonged perhaps by Evers' curious insistence that, sooner or later, the sun would have to emerge.

"That's my place up there—see it? Just to the left of the Chiesa Nuova."

High on the honeycombed hill, the houses stacked in tiers reaching beyond his sight, Gerson recognized the faded pink stone of the chapel. Beside it there was a cluster of walls, domed and tile roofs, a few glass-fronted shapes. (Somewhere near there, earlier that morning, they had unloaded Evers' few belongings.) But although he nodded, responding to the appeal, he could not tell which one it was.

"I've heard there's a path that goes all the way. Nothing I'd want to climb, but it should be useful coming down—to shop or to the beach."

Evers moved farther from the water, as though drawn in that direction. Gerson waited a moment before he followed. The house, though not visible to him, was a reality: but he wondered if there actually were such a path. The doubt came as he thought of how they had unloaded the car: hauling suitcases and cartons down flights of stairs, through a narrow alleyway, across the rock-strewn ground. (The car had been parked directly above, at the end of an almost impassable dirt road.)

They went on at a slow pace, crossing the packed, polished stones, the gritty black sand. At a distance they could see a few boats high in their wooden cradles, the faded, flaked boards indicating the long period of idleness. A few months from now, Gerson thought, there would not be room to turn around. He imagined them moving past the standing and the prone, threading their way through the maze of oiled bodies.

"It seems important for me to be close to the sea. No matter how long I stay away, I always come back."

The carved features, the weathered flesh were there to confirm it; and Gerson knew that this came, not from lying in the sun, but from years spent as a seaman, a commercial fisherman. The boats, he thought suddenly, could be scraped and repainted, but for the man renewal was another matter. (At any rate, Evers was here now in a very different kind of role.)

"Starting again doesn't bother me as much as I thought—maybe because I've done it so often."

"Well, I hope things work out." Gerson started to say something more but checked himself. All this sounded as though the move were by choice, by intention. Yet it was clear that his leaving the city, severing those ties, those reminders, had to be connected (whatever else was involved) with his wife's departure.

As Evers stopped to light his pipe, Gerson turned toward the long, curved shoreline. At a distance, those cliffs, that mountain rising from the edge of the sea could still suggest what had been and belonged here—but how long would it be before there too layers of houses blocked the view? He sensed and waited for the announcement. When it came, Evers asking if he wanted to start back, he could only say: "Any time you're ready."

The socketed eyes rested briefly on Gerson's face—not long enough to be interpreted. Then Evers turned once more to what was above them: white walls, brown tile, and framed glass stained by the sun. When he spoke again, the eyes were vacant and the voice level and controlled.

"Doesn't look much like a fishing village now."

"No, it doesn't." Gerson hesitated; before they went on, there was perhaps after all something that could be asked. "By the way, when did you first come here?"

"Oh, about two years ago—more or less." Evers moved with the words; the timing suggested this was to avoid the next question.

Following a step or two behind, Gerson wondered if, in spite of the casual answer, the attempt was to relive, to recapture something that was here a long time before.

As Evers increased his pace, Gerson made no attempt to close the gap. The shops, the compressed houses, were already close enough to start him thinking about the return. It was probably too late now, he thought, for any of the things that might have been said.

2.

As they climbed the wide stone stairs, footsteps echoing, it was a while before either of them spoke. But they had gotten used to longer (and more difficult) silences on the drive down. For Evers this was not unusual—in the last months especially, there was less and less that needed to be said. Gerson, however, still felt that some effort at communication was expected or required. . . .

Leaving Rome, they had been confronted with the jarring noise from crowded streets, traffic coming from all directions, signs to be watched for and interpreted. With these and other distractions, it seemed easier to admit that whatever they had to say could wait. Going past the streaked monuments, the rust-colored buildings, they remained occupied (whenever the noise permitted) with the internal surroundings of their separate lives. Only when all this was left behind, and they entered at last the open space of the highway, was any sustained speech possible.

It had been almost two months since they had seen each other, and for once they were not confined to a room full of voices. The time that stretched ahead—five or six hours from Rome to Porto-Vecchio—was more than needed to cover their activities during this period. Beyond this, neither of them knew what might be said, what would remain unexplored.

They started this way: with books they had read, galleries visited, films they had seen or missed. (Evers' brief report, at this point, could be ascribed to his recent illness, the weeks spent in bed.) And from there went on to news of acquaintances: those greeted and said goodbye to, part of the shifting tide, the transient element in the ancient city.

It was not long before they turned, as if to fill in the empty spaces, to the landscape itself: this terraced hillside, that vivid valley, those bare and brittle branches. This too went no further than what it suggested of other times, other places. But then it seemed that, for Evers at least, something else was involved. He tried to express this, making a distinction between the natural and the created landscape, between what belonged there and what man had contributed or taken away. When this brought no response, he turned toward the window—as if the sight itself might confirm what could not be put into words. (Even during that blinding rainstorm, he continued to stare through the glass.)

It was well past the second hour—nothing said yet that opened or closed any doors—before the talk turned to the move itself, the purpose of the trip. It started with Gerson asking about the pots and bowls on the back seat. (They had just crossed a rough place on the road, and he wondered if anything had been damaged.) Evers only glanced there, said he was sure nothing was broken. With a rare, dry smile, he added that in any case he could always make some more. He mentioned then that there was a kiln in the house at Porto-Vecchio—used originally, the owner had told him, for baking bread. This was an unexpected piece of luck, since his idea was to do this commercially, as a source of income.

Gerson had noticed some of these pieces in the Rome apartment, knew that Evers turned them out in his spare time. But it had not occurred to him that it was a serious interest—certainly nothing that Evers would consider giving up his job for. The job, he recalled, paid rather well, seemed to involve no more than that easy kind of institutional selling.

As Evers went on, saying this was something he and Julie (his wife) had planned to work on together, it occurred to Gerson to ask about the separation—not only that the opening was there, but because he sensed it was somehow expected.

Evers delayed his answer, cleaning, packing and lighting his pipe. Then he spoke slowly, between puffs, as if trying to figure out what had happened. As he told it, they had both been aware for some time of the growing estrangement. For a while they had avoided discussing it; but even when they were ready to talk about it, found that they were not able to get at the source.

It was not until much later, Evers continued, that he realized how much of it was due to the difference in their ages. He had suggested the move in response to what he recognized as an increasing need for privacy, for withdrawal. She had agreed at first but then, as the time grew closer, began to express certain reservations. Finally, it had come out that what was important for her was to be where things were happening, close to all that stirring and striving of life in a great city. (Julie was still young enough, he explained, to feel that there was still something to be discovered.) She had not announced her decision, however, until it was almost time for them to leave.

Evers stopped as suddenly as he had begun. It appeared from the shrug, from the way he turned his head, that this was all. He seemed willing, at this point, to listen to whatever reply could be made—or to let the silence accumulate. But after a few moments, with a quick glance at his companion, he suddenly expressed doubt as to whether this made any sense, whether it explained anything. (The note of appeal contrasted with what up till now had been a flat recital.)

The question came while Gerson was still trying to connect all this with the image in his mind: that small-boned, soft-voiced, delicate one—remembered as leaning toward her husband, following him with her eyes—was she capable of that much will, that much desire? He limited himself, however, to something closer to what Evers might want to hear: people had different needs at different times—even with goodwill on both sides, sometimes these things could not be resolved.

Evers took the reply more seriously than Gerson had anticipated. He said that while this expressed part of their situation, it left out a great deal. He knew that Julie did not want to stand in his way, and he wanted her to have whatever was necessary for her own fulfillment. Certainly they had taken different paths before—and been able to work out some kind of compromise. But the difficulty this time was that he had, in fact, come to a place where none of the usual goals seemed worth striving for. Not that he felt defeated or despondent, but perhaps ready at last to accept his own limitations, his inability to change anything. (How could he expect Julie, at her age, to share this view?) All he could do then, it seemed, was to acknowledge her need, and for himself to find and follow his own orbit, wherever he had to go. . . .

Listening to this through the throbbing noise of the engine, Gerson did not know what further response to make. Certainly there was nothing, either in what came before or in their previous meetings, to prepare him. (How was it that it all sounded, at the same time, both too intimate and too remote?) He said something to convey his interest and sympathy—but not enough to invite any further disclosure. Yet even as he spoke, an insistent question echoed: in a situation like this, how could one tell who had been abandoned?

As the sky darkened, Gerson shifted his position, tightened his grip on the wheel. He directed his attention to the traffic, the trees—anything that might offer a distraction. But in the silence that followed, he knew that something had been asked for and denied. With this, he felt an almost intestinal stirring—part resentment, part response to some unnamed threat.

As the wind mounted and at last the rain began to fall, suddenly there was an even more pointed question: had Evers understood what this attempt to lead a self-centered, self-contained existence might cost? At least one thing was clear: with her departure, Evers had already paid the first installment. And leaving his job, the closed circle of their friends, it was certain that others would soon fall due.

3.

They had reached a level place at the end of the first flight before Evers finally broke the silence. In a quiet, almost solemn voice, he suddenly asked if Gerson would like to stay for lunch. The question came as they stood beside a church with barred doors; most of the row of small shops next to it were closed also, the others marking time until the season started.

Gerson did not understand why the invitation came now; he had said earlier that he planned to leave about this time. The watch on his wrist read a few minutes before one; he was not hungry, though—and there were several places to eat along the way.

"I'd like to get back before dark," he said. Then felt it necessary to add: "Madeline said we'll be having company for dinner." It was only after he spoke that the image of Evers, eating alone, occurred to him.

They started climbing another, longer flight; beyond there, in the first flat open space, the car was parked. On the way, Gerson noticed the torn, faded posters that covered the walls on both sides of the narrow walk: the events they announced all belonged to other years.

The car was already in sight—Gerson moving ahead was going toward it—when Evers reached out, touched him on the arm. "You forgot to buy those plates."

Gerson blinked, then slowly nodded. He knew that he should be grateful for the reminder—at least it saved him an explanation—but he was already looking forward to the drive home. (What echoed was Madeleine's voice as she specified where to buy them: that special shop across from that particular hotel.)

A moment later, they had changed direction, entered a street that angled upward on their right. Farther along, passing one of the few empty lots that faced the sea, they stopped for the changed view. Gerson noticed how from here the beach appeared compact, diminished—different from the place where they had walked a short time before. Evers, though, only glanced there; once more his attention shifted to what was above them: the location to be made beside the chapel wall.

"There it is—right in the middle of all those vineyards." His voice went higher, rising in self-sustained enthusiasm. "And what about that garden? I told you, didn't I, that Paolo said I could have all the vegetables I needed?"

Turning in response to the demand, Gerson found that even from here he could only guess which one was indicated—beyond that, the effort was wasted. And as for the garden, the image that remained was of the rows of crooked stakes, marking the flat, dry ground—where something might, or might not, grow in another season.

—

In answer to Gerson's question, the woman behind the counter nodded vaguely toward the back of the store. Moving there, Gerson scanned the plain wooden shelves. Flat, unglazed white, he told himself, the thin blue border painted by hand. All that was visible were these rows of glossy factory pieces: produced by and for the same taste. (Was this something Madeleine had invented—or seen some other place, some other time?) It was Evers who finally located them, dusty and almost unreachable, at the back of one of the top shelves.

When Gerson set the plates down on the counter, Evers asked the woman where they were made. She told him they came from a small town a few kilometers south of there. As she wiped and started to wrap them, Evers said: *"Conosci la casa di Paolo Orlandi?"*

When the woman replied that she knew the house, he told her that he was the new tenant. At this she nodded and smiled, said she hoped she would enjoy his stay.

"Anch'io sono una ceramista."

The dark eyes narrowed for a closer look. *"Ah sì, va bene."* Then the smile broadened. *"Durante l'estate sono molti turisti. Ne comperanno molti di questi."*

Gerson still found it hard to believe that Evers was serious about this business of pots and bowls. It was possible that, as the woman said, it could bring in some money during the season. But for anything beyond that it was unrealistic to . . . Suddenly there was the image of the cell-shaped oven set deep in the basement wall.

Standing on the cold, stone floor, looking out across the slanted, vine-covered field, for a moment it had seemed that Evers was already at home: *as though the place were somehow intended for him. . . .*

The parcel was on the counter. Evers was at his side saying something. He shook his head to indicate that he had not heard. Evers repeated the question, this time in a louder voice. "Do you mind if I buy them?" And went on before he could reply: "I want to make some plates for you and Madeleine—but that'll have to wait until I get things set up. In the meantime, please accept these as a present."

Gerson nodded, thanked him. But as he picked up the package, started toward the door, he wondered at the gesture: Evers should be buying what he himself needed—from what they had unpacked, there wasn't even enough for him to get started.

As they stepped outside, Gerson blinked at the reflection of sun on white walls. For a moment, as he shielded his eyes, he felt as though something had dissolved and disappeared. What would it be like, he wondered suddenly, to start at fifty or fifty-five in a place deserted in winter, submerged in summer? He understood then what his flesh had recorded earlier: as if he himself were facing this—but with the cold knowledge that there was nowhere else to turn.

◆

Gerson unlocked the car doors, carefully set the parcel down on the back seat. As he started to get in on the driver's side, he saw Evers still standing there.

"I think I'll walk the rest of the way."

It took a moment before Gerson realized that Evers was ready to say goodbye. It was as though he had not expected it—instead of the relief he had anticipated, there was a sudden reluctance. All at once there was more to be discussed, a range of things left unresolved.

"That's still quite a climb," Gerson heard himself say, "Why don't I take you up to—at least to where the road branches off to your place?" He stood with his hand on the car door, still not sure what brought the reversal, what it meant. And then he said: "I was thinking we might have one last drink. . . ." He felt the warmth suffuse his flesh, but had to go on: "We could stop by that bar. . . ."

At first, there was only the distant smile, the slight movement of the head—nothing else to show what the offer meant. The smile faded, though, along with what flickered in the eyes. Evers spoke then with a slow nod, making the decision. "Thank you for that—and for all the help." He went on quickly: "But I know you have to get back. . . . and I might as well get started on what I have to do."

They talked for another moment: Evers asking when Gerson thought he might come down again, getting the reply that it might be a month or more.

"By that time, I might have things in pretty good shape. If you and Madeleine can come for a weekend, I should be able to put you up. Just let me know a few days ahead. . . ."

They shook hands and said goodbye. Gerson, entering the car, turned the key, listened to the roar of the motor. His last view as he started up the narrow, spiraling street was of the man framed in sunlight and planted on the stone.

4.

He drove fast, and did not stop to eat on the way. He felt as though he was being hurried along by all the unanswered questions—none of which would disappear until his return. Once more, he tried to explain his involvement, going back now to Evers' phone call: the hoarse, weak voice telling of his illness, the departure of his wife, of being forced to move—the whole impossible situation. (And why was the call made to him? Certainly there were others closer to the man, on whom there was at least some kind of claim.)

Gerson turned toward the landscape; beside him now there was, incongruously, a stand of first-year trees, their slender rods growing out of season, rising from the over-aged, over-cultivated land. Somehow this was one of the sights they had missed on the way down. (Perhaps during that slashing rainstorm. It was still a source of wonder that, after an hour or so, Evers' prediction had been confirmed: the strong, clear colors of the late sun spread through that winter sky.)

In the silence of this vacant, sun-filled afternoon, there were echoes of that remote, detached voice. *Free to live and free to die.* That was Evers asserting the need for the individual to select and move within his own orbit. Gerson went over it again, telling himself this was, after all, something he should be able to understand. (Was it the same thing for Evers as for that small, fragile woman? If this was the case then, perhaps, forsaking each other, neither had been abandoned.)

Gerson pressed down the pedal; ahead the black surface offered the straightest, shortest way to his destination—yet one sharp turn of the wheel could change that, too. It was one thing to talk about orbits, but what happened when one was alone and needed help? How had Evers gotten through those long feverish afternoons—wasn't it almost certain that someone had sat beside him, offering the touch of cool fingers, the sound of a living voice?

Free to love and free to kill. The changed words, his own paraphrase, appeared without thought, without preparation. He responded suddenly with a loud yawn; he was tired of all this—whatever it meant, it belonged to what was behind him. . .

Sometime later, realizing there was more than enough light for the distance that remained, Gerson eased the pressure. As the car slowed, his breathing adjusted to the pace. Leaning back in the seat, he assured himself that in any case Evers' move could only be temporary. The garden, the vineyard would all disappear; in their place would emerge rows of interlocking walls, carved from what was left of the mountain.

The car shook as the tires crossed a rough place on the road. (Was it the same one?) Gerson turned his head toward the back seat; the quick glance assured him: the plates were where he had left them. But somehow the idea of their being in pieces stayed with him. It took some time to trace the distant echo, something an archaeologist once told him: from pottery fragments one learned the story of what had been—more than from anything shaped in marble or cast in bronze.

Gerson loosened his grip on the wheel, smiled at the image in his mind: Evers offering his pots to some tourist, trying to explain their value in these terms.

The plates were where he had left them. It was the absurd that echoed now, replacing what only a moment ago had seemed portentous and meaningful. But it reminded him that, after all, it was Evers who was responsible for their being there. The irony of it was that, while Evers was eating alone, the plates might be used that very evening. But more likely, he admitted, what Madeleine had in mind was to display them on a shelf—something else to decorate the rooms in which they lived.

Notes on Beato Angelico

What might be expected of such men if they happened to find themselves in the presence of living beauties, *with their lascivious ways, soft words, movements full of grace and ravishing eyes—when the mere* counterfeit *and shadow of beauty moves them so much?*

—G. Vasari, *Lives of the Artists* (1550)

1.

As the wide steps of the ramp-like staircase filled with the departing crowd, he knew that he could not delay much longer. He stood at the top of the descending spiral watching the movement; then, peering down through the oval-shaped space, he noticed a reflection of light upon metal: the altar floor littered with coins. His attention held there; he recalled vaguely that the meaning had been explained—perhaps more than once. He shook his head; what concerned him was not the lost memory, but being so easily distracted: there was something else on his mind.

He turned, moved a step or two, looked back toward the thronged, half-dark corridor. It was from there that he had just come: from the huge gallery located at the other end. It was in that long, double row of rooms, walls covered with the paintings of six centuries, that the encounter had taken place. (To locate it more precisely, in the first half of the fifteenth century.)

It had happened, he told himself, not by accident, but because he wanted it to happen. (*At least that much,* he thought, *should be clear.*) And if nothing more was involved than the brief conversation, it was because he had limited it to that: letting her drift out of sight—when it was already clear she had no objection to his going along.

He shifted his stance as the bulky presence of the gray-uniformed guards, moving into his line of vision, blocked part of the view. He noticed, though, how they stood beside the rusted iron turnstiles, unaware of or indifferent to being in the way of those who were leaving. For them, it was another day, another crowd; as soon as the corridor emptied, they could go home.

He glanced at his watch, noting the minutes that remained. It was possible, he thought, that she had already left. Yet since he had come almost directly here, and when last seen she was heading toward another part of the gallery, it was not likely. To lessen any chance, though, of missing her in the crowd—that suggested a special kind of irony—it would be better if he stood closer to the entrance. . . .

He surprised himself by turning back instead to his former view of the staircase. This time, he watched the departing throng of priests, tourists, children, soldiers, a question forming in his mind as to what had brought *them* here. A few moments later, he recognized that this, too, was a distraction—as earlier, with the sight of the coins. Rejecting it, he forced himself to consider what he had so far been trying to evade: the meaning of the encounter. . . .

It was easy enough to recall, once he could face it, how it had started: the inviting legs flashing into his sight from the other end of the passageway. Nor was there anything complicated in his response. For evidence, there was the dry mouth, the wetting of his lips, as if in anticipation of what might be tasted. But it was also true, he had to admit, that at some point it had turned into something else—precisely what, he was still reluctant to define.

He placed his hands flat on the pitted stone of the curved ledge; leaning over, he felt his heels rise from the floor. He put his weight down, digging in with his fingers, to steady himself. It had started, he realized, before he had even arrived. The encounter could not be explained, at least not beyond the obvious, without some reference as to what had brought him here—or rather brought him back.

Had he come then looking for *something*? Something he had missed on his previous visits? It might be significant that, unlike the other times, he had passed by the other floors of the museum—all the statues, vases, antique jewelry—and gone directly to the gallery. It was easy enough to explain this by his late arrival (about two hours before closing time). Yet it appeared now—in view of what had happened—that this was not the whole story.

All at once, he was presented with the unwanted, unasked-for insight. Coming as a statement of what he was *really* thinking, it tended to cancel out, by its very simplicity, what he had felt was complex and unsolvable: *he was not waiting for her.* And this meant that he did not want to, or did not expect to, see her again.

He lifted his hands off the cold, porous stone, rubbed one palm against the other. It seemed now that he had known all along that nothing would come of it— that nothing *could* happen. (After all, he could not entirely push out of his mind the fact that, once he stepped outside, someone would be waiting *for him*.) This made it sound though like the end of some important, extended relationship. And yet, as the time was measured on his wrist, how long could it have been—fifteen minutes, a half-hour?

The time was being measured for him now in a different way: in the empty spaces visible in the corridor, in the quieter, more determined appearance of the figures on the staircase. Soon he himself would be on the descending spiral, adjusting his pace to theirs, to emerge with them somewhere on the gray, tangible streets.

Was there any other choice? He could not go back through the rusted turnstiles, toward what was already consigned to the past. (What would happen if he tried to explain to the guards what was on his mind?) He could only stand here, for the moment at least, unable to move in either direction: *between the two women.* Between the elusive image and the familiar face that was central to his existence.

The question that was not a question, the decision that was not a decision, pressed on him. For he remembered now what he had seen (less than seen, more than imagined?) when *this one* had finally turned in his direction. He had to admit that it was nothing like what he had expected or hoped for: the small dark eyes glowed behind the odd-shaped lenses, expressing something quite different from what the flesh had offered. There was even, on closer view, something wrong with what she wore: the black and white jacket and skirt suggesting the fashion of another country, another time.

He reached into his pocket, pulled out a pack of cigarettes. It was only when he started to put one in his mouth that he remembered: *e vietato fumare.* Returning them, he corrected himself: this reaction had come, not at that time, but only *after* she had responded to his remark about the painting. It had come, in fact, in the middle of what had begun to sound like an impersonal, undirected monologue. . . . He had listened in growing wonder, only gradually finding a current of meaning beneath the tide of words. What it suggested was that for her, art was inseparable from religion; her affection for the past indicated a withdrawal from the present—and included in that was a denial of the flesh. (Thinking of the waste of what she possessed in such ironic abundance, of her feeling for the painter dead four hundred years, she seemed to deserve the name: *lover of death.*)

Had she at any moment, during this long outpouring, been really aware of his presence? He had tried several times, in different ways, to let her know whom she was talking to. But there was no evidence, as he thought of it now, that she had ever heard him.

She had spoken—and then her voice had stopped. With a look over her shoulder, which he was free to interpret or to ignore, she had moved on. The impression left was of some kind of invitation—but did it include anything to be shared by the bodies of a woman and a man? She had gone then out of his sight and into a place where, even though a few steps would have taken him there, he was not prepared to follow.

2.

The sight of those fantastic legs had stopped him when he was already on his way out. He had gone through the gallery at that forced pace, conscious that there was time only for that hasty overall view. He had lingered only in the immense *sala* in front of the Raphaels—admiring the paintings, but finding that the tapestry left him cold—and in that narrow, shadowed space illumined by a Leonardo. Leaving, he was taking with him a sense of disappointment; for once, the great names had nothing to say that he had not heard before.

It was in this context then that he had reacted to that brief glimpse of the seated woman: from the raised hem of that black and white skirt, issuing its indolent, unselfconscious invitation, the color of flesh had extended outward. The stunned eyes had sent a message to the confused mind: was it possible, with all that he knew, something could still be discovered *there*?

He could not, though, as yet permit himself to change direction. For one thing, as he had often learned, what swelled in the mind today shriveled and disappeared—seen by the cold light of tomorrow. And so he temporized, turning back to what was on the wall in front of him. He saw no more, though, than was there before: the same mediocre, stilted landscape. He did not need to read the title, remember the artist's name; one glance told it all: figures floating through an endless garden, trees swaying in the misted, scented air.

He turned his head finally; where he had looked with desire, there was the empty chair. He nodded his head at what the sight confirmed: it was like him to delay long enough *to make sure* nothing could happen. . . .

Arriving there, he told himself that he should accept it now: the first view of her was also the last. He surveyed the small, square room: in front of him, the staring dark-robed saints appeared flat and unaware against the gold-leafed background. He moved away; in the corridor, there was no other presence but his own. Suddenly, out of some forgotten place, the harsh memory stirred: so many long, stone corridors, so many bright canvasses strung from invisible wires, covering the flat, neutral walls.

He put the thought into hard, clear words: *that was the hunting ground.* It was part of his personal history that, moving past the paintings, he had found something beyond the artist's intention: the living flesh making him forget what the narrow frames were supposed to contain. The shadowed faces, the darkened names (not to mention the breasts, lips, thighs) flickered for a moment—but it was all long ago and far away. Little more remained than the abstract knowledge that those encounters had actually taken place. He could believe it, though, when he thought of how the setting lent itself to precisely this kind of contact: just their joint presence in this or that *house of culture* established the common interest, suggested that other things might be shared. . .

He was in a room where the paintings, placed next to and one above the other, blurred and overlapped. He shook his head, blaming the poor arrangement, the inadequate lighting. He looked toward the high, narrow window on the opposite wall, instinctively tracing the light to its source—and it was at that moment, while wondering what kept him there, that he sensed her presence.

Moving quickly toward the next room, he saw her standing there, facing the wall. Comparing the image projected on the screen of his mind and what was being measured by his eyes, he found the figure shorter, more *life-sized* than he had imagined. He missed of course the sight of her face—but he decided that, while he sorted out his feelings, it was probably better this way.

She stood there concerned and devoted, in front of that same small painting. She stood there for a longer time than he could have believed possible. And when she finally turned, taking only a step or two, he offered his face. Waiting for his presence to be acknowledged, he took a long breath and held it.

Then with a now-or-never feeling, he exhaled the words. Hearing them, he could not tell whether the sound was that of a statement or a question. At the same time, though, something else echoed in another part of his mind: devoting that much time to that one painting, what could she have seen that he himself had missed?

3.

Her brief answer came without hesitation, as if the casual observation invited the casual response. It needed only that further glance in the direction of the canvas, to make it clear what she felt was being shared. It came then as an afterthought, when she added: "For me there's no one quite like him."

At least that was what he thought she said: getting used to her face, the words almost slipped past. (There was also the strange accent to be traced.) He thought it best, under the circumstances, to admit his confusion.

"Beato Angelico—Fra Giovanni, the good friar of Fiesole."

The Blessed Angel. The way she spoke the name conveyed all the reverence of one who took it seriously. She confirmed this, a moment later, by telling the story of how the friar had refused the chance to become an archbishop. He tried again to clarify things by referring to the man as a painter. (He still could not place the accent.)

"It's not easy to explain. . . ."

He understood then, as she hesitated, that she was still trying to find words— perhaps part of the effort was for what had to be translated from her own language.

"I'm sure that there were better, more important painters. But for me he has always this special meaning—how can I say it?"

She moved closer to the painting. Her hand reached out and for a moment it appeared the long fingers were poised to caress it. "Perhaps this way: here the artist and the man cannot be separated. There is nothing, no ambition, no desire, that does not belong as much to one as to the other. The painting takes this shape from the faith that he had to express."

The slight movement of her shoulders indicated that she did not know, after all, why this had to be put into words. He said then: "I understand that. But how does that make him different from the other painters of his time? They all praised the same God, feared the same devils. Because he chose to enter a religious order and they didn't . . ."

He left it that way as he noticed that her eyes had not moved from the wall. And when she spoke again, her voice came from a distance, veered off in another direction. "That's when I would have wanted to be alive. When one could know and feel where one belonged—part of what existed, of what came before and what came after. And not be ashamed to express this either: it could come out in every brushstroke, every shape of the stone." She stopped, turned to him. "You don't think *he* painted for his own glory, do you?"

"I know very little about him—as a man or as a painter." This, though, he realized, had a defensive sound. He said with more emphasis: "I think that any artist, no matter how religious, would have to express something of himself as an individual."

Her head raised in a gesture that expressed both inquiry and defiance—at the same time, it revealed to him more of the line of the neck, the slope of the shoulders. "Fra Angelico painted as naturally as he lived and breathed. If he had never signed his name to a single canvas, his work would still say the same thing: this is how man serves God—and there is no greater privilege, no greater joy."

He felt the stir of resentment, admiration turning to anger as he thought of the waste: the flesh that invited, the mind that denied. What it amounted to was this: the body could not be transcended—it could only be deprived.

He glanced toward the high, narrow window. There was even less light; too early for darkness, it could only mean that somewhere out of sight the clouds had thickened. If he had not changed direction, he might be outside now: looking up at that sky, waiting for the rain to fall. (When that happened, the one he had arranged to meet would have to seek shelter inside.)

He was not aware of the exact moment when she turned and, giving up the focus of her attention finally, went on toward the next room. All he could tell was that, without choice or decision, his motion somehow coincided with her own.

—

"These few rooms mean more to me than all the rest—all that show and magnificence—yes, even more than that ceiling in the chapel. . . ."

He noticed that, as her attention again turned toward the walls, nothing here absorbed her in the same way. Strangely, though, he approved, would not have it otherwise—as if the transfer of her affections, coming this soon, would show her as fickle, disloyal.

"I know there are some who talk about men like Angelico as—what is the word?—'forerunners.' As if all they did was to prepare the way for the others: for the 'really great' names. It isn't true: what they had was very much their own. And if they lived in a time when one saw little of the outer world, it only meant that their inner life took on so much more. . . ." Her voice trailed off; she left it incomplete—as though if this were not clear, nothing she could add would make any difference.

"We seem to be looking in the same places, but not seeing the same things." There was that edge in his voice—on the inside it sounded like he was shouting— that suggested retaliation. But for what, he wondered. For taking his presence for granted, for promising what she was not prepared to deliver? He knew better, though: this one had created for herself a perfectly delineated, self-contained past. No more room there for him than for anything else associated with the harsh, imperfect present.

"And what is it that you see?" Even with the question, the tone remained impersonal; even before the answer, it was clear, his words could not penetrate to where she had retreated.

"For one thing, I can't forget the violence that surrounded their lives. I think that it was the torture, the guilt that produced the ecstasy."

This time, the smile was clearly that of the believer; it showed patience, tolerance, even something like affection—that special kind reserved for those to whom the light was denied.

"Oh, we take that for granted. But of course that's only the surface: the pain without the meaning. That's like—like calling the surgeon the man with the knife. Without asking or caring what infections or corruptions have to be removed."

He thought of an answer—but the words disappeared as the image flashed in his mind: the curved flesh flat on the long white table. She lay there, under the concentrated cone of light, surrounded by the masked, sterilized actors. And it was understood that no one held her there—this then was what the flesh had come to: choosing *that kind* of penetration. . . .

They stood now in a different setting: not the flat, neutral walls, with one painting stacked above another, but a shining expanse of marble surfaces. (The eye had to move past the reflection to find the canvasses.) He was aware of something else here that had to be solved—but there were no clues beyond the huge ornate mirror, the gilded clock, the painted porcelain.

Watching her move beside the expansive stone, it came to him that he was seeing her now where she belonged: *in a room like this*. She filled this space, where nothing claimed her attention, in a way that the cramped rooms, with their dark-robed saints, could never have suggested.

"Lorenzo Lotto. Melozzo da Forli." He heard her voice at a distance, murmuring the names. At the sound, there was a small stir of interest. These names had some meaning for him; they were *discoveries* he had made here, in this very room.

"Do you know their work?"

He hesitated; here was something that might be shared. He said: "I've seen these before." As for the rest of what he might say, that would take, it seemed, more of an effort than he was prepared to make.

She stood now only a few feet away, a glowing presence in the darkening room. Her eyes, though, already gauged the distance to the marble-framed entrance. Sensing the decision, he told himself that the space between them was not meant to be crossed. Yet he felt that, as at the beginning, it was again now or never. This time, though, the rhythm of his breathing was not affected; it went on, inhale, exhale, in the same steady pulse that sustained him.

He did not move when she moved. After all, it was only a thin, invisible thread that stretched between them, and when it snapped, severed by the vibration set off by her footsteps, he knew that it could not be repaired.

━

In the empty room, responding to the silence, there was both a presence and an absence. Within the limits of what filtered through the deprived senses, one thing was clear: he had after all joined her in denial. If this could be explained, it could only be with the recognition that her terms were too high: she asked for faith, payable on demand. He could only offer this: the artist's need was for whatever could keep the brush in his hands. *Faith or fiction*; what mattered was how long and how well it sustained him.

Turning in the opposite direction, he once more confronted the glittering surfaces: the enameled vase with no flowers, the clock that had stopped centuries before, the porcelain figure that had never known the reality of motion.

Above his head, as he reached the far corner, there was once more the ornate gilded mirror. It was too high, he realized, too far out of reach—no chance that it could have reflected the sight of the two of them standing together.

4.

He was on the spiral now, lending his body to the downward motion, following those for whom there was only this one direction. He felt as though he were being shuttled between the two women: between the brief, ripe image and the face he could recognize at any distance. He went where his footsteps led—along a course determined by this simple vertical motion. Was there any other way? He thought of those immense shining corridors that extended outward from the staircase. At least there, moving horizontally, one might feel for a while, as he went on, that there was more to come.

Three floors of history. He ticked off the contents, skimming the catalogue in his mind: the Egyptian Museum, the Greek and Roman statues, Etruscan vases, parchment maps, illuminated manuscripts. Not only could it not be indexed, but even the idea of all this profusion produced a numbness, a sense of fatigue.

Across the long shining corridors. He thought of where this accumulation had come from. It had passed from hand to hand, from one epoch to another—collected by an army that changed banners, changed rulers, but marched always under the same slogans. His own motion was contained within that larger movement—did it matter then which way he went, what choice was revealed by his present course between one woman and another?

The hunting ground. He did not know at first why this echoed again, what connection there could be between the sensual self on the prowl, and what he had just seen charging across the pages of time. It might be, though, that what he was after, as well as what filled the glass cases, decorated those magnificent walls, could be considered as *trophies.*

As he descended now, a dry smile appeared on his face at the extravagant comparison between his own out-of-season *hunting,* and the wars that brought these priceless treasures. And as if this were not enough, there was also the thought that he had gone by all of this in the single-minded, *simple-minded* idea that by seeing less he might be able to understand more. There was more to be learned from his presence here on the wide steps, hemmed in by the departing crowd on their way back to the literal streets—*after all, wasn't this what one always came back to?*

(Away from the anonymous faces, he could only turn toward the vision in the black and white dress: where was she now? Perhaps where he had left her—somewhere near the end of the fifteenth century.)

Reaching the first landing, he remembered the first time he had come here: that was when, in his ignorance, he had tried to see it all. He shook his head, wondering at the ridiculous figure he must have presented: his feet dragging across the corridors, eyes turning in all directions; and all the while, looking for an end that was not in sight. . . .

—

Nearing the bottom of the spiral, he came back to where the coin-splattered altar floor was the most immediate thing in his sight. Pausing there he watched a thin, dry-faced woman holding a child above the rail that enclosed that space. He saw the fingers open, the money fall without sound from the small, flabby hand. He went on. Perhaps for the child, he thought, there might still be a saint—*or talented friar*—to shape and prolong the dream.

At last within sight of the entrance—the gray air a curtain across the unknown—he noticed the huddled figures. The colored umbrellas, the wet hair, were signs of what was waiting for him outside. (It meant, too, that the woman he had arranged to meet would not be on the steps.)

He moved slowly, feeling the press of bodies, the anonymous flesh. It made no difference, he thought, how close they came together: whatever brought them here, occupying the same space at the same time, it was not enough to relate one to the other. And then it occurred to him (thinking of that remote figure) that the reverse might be true: that *intimacy* might be achieved with what could not be touched.

Under the impact of this, feeling the force there of something beyond his understanding, he tried once more to summon that image: but it was already too far behind him. All that formed was this weak flicker, this flesh turned to shadow. And in his mind's eye, black and white ran together, dissolved by the steady falling of the undeniable rain. Nothing could keep the raised hem of that bright silk from unraveling, the thin threads from fraying, from falling apart.

It would be cold outside; in contrast there was, he discovered, an unusual warmth in his own body. Bringing his hand to the side of his face, the touch confirmed it. It occurred to him that the woman who waited might notice the flushed cheeks, might want to know what they meant.

He was only a few steps from the opening when he sighted the medium-sized figure in the neat brown suit. For some reason, he noted with surprise, she stood facing the street. (As the other, in front of the wall, had faced the past?) It was there, he thought, that they would soon be together. Walking beside her, he might notice the legs: straight and short and fleshed to the size of his imagination.

He stopped and stood there. In a moment their eyes would meet—one glance that proclaimed their mutual existence. The first words, he knew, would refer briefly, lightly, to the real events of the few hours of their separation. Then before she could notice and comment on what remained of the lighted eyes and heated face, he decided that he would ask her again about the coins.

The House/The Doors

1.

It is tiresome to go through this again, but with the renewal of the contract a public statement is expected. Not that I intend any elaborate explanation: considering the available material, that would be a waste of time. Enough then to limit myself to routine matters—past performance, cost accounting, etc., and the usual paragraphs summing up procedures and the rationale of a realistic admittance policy.

One thing I have no intention of including: any response to the standard complaints of "unfair treatment," the "rigid" nature of authority, etc.

When I first started, these appeals were often touching, even upsetting, and I spent many hours with bewildered petitioners. But it always came back to the same point: whatever rules or laws left them outside had to be unjust. It never made any difference that documents were produced—some of them ancient scrolls—that set forth the basis of entrance and tenancy.

It has become clear then, at least from this standpoint, that not much has changed. This in spite of the "urgency" of recent public outcries. One has only to look at the crude, hand-lettered signs carried back and forth in front of the more widely known entrances to realize how naïve the illusions and expectations.

2.

As it turns out, I may have to say somewhat more than I originally intended. The recent publication of M.'s *Treatise on Admission*—which has reached a surprisingly large audience—may call for a detailed reply. Not that I anticipate any difficulty dealing with the "charges." Typically, M. presents a view almost entirely from the outside. And concludes with a melodramatic "exposure" of the false decorations—tinsel, plaques, scrollwork—that hide the "true" nature of the Doors. No wonder that, deluged with these journalistic "revelations," the rage and frustration continues. . . .

3.

I have decided, after all, not to respond in kind, to issue nothing more than a formal statement. If M.'s work, with its trivial oversimplifications, can gain acceptance, there's no use even trying to allude to symbolic manifestations.

(Note that B., a sensitive and imaginative observer, issued some eight or ten years ago a fairly lucid account, describing the interior, including some rather ingenious alternate floor plans. And the response? Some three or four hundred copies sold; the rest presumably still moldering in the warehouse.)

So it is best to limit myself to routine information—although to avoid dullness, I might include a few anecdotes of those who have approached, and even come through the Doors, during my own brief tenure. It is hard, though, after these years of service, to avoid some expression of personal feeling. One would wish to say something, even though it be misunderstood, about the negative image of the Doorkeeper that casts him as an enigmatic or even sadistic stereotype.

4.

Somewhat against my better judgment, I spent the morning giving vent to these feelings. (Knowing of course that none of *this* will ever see the light of day.) And I must say, just getting the words on paper makes me feel better. No one knows what it's like being on call, held responsible for decisions and procedures handed down through—could one ever count how many?—councils and echelons.

And all this has merely to do with street-level activity: contact with floors above and below, entrances into basement and garden, being severely limited. And as to that further realm, *Corridor Control*, that reaches one only on the rarest occasions—through the briefest of unsigned memos.

Before going to sleep, I again tried to put some of the experience into words. But this time, instead of feeling relieved, I was more distressed than ever. Needless to say, I spent a most difficult night, getting up, pacing back and forth, putting lights on and switching them off. Also I kept hearing noises—as though the house itself had suddenly become responsive, walls and windows taking on a strange kind of vibrancy.

5.

I have stopped answering the knocks and the bell. This I accomplished with a rather curt note tacked above the main entrance: *Come back in a week*. I was able to do this, since this is traditionally a slow time, with most of the week devoted to taking inventory.

The rest, the relative quiet have already provided a refreshing interlude. This afternoon, after a gentle, ease-producing nap, I awoke with a memory undoubtedly connected with my present situation.

It took place some years ago in another country. The woman at my side (it must have been R.) listening attentively as I described the feeling of being hemmed in, not knowing where to turn. Her reply was something to this effect: *At times, a door appears where there is no door. The door opens at a place and in a way for which there is no expectation, no precedent.*

Strange that the whole experience should have been so completely forgotten, pushed back so far into the recesses of the mind! For as I think of it now, it seems entirely possible that it was precisely this encounter, coming where and when it did, that started the turn of events, culminating in the decisive move from outside to inside.

Lying here unable to sleep, I have reflected further on the circumstances of that conversation. It took place beside a famous lake in the province of W. Above us was the Castle: the summer residence to which the faithful still make pilgrimage. Close by there is a Museum in which are stored specimens of the long, narrow boats in which the "Barbarians" once set sail. And of course not far off are the ruins of the Temple: the same "sacred grove" described in F.'s classic work. It was there that the rituals took place: the trees worshipped, the kings murdered.

It seems necessary to return to the house on the street, the street in the city. And to such mundane matters as the repair of warped doors, the recovery of missing keys. I should note here the special and faithful assistance of C., who is certainly much more than a highly skilled carpenter and locksmith.

But this only calls up another memory: the afternoon C. forgot about the sealed-off passage that leads to the lower basement and stepped off into that dark space. I found him hours later, his right leg broken. . . . Note how many of my current difficulties began at that point. For soon after his recovery, he applied for a transfer: it seemed that *after the fall*, he could never regain his old confidence. And since it proved impossible to replace him, I was forced to take on tasks for which I am almost completely unsuited.

6.
This morning I removed the notice from the door. In a short while, I suppose, the knocking and ringing will begin. I have already mailed a brief statement to the press. It says no more than what is available in previous statements. As such, it should serve to establish the continuity of policy. It emphasizes, as is only proper, the need to maintain standards, to keep a consistent ratio between available space and the number of applications that can realistically be considered. . . .

The Graduate

1.

Now the decision is made, I wonder at the long delay. Of course, there is the handicap. But at long last it's becoming clear that—one way or the other—all are handicapped. And the doubts, the rationalizations? Perhaps no more than masks for pride, for willfulness. As the Instructor says: *The Stones are hard and dangerous—but how else cross the river?*

It remains now to proceed with courage, with full confidence. Enrolled in the Course, the rest will follow: step upon step, until I reach the other side. (*How long*, and in *what direction*, are questions that need not be asked.)

There is no chance, I realize now, of this being merely another detour, another waste of time. It is rather, at long last, the best chance of finally entering a different space. As the Instructor says: *Concentration, Coordination, Convergence.* These are the key words—not words really, but states of being to be achieved.

2.

At last—today it begins! I am indeed looking forward to the weeks of intensive training, designed to promote the quick, deft movement that implies true inner balance. (So much more, really, than mere self-defense.) My attention now should be geared to this—and nothing but this. For it is the *Process* itself—(am I quoting again ?)—that shapes and forms the outcome.

Thus, obtaining the Certificate is the smallest part of the Task. More important is to perfect the Instrument. To come to that point where, at last, one begins to move without conscious effort, without will. As I understand it, this can be as true for me—perhaps now I can accept this—as for the *sighted* members of the class.

3.

The time has gone by quickly. Just as expected, the routine, the discipline are indeed making a difference. Not only the gain in poise, in self-confidence—overcoming that initial awkwardness—but a certain *stamina* beyond anything I might have guessed. I can hardly wait for the day to start: what *new* discoveries lie ahead?

4.

. . . Something is going on that I do not quite understand. For some reason the class is smaller now than when we began. It seems some sort of "separation" is taking place. No one has actually been dropped (how rigorous the initial screening!), but rumor has it that some "more passive" members are being assigned elsewhere.

5.

The separation has indeed taken place. As to what training the others (*more passive?*) have been assigned, there is no word. The choice, however, has been made clear: this morning, right after breakfast, our diminished group was summoned to appear at the Supply Room. After some short delay, our names were called. We were then issued: Mask, Foil, Protector, Tights—the complete Fencing Costume!

After the initial surprise, I found I was not the least perturbed. A few moments of questioning: wasn't this a strange way to achieve inner harmony and balance? Yet on reflection it became clear that, at a certain level, this must be what is required.

Only those who still cling to the mundane level of expectation and desire—it now seems obvious—are unwilling to admit the urgent fact: it is precisely *here* that the Path divides.

6.

. . . As the Instructor predicted: *parry, lunge, thrust* are becoming part of a natural repertory of motion. And along with this, the Foil itself seems to be part of the body—an extension of hand and arm. Thus I have noticed, when it is *not* there, I begin to miss the weight. One thing, though, continues to puzzle me: how is it I know almost at once when the Instructor leaves? And as a corollary, that I do less well at such times?

7.

I am not quite sure how this has happened, but I have become almost unaware of the presence of the Others. Perhaps this is because I have now been officially assigned an *Opponent.* While somewhat unexpected, this must represent some recognition of what has already been overcome, some transition to a "higher stage" in the training.

. . . What is intended by these daily "practice bouts"? In the absence of any direct indication, I cannot help some slight feeling of suspension, of unease.

. . . It has occurred to me to ask my Opponent. This is not, as I understand it, strictly forbidden by the Rules. Yet how could I—considering it further—invite the cooperation, the confidence of the very one chosen to oppose me?

8.

So there is to be a *Contest!* Not of course anything like those advertised vulgar spectacles of the outside world. This is rather to be a subtle display (*an unfolding?*) of skill and grace, more like a dance than a parody of warfare.

I learned this after taking the drastic step of speaking directly to the Instructor. A step that was prompted not by any inner doubt, but by a natural concern for what is, after all, a serious physical handicap.

—Remember: the foils are tipped. He said this in the most gentle voice. And this encouraged me to go even further: to ask about my Opponent. Once more I was not disappointed. I could almost hear the smile in his voice: *But of course you're evenly matched.*

It took a few moments to sort this out, to grasp the meaning: *So we have to imagine each other?*

As his voice came back with some more soothing words, somehow my hands moved toward my face. I suppose he left just then—at least the warmth of his presence faded. My hands kept moving; I touched and rubbed elbow, wrist, neck, chin. The flesh itself was solid, warm—nothing of the cold dark I felt inside.

9.

No victory, no defeat. I should have known. *Evenly matched.* I should have known. *Contest is not Competition.* (The very words of the Manual!) I should have known. . . . But in my mind's ear, sounding again and again: padded feet thumping on the wooden floor. And from afar, derisive voices, mocking laughter . . .

10.

How did it come about? I cannot tell. All I know is that I have no further need— that much is clear—for that discipline, that motion within a confined space. I am resigned now, not only to leaving, but returning where I came from. *Back there!* Once more tapping my way through the noise and fog of one city or another.

As for the training, perhaps it may serve (if not as intended) to ease my passage there. Through crowds and traffic, my steps can be less fearful, more directed. It will be good to take hold again (how long it has served me!) of my own red and white cane.

I am eager now to relearn the grasp of it. Will it again fit neatly in my hand? Can it too be held with such confidence, without feeling the weight? Is the task then to reclaim the loss—the true replacement for that long-desired, dreamed-about, perfectly balanced foil?

The Man Who Was

1.

Now we're into it, where are we? As far as I can see: close to being deadlocked. Maybe the issues are confused, but the lineup is pretty clear: the Strategy Committee, starring Agnes, Luis, Claude, vs. the Festival Committee: Frame, Shade, Brand. And good, solid old Bourgnon—right in the middle.

I look around, try to get my bearings. Here we are in *the theater*—where we belong—deciding whether the show must or must not go on. But is this a question that belongs in the real world? Somehow I keep expecting the thick blue curtain to part, the flat white screen to appear. And in a moment, the lights to dim, followed by the music, the familiar, reassuring dance of images. . . . But we ain't after all in Plato's cave. No sir: we are in fact at the Trianon, this gorgeous town's leading cinema—*sin amor*—among colleagues and fellow workers.

So far, there's been a lot of noise—airing of voices. But what's really going on? Oh, I know what the issues are supposed to be: freedom of expression, the right to exhibit without review, etc., etc. But right now it seems more like a clash of personalities: Luis and Claude representing "radical charisma," Frame and Shade the well-worn stable virtues—or more conveniently: "establishment."

I have a strong feeling that Luis and Claude are going to have it their way—turn the whole thing upside down. That the Festival's going to be canceled. Hard to believe that's what they really have in mind. Protest? Against what, against whom? My guess is—in terms of what they have to gain or lose—ultimately against themselves . . . Might take it more seriously, but when I hear Luis say *fellow workers*, I think of the guy who played the part in *The Organizer*. And I start wondering: is it early Eisenstein, or late Chaplin?

—And inside, how goes it? Not nearly as upset as I thought. Of course the expense of coming here and going back. But more than that, much more. *Did you have something going this time?* No, I didn't. That's all it takes. They look at you; their eyes flicker, heads turn away. A highly expendable business. Always was. Now even more so. So it comes out like this: you were in it—one of the voices they all listened to. Now maybe you're out of it. And what happens inside: *is it over, has it moved out of reach?*

—

Ah, now they're getting up. People starting to leave. A few more speakers—but who cares? No decision till tonight's meeting: that's for sure. I'll wait a while; observe what's going on in this classy *Emporium*. There's a word for you—maybe out of style, but well chosen: the marts of trade. Flesh and film. Any buyers, any sellers, any takers today? It's the same old story in the same old way. . . .

—Notice please what you're up to. Your body in this chair, starting to tense up. The chair, the furnishings: brown velvet, red plush. Curious that—no matter who makes what speeches—the preferred setting has a touch of elegance. Do I hear in this the old nostalgia: having to have it mean something? *Organic form, that unbroken line* . . .

Mary, dear, I wave, shrug in response to your questioning gesture. *C'est la vie. C'est la guerre. Vive la Revolutión* . . . Can't say I expected this—that quick turn from relaxed boredom, the drone of words, to this: rhythmic applause, feet stamping, chanting. And all at once, there's your avant-garde—turning into a Stadium Crowd. *We want Bourgnon.* Will they get him; will he respond to this kind of pressure?

. . . Well, would you believe it? Here he comes! White handkerchief in one hand, rolled-up parchment—or document—in the other. Going to try to read a statement. Anyone ready to listen? Not enough to make it possible . . . And there he goes. That's Bourgnon for you: he'll give it a try—just that much and no more. Notice the dignified shrug, little bow toward the Strategy Committee. Letting them know: it's in your hands, up to you now.

——

Just a bit longer—then off I go. But where to? There's a bar in the lobby. Not far enough: the same faces, voices, questions. Back to the hotel? Too early in the day. Favorite chair at the favorite café? Perhaps, perhaps. Maybe down to the beach—no, still too much sun.

—So what's with you? Fact is: I'm getting depressed. You know why, don't you? I suppose so. Fact is: in spite of everything, I still feel I have work to do. Pretty bitter when I see them moving in, taking over. Resent their taking credit for what were originally my own ideas. Claude's scene with the epileptic child: shots of the skewed walls, the enormous mirror. What Luis did with the crowd trapped inside the Cathedral. And so many more. Of course, we all borrowed—or took—from somebody. In one sense, the history of this or any other art . . . So, what then? Heading back on the old self-pity road. Singing the missed-the-boat blues.

—But you're forgetting something, aren't you? Forgetting what? What the ugly, dried-up peasant woman said. *Saint's eyes. You have saint's eyes.* The voice of ignorance. No, not at all. Fact is: you can't fool those people. Right out of the damned earth; baked in the mud beside the yellow rivers. So what? So that's there, too. You mean: *was there.* Oh hell: is there any bottom to it—what a piece of work are we? We'll find out.

2.

Well, got out of that damned seat anyway. Any better off here in the lobby? Faces, noises, voices. *The power of babble?* At least the bar's close by. So far, no one's come over—all vaguely familiar, but no one in particular. More Levi's and sandals than last year. What was I saying about elegance? Change is the number: customs and costumes. *Autre temps, autre moeurs,* as the wigged ones used to say . . . Do my eyes deceive—those two standing close in conversation? *Lucille and Claire.* The names repeat: which Lucille, which Claire? You know, you know very well.

—These ladies would like a drink. Too early in the day? Never too early, never too late. *What did you think of it?* What did you? I think we should all pack up our wash 'n' wears and go home. But wouldn't you rather stick around and see the fun? No fun for me. Have to take it seriously: a lot at stake here—not just careers, either.

—All right: say somebody's got to go out on a limb, while somebody else has to stay home and mind the store. It's a division of labor: some have to harvest the apples; some have to upset the apple cart. But here, harvesters and upsetters are the same people. So you can't join "militants" or "conservatives"—as if these were real issues; as if this were the real world. . . . So much for the outer voice: my contribution to "acceptable" or "outrageous" opinions. Fact is: I really like all of them—dealers in flim-flam and illusion—and particularly these two.

—So what? So sip your drink—and by the way, how come you didn't develop a taste for this earlier? Meaning what? Meaning God knows you developed quite a few others . . . Have you forgotten, then? What this time? What the fat man said. *Not into unclean hands.* Go ahead, tell me the rest. *Not into unclean hands does blessedness come.*

And so we say goodbye. Arrange to meet: late lunch beside the beach. Good to see again—beside the sea—catch up on things . . . Talk about feline grace, here it is. And you know what hits me—right here, right now? I love these two. I have for years. Fact is: we like and respect each other. After all this time . . .

—You must be kidding. Your real affection is for that glass and what's in it. *Margarita!* My newfound salt-rimmed love. Want to hear something funny? I've exchanged *Margaret* for *Margarita.* Wife and kids for soothing balm for my soul. Your soul, your ass. What about this one on your right, and on your left? Well, on the right, friend only. And on the left? There too, old friend. Will the witness raise his right hand: did you or did you not? All right, I did. But that was long ago—and in another country.

3.

Good to be horizontal again. Small room with a view. Not what you're used to, but not bad. A bit of quiet, bit of rest, before we again go forth. Best thing about these countries: that afternoon break. Like too the way things come back to life in the early evening. And through it all, the breeze from the sea: the wind that soothes. But also the wind that stirs, the uneasy wind, the wind of madness . . . Yes: it blows, then it stops; voices and faces come and go. But on occasion a bright, undeniable moment: all light and shadow.

—What are you talking about, saying now? You forget so much, so easily. And what this time? Was it that scene of candles and flowers—no, not that; not in any of the films—neither yours nor theirs.

—Go back a little further: to that very place, that very moment when— when light turns into shadow? Do you know now where we are going? *Madre de Dios. Be with us in this hour.* Now I believe I do. Back then, back there. To the green country . . .

—Deserted gray stone: the Monastery. How it was that afternoon—deep in the summer of betrayal. Coming to that place: nowhere else, no further to go. There in that square space—low ceiling, black beams—at the end of that long narrow corridor and there it was: double rows of circular holes—about fifty on each side—the squatting monks performing their sanctified bowel movements: catch them right there—wiping hand ready to descend; zoom in on those sun-stained faces . . .

—*You know what else? Can you see it now?* It comes back, all right—that scene and what came later—fact is: it never goes away. . . . The birds in their incredible plumage: the stillness of that afternoon, the drugged smell, thick wet air: those men in white cotton pants, loops tied at their ankles, the sandals with rubber-tired soles bent almost double among the rows of spiked plants . . . You saw it then as you walked the cool gray corridor: *the thorns, the crowns of thorns!* Left over they were from the last procession and ready for the next: crowns guaranteed to fit any size head and—right there stuck into racks on the pillars: split straps of leather: *the whips—dammit, the whips!*

—What happened then to your upholstered flesh, your nice tidy brain? In the name of the Father, and of the Son. You stepped back into the cool shadows. And you said: forget the cameras. Let me out of here—right now! And all the way back, feeling it beat inside your skull: white-robed, black-robed figures clad in the thinnest of cotton crouching in those sun-darkened fields, those green spikes rising, those curved blades ready to descend.

4.

Beside the sea. The beautiful, bountiful sea. Good choice, good time: place not crowded; few stray tourists—mostly Europeans—few long-haired youngsters: origin, destiny unknown. Deciding where to sit: Lucille pale, worried-looking; Claire tanned, energetic . . . Shall we eat here or inside where it is cool? Inside: we can look through the tinted glass at the boats tied up alongside. How about right here? No, let's take the next one over. Once a director, always a director. Water in a glass; the size of these menus: to impress the tourists I suppose. *Parlez-vous?* Only when

I have to. A small steak? Not a bad idea. You trust the lettuce. Of course . . . Our voices go on like this: a little higher, little lower, little younger, little older. *Lucille and Claire*. How long has it been? Long enough to draw these lines—from here to there—across our faces. To darken these eyes and lighten this hair . . .

What are they saying now? Something about this one, that one. Hardly any need to follow the words. Same old story in the same old way: success, failure, appearance, disappearance. And how is it we happen to be sitting here, in the role of survivors? Battered, bruised around the edges, but nevertheless . . . *Dom's dead*. Claire saying it, looks at me expectantly. Words fall across the table—beside the bread crumbs, knives and forks, the stained cloth . . . Death without surprise—almost without grief. Lost touch; didn't even know he was sick. Thinking of it now: without surprise, because he never—in fact—resembled a survivor. Without grief—because? Man on the run, he done fell down. *Dom: the perennial assistant.*

—You blame his wife? I don't: all she wanted—once she made the choice: a home and kids. And she did it: gave up her career—after some really fine performances. Stuck with it; played it straight. Changed the diapers: scooped shit out of the soft white cloth. Baked the bread; and cooked the pasta *al dente—if you please*. And what about him—wasn't that enough? For a while; but then he gave up the job to peddle that absurd idea: *Oedipus Among the Ruins*. Some silly notion about modern tragedy—with a Baroque background! *Dead*. Ain't nobody gonna film that scene. . . .What were you saying? The check is mine—all right, ours. Money easier to share than grief. Yes, indeed: let's go down to the beach. A few minutes to change, and meet you—second thought: be a while, few calls to make.

5.

Lying on the sand here between them. Lucille and Claire: lines extend from here—all the way back. Brings back the time I said goodbye to Margaret and the kids. Lines extend: to things I would not look at, not want to know about. . . . I see now what is coming my way: the child throwing a ball into the air, small dog making a mad dash toward the sea. *Mare Nostrum*. Circles like a noose around our throats. Yet without this sun we would—how to say it?—still be frozen solid: memory lost in the ice. Thanks due for this—and for ships like swans that crossed this water . . .

The two with their heads together: so close and yet so far apart. The lines extend, come together, diverge. Claire: the man from Istanbul. In the market for "feelthy pictures." How did she handle it; what did it do to her? *Not into unclean hands?* Only from a distance, lacking the particulars, is judgment possible. Rush to her defense: the exception, not the rule. And besides, the distributor is just a funnel for supply and demand. Might as well object to the man from the Philippines in the market for *Hercules in Chains*. Strong man against the oppressor. Millions see it that way: the rising, as fantasy, is genuine: their hopes and fears . . . For the "great unwashed," sex and violence in a simple, straightforward form. Fact is: I respect that. What's suspect to me are the refinements—symbiosis of voyeur and exhibitionist—disguised as philosophy, metaphysics. That son-of-a-preacher from the North is their baby. And the French, the Italians—Luis and Claude among them—following along. Throwing rocks at the Establishment. And from the other side? A flurry of dollar bills. Subject can't even be mentioned—not even here—without having a label pinned to your back. . . .

What does it come to? How the hell would I know? Maybe the kids see it clearer, understand it better. Bill and Gwen and Mary—it's their world now. Last year: Bill hitchhiking across Europe. Find out later he was ten miles away, wouldn't come to see me. *Margaret's letter*: they're our kids—but no longer kids: having become themselves. Making it up as they go along. Far from us as possible. Making it up—all right, let it be. So far, thank God, no disasters. One abortion par for the course. Not into hard drugs—dear Lord, please keep it that way.

—Wait a minute, you're forgetting something. What is it? What happens when you turn your head the other way? As for instance? In the direction of Margaret's mother: hands shaking, mottled skin, blue spots, purple veins. There's *mush* in your future. Sans this sans that sans everything. . . .

—*Sex in Sweden.* Claire talking. Strange combination of somnolence and energy. Denies herself nothing. Man is there to be slept with. And yet—beyond the fucking machine—where do her paintings come from? Because they're well done? No, more than the skill: the economy, the integrity. There's an irony: the dirty pictures she sells pay for the clean ones she makes.

◆

Beside the beautiful, dutiful sea. Reminded of those flesh-and-sand epics—another name for them: can't remember. Asses to asses, dust to dust; if the tops don't get them, the bottoms must. I would romp there—not now of course—but in the old days . . . German girl chased around the ship. Ballet dancer and the beast. Used part of that in the film; no one ever guessed—but it came back in a dream, as deep distressing fantasy. And she the original—Helga or Magda—quite witless: saying no, no there's some mistake. Turned out very funny: saving it for the man from Carrara, who promised to carve her form in imperishable marble. And she believed it . . . I wonder if they still do—as for instance, Miss Bikini over there, leaning toward Mister Shoulders . . .

—Over there the sky darkens. Beyond other places, other times. Close eyes for a moment, and what appears? *Lucille.* That day at the lake. Above us, the castle on the hill. And below, in a grove of pines, the museum with the Viking ships . . . What set it going? Can't remember. Something about a film; some Italian town that had a special meaning for her. A flow of words—almost incoherent—let loose. Listened for a long while, then finally said: *Sometimes a door opens where none was before.* Did I say that? Must have. Not knowing, though, whether it meant anything, anything at all. And her response? Stared through her glasses at me—real hard—trying to decide something. Then, kind of incredible, shivered and swallowed, breathing heavily, noisily through her mouth. And I could almost see the tension going out of her.

◆

What are they saying now? Doesn't matter, I suppose. More important: we're here now; something has been saved that makes it possible. Of course I'm hiding something—as usual. Fact is: I never played it quite straight, never really dream for dream: you let me in yours, I'll let you in mine. . . . Claire's talking about her daughter. Lucille, childless, maybe not that interested. The kid's grown now, off to school. Saw her last in Paris: chubby, silent, an enigma. Must be a disappointment. Interesting thing about Claire and Lucille: both married only once. Quite unusual in this bunch . . . A funny thought: send Claire as liaison between Luis and Claude and Bourgnon. To take it more seriously: knows the business from A to Z; bought some of their early films—when no one else would. But also a certain—bed-knowledge?—to cut through the pretense: why don't you boys try to work this out. . .

Something phony going on, isn't there? Yes, the way I keep trying to downgrade Luis and Claude. Fact is: I admire and envy a lot of what they've done. Things they've been able to accomplish, I could just barely touch. So much of my own stuff—especially the early ones—just gorgeous spectacle. Remember that damned thing with the Mexican general and that silly woman—God, I must have been young!

—But don't knock it all: burning that church was a beauty and the woman giving birth on that hill—all those lovely angles—the sun solid as white stone: almost total silence, the men riding their horses like dancers—*I want to see sweat on their moustaches. I want the absolute reek under their armpits.* . . .

—Turn your head, please; turn it further. You and Claire. The first time it happened . . . *Of course, dear, of course. I know you can't be bribed. Just come to dinner and we'll talk it over. Discuss the details, wrap it up in a few days.* . . . Not too much to ask, was it? And actually we had a good time. Not any strings, after all. Signed it that night, and was free to leave . . . What did she want then, what does she ever want? Ten years before I finally understood: no shortage of men; bigger, more important deals. It was *the bond* she wanted. One or two nights—even a year apart—would do it. And that's how it went: the token once given acquires a deeper, more lasting meaning. Over the years, she would call two, three times a year, just to keep in touch—make sure I was there. And I see now it's given me something in return:

times we all need the voice that says: I'm here, I'm listening. And I suppose that was the contract—better perhaps for being unsigned—and I suppose there are worse, much worse.

—

Seem to be drifting off. So easy to be with these two: no pretense, nothing that needs to be said. The Festival, the films, all the striving—really behind us. And ahead? Depends which way the wind is blowing . . . *Margaret, dear Margaret.* How is it there on your sun-drenched island? The good, the peaceful life—yours at last? The kids grown up and gone: time for you to be yourself? But I forget: Alex and his kids. Close enough to be—how would he put it?—*dropping around* all the time. *Alex.* That man wears the most beautiful shirts—and never sweats. Even more beautiful, I imagine, are his account books. I speak now of old money—untouched by human hands. . . . Margaret in the garden: becoming quite an authority on the late-blooming this, the early-blooming that—and I think is going to make it. The last two letters downright friendly. Now that we've reached this point—the latter years?—doesn't blame me for the kids anymore . . .

—Forgetting something? What do you mean? I mean what was there: right at the beginning. . . . Swimming toward the shore—trying to prove something—*almost let her drown!* What kind of game was that—watching her struggling after you—distance getting wider all the time. All that crap about how strong she was—fifty times across the pool—damned well something else. Fact is: knew she might cramp up in that ice-blue water—how the course of her pride ran: the fatal defect measured exactly to the point. You moved then—oh yes indeed—reached her, pulled and lifted as the rage mounted; got her ashore; fell face down on the sand, rescue and killing all wrapped up together. . . . *Attention please: return to present:* eyes open to verify, to validate. Lucille and Claire. No trace of Margaret in either of them. Different characters; different scenario. For here upon the sand, you see before you: children playing, a blue silk kite dancing overhead. And over there the eternal fat man: *not into unclean hands*—sipping beer and—believe it or not—reading Gide in French.

What the hell is it all about? Loving and killing. Loving by intention—killing by neglect. Is the difference important? Who was it then played those unmentionable games: screwing them down on the hardwood floor? Younger then: more need to punish. Explains nothing. Anyhow, time to read what's on the page. Time to let the male lead take over—as it takes place right now, not ten feet away: Mister Shoulders, I give you Miss Bikini. . . . Margaret and the kids. Almost ready now to love Bill. Whatever way he decides to go—swallow as I say it—still tastes bitter. And Mary, Gwen? There too: they have their own burdens, their own horizons. Time for the incestuous father to retire to the wings. Great cloak wrapped around his shoulders—combination of king, shepherd, ancient prophet—retreats into the forest—clack, clack, cut-cut: we'll print that.

Wide awake now. Our voices join again; back now on the subject that unites us most easily: our professional lives. Lucille asks about my plans—pending the outcome here. Tell her, in any case, this is my last year on the festival circuit. After this, one or two a year—just to keep in touch. Claire smiles, says nothing. Lucille objects: she's heard it before. But I go on: time for the new breed to take over. Wyscinski at twenty-five—imagine—writes, directs, produces. Brilliant shots, incredible tempo. Lucille objects: where's the story, what's the value system? Talks about the last one: couple making love in shadow of national monument: *To the Fallen Heroes.* Ironic comment—courtesy of explicit sex—but what else does it offer?

Of course of course. As she says: a certain freshness, spontaneity; it can be done. Fact is: I've done it myself. Camera moves on its own—whole thing fluid—something catches your eye—starts to track it down. So far it's knowing the instrument, tools of the trade. But a different question: is the man holding the camera—or the camera holding the man? Objectivity a myth: lens a glass eye—the real one a soft jelly—and where is the man—apart from the machinery? He is as he was: where he came from . . . Haven't I as a kid come out of the darkness into intolerable light—not knowing where the hell I was—what I was made of—what I left back there in the theater—where my real life began—where it ended.

It looks like Mister Shoulders is going home—without Miss Bikini. And we're still here—but not much longer—beside the restless, emblematic sea. The view up close: striped tents, folding umbrellas. Not too clear: sand on my glasses. Lint from the towel as I wipe them . . . Claire's face and shoulders: still firm and unyielding. Believe it or not: close to fifty. Lucille five or six years younger—no comparison really: sex, love not that important to her. What's the best, the worst of this or any age? No way to tell, really. At one point, I suppose, mind, heart makes the rules: the body goes—as we imagine—where it can: not only sex and love, but dive off a cliff into the water. Then at some point—reports begin to filter back—can't go that way—stay home and pay attention: little twinge at back of neck, quick tightening across the chest . . .

Good to be off the beach. Hope I didn't overdo. Pink around the edges— not too bad. Look at this: soft, white spread—and at this: soft, cold and hidden among the dark hairs. May never come out of hiding. Swear though that if and when—from now on—must be with someone that means something. Cold hand brushing off the grains: whole range of sensations never experienced before . . . Started when I arrived at Hospital. Looking up as they wheeled me in. Nurse standing there: *Oh it's you. We've been expecting you.* Marvelous line: filming the scene, you could never make it up—only some actor—into the part—could ad lib it . . . Distractions, detours, and cover-up: the mind a dog with a bone, cat with a ball of twine . . . *Sensations*: that day and the days following: probed and stared at—follow the green line to the X-ray room—the blue line to the blood lab. Nights between the strict white sheets: the touch, the smell of things—both terribly deprived and terribly enhanced—a single ray of lovely light coming through the high narrow window . . .

Wonder why we didn't go in the water. Maybe it's that we meet so seldom now—seems important to have a few hours apart from the crowd. Yet when we're with them, we sound just like all the rest.

◆

Claire driving; Lucille staring out the window. How serious, absorbed she looks. Lucille never quite made it in this business; maybe never quite wanted to. Something there I'm forgetting again—what was it? *That day at the lake.* But of course: found out the rest of the story later. A lot more involved than I imagined: a door opens, a door closes. *Learn to live with the losses.* Did I say that to Lucille? Doesn't sound like me. In this case—strangely enough—loss of a place, not a person. *Santa Vittoria.* Small town couple hours from Rome. Her own discovery: working then as trouble-shooter, scouting locations, contracts, suppliers, etc. Kept this one for herself: spent weekends every spare moment; good place to hide—away from the crowds and noise. Visited couple times; liked the town but not enchanted. Promised though to be there—forget what time of year—for local procession . . . Arrived on clear, cold day in time for their return from ceremonies on top of mountain. Sound of shoes echoing on cobblestones; exultant voices, faces singing some deep hymn of recovery, of renewal—flow of their bodies through the channels of the high-walled winding road. And then at the plaza: the end of it, after all they'd been through . . .

My God, I'm forgetting: *Lear, her painter friend.* He was there, marching right along with them. That's right: one reason I went up there: she was worried about him. *I'm going native,* he'd told her. Started acting really wild. And I was there when he almost fell through the door—eyes staring, almost incoherent babble—pieced out what happened: twelve miles there and twelve miles back: carrying on the way sacks of stones—weight of their sins—dropping one at a time at designated places—and somewhere on the mountain: outdoor theater: scenario, script: *One Cross, Two Thieves.* Not underground, not avant-garde, but far out, far under the glass-blue sky. And my God, it was like being back there again: with the whips and the crowns. . . .

Whole thing is so damned complicated. On one hand: wished I had what sent Lear up the mountain. On the other: such men are dangerous . . . Even that's not all of it: the other question: can loss of place also bring loss of person? Lines that spread from here to there: inscribed on Lucille's face. Because she did it: brought Grundig there to make that crappy film. And a few months later, her letter: whole town's ruined, corrupted. Went out and hired those clean, exultant faces as background extras; stock, costume peasants . . . Still not really fully aware of her own part in it. So, what's the good of talking now—of course she wants sympathy—wants to blame Grundig for the betrayal but I'm not up to that.

6.

Favorite chair at the favorite café. Actually one of several, next few blocks: the heart of Cinema Row: Café This, Café That, Café Other. A careful choice: who is seen where at what hour. Movement from one to the next: the swarm of hopefuls. Talk about *processions*—the profane counterpart? Well, look here: yesterday's rising star. And today? Available at a price. And over there—across and down the line—girls on the striped swings: for hire . . .

—*Café Other.* Once more life imitates art: this canvas-backed seat named: director's chair. Light dry wine with twist of lemon. Not drinking now, but sipping. Worried for a while; but still able to taper off, set limits. The choices present the man: self-serving or self-destroying—I seem to be learning. . . . Trying out the observer's role: watching the world go by. So far no one I particularly recognize—but all terribly familiar: tourist ladies, bit actors, con artists: air and dreams for sale . . .

The air softens, darkens. Through the roar of traffic, the swooping, soundless birds. Afternoon at the beach: good or bad idea? Not bad: didn't overdo; more restored than taken away. Be prepared now though: it is the hour when—at any moment—the Furies may descend. . . . Notice waiter: young, careful, attentive; no trace yet of the boredom, arrogance of the others. Order couple sandwiches—egg salad, ham, white bread: eat light, stay light. Face beside me—next table—looms into view: peers over glasses, washed-out hair, gestures with cigarette. I strike and hold the match. It could start just this way: eyes meet, the flesh invites—days long gone: memory of an elephant. Still it pervades the atmosphere: sniff what you no longer touch, no longer taste.

—*So, how are you doing?* Not bad, not bad. It appears that the Furies are not coming—not this time. That I can be here and still out of it: quiet place midst of the uproar. Rest at the hotel earlier damned good idea . . . Who's that waving at me, or those people over there? Something stirring in the air—wait a minute, there they go: *Wyscinski and Manheim*. Just a glimpse of their hard, purposeful faces. *The new breed*. They go where it's going. Looking ahead I can see—through their eyes—Luis and Claude as romantics. It's that three-part thing: old men, young men, the children. That's what I have to realize. Wait around until Wyscinski asks a question. Let him know I'm not the enemy. Something could happen then: *over the hill, and through the dale, to grandfather's house we go.* . . . Fact is: they're scrambling for the same prizes as Luis and Claude. Even if the Festival's canceled here, it'll be the same next time: man to man, head to head, coming down to the wire. . . . *Am I really out of it?* That's the big one. Resigned to role of "elder statesman"? Very funny. Times when I want it so badly my hands sweat. Other times when I'm ready to sit by the fire. Old hungers not to be denied—yet slipping out of reach . . . Lucille's response when I wrote her I had some new ideas: send anything you can—an outline, even a few paragraphs. Just what I used to tell someone I liked who sounded desperate . . . Fill the glass, sip slowly. Nibble the little-old-lady sandwiches with the crusts pared away. Evening not far off; the day shifts, plays itself out; the circle starts to close. Two or three more days and that's it—aside from the Festival, certain contacts will or will not be made. If something happens, fine; if not, forget the whole thing. Could go back to writing—for chrissake don't mean my memoirs. Teach somewhere: film department, some college, university. Theater, too: direct student productions—summers off, taste the academic life . . .

—

Inevitable, of course: one or the other had to find his way here, notice the empty seat, invite him or herself to sit down. But in this case *Mario*: one of my least favorite voices. Part of an ear I lend him—as he talks:

. . . So Manheim's the real fire eater. Up the rebels. The others know—come right down to it—be cutting their own throats. You know: we've worked our asses off to put the Festival together. Now a few hotheads—all right, take that back: maybe the gesture's important. Still it's a political gesture. And people like Luis and Claude—wouldn't they be the first to holler about political interference? Know what I mean? They asked for support, backing to make the films. And lots of people got involved, contributed. Sure, some had no choice—but some came in because it's Luis or Claude or Ray Herron. All right: leave you out of it—know you're not showing this time . . .

—Well, he's gone. Not far, though: see him there, four or five tables down, making another stop. Bird of passage; wet finger to the wind. Remember him working for Brand few years ago: assistant to the assistant—*like Dom, who is now dead*. But this one in fact may be the survivor par excellence: crumbs from any table. . . . Remember the good ole days when Brand had them charging up the hill, charging down again? Those immaculate, heroic wars. And when that gave out—what next?—how could I forget: mad sister locked in the closet; screams in the night—modern Gothic. But as a person Brand's likeable, good administrator. Went out of his way to be helpful, still keeps in touch . . .

—Why are you going through all this? Because Brand represents an alternative. *Like a sellout*, you mean? Maybe so. If I could only be a little more stupid, self-deceiving. Or on the other hand, ready to go all out—no, I've done that: taken all the risks. More a case of where I've been: too many faces in too many places. And too many voices—all saying: *Listen to me*.

—

The lights are coming on. And so—it appears—is the bad time. Strikes me I went through it last year. Strange, I can't remember: was it Munich or Brussels? You go from here to there: bombarded with sights, sounds, voices—claims and counter claims. And somewhere in this, like a big dark hole, you start to disappear. . . . Don't look at the glass: you haven't had that much to drink. Not what's in your hand, but what's in your head. Keep thinking that trouble "behind the eyes" has something to do with it. But remember what the Doctor said: whole organism's overextended. Wonder, though, what it is when water pours from the eyes—as if in deepest mourning. As if I left something back there at the hospital. Nothing tangible like a liver, kidney, spleen. Rather some old myth of immunity, of invulnerability. Look how far it traveled—long past its time—before being laid to rest. . . .

—Look at this one: young, self-assured, shining face and bones. Am I to see this now: over and over again? And you know when it started? Yes: late last spring . . . Coming out of the hotel, young woman with straight black hair, wide skirt, flowing cape, sweep of a dancer. I wanted to reach out, put my hand in hers, walk off with her. No sex in this—I swear—but a curious deep recognition—as though—whoever she was—carried within her—in no separate place—my deepest self. *Gwen!* I reached into my pocket and came up with Margaret's letter: Gwen had gone off somewhere—no forwarding address. What got hold of me then—resemblance or apparition—didn't matter. What mattered was that so quickly—in the next few moments—I was plunged into some vortex of defeated dreams—all that might have been. I was close to the edge then. . . .

7.

Good to be in motion again. Too damned long sitting in that chair. Moving target harder to hit. About six blocks to the theater. Meeting won't start for about an hour. Still might turn around and change direction. But I might run into someone: pretty awkward to explain: so close, but not attending . . . *Agnes*. No question now: words to be exchanged—more than the time of day—always forthright. Stands close to Luis and Claude—but her own woman . . . Together for a bit; then she rushes on ahead. And from this brief walk beside her I learn: Frame and Shade are leaving— not waiting for the meeting. Frame back to London; and Shade to Switzerland . . . Shade's sense of what's permanent, enduring: wars come and go—old waves, new waves. But a numbered account goes on forever. . . .

A few more blocks. No turning back now. Time for a drink in the lobby. Maybe just one, a light one. Going—for what reason? Why, just to be there: to be inside rather than outside. Somewhere, as the man said, is better than nowhere. And when it comes to a choice, what will you? I'll sit firmly on both hands. . . . *Bourgnon.* Unmistakable—even at a distance. Moves well for that almost two hundred pounds—solid on the hoof. One thing I know: if I were getting into something big and needed advice, he'd be the man. Not so much for the money, as for the intuitive sense: who to talk to at what hour in what tone of voice. *No patience with anything the least bit suicidal.* That's what Luis said about him. And I recognize there: power without waste—a combination I never quite had.

—

Getting closer now. Light sweat: hands and forehead. And water from the eyes: the healing fountains? Not quite the Furies—but some related little devils: first cousins? Think of what you were—and are. Fact is: I stood for something. Helped make some of the better things happen. In any case: no monster . . . *Was that Claude?* Can't really tell: his stride, way of dressing—but gone too fast. As everything seems to be going—too fast. The circle closes, whirls away into orbit: success, failure, appearance, disappearance. . . . No monster? Have you forgotten? *Two on the bed and two on the floor.* What kind of game; who was that man? Gone, gone forever.

—Well, friend, you've tried a little of this, little of that. Dipped your feet in an icy stream; plunged into snow and rain; dried yourself by the fire. Close then to a creature and child—almost forgotten, but strangely now returned to sight. You see now—don't you?—something that gets lost in the crowd. Something that never got into any of the films—yours or theirs—except for a touch here, a moment there. There was a man—there is a man—who wandered down the hill, sought shelter in a cave. Not a place of blue curtains and wide white screens—but of bats and bears. And who climbed again—through the narrow entrance—into glaring light. Wandered then until he came to where the grass turned yellow, the black hills hardened into stone. *I can still do it—I think I can.*

—It all turns—doesn't it? on what the Nurse said: expecting you. On that oval face blue eyes: neutral but of course *professionally* finds it interesting. But does it turn too on what the fat man said: *Not into unclean hands?* Deliver us as we are delivered: into clean and cool and steady hands: handle the camera—as they handle the knife. . . . But even more it turns—in some random, awkward hour—on what happens when your fingers reach out and touch an empty space. Mouth open to no expected sound, but from far off, massed chorus of birds and maddened sirens—and something deep inside—by utterly unknown means—relays the information: they are coming closer, closer.

Afterword to *The Edge of Something*

Of the Fictions, the title story "The Edge of Something" and "Notes on Beato Angelico," written during a stay in Italy (1961–64), are unchanged. "The Man Who Was," originally from the same period, was rewritten in 1975. The three parables— "The Contest" [Editor's note: see p. 66, from *Truth, War, and the Dream-Game*], "The House/The Doors," and "The Graduate"—date from 1970–75, following the publication of those collected in the volume *The Scale of Silence* (*kayak*, 1970).

The appearance in a single volume of work written at different times and in different genres invites some question. The unifying element is partly suggested in the epigraphs and in the title: the sense of "something withheld," something that remains "about to happen"—beyond the confines of the page. (Not "withheld" by the writer, but by the nature of surrounding circumstance: the dominance in the human situation of the "unknown," the "incomprehensible.")

But as the dialectic works, shifting perspectives also play their part. While this led to the rewriting of "The Man Who Was," it called for a different choice with "Notes on Beato Angelico." In the first case, relating the still viable issues to a "present & actual" world—even though the view is largely "retrospective"—required the rewrite. In the second, my decision was that the "symbolic panorama" of an encounter within Museum walls was better left as a deliberate anachronism. Finally, while rewriting "The Edge of Something" was not an issue, I want to note the year of composition: 1963. The situation of the protagonist was viewed then—it was still possible—as an "isolated instance." Not the social phenomenon it has since become.

—L. F.

Through Deserts of Snow

(1975)

Finally, how can we believe in the meaning and the dignity of these delirious images that—in the darkness—we shape out of the ashes, for an instant?

—Ivan Turgenev

For whereas in the life of mankind the mythical represents an early and primitive stage, in the life of the individual it represents a late and mature one.

—Thomas Mann

There is not a shred of fiction in the following tale.

—Nikolai Leskov

1.

It happened in N., a small town in the province of Y. It was a market day. From all directions came the voices of buyers and sellers: the shrill good-natured jibes, the raucous offers and counteroffers. All of this fret and bustle, however, came to a sudden stop as the air was pierced by a loud, agonized cry. . . .

This was what was passing through my mind as I turned the pages: the typical opening of some nineteenth-century Russian short story! Yet this was not a period piece I was reading, but my own notes, dated from about a year ago. They recorded, I had to remind myself, the experience of a man who lives in our own time. (Stephen X., since that is the name I used.)

Reading further, I recalled that the encounter was not at my initiative and that, as it turned out, we did not meet again. It was evident that I had been impressed, moved enough to record the occasion—not enough, though, to have felt it necessary, in all this time, to review what I had written.

Why then this belated reaction, and why did it take this form: transposing a man's experience into these faded literary echoes? For while it was true that the setting was Russia; there was nothing, as I recalled, that preceded the First World War.

It came to me then that, while speaking, he seemed at times to see himself as a character in fiction. I found myself turning the pages now, as if looking for some confirmation. . . . And there it was: that part where, describing his second escape as a prisoner of war, he talked about making his way "through a Tolstoyan snowstorm."

I had only to look a little further to find other sources for this uninvited fantasy, this entrance into a landscape known to me only through the words of dead writers. But having gone this far I found myself asking (it seemed inevitable) whether anything could be done with these notes: whether they could be given any shape or form—in the language of our own time, of course.

But as I read on, the impression was once more of the remote, the formless, the unbelievable. There were elements of melodrama—which I would not attempt to handle. There was also, in the nature of the material, a need for some kind of catharsis—which I would not be able to supply.

I closed the notebook, tossed it on the desk. And for some reason, a few moments later, closed my eyes. It was some time before I was ready to admit that, far from having finished with it, I was faced with some insistent further demand. Something was impelling me, beyond these notes, toward the room in which we met: *that view of him standing beneath the immense chandelier* (how could I have forgotten those absurd glass petals?), *the light of another time falling across his face.*

More of it did come back: the six of us in that narrow room seated on those misshapen, uncomfortable, probably fake antique chairs. Our wonder and disbelief as we listened to that remarkable outpouring, that extended, apparently unmotivated monologue. Light reflected on slabs of streaked marble—even the floors covered with this shining expensive stone. And it was through these distracting surfaces that we noted the nervous smile, the small, soft hand wiping the round, creased face. (It was cold in that room, was it not?)

We could understand that this was what he had to remember. He was reliving, as probably many times before, those peak moments. But the telling of it there and then also had to have some special meaning. I recalled, without at first making the connection, our host saying that *as a writer* I might find him interesting. It did not impress me at the time: that kind of statement is easily made, easily forgotten. Now, though, it struck me—and I matched the insight by opening my eyes: Stephen had wanted this heard as something *by which he could be remembered!*

And I thought: We share that, do we not? We offer our names, present our faces. We place hands on the flesh of those close to us, leave them long enough to imprint the touch. Less lovingly, but with as much desire, we carve initials upon the walls of monuments—and even urinals. And always with just one idea: to establish our presence in the hope that our absence will be noticed . . .

2.

. . . Night before last at the F.W.s' for drinks and dinner. Not at all what we might have expected. For one thing, they were both so subdued—none of the tension that was so noticeable last time. But then the whole evening was strange: suddenly finding ourselves in the role of listeners. (Considering the situation, we were all bound to appear more passive than usual.)

The Long, Unhappy Life of Stephen X. Hearing him hold forth, there were times when this is what it sounded like. But it seems now this would be unfair: there were few complaints or bid for sympathy. He told it mostly as though he himself were puzzled, as though inviting us to share the mystery.

How did he get started? I must have missed something, for all I remember is that it was not long after dinner, that we were drinking brandy, smoking cigarettes. The rest of us were seated; he was standing near that huge, ugly chandelier. F.W. must have said something to prompt him—not with any idea surely of this kind of response. (Note that up to this point Stephen had said little, appeared shy, reserved.)

As for the *why*, I'm even more in the dark. I felt, though, that, in some way it had to do with my being there. But also somehow with the presence of the child. (Althea, the F.W.s' twelve-year-old, is a charming, rather fragile girl.) At least that is how I interpret his speaking so often directly to one or the other of us.

In any case, there we were, suddenly witnesses at the unfolding of a man's biography—as much at least as he chose to tell. Were we surprised? Perhaps not at first, not until we realized this was going way beyond any normal expectation.

As he began there was some hesitation, trying to find the right tone. But almost at once there was the composure, the ease that comes with long experience before an audience. For even though it was personal history, it was told in the manner of the social scientist (which he is), the events presented as if to illustrate a case in point.

It was not long, though, before the image shifted. He was standing there, speaking in that modulated voice, saying things we were not surprised to hear—and then there was something else. It came to my ears at first as a small flaw in the tone: wasn't this being said too easily, wasn't it too well arranged?

One moment then it was all contained, secured within the walls of the familiar. The next, the whole thing went off—all the way toward the bizarre, the unexplainable. (Althea at some point here was reminded by her mother of the hour. The narrative stopped while she said goodnight, bowing gravely to each of us in turn.)

Did it make any sense? It did if we considered that, as a man of seventy looking back, he might feel some urgency about exploring just those areas of *unknown territory*.

Remember that this was someone who had been pushed to the limits, who then emerged, following routes not recorded on existing maps, as a battered yet apparently intact survivor. Was it so strange then that, along with the more immediate questions, his story might extend into such things as the nature of reality, the relation of the known to the unknown?

Enough of this. I want to come now to the material itself. I'll start with the first thing that comes to mind—worry about sequence later. We can skip all that "introductory" material, begin with something where he seemed to come to grips with whatever was bothering him.

◆—

". . . There's no way to tell you how long a winter that was. The morale was low enough even before this; now we were getting close to the bottom. With no food, no way to keep warm, we only managed somehow to stay alive. What kept us going was having something to trade, some service to offer—bribe a guard, make a deal with some peasant.

"But the time came when there was nothing left. That was when, starting each day, we wondered if it might be the last. It was about this time, as I recall, that we began hearing all kinds of rumors. We paid no attention at first: some of it we'd heard before—and eventually one canceled out the other. But then we noticed the change in the guards; how they would just shrug and look away when something happened. And when their uniforms started to fall apart, it seemed that, while they hadn't reached the same stage, they too were no longer soldiers.

"You might wonder why, at this point, there weren't more who tried to escape.

Well, even if you got out, where could you go? In the middle of nowhere, with those thin rags, how could you get through those deserts of snow?

"It was only at this point of desperation that we finally managed to take some kind of action. A number of us got together, decided to equip one man with whatever food and clothing we could gather, send him off to try and get some kind of help. Not much of a plan, but the best we could do."

Stephen went on then telling of his selection for this desperate, directionless mission. But I noticed that he avoided going into detail, gave no basis for their choice. We can only guess then what it included: the already demonstrated ability to survive, some special combination of courage and cunning. Yet with all this (and how was this decided?), it had to be someone who would honor his promise to return—even when his own safety was involved.

———

If this were a straight narrative, we should have to fill in what happened directly after Stephen left the camp. But the way he told it, there was no way to follow him across those *deserts of snow*. At times he himself indicated the failure of memory; sometimes there was just the gap, the unexplained leap across space and time.

He spoke for instance of his arrivals, of the incidents that centered around them. But what about those limbo-like intervals of undirected wandering? It seemed that what he left out, perhaps on purpose, was any reference to what he endured along the way.

So we have to imagine his passing through a succession of those bleak, empty villages, viewing the dazed faces of old men, women and children, himself one of that growing army of the dispossessed. And to add the days and nights of a fluid, lost time—not only his own disorientation, but what was happening all around him: a vast nation, a complex social structure, starting to crumble. Only then can we pick up his voice again, hear it in context, with all the reverberations:

". . . This was more of a city than the others: more people, more buildings. But the atmosphere was the same: the same drabness and confusion. I found myself on a wide, muddy street, moving along with the crowd. There was a sense of drifting, absence of purpose. We walked with our heads down, not looking at anyone or anything, into the wind.

"Like them, I suppose, I was not thinking of anything in particular—wondering if somewhere there was a warm place, something to eat. At some point, though, I realized there were fewer people about—the street almost deserted. I knew that when the beggars and drifters disappeared, there had to be a reason. I did not make the connection though until there, just ahead of me, was the bulky, well-fed figure in the uniform.

"What happened then is hard to explain. I knew that I too should be leaving. But for some reason I just could not make a move."

The policeman, Stephen said, came close enough to notice him, but then made no further move in his direction. Stephen stood there as if rooted, openly, defiantly studying the figure of authority.

It came to him then that, more important than anything that might happen to him, there was something he had to find out. "I had no idea at that moment whether I was giving up, or whether I really thought he might be persuaded to help." He moved then in the direction of the uniform.

At his approach, coming so directly toward him, the Policeman appeared startled. When Stephen spoke, the man seemed to have trouble finding a point of reference. As someone with authority, we can imagine, his position had been clearly defined. But this could only be exercised when the man before him responded in the accepted way: within the range of respect, fear and flight. Stephen's appeal, though, went beyond the symbol to the man who wore the uniform: husband, father, brother, child.

What was strange about this, as Stephen told it, was that he was able to speak so deliberately, in such a calculated manner. "As if I knew I had to strike at some vulnerable point. The target, I decided, was where the sense of humanity was most likely to have been preserved. I asked then whether he had any children."

The startled answer was that he had: two boys, three girls. Stephen said then that he hoped, if he survived, to someday have a family of his own. He went on, telling of his dreams of peace. When the response finally came, it was the man himself who spoke, asking what Stephen wanted.

As Stephen told him, the Policeman finally muttered that he might possibly be able to do something—he could not promise anything, but there was a place where one might find food, a place to sleep. Then with a brusque gesture, he motioned to Stephen to follow him.

They went through some of the back streets, coming into a kind of red-light district. They stopped in front of one of the houses, the Policeman asking him to wait there. He went inside, and a few minutes later emerged with the news that it was all arranged. When Stephen attempted to thank him, he brushed it aside. "I'm not doing this for you," he said. And before this could be interpreted, he went off down the street. Watching the retreating figure, Stephen said that, strangely, there was more authority in his walk than when the sight of him had cleared the street.

One might have expected more details about what went on inside, how Stephen responded to the atmosphere within those narrow, steamy rooms. Nothing about this, though, nothing about how he felt, as a non-paying guest, concerning the business being conducted all round him. One imagines the change of scene as rather bewildering, moving from that desert of stark, hungry men to this oasis of abundant flesh.

How long had it been, one wonders, since he had felt desire? Since he had dreamed the shape of a woman, believed that warmth would again flow through his own body? The only clue as to what happened, what it meant to him, came as a kind of afterthought. "I was treated royally," he said. And then, as perhaps the recollection touched him, his eyes and mouth registered a brief, almost invisible smile.

—

Stephen remained several days: long enough to restore the remembrance of what the flesh had once meant. When he set out again, it was as a man somewhat healed. For a while, the world was again filled with faces; the search no longer for the impossible, across a landscape in which there were no directions.

"Unfortunately, this didn't last very long. Once more I became part of that endless procession of people in flight. But along with those dazed faces (children without mothers, mothers without children), something else now came to my attention. For the first time, I noticed men in uniform without guns and—just as strange—men in working clothes with guns."

How long a period this covered, again, he did not indicate. With the same absence of connections, of what was endured, he went on. Finally he found himself in the city of N., in the province of Y. (Pronouncing those names was no problem for him—but we'd better not try it here.) It was there that something happened that made him forget the sights and sounds that belonged to the time of upheaval:

—*Market day in the city of N.* Buyers and sellers playing their accustomed roles. Prices being quoted, offers made and rejected. The bargaining going on. The voices begin to echo, take on a ritual sound. Suddenly it appears that here nothing has changed: this small-scale turmoil is self-contained, shuts out the larger noise of war and revolution, the crash of falling worlds.

It was while this was passing through his mind that, from somewhere not too distant, an anguished cry split the air. He turned toward a sight that attacked his senses: a peasant was beating his horse: decades of betrayal, of hate and frustration, summed up in that gesture.

As the raw cracked fists drummed upon the stretched skin, it was an overwhelming question that started to beat within the tight bone of his own skull: *What crime had the four-legged creature committed—as seen through the eyes of the two-legged creature?* There was, it seemed, no answer. Stephen wondered if anyone else saw it this way—or was it just his own distorted vision?

It seemed that for the others this too was part of the spectacle. Within the context of buying and selling, no more than a distraction, a momentary diversion.

He thought: if the whole structure were to split wide open, this would still remain. With all the talk about truth and justice, good and evil, there was just this: the animal being destroyed was one thing, the price of potatoes was another.

"I don't know why, after all I had seen, this triggered my reaction. As if I had come to the end of something—something not even the war, the prison camp had reached. I realized then that others, in different ways and for different reasons, had come to the same place. If it took longer for me, perhaps there was some residue of belief, some ingrained, inherited optimism that had to be overcome. Anyhow here it was: the basic, interchangeable face of man-beast, beast-man. And what made it possible was this unity between rage and indifference: one could not exist without the other.

"I remember that I suddenly felt very tired. I had wandered past the market-place, found myself standing alone in a flat open space. In front of me there was a mound of snow; I stood staring, finding the white shape open to interpretation. I felt then that it would never melt, that finally here was a winter that would not end. Why had I taken it for granted that it was necessary to go on? It was time—now or later made no difference—to just lie down. And I could think of no better place."

Stephen said that he awoke in a large, empty room. Above his head, dark, heavy beams crossed a white ceiling. Light from a distant window indicated it was day. Beyond this nothing could be defined. . . . The deep silence lasted until, from a distance, there was a vague, meaningless murmur of voices—nothing that suggested communication between one person and another.

For a while his eyes closed again; when they opened, there seemed to be a figure that now formed part of his sight. Was that an old man standing in the doorway? Because of his condition, and because the figure did not move, he remained uncertain.

Later, though, he came to accept the reality; his eyes focused on the long white beard that spread down the front of the faded red silk dressing gown. Just then the old man stepped closer. Stephen saw him as tall, erect, gnarled—the whole impression was of something almost biblical. And then he heard the voice—the ringing tones confirmed the image—and accepted that the words were directed to him.

"My servants—I should say my former servants—brought you here. My name is Gregory Nicolaievitch, formerly a merchant of this town."

Stephen wondered vaguely why the old man identified himself in terms of what was past. Then as he went on, supplying a few details of how they had found him, Stephen found himself resting more comfortably: his presence here, after all, was no more strange than so many other things encountered in his wandering.

The old man then told more about himself. He said that he was a Molokan, a member of the religious sect that called themselves the *Old Believers*. He had *for-*

merly been a man of great wealth. But now everything was gone: the furniture, along with the servants, had disappeared. He could not, of course, blame them, since they had only responded to events, to a power greater than their own. The outcome of these things, after all, was finally in *His* hands. (The ultimate design, the pattern, would only become clear when *He* willed it.) All that was left now, for his wife and himself, was this empty house. He gave thanks, though, that God had spared them this much.

After a pause, he asked how Stephen felt, whether he would care to say something about himself. Whatever he might want to put into words would be heard without judgment. Above all, he need not feel that he had to explain anything, only to satisfy "the needs of his own spirit."

Stephen said that, responding, it was at first like talking to himself. The old man stood there straight and unbending, saying nothing, giving no sign that the words reached him. For the moment, though, Stephen found just the sound of his own voice reassuring.

But then some time later, between cups of tea brought in by the old woman, he began speaking louder, faster, feeling a greater need to communicate. In spite of what the old man had said, it was as though all he had lived, felt, thought was being weighed in the balance.

When he finished, the old man still said nothing. He waited a few moments, still unbending, then turned and walked away. He went as far as the opposite end of the room. Facing the wall there, he pulled back a long, heavy drape.

Stephen could not tell, at this point, why he raised his arm, what his fingers were doing with what seemed to be a metal knob. (It crossed his mind that for the first time he had been able to put into words something of what he had endured.) It was only when the old man stepped aside, revealing the safe door, that the meaning reached him.

A few soundless steps later, and the old man stood before him. The figure was no longer so unbending, so remote. Suddenly close to his eyes were the bent fingers—and the creased paper heaped on the wrinkled palms.

Stephen stared at the mound of banknotes. Trying to interpret it, all he could do was move his head from side to side. But whether this was rejection, or only disbelief, he did not know.

The old man's response was to thrust the money toward him. "You must take it." And now his voice took on a hard, flat quality. "My wife and I are old. We have had a good life. I can assure you that we have more than enough for the time that remains."

Stephen said it was just this that brought him to the edge of refusal. It occurred to him, in spite of the assurance, this was indeed all they had. And then the full meaning of the gesture struck him. Under the tide of emotion, he felt about to be engulfed. All the carefully learned lessons (that special combination of courage and cunning) were being swept aside. And he had nothing to fall back on, nothing to keep him from drowning.

He only found his voice with a rising, unexplained anger—the only way to fight back the tide. He spoke wildly, without restraint. "What this means is that you have decided to give up. And because I have no choice, you think I'll go along with this. Let me tell you: this is not a gift but an exchange: my life for your death. Not generosity—but an act of despair."

Gregory Nicolaievitch did not seem surprised or offended. He nodded while he listened, the glazed light-struck eyes taking it all in: as if this too was expected, foreseen. Then in a softer voice, he said: "I am sure there are good reasons why it seems this way to you. That this is not just anger speaking, but your whole experience. But I must also say that I have lived longer than you." He smiled, as if in response to some intangible, remote memory. "Long enough at least to have been on the side of both giving and receiving. As a merchant—I must speak frankly—I have known what it is to cheat and to be cheated. One thing though I have learned: finally a time must come to balance the books. That is why I can tell you: that time for me is now. I hope you will understand, my friend, when I say that you are wrong: it is not despair—it is love."

◄

We're in for some confusion here. To tell it the way it happened, we should have noted first the story about his *previous* escape. (Did *he* tell it this way, or is this how *we* remember it?) In any case, if we were writing it, the order would have to be reversed.

—Shortly after his capture, Stephen was placed on a train with other prisoners of war. They were being transported to a camp far in the rear of the advancing front. They had been in motion for several hours; Stephen had struck up a conversation with the man next to him. The man had suggested they ought to try and make a break for it. (The moonless sky indicated they might have a chance.) After some hesitation, the sharing of a cigarette, Stephen agreed to take the chance. . . .

When the time came, the train slowing down as it rounded a curve, they leaped out into the night. They landed on a soft slope, rolled down a few feet, reached the bottom dazed but unhurt. A few rifle shots punctuated the darkness; some vague shouting followed—the voices metallic, meaningless in that vast, empty space. They listened, felt strange, disembodied as the wheels clattered on, the train moving toward what (just moments before) had been their own destination.

They finally realized that it was gone—even though it still echoed in their minds: not only the sound, but the physical presence from which they had been severed. At last they got up, tested their strange legs, moved out into the night. They walked slowly, carefully, adjusting their pace to the prevailing uncertainty.

For hours they went on, guided by stars for which they had no name—out of their known positions, displaced as they were. Their goal was to reach the German lines. (Stephen was in the Hungarian Army, allied with the Germans.) And their only chance was to make contact some time before daylight.

It happened just as the night was wearing out: coming into a small clearing, they were startled by a strange noise. They stopped and listened; the night had been full of noises—but nothing like this. Hearing it again, they had to accept the reality: it came out of the mouth of a human: someone was yawning. (Absurd, because it belonged within walls: a man turning away from the fire, seeking the comfort of his own bed.)

They dropped to the ground, made themselves small as possible. They remained quiet, motionless—yet soon realized they could not just lie there, waiting until the spreading light caught them. . . . Some time later, raising their heads at the snapping of a branch, they sighted something in motion through the dark leaves. They gestured, whispered; decided to take the chance: to address the shadow.

It was Stephen who called out, speaking in German, hopeful that it was the right language. He tried to make his voice as soothing, as believable as possible. There was a long wait, no reply. Around them were the sounds of the awakening forest, light thinning, changing the color of the trees. Finally there was a rustling, cracking of twigs, and through the leaves, they at last glimpsed the dark, descending figure.

A few moments later, on the ground before them appeared a German soldier's coat—with a man somewhere inside. As a combination of soldier and apparition, the figure was less than five feet tall. When they could focus better, they saw, peering through the folds of thick cloth, the wrinkled circus face. (How old *could* he be: thirty, forty, fifty?) There was no doubt, though, about one thing: what the little fingers held, kept pointed at them, was a genuine, full-sized rifle.

"Would you kindly inform me as to who you are?"

It was hard to believe their eyes, even harder to respond to the squeaking-toy voice. Stephen, when he could finally speak, tried to answer the question. (It did not matter that he was repeating himself, using the same words he had addressed to the nearby tree.) He went on for some time, adding whatever came to mind that might help to make their presence believable. But while speaking, he kept wondering at the clarity of this curious dream. (Surely that rifle could not possibly hold real bullets.) At any moment, if this went on, they might find themselves surrounded by other gun-toting dwarfs, apparitions of various shapes and sizes. Those creatures might appear—he could not help pursuing the image— as when last seen: *sprinting through the forests of his childhood.*

When Stephen finished, the little man at last lowered the gun barrel. "So you've come from over there," he squeaked. "Well, that's certainly a long ways off." He opened his mouth, started to say something more; what came out was another loud yawn. "Excuse me. What was I saying? Oh yes, there's one thing you must take care of. . . ." He stopped, noticing their position. "But please stand up—you'll catch cold lying there." When they complied, he said, "You must be sure to set your watches back an hour." And added: "Summer is over, you know."

—

I think I understand now the source of our confusion. It becomes clear as we recall the "episode of the dog." This of course took place some months after that encounter in the forest. To set it straight: the little man took Stephen and his friend to the nearest outpost. Before they could be sent back to a place of safety, there was an attack. In the course of it, Stephen's companion was killed, and he himself recaptured. He was sent then to the prisoner of war camp. (From which he later started out on his trek across the "deserts of snow.")

What must have happened then is that we pushed the "dog story" further back in our own memory. No point in dwelling on this: considering the nature of the material, the "resistance" is not hard to understand.

—"I should tell you first that I'd never had a pet of my own. My brothers and sisters had dogs and cats and white mice—sometimes our house was a regular menagerie—but I never got interested. I remember too that this was something they used to tease me about—not that I minded: it was all just a part of growing up.

"Where was I? Yes, well, all that's important here is that when this dog attached himself to me, it was certainly without my encouragement. From then on he was almost always at my side."

After trying to discourage the animal, Stephen finally accepted the situation. He found himself sharing whatever there was to eat—still grudging the scraps that fell from his fingers. And if his hand never reached down to stroke the matted hair, it was *the feeding* (he told himself) not the feeling, that was important.

One day as Stephen returned from a work detail in another part of the camp, the dog did not appear to greet him. He looked around, tried to forget it, but the continued absence bothered him. He asked several of the men; the replies were brief: heads turned, eyes looked in another direction. He might have accepted this, he said, as the usual indifference—except for something in the air that enveloped them.

He started his search, wandering in one direction and another. Just before dark, approaching a small dry gully, he stood before the smoldering remains of a fire. Watching a thin thread of smoke disappear into the neutral air, it came to him that he would not have to look any further. The light lasted long enough for him to discern, among the gray powdered ash, a scattering of bones.

At first, the thought came that at last his obligation (incurred, after all, against his will) was finished. The next slice of dry bread would go into his own mouth: no more looking down, responding to the mute question. (If his hand had never soothed, at least it had never punished.)

But then as he raised his eyes to the empty darkening sky, he realized that somehow it was not yet finished. Before he could walk away, once more to walk alone, there was, it appeared, some final claim. Stephen said he was not sure what happened then—could never be sure—but this was the remembrance:

Kneeling, he extended his hand into the soft still warm mound. He probed, sifted the gray powder. He stopped, shuddering at the touch. He waited, then forced the fingers to close, and a moment later, the arm to raise and the eyes to look . . . There in the palm of his hand—something he could not contain, and certainly could not throw away—was the dog's heart. *It was still beating. Holding it there, so close to his own pulse, he would have to wait until it stopped. . . .*

The awe in his voice, even though he tried to control it, was unmistakable. What kind of fantasy was this? More important, what could explain its persistence, after all these years? We could neither imagine what called it forth, nor what kept it undiminished. But one thing was clear: this was not told just for the effect. The man before us was not aware, at that moment, of how his words echoed, what it sounded like to those who heard him.

Note that this feeling of wonder seems to exclude the more expected, more familiar emotions: it suggests no guilt, offers no rewards, deals out no punishment. . . . *Echoing in that narrow room*: the flurry of small, self-conscious gestures. Someone squirming in his seat. Someone clearing his throat, coughing into his hand . . . With the glass chandelier swaying over our heads, with light splintered on all those distracting surfaces, what else could we do—except act as if we had not heard what he had heard?

◆

The story about his mother, at any rate, came somewhere near the end. My first thought was that since it dealt with an earlier period, that of her childhood, it should be at the beginning. (Aren't we making too much of this whole question of sequence?) But now it occurs that, following the rest, it does move into a larger framework: passing from what he remembered to what she remembered adds another dimension. *(A view of Terror as part of an enduring inheritance?)*

Note again that Althea had left the room long before this. From a distance, we heard the record player in her room: a voice not much older than her own mourning for a hopeless, lost love. It made an interesting counterpoint, for a while, to Stephen's recital. But then it got to him and he stopped; for a few moments there was a bewildered look on his face. Then F. W. got up, went into the next room, took care of the intrusion.

(We mention this because, if one thinks of *her* listening, the time span can be extended as far forward as the other goes back. Of course, *considering the nature of the message*, one can only hope that she in turn would not have this to transmit.)

—Once more we are in Russia. Stephen's mother was about five or six when it happened: in the time of the *Great Pogroms*.

One afternoon on the outskirts of the ghetto, a group of women and children were being harassed by some Cossacks. Swinging their whips, shouting, they herded their prey, kept them turning in all directions. At one point a thin, pale nun approached, witnessed the scene. She stood motionless for a while, but as it seemed "the game" was becoming dangerous, she stepped forward.

Ignoring the shouts, the curses of the horsemen, she called to the women and children to follow her. She led them, as if this were some pilgrimage, toward a shrine recently built just outside the ghetto. As they reached the entrance, the Cossacks rode up, circled the air with their swords. This time the nun raised her voice, spoke with anger:

"You see before you a new shrine. It was built to honor Him who died that men might learn to live in peace and love. You have shown that as far as you are concerned, that death was in vain. But I will tell you something else: if you stain this shrine with Jewish blood, you will spoil its power to heal for generations to come!"

The swords continued circling. But slower now, as if no longer sure what those arcs of steel were supposed to enclose. And at that moment something happened—one need not speak of miracles, for a simpler explanation is possible: the horses reared, bolted, took off in different directions.

It was not long, in any case, before the iron tightened inside their jaws forced the fractious heads to turn. Coming back, the Cossacks lined up as if in military formation. But ready to charge, they saw no enemy in front of them. Those moments of delay, as it turned out, were enough. The intended victims were already shepherded inside; a wall, a door, separated their flesh from the raw edge of steel.

It was there, in that sanctified darkness, that the child tried to understand what flickered in her mind. Seeking definition, she listened to the low, timeless moans rebounding from those newly built walls. The sound touched her; she felt it as the fear that passed from flesh to flesh—bringing a closeness she had never known before.

Something appeared then that, considering her age, she could not have known to look for. Whatever it was, wherever it came from, she responded on the deepest level—as though it entered through her pores: "It's dark in here, Mother. I can't see how to die in the dark."

—

For the final episode, we again swing across time—now, though, toward the present. Once more, all we have is a small incident to represent a whole period. At that point, considering the hour, the fatigue of both speaker and listeners, we could not expect much detail. (Let's not forget, though, that the ear, as well as the memory, is selective. We were ready by then, certainly, to reject more than we were to retain.)

     —Germany: The Second World War. Stephen, as a Jew, was sent to a detention camp. Later, his name was placed on a list of those to be shipped off to Auschwitz. Somehow he became the object of attention of a certain Lieutenant M., a former schoolteacher. (They had this, anyhow, in common.) In a few very brief encounters—surprising that even this was possible—a contact was established.

     Not long before Stephen was due to leave, his name disappeared from the list. What happened was that the lieutenant (no need to mention at what risk) faked an order for his transfer to another camp—one that was not an extermination center.

     Stephen said no more about this, did not indicate whether there was any further contact. Passing over what he went through, including how he was able to endure another period of internment, he went on to what happened after the war: coming to the United States, starting a new life. But this too was only touched upon; what he really wanted to tell us, as it turned out, was about his going back.

     The decision came after many postponements, after a long, continuing debate with himself. There was, of course, the natural reluctance to return—even to that continent, let alone within those borders. But he had set himself the task of finding the man who had saved his life. (Note that for the second time, someone in the uniform of the enemy had helped him. Also that the *ally* in one war becomes the *enemy* in another.)

     The view then is of him going from town to town, once more wandering without direction, and with little more than the man's name, the dim memory of the rather ordinary face, to guide him.

     How long was it before he finally gave up? Before he admitted that that confrontation would not take place? He did not mention a day or a month, did not describe the occasion. He barely suggested the nature of the loss: the dream of listening to that voice, searching that face: comparing it with what, over the years, he had had to invent for himself.

     So once more we are forced to add something to understand the trauma of the return: the odor of memory persisting, seeping through the immaculate, functional structures of the present. And there is this image of him standing somewhere on that soil asking questions—since the man himself was gone—of the cloudless empty sky. And perhaps at one moment or another, breathing in that air, thinking of ovens and the smoke that clogged another sky.

What does it all indicate? Without trying to put it together, we cannot tell. Perhaps we'll get around to it some day, perhaps not. At present there is just the notion of some vast formless odyssey. Neither a going toward nor a going away from—a journey in which the motion itself (*self-sustaining?*) may be all there is to understand.

To round it out, we should say something about what Stephen is doing now. He's teaching a social science course at a Catholic university. The first irony in this is obvious. The second, which appeals more, suggests that in the course of his lectures he is certain to be called upon to supply categories for human behavior and experience.

Considering what he had lived through, the imposed order, those charts with the patterns they trace, may have become a necessity. And yet as we heard it, moving with him through those *deserts of snow*, it was the elusive, the ambiguous to which he kept returning.

Finally, we should note that, even with the omissions, there remained a sense of continuity. Echo of it when he said near the end: "After all, it's the same human material." That said without judgment; but also without resignation—the search goes on.

3.

This more or less is what the notes contained. Looking through the stack of typed pages (much neater than the scrawl of my handwriting), I wonder if anything has been accomplished. It seems that, as expected, some things are clarified—others left unresolved. Most unfortunate is that, against the background of those vast events, the figure remains at a distance, not the particular face we are bound to recognize, but the generalized features of the archetype.

We can only say, regarding this failure, that we have not yet understood what is being measured—and on what scale. It is significant, in this respect, that Stephen X., *the man himself*, had so little to say about what it was he had endured. For in presenting it as something unsolved, in that dispassionate tone, he inevitably lost much of our empathy and identification.

Even as we write this, however, something else comes back: a direct memory not included in the notes. It happened that, as we were going toward the door, Stephen said: "As a reward for your patience, I've decided to make you all honorary

Hungarians." That he chose to end the evening on this note (that smile on the face of one who had *been there*) perhaps says as much as there is to tell.

For beyond this, what *can* be said? Once more the example of the man himself invites our silence. For as we understand it, all he asked was that we shift our attention from the teller to the tale. Perhaps also that, following the way of wonder, we try to look beyond the face of terror.

Considering this, suddenly the mind veers in another direction. All at once, we are caught up in a tide of emotion for the whole experience (*to have lived through all of this!*) and, incredibly, find ourselves mourning for what we have missed. For all that which, separated by time and distance, remains outside our reach. We begin to dream, to rearrange events, to explore the turns not taken—but then before we drift too far, drop anchor in the present.

But this is not the end of it. (The mind turns where it needs to turn.) For it has occurred to us that, having crossed the strict borders of the literal, we may have earned *the right* to claim a much wider acquaintance: to enter the realm where the pale, fearless nun, the vulnerable policeman, the compassionate lieutenant, the Bible-limned figure of the Old Believer, belong also to our own experience.

Market Day in the city of N. Is it possible that, since we have come so far, our presence is not unexpected? That at any moment now, a loud cry will startle us. That we will look up, eyes filled with wonder, at the sight of that peasant beating his horse . . .

We know better—at least in our more rational moments. And yet we sense that, although the uniforms change, it is the same army that passes. The dogs are a little fatter perhaps, with more meat on their bones. (If we had to make a meal there now, at least we should not starve.)

Through deserts of snow, through Tolstoyan snowstorms, must we then our own selves pass? It does not seem to matter, for we are placed among the survivors. It is in fact already settled, return ticket in our pocket, that our journey is for the full distance. (In the middle of the forest, an old dwarf is waiting to greet us. His loud yawn is the guarantee that once more we have reached friendly territory.)

We can stand then with Stephen X. beside the glass chandelier, exchanging remarks with others of this select company. (The presence of *the child* need not inhibit us: it is time she too learned whatever there is to be heard.) Faces all around us, waiting for the next speaker. We hold a glass in our hand—is it our turn? While we hesitate, bringing the rim to our lips, we sip the liquid of forgetfulness—yet somehow it only brings remembrance.

Among this company, we wonder now, where is the "man with the notebook"? If he is no longer among those present it must be because, at the last moment, he recognized the intrusion. That is, in preparing the images with which the others could identify, it became necessary for him to disappear.

Whether that is so, and whatever the reason, it does not seem to matter. By his absence, as it turns out, we have gained something—put it this way: the right to enter the city of N., located in the province of Y., any time we choose. But not as ourselves, of course, not as anyone visible and with a name.

The Book of Glimmers

(1979)

For the Reader

I have imagined you opening this book, wondering at the sight of short paragraphs, unfamiliar headings. But the space between writer and reader, I suppose, is not easily crossed. For, whatever the difficulty, the reader may prefer the encounter with the text without the intervention of a preface.

And that is in the spirit of what I call *glimmering*. The experience is of an *abrupt entry*, without foreknowledge. You start without the usual paraphernalia— material gathered and organized—considered necessary for even a modest journey. (I have, however, included "Notes & Work-Points" and a brief afterword to suggest where we are coming from.)

Dream and thought form an uneasy combination. We have no common expectation for what we "think about" and what we can only "dream upon." The search for a single thread, for definition, is usually considered apart from the "vagueness," the multiplicity of dream and reverie. Be prepared for an effort to weave them together.

And even if this does not succeed, I hope there is a paragraph, a phrase, even an aphorism to set your mind glimmering toward *what may or may not be there*.

—L. F.

Glimmers One: Unfinished Circumstance

. . . unfinished Circumstance. . . an Estate / perpetual / or a reduceless Mine
—Emily Dickinson

The Nature of Glimmers

1.
What is a "glimmer"? Less than a notion or a guess, it is closer to an "evanescent intuition," to an "obscure intimation." Let us say that it exists—derives from and goes back to—in a different realm: that of "Flicker/Flutter." Observe it then as real or imagined in the dynamics of time itself: Not Yet . . . Not Quite . . . No Longer. Join the "not yet" with the elusive, but sturdy AS IF, and we may have a "bridge" between Appearance & Reality. So our "glimmering" shuttles between realms of the tangible/visible/expressible—and the intangible/invisible/inexpressible. The particular glimmer then hovers on the edge of perceiving, sensing, knowing. Peripheral to vision, we may on occasion: "dream it into being." But its basic nature is to be most often "irretrievable."

2.
I'm tempted now to call it: "What/Where/When"—for which we seem unable to find the appropriate: "How/Why." It brings to mind the phrase: "A Series of Noticings"— which may be available to the patient bird-watcher as well as to the artist.

3.
Considering then "all that glimmers" being as much in shadow as in light, we need to confer value on what we cannot encompass or understand. For this I propose: (a) *It is* what you make of it; (b) But it is *also* something more & something else; (c) We shall *never* get to the bottom of it. And the corollary of this:
> The effort of the Intellect is to *explain* the Mystery.
> The effort of the Imagination is to *express* the Mystery.

◆

The Dream of Language
This was our human dream: that within language could be found the possibility of peaceful and fruitful coexistence. That the spoken or written word, reducing distances, providing names for the unnamable, unthinkable, might throw back the edge of darkness. But in time the word "became the sword"—vehicle for threatening & ambiguous gestures it could not withhold.

—

On the Grounds of Being
Where Being/Nonbeing maintain vital connections with Source and Horizon, Doing occupies a secondary role. Where they do not connect, the dialectic brings the sense of dread, of void. Still, this might be worked out, mediated, in terms of "Being as Belonging"—under conditions where "caring & sharing" remain effective as prime motives. What cannot be worked out—since it occupies a different continuum, relating to the goals of a materialistic, pragmatic culture—is what spreads across: Being-Doing-Having-Achieving.

—

What is Art? Art is the work itself—the tracing that remains—after the hands have done. Art is what is implicit, necessary—even where there are no hands.
    This is what Art incorporates:
    1. The Spirit Within: Image & Idea fused with the force of Event—the sense of "what has happened" absorbed into the larger context of: "what might have happened."
    2. What Is Happening: the unfolding of what is at first unexpected, and then inevitable, which is analog to the "real world."
    3. The Next Step: even after the "outcome" is presented and fulfilled, the sense of something further that is "about to happen": carrying over into the mind and life of the viewer, listener, reader.
       Not silence but gesture. Not gesture as sign or symbol, or "speech performed," but *being itself* as felt experience, made manifest.

—

The Why/The Why Not
Heidegger's *Why?* Picasso's *Why Not?*: Heidegger calls this the first question of Metaphysics: "Why is there something instead of nothing?" Picasso's "Why Not?"—reported as a favorite phrase, expressing his stance toward experience—may be heard as the artist facing a task which may require a "leap of the imagination," even a fall "into the unknown." Comparing the two, then: *Why* asks to be explained. *Why* is to "look before you leap." *Why Not* seeks surprise & discovery—expects the random & the wayward as part of a "calculated risk"—accepts the presence or absence of causal connections as a *given*: whichever it is, it belongs to the "new territory."

—

The Who as What/The What as Who
When Duchamp said: "Art is what the Artist says it is," the note of defiance expressed

the sense of freedom. What was probably not foreseen in this is the concomitant: "Is the Artist *who* he says he is?" The question goes deeper than our contemporary situation, uncovering a perennial uneasiness within the basic archetype: that of the "Impostor."

Within the larger context of the individual and the environment, we find at work all that tends to turn subject into object, object into subject. ("We do it all for you" is a current advertising slogan: *We* is the corporation that sells hamburgers; *You* is the tenderly cared-for consumer.)

What is being played upon here is a metaphysical pathos that may have a primordial, animistic source. Consider that personification is used to "animate" the inanimate, to humanize and make the environment less threatening. (And whatever happened to Ruskin's "pathetic fallacy"?) The manipulation then of the "collective unconscious" precisely in ways to defeat and degrade its deepest longings.

Individuals suffer from, survive through Institutions.

Institutions suffer from, survive through *Mystiques.*

—

The And/Or Situation

For a long time I felt, as did many others, the inadequacy of an "Either/Or" view. It seemed then that the "duality," the "polarity" could be better dealt with as: "Both/ And." But the flaw there, it would seem now, is that the thing & its opposite are still considered from the standpoint of their distance from each other. Preferable to this might be a view that shows them as "intermittent" as "intermingling": life and/or death. (*Bios* contains them both.)

Still, what could be more difficult to accept? This is just where the "tolerance for ambiguity" is under severest strain. The need for directions, for goals, for answers, for diagnosis insists: it has to be "this or that." (*This* excludes *that.*) At issue is the whole notion of choice, will, and decision—along with the sense of value, the hierarchy of the more or less "important." Even more threatening is the suggestion that, where it doesn't matter whether it is "this one" or "that one," the individual is made to feel replaceable, interchangeable.

—

One often has a strong sense of "the truth" of something that cannot be proved—or even adequately illustrated. This is the case with my notion of:

1. *A Dream in Time*
2. *A Dream Out of Time*
3. *In and Out of Time*
4. *In, Through, and Beyond Time*

The best I can do is to equate these with:
1. The Linear or Literal
2. The Classic
3. The Romantic
4. The Metaphysical

and look to the poems, the paintings, the sculpture—monuments & ruins—that embody and suggest correspondences for: Legend, Myth, Symbol, Allegory.

—

Forms of Reality: The Given, The Created, The Substitute
This would be most difficult to illustrate, but we are fortunate in having Marianne Moore's famous poem "On Poetry," which deals with it directly. Here are some relevant lines: ". . . when dragged into prominence by half poets, / the result is not poetry" (The Substitute). Instead, we must have "imaginary gardens with real toads in them," "hair that can rise," "eyes that can dilate" (The Created as the Real). But we cannot neglect, must also include: "business documents & school-books" and statistics (The Given).

On a less serious note, these three orders of reality are indicated in an old joke: What's the difference between the neurotic, the psychotic, the psychiatrist? The neurotic builds castles in the air. The psychotic lives in them. The psychiatrist charges both of them rent.

A favorite quote from Hart Crane—"As silent as a mirror is believed / Realities plunge in silence by"—indicates for me the ambiguities, the constant shifting and dissolving of these forms.

—

It may be useful, at this point, to offer a "trajectory" or "overview" of my own thought process. With the sense of certain "stages" or "turning points," this now appears:
1. What Ought to Be (1935–61)
2. What Could Be (1962–75)
3. What May—Or May Not Be (1976–)

Note: The specific date attached to What Could Be (1962) refers to an insight that came while reading Kenneth Clark's *Landscape into Art*. Clark's reference to Ruskin's "three types of perception," using the example of the primrose, suggested to me an "imaginative realism," as a *what could be*—between the literal realism of *what is* and the idealism of *what should be*. (The literal could diminish the flower to "mere presence." The ideal could dissolve it by seeking a form it did not have, and could never achieve—Shelley's "bird thou never wert," might be an example.)

Further note: As I began to write the *Glimmers* in 1976, and I got more in touch with multiplicity, with the random and the wayward, I realized this was the stance I was taking. The line that summed this up for me: "It takes a thousand glimmers to make a light."

Going Toward/Away From

(As an example of "what may or may not be," the following is presented more for its "speculative flow" than for precision of thought or language.)

1. We seek revelation, enlightenment, and forget the continuum that starts with the opaque, ends with the transparent.
2. Who is "We"? In one sense: I plus Thou equals We. (But with species identification, "We" enters the generalized realm of the human. And at the level of survival, the "I" turns from a specific person, to the "one who" has these basic human needs.)
3. *Someone, Something, Somewhere*: In terms of Necessity: I must be someone; I must have something; I must belong somewhere. The specificity of this, however, breaks down in the contradictory impulse toward freedom, toward the universal. For although "some" is better than "none," the desire for "this man's art, that man's scope," brings in the unconscious substitution of "any" and "every"—an endless source of confusion.
4. Language dreams: sometimes on the scale where it creates a castle, a throne. Having created the "Court," it sends for dancers, clowns, tumblers, sages.
5. Airing voices, we contrive and complain. Only later, in distress, do we remember—with gratitude & relief—that the reservoirs of silence remain intact.
6. Once more: Who is "We"? This time in terms of location, of belonging: within the tribe, within the "community of solitudes." (Note: subject for a separate reflection, as a "spin-off" from this: Landscape & Community.)
7. We have fallen out of History and into Time. Out of time and into Space. With "space stations" and "space shuttles," technology may provide some useful metaphors. But the basic activity of the mind requires a dialectic between: Making Alike/Differentiation. In undifferentiated space, we are more lost than ever.
8. Without Time—our cleverest invention—we lose also the related: "sequence" and "duration." (The perishing ocean is not "eternal"—merely dying.)
9. Without sequence? Choice and no "consequence"? We are deprived both of "one following the other," the sense of hierarchy, of precedent, and of "one following *from* the other," the sense of causal connection.
10. No more mystiques. Accept instead the varying proportions of "trial & error."

The pitfalls & pratfalls that remain—even increase as we venture into "unknown territory."

—

Light on the Table

1. Plato's view of Art as "re-presenting:"
2. God's absolute idea of the table.
3. The Carpenter's replication—scaled to human need and understanding.
4. The Artist's vague idea of God's idea—or perhaps the Artist's "blending" of the primary God-Spirit, with the Carpenter's "rough materials."

Note: The issue is still debated, still unsolved. Although from its inception, modern art attempted an alternative: the Artist paints a painting—not a table. Let God dream the table. We sit down—we eat (cf. Prévert's poem: "Picasso Goes for a Stroll").

—

Culture/This Culture

Ortega calls culture "a treasury of principles." But makes the distinction between situations where culture is "at the service of life," and where life is at the service of Culture. This suggests we need also to distinguish between *this* culture and Culture itself. (As metaphor, I prefer *reservoir* to *treasury*. With the latter, the negative drain can bring us to "bankruptcy." With the former, to "pollution" and to "drought"— both closer to the sources of dread, of void.)

—

Culture vs. Self

More on the effect of this culture, and the negative reaction transferred to Culture itself: when the givenness of the environment is so entrenched, alternatives seem impossible, the Self is prevented from ever viewing—not to mention realizing— what might be a "natural shape," "natural bent."

—

Culture vs. Creature

The basic, primordial conflict between a "culture self" and a "creature self," between "culture consciousness" and "creature consciousness." The familiar associations here are that the "culture," through various systems, institutions, superstructures, is imposed upon the "creature." (All that is "instinctive" on one hand, all that is "acquired" on the other.) Less familiar may be the notion that the "creature" inheritance involves more cooperation than dominance—more dialogue with things and fellow creatures: the ecological balance does not imply the "peaceable kingdom" or the "noble savage," but it does suggest another kind of communication, as a prior condition for living on this earth.

Two Problems of Culture
1. How to save the "baby"—while throwing out the "dirty water" in the tub?
2. What are we to do about: "old bottles and new wine"? Playing with this: Can the questions be joined as the single problem of "container & contained?" Suppose the container is the Body. The contained is Spirit or "vital fluid." We might be ready, at this point, to pronounce the "vessel" suitable for either the mundane or the cosmic voyage. But the immediate view produces a quick deflation: of the cast-off, the discarded—*no-deposit & no-return*—littering spaces between the houses (cf. Collingwood's phrase: "the corruption of consciousness").

The Population Problem of Words: *Too Much Is Being Said Too Soon by Too Many (and Too Often!)*
The Poet has Opinions—just like everybody else. Necessary at one stage, many are later disowned, discarded. Some are remembered, however, preserved as "curious relics"—to pick up and stare at—sometimes with wonder, sometimes with indifference.

The Poet who becomes his own Philosopher is all too often like the lawyer who defends himself: both have *fools* for clients.

The Human Condition: *Beyond the Name & Number/We Forget & We Remember.*

(And of course we are "forgotten & remembered"—most often, as we think: in the *wrong* ways, for the *wrong* reasons!)

To Be Included—but not enclosed—*Is a Condition of Our Freedom.*

Gift Without Burden
"'Tis a gift to be simple / 'tis a gift to be free." We have come a long way from "self-anointing"—guaranteed by suffering and pain—as a privilege of rare talent and genius. Now it seems that "magic ointment" is on sale at your corner drugstore—or direct from "J. W. Wells, dealer in magick & spells." (One shilling per box.)

——

About the Word
Having lost sight of its ends, the Word lives now entirely beyond its means.

Having lived for some time beyond its means, the Word has lost sight of its ends.
(Also: The World?)

——

Suicide: A Leap to the Wrong Conclusion
(Note: When I quoted this line to a friend, she remembered one on the same sub-ject—without being able to name the source: *Suicide*: someone who takes his own life—*too seriously*.)

——

Crossing Time
The sense that we have crossed some fundamental barrier—are about to cross oth-ers—has given rise to such expressions as "post-human," "post-history." If this is so, how can we distinguish the possibly different kinds of being that might be present or might appear in "radically different"circumstances? The invented words may be useful here: Today's being: "Mono-Morph." Tomorrow's being: "Duo-Morph." After tomorrow: "Poly-Morph" or "Trans-Morph." Another version of this: *Yesterday's being: Human. Today's being: Earthling. Tomorrow's being: Spaceling.*

Within this perspective, the difference between generations may be as great as between one species and another—or inhabitants of different planets. The extreme statement seems necessary as we approach a tomorrow in which the "scientific" manip-ulation of life processes bring life spans and life forms closer to a synthetic context.

We may also call this view: "the death of perspective." For it leaves us only with a clear, reasonable saying of "what we were"—with no more than the vagu-est guess of "what we are"—or are going to be. (Note: the major media effort—from magazines to newspapers to television—and the corporation slogans that have turned "merchandising into *legendising*.")

It may also be possible to apply these notions to some recent history: (par-ticularly to the phenomenon of the "hippies" and the "counterculture"): Let's arbi-trarily say that the "Post-human" makes an appearance in the sixties. That it is then superseded by the "Neo-human" in the seventies. And the reason for this? The initial effort of the "Post-human" is to separate itself from the "intolerable image" of its predecessors: *nothing like us ever was*. But then finding the "totally unprecedented" brings with it the even more difficult sense of "cosmic alienation," it becomes nec-essary to switch to *something* like us always was.

Thus there emerges the "Neo-human," with the essential recognition that it cannot survive without its human residues. It must fashion a new image, new modes. This is signaled when the "advance elements" discard beard and long hair, find outlet in a new "elegance." (Note: the scruffy seekers continue to appear in Levi's and sandals—but this may be only up to a certain age—or as "weekend clothing.") And at the same time—and here is where it diverges more significantly—there is a search for "selected persons," among the older generation, to serve as models, as acceptable, even admirable predecessors (artists, poets, ecologists).

Sensing the "trajectory" of all this, we might say: the "Throw Forward" of the sixties, experiencing an intolerable "fall into the unknown," not only withdraws but adopts in the seventies the strategy of the "Throw Back"—a metaphysical "reversion" that occupies itself with nostalgia, with antiques—even with "ancestor worship." (A variation of this might bring a shuttling Back & Forth—exhausting and frightening with its pull toward opposing directions.)

Question: Where *every* one is vulnerable, is *any* one? Note how this "cuts away" the traditional ground of the poet, the artist: that of being *specially* vulnerable.

On Consciousness & Imagination

Some different criteria to help distinguish the work of Consciousness/Imagination: As currently used, Consciousness "seeking" and "expressing" is more at home in the transitory. Its mission is to "go into" itself, to explore itself. The movement of Imagination at first appears also to "go into" itself, but it does this only as prelude to a further outward motion. This is to integrate, to work upon, even to transform what is "already there," "already out there." Thus, characteristically, Consciousness is an *extension* and Imagination a *preservation*. Consciousness needs the *excitement* of the "emerging novelty." Imagination needs the reassurance of the correlative between "in here" and what has been, is now, and will be "out there."

The Well/The Will/The Vision (borrowed from a chapter in J. L. Lowes's *The Road to Xanadu*): *The Well:* container for the "living water" of the Spirit—where all we have "received" is stored. *The Will:* by which we organize and transmit the "materials" of creative expression. *The Vision:* the inner sense of outer things. The combination of these is used to develop "scenes & panoramas," "landscapes & inscapes" that include the Known, the Unknown, the Unknowable.

Dream Creature/Waking Creature

As an alternative to the view previously expressed, which places the "monomorph" of today as subject to be superseded by the "polymorph" of tomorrow—the "earth-ling" by the "spaceling"—is the sense that whatever *is* is implicit in what will be. The earlier view then could be seen as a "construction" of the *Waking Creature*, with its need for "Order" as contained within established Space/Time boundaries. But the *Dream Creature* has other needs: in its fluid world, there is neither "crisis" nor event, but constant, limitless passage and transformation.

—

Symbiosis/Immunology

Relating to the above, but with a focus on human vulnerability, its kinship to other "life forms," is the special awareness that our basic notions and metaphors stem from the fundamental situation of life lived on the land. This is in effect an "Immunology": we keep apart basically not to become "physically" or "spiritually" infected. The history of plagues, of primitive peoples destroyed by diseases of the "civilized," deeply embeds this in the "collective unconscious."

But life in the Sea exists by a "symbiosis," with a clarity and transparency that leaves hardly any room for "Immunology." A shorthand notation on this: *Symbiosis*: Part of—not apart from. *Immunology*: "The Plague"; "The Fall" (Camus's metaphors).

       Symbiosis: *Sea/Dream*   Immunology: *Land/Waking*

—

Just Glimmering

The situation of this moment. Of what is immediately before us. I become aware that, in preparing this "condensed" text, what has largely survived so far is the more "conceptual" material. The accent is on "propositional" truth—this somewhat at the expense of the "feeling tone" of the more confused, wayward, sometimes playful, sometimes painful search for the "felt truth" of the original text.

Something happens in the writer's mind. Something happens on the page. Something comes off the page—into the reader's mind. The "bare bones" of the situation seems mundane, obvious. And yet we come back to it again and again, making adjustments, trying for a better balance.

One way of getting at this is to look at one of the haiku of Basho: "Ancient pond / frog jumps in / water sound." One translator makes the point this could also be "Ancient pond / frog jumps in / *plop!*" (We are not concerned here with lit-erary merit or the exact number of syllables.) And this gives us the choice between putting the *plop* on the page—and making it happen in the reader's mind. This remains an issue, with the current feeling that language has not been explicit enough, or daring enough. But I recall coming across a reference to a newspaper review of one of the early editions of *Leaves of Grass*, in which the reviewer com-plained that "Whitman has brought the slop pail into the parlor."

If we refer to the much longer history of Chinese poetry, the view that emerges is of a pendulum that keeps swinging between the "implicit" and the "explicit."

But coming back to our own present, it would seem the self-conscious avant-garde, with its insistence on the explicit, might be offered this longer view: The *shock* of yesterday is the *schuck* of today—the *schlock* of tomorrow.

◂

Endless Reproductions (cf. Walter Benjamin, "The Work of Art in the Age of Mechanical Reproduction," from Illuminations*)*
Endless reproductions in print, record, film, tape: playing or showing it "again and over again." No recognition here that, as Whitehead said: "Fatigue is mere repetition." The effort instead to make everything instantly and constantly accessible: to be retrieved at will, reenacted at the push of a button. This possibly starts at the level of "reassurance"—images against the void, the literal "nowhere"—but then goes so far as to stir the unconscious with "intimations of immortality."

There is no longer any way to calculate the effect of the distortions to the perceptual system. Time can be spliced, edited, replayed, reassembled in a bewildering jumble of "before, during, and after." Thus technology substitutes the trivial, unnatural "again" of the late, late movie for the spirit-echoing depths of experience. The sense that something truly endures, that can be called back, called upon, when needed: the most stirring images of art and religion.

◂

Poetry & Metaphysics:
"Does it not seem that there must be a ground common to metaphysics and certain types of poetry? . . . Is it a pre-linguistic experience?" (question addressed by F. C. Copleston to Jean Wahl in *Philosophical Interrogations*, Harper Torchbooks, 1970).

My first reaction is to be pleased with the way this is phrased. A second look brings the thought: the "common ground"—what is that? A third suggests a "feeling" that grows through silence—to be content as "contained," or to seek expression. . . . The wind blows across the ground. With or without voice. Within or outside the range of our hearing . . . But if we move from this to the question "Can something grow here?" we take a significant step. We are then looking at the "ground" as a place for *cultivation*. And we are preparing to "say something" or do something that will alter what is originally and inherently "there." There is not only what is to be used, "brought to flower," but what may be wasted, destroyed. Taking all this into consideration, we need to distinguish carefully what to touch and to leave untouched: *Metaphysics is to Poetry as Soil Conservation is to Agriculture.*

◆

On Viewing and Vision

Viewing implies a viewer. Does Vision imply a "visionary?" It is understood that Vision implies "seeing beyond" the Visible—toward what will be but is not yet manifest. But even here we need the further distinction between what is "predictive" and "prophetic."

Predictive: a far-reaching interpretation of data that is already, though perhaps only slightly, visible.

Prophetic: derives from and relies upon "the intangible, invisible, inexpressible" as a primary source: the *judgment* of the Hidden upon the Manifest.

(Whitman & Blake wrote about the evils of industrialization. Whitman's essay is full of foreboding for the future: centralized control, pollution. But the tone is rational, although despairing. Blake's charged, ecstatic language is often compared and linked to Whitman's—in this instance though, the expression is quite different.)

This is somewhat of a detour, and the distinction may be only of minor value. (As with the sometimes useful distinction between "rational" and "irrational" vision.) More to the point, to come back to the dialectic: viewing is not necessarily even *seeing*. And at its highest, most perceptive—when it brings the sense of "seeing through"—is still not Vision. For as previously noted, this only activates the tension implicit in the further dialectic between the Transparent and the Opaque.

It may be useful then to offer this—however limited and over-simple—"definition" of Vision: "Vision is the force that correlates and sustains the inner sense of outer things—even when it cannot project or find corresponding images to relate the parts to the whole."

Glimmers Two: Weights/Measures/Affections

To measure is to know.

   —Lord Kelvin

*To measure we need to know not only the influence of the observer,
but of the observing system.*

                    —Fritz Capra, *The Tao of Physics*

Care is the condition for being in the world.

                    —Heidegger

Glimmers Two begins (December 19, 1976) on the following subjective note: Woke this morning with stream of images, notions, residues of imaginary encounters and conversation carrying over from sleep. Along with this, some vague thoughts about the "unconscious." Wondering how the "therapies" and the "psychologies" manage to structure what seems, at these times, so utterly random . . . Noting also how the pleasant sensation that goes with the "streaming" contrasts with the need to "signify," to "construct," to make use of. It occurs to me that the whole effort to "differentiate further" is constantly at odds with the "givenness" of this other, creaturely existence.

   . . . Thinking more now about the reader: hoping the present effort goes more smoothly, with fewer "detours." But *Glimmers* are Glimmers: connections are made and connections fail. Something rises to the surface; something gets away. I summon a word, an image; for a moment I feel its presence—almost within reach—and as quickly it is gone. No point in asking: where from, where to? I can only try to be alert, attentive for the next "member of the throng" that comes this way.

   Of course, more is involved. Whatever is going on around me, all that has gone before, whatever yet remains to be. Staring at the page, I cannot see the "next word" before it is ready to appear. I have tried saying *Speak, memory*. But the "instrument" fails to respond. Something ironic in this, as I recall the line I once wrote: "How easy it is to move from memory to invention." And what is the "player" without his chosen instrument? A question I never cared to answer—even less so with the fading of the senses that goes with this age.

   More to the point, though: I have not been that interested in my own life. But the "dance of ideas" is one I have tried to follow. And if I continue searching, it is not for what is mine to claim, but for whatever there is to share.

   Let me put that to the test: an early memory is that of seeing the Cocteau film *The Blood of a Poet*. One scene in particular returns: card players seated at a table in an open courtyard. They shuffle, deal the cards, oblivious to the falling snow. . . .

Leaving the theater, walking in the snow—*real snow this time*—I too was oblivious, under the spell of having "entered another realm." As it turned out, I had not far to go: a small street in Greenwich Village. My cousin lived there. When I told him about the film, he said there was a poet living next door. I was still too young for the name to mean anything—but it did a few years later: e. e. cummings.

Now here's the temptation toward anecdote, toward the "legend" of the self, for which one only needs—or so it seems—a few names that reverberate. (Another to include here would be the well-known art critic who wrote one of his first published essays on the showing of this film.) But the reminder comes that, as presented, there is not enough to merit attention. One has either to elaborate or go on to something else. Of course one has first to believe in the "reflected aura" of the "glorious company," to be sure of the resonance of the names.

But that means to risk the "radical erasure," the cancellation, imposed by a new generation that has its own "names to remember." To risk also the mocking echo: "Who he? Who she? Who they?" And it means the special kind of foolishness— besides the brief "entertainment"—that comes with reaching one's *anec-dotage*.

So much indeed for the *Path of Biography*.

Does it matter "who" writes these lines? To some extent, yes; to some extent, no. As long as the "feeling tone" is right, it only matters that the voice of one who feels, suffers, rejoices, is retained. For the effort that must be made is to preserve the "human residues." And the choices, along this line, that suggest wherever possible a "one-to-one correspondence," tracing the presence of a sentient being.

The minimum resolve here is to "do no harm." Not as easy as it sounds, since we have no sure way to tell how anything we say is being heard.

Further reflection on "who" writes these lines: There is, as we consider the range, the tonality, of verbal expression, what is available to one who sees, hears, says, remembers, forgets. The ordered seeing of "poets," "storyteller," even "reporter," shifts to the more ambiguous: "witness," "observer." The contrast also between the transient account and that which survives is given more "lasting form."

Cause for wonder here at the origins of myth & mystique of the "special being" of the artist—who in one sense is working with the same materials as the undistinguished, the unknown, the forgotten, producing combinations & arrangements of word & image we have learned to call "Art."

—

The Gift That Disqualifies

What is it like to come to a place where there is no need to know, need to prove? In relation to poetry, to language, the sense of what is concealed "within the word" keeps growing. At best, I have caught only a glimpse of what might be said, heard, written. Eliot wrote: "Understanding begins in the sensibility." And I have to concede a whole range of "sensibilities" whose origins and orientation are so far removed—not only outside, but within this culture—that my response is often mere guesswork.

―

On Sacrifice & Discovery

1. Does it make a difference which comes first? I had considered the natural order to be: "sacrifice first, discovery later." But then remembered the example of Freud who made his discovery, then almost had to sacrifice his career as a successful physician, as his work disturbed, threatened prevailing theory & practice.
2. Those who were "lucky" enough to make discoveries of a kind welcomed by those in power in that time & place—and given generous rewards. (Curious that there is presently an expectation that this should be the rule—rather than the exception.)
3. Discovery without acknowledgment, without recognition within the individual's lifetime.
4. Discovery as something one stumbles into—suddenly "noticing," or looking in an "unexpected" direction.
5. Discovery without effort: as when newly available technology provides an opening into areas previously closed (cf. Dannie Abse's poem, "Letter to Alex Comfort," an amusing, incisive account of the noted scientific "discoverers").

Strange that, as I am writing this and open the anthology to check on the poem, the book should fall open to a quote from Marianne Moore: "To be trusted is an ennobling experience, and poetry is a peerless proficiency of the imagination. I prize it, but am myself an observer; I can see no reason for calling my work poetry except that there is no other category in which to put it" (from *The Modern Poets*, edited by Brinnin and Read, McGraw-Hill, 1963). This echoes what I wrote earlier about "the ordered vs. the ambiguous seeing" of the "poet," the "observer"; it provides also a rare, rare example of *the Gift that disqualifies*.

―

On Impulse & Improvisation

A closer look at these familiar words often brings the view of what we have wrongly taken for granted. Note first that *spontaneous* is used in a positive, and *impulse* usually in a negative sense: one "gives way" to impulse—only at some risk. Further, to give way "entirely"—beyond instinct & reason—may invoke all sorts of dangers.

And improvisation? It must be used with caution, in situations where "knowledge" is insufficient, data unavailable. In contrast to this I suggest the existence of two basic procedures:

1. When in doubt—join something.
2. When in doubt—improvise.

What might be added is the necessary practice to improve improvisational skills. The combination of experience and intuition, with a feeling for context, may suggest how far the testing of inner strengths can go—along with the recognition that, in any case, there is no escape from *contingency*.

Recent Encounters

Some recent encounters bring back once more the sense of "remarkable coincidence," of "intertwining lives." Beyond description & explanation, we wonder how events are initiated, the role of our presence. We speak a word, it falls somewhere: a seed within the ear. Beyond our sight a wheel turns. A distant observer sees it, decides to set a wheel of his own in motion; then another & another. Soon the whole world is turning. . . . Someone in another country, another time wakes up in the morning, notices the presence of the "turning world." Imagine this unknown "future friend," "kindred spirit," as he yawns, stretches, wonders: What could have set it in motion?

Durable Goods/Personal Things

Within the context of Western culture, the often contradictory pursuit of The True, The Good, The Beautiful—and the metaphysical pathos which relates them to The Lasting. "Goods" as what makes living possible & worthwhile, and as "merchandise." Somehow this reappears within the personal milieu as "treasured objects"— treasured to the point where, as in Nazi Germany, they could not be left behind. This "symbolic furniture," combined with or given the status of "ancestral tokens," is often powerful enough to embody and dominate the life of the individual.

Sightem: The weight of three doves / bodies geared toward winter / on the slanted branch. *Reflection*: Thus as I look out the window, I am *gifted* with the sight of what is there. But with a change of mood, I perceive the "darker side" of seeing. Negative phrases to express this: *The Tyranny of Sight/The Arrogance of the Visible*.

1. In the "arrogance of the visible," Image takes the place of Idea and Ideal. Image proliferates into images that are mindless and "without consequence": war, murder on television.

2. In the "tyranny of sight," Everyman becomes a photographer, scurrying around, determined to leave no stone unphotographed. It never occurs to these stalkers of "bird & bush" (Wallace Stevens, "Anecdote of the Jar") that what we publish takes from darkness—as from wilderness—what cannot be replaced. Silence, the invisible are also dwindling resources to be protected: essential components no longer to be considered apart from physical survival within the ecosystem. . . .

In reworking these *Glimmers*, the question of what to include, what to leave out, is ever-present. The following reflection on personal pronouns seems borderline: worth including for latent content: Where is the "you" of yesterday?

Sometimes it reappears as the intimate "thou": sometimes as the distanced, negative "other." It can also be placed in an intermediate position between "I" and "We." There is also a feeling of association, and one of disassociation: "Whoever you are, your gods are not mine" (Nelson Algren); "When I am told I must be for or against—in that case I am against" (Camus).

Out Of/In To
A whole cluster of reflections starts with the observation that the word *emerge* is e/merge: out of/into. With this "humble" beginning, insights expand toward the larger theme of Access/ Refuge. And as a related configuration: Entering Into/In Trance/Entrance. Since these are ongoing, this must be considered a tentative saying:
Entering Into:
1. *The unacknowledged "compact" or "contract."*
2. *A wider, deeper space.*
3. *Crossing the boundaries, barriers to approach:* Another Realm.
4. Further penetration that leads to the *colonizing* of what was considered "fantasy," the "undiscovered country."
5. The other person, the other thing: excessive empathy: "You are myself." (Note: the inevitable concomitant: being, entered, possessed, "taken over" by demons and spirits—perhaps to an extent where "exorcism" is called for.)
6. Into the "symbolic dimension"—the self transcended, transfigured, metamorphosed.

Access/Refuge
The polarity of—it seems at first—the "Open" versus the "Closed" door. The need for "freedom" on one hand, for "shelter" or "sanctuary" on the other. Observe, though,

how the two—as it were—begin to dance toward each other, until it seems possible to say: "Access is Refuge. Refuge is Access." (Not only do we "hide and seek"—but seek to hide, and hide to seek.) And note the potential benefits of both: *Access* to the Self: possible enlightenment. *Refuge* from the Self: from the burden of excessive self-consciousness. (Note further: the role here of "The Mirror" and of "The Lamp." The Self that absorbs light reflects the Image; the Self that provides light *projects* the Image.)

—

Entrance/In Trance: Briefly on these two: *Entrance* is the term used by George Kubler (in *The Shape of Time*) to distinguish what is available to the artist in a certain place, certain time: "greatness" may have more to do with opportunity than with talent. Thus at one level, the artist follows his "lucky star"—long before his more serious encounter with the "Necessary Angel." But this may also be accompanied by, or even produced by, some extraordinary state of mind, of extended intensity, with his behaving as if *In Trance* (note Eliot's remarkable line: "Till human voices wake us / and we drown").

—

Location/Direction

A brief note on what could be the subject of an extended reflection: *Location* implies the convergence or conjunction of time and place. *Direction* implies the "active seeking" that precedes this. The difference between *in process*, and *in situ*, the "where" that is already established. The frustration and fear when both are "missing" is based as much upon an expectation as upon a need. When Ortega says: "Man's natural situation, his life, in itself *is* disorientation, is being lost. . . ." the word *natural* resonates: so contrary to what we wish and expect—as if we were being told "order is disorder."

For a condensed view, I note the favored words of a friend: *Route, Root, Range.* These seem now to relate to Direction, and to *Getting There*. My own favored three— *Scope, Scape, Scale*—more to Location, and *Being There*. And that this is not merely a "word problem" was expressed to me recently by a physicist: "We're not sure where 'there' is." Gertrude Stein's "there is no there there" is the inevitable echo to this.

—

Discovery: Promise & Menace

The sense of Discovery may be perceived: "as if for the first time." Excitement is added with the sense of the unique event: "the first and only time." But with this is implied: "never before/never after." This can suggest a "break" in the vital continuum between Source & Horizon, which could bring Terror/Dread (Kierkegaard on Dread: "When the impossible becomes possible"). This gives us another example of how faulty is our sense of Polarity: in this case the assumed distance between Promise and Menace.

This dialectic between "Promise and Menace" appears as a constant of human experience—almost at its center. But our view of it changes at times when the "apocalyptic" makes an appearance. A fine discussion of this in Frank Kermode's *The Sense of an Ending* (Oxford, 1967). Here I want only to work with three memorable phrases from that book: *solidarity of plight, diversity of state, parody of paradigm.*

Linking these then in condensed form: The "parody of paradigm" operates when existing models wear out so quickly they cannot sustain belief, and so become subject to "takeover" in parody. At the same time, the largest part of the world needs concern, compassion; and for this we seek to connect with those in like condition, recognizing our "solidarity of plight" with victim, refugee, exile, outcast. As for "diversity of state," in my view, this can be preserved when and where individual identity coincides with this collective responsibility. What happens, though, when "solidarity" and "diversity" are separated, set on opposing courses? Kermode illustrates with the situation of modern art, where he finds: "inconceivable diversity of state, without solidarity of plight." He calls attention to "fictions without ritual"—a world in which image is set against image, word against word. I have seen this happen in work that, almost by design, expresses the grotesquely trivial. My understanding is that *Devotion, Indulgence,* and *Necessity* are essential to the creative process—kept in some kind of balance. But "diversity" per se relates to "indulgence" per se—and the resulting proliferation without quality or meaning.

Each word carries—within itself—the weight and history of the language.

◂

A Brief View of Necessity
   1. What we can live with.
   2. What we can live without.
   3. What we cannot live without.
(Note: Who remembers and would care to identify any collection of words—even a small phrase—they would want to call: *indispensable?*)

On the larger issues, I would relate the above to Whitehead's statement that life has a "threefold urge:"
   1. to live
   2. to live well
   3. to live better

Consider what is often presented as the "subjective" necessity: What I want to do, or need to do. Contrasted with the "objective": what needs to be done. While this is somewhat simplistic, it leads us to the perennial question of "Freedom & Necessity." Engels called freedom the recognition of Necessity. This can be paraphrased: What I want to be/What it wants to be. Note the possibility, beyond conflict, of an onto-logical mutuality here: considering both my "right & need" and its "right & need." Note also the devious way that self-interest conceals its pursuits: what I want it to be—which could bring about "its" destruction, not only from passion & desire, but from no more than a whim. (See, for example, Francis Ponge, Taking the Side of Things. Ponge's eloquent poems and prose poems reveal this as a basic stance toward experience. Showing what is within "bread" or "table" or "pebble," Ponge also shows how we diminish the object by making it "there for us," instead of "just there.")

The Hidden/The Manifest

The "Hidden" as the Source from which the "Manifest" is derived (The Reservoir.) It is as if, preserving the Secret, the Mystery, we keep intact the quality and level of the "living water," maintain a suitable home for the *fish*. While we may, on occasion, drop a line into this reservoir—even catch and eat one of the fish—we retain a spe-cial affection for "the fish that got away."

The Silent/The Articulate

"Whoever seeks to gain his life will lose it." Related to the above reflection on the Hidden & the Manifest is this view of irreducible paradox. I have before me a book with the title: *Raid on the Articulate*. It is by J. D. Crossan, and bears the subti-tle: *Comic Eschatology in Jesus and Borges*. Crossan's study of their parables shows their affinity rooted in paradox—and how this is subverted by glib commentators (including the Apostles) who present an ordering of the world in terms of "prob-lems" and "solutions."

Another Word on Necessity

While I wrote earlier from the standpoint of Being as Doing, as Having, something needs to be said that considers Being in its more fundamental sense: *as Being*. This takes us away from "What I want—or need," to the related questions: Do *I* have to Be? Does *it* have to be? Note that the "revisionist" or "reformist" will add: "this way" or "that way" (bringing us back to "problems and solutions"). While the "radical" view implies: "at all" (cf. E. M. Cioran, *The Temptation to Exist*). Note also that we are using *it* here in the sense of the man-made institution or system—not as we did before, as the "natural object" that needs to be preserved.

To sum up, then: *I* do not have to be. *It* does not have to be. With this understood, imagination and intuition begin their search for alternatives: for what *can be*. For improved forms, for more congenial conditions to replace whatever now tends to diminish and to dissolve.

➤

Toward a Definition of Event

First, to locate "what is happening" between what "has happened" and what is "going to happen." (Consider also Aristotle: What *has* happened is History. What *might have* happened is Art.) Note that the usual view of the writer positions him in a "closed room." This suggests that the imagination works on the past to create something "believable" in the present, and capable somehow of affecting the future. But attempt some alternate positioning: the Astronomer at his telescope; the "prying neighbor" stationed at the window; the "cinema vérité" photographer tracking a single figure through dense crowds and traffic. Obviously, the stance, the angle of vision, affects both the content and form of what is contained within the "unfolding moment."

The dilemma is expressed again by Aristotle: to find in that which passes, that which does *not* pass. (The lasting *within* the temporal.) Let us try to restate this, closer to what we perceive: "Here now it is" fades and turns into: "Just there it was." We may be saying only: these are the limits of perception, of expression. Calling attention to the "time-bound" nature of imagination itself. And to test this, it may be necessary to say: What if we agree *nothing* has happened—(nothing new under the sun)—and therefore, nothing is going to happen?

Having articulated the "absurd" proposition, we may risk a further bit of "nonsense"—in challenge to Heraclitus: "You can't step in the same river *once*." Thus there is no sameness *as such*, any more than (in the ever-changing river) there is any "succession" where we can discern: "before, during, and after." We are left rather with the unceasing flow—which we are and remain part of—never apart from. Event then is another "construction" imposed on Nature and Reality, for a kind of ordering that contains sequence and duration, that confirms our need for patterns among the visible.

➤

Being & Existence

Variations on a familiar theme: Existence, as we regard it now, faced with the "intolerable," begins its search for *Refuge*: for sanction and sanctuary within these "given structures." Being, for its part (wanting to enlarge what Existence would "diminish"), seeks *Access*: all the ways of entering a whole variety of realms. The question of Existence is bound up with the "appropriate or necessary" mode: to exist—this way or that way. The question of Being—as intended here—is posited as essence, without alternative modes: Do *I* have to be? Does *It* have to be? (The "variety of realms" mentioned above is not a contradiction, since these are not conceived or fantasized in existential terms; they are rather "different orders of being," located on a larger scale than: "me and my lifetime," in what is "beyond" or "elsewhere.")

This may suggest that what cannot be altered within an existential framework may have to be "suspended" or "removed." And from this we may gather the double view:

1. There is nothing to be done—leading to negation and despair.
2. Coming back to the thing "in, of, and for itself," the *being* of things, we can invoke the radicality of "letting be."

This may at least bring into view how we ourselves supply metaphor and reality for—what makes existence so intolerable—intrusion, for invasion.

On Aphorisms

I have included a few here, survivors of the original text. But most I have discarded—not that they now seem unappealing, untrue—insofar as they suggest "knowing" rather than "glimmering." What follows now is a "linking" of several related sentences with "glimmer intention"—even though with "aphoristic sound":

1. We are what we eat, what we dream, what we worship. From this "core situation" come conflicting images that cannot be reconciled, resolved— ingrained in the human situation, therefore, are elements of what is basically "intolerable."
2. To overcome this we invent, imagine, various structures and concepts—and the myths, symbols, rituals to make them possible, appealing, enduring.
3. What emerges then I have called the Conspiracy to Pretend (that we do not in fact "eat what we worship") and a Resolve to Believe (that with ritual we can transcend the intolerable fact). Between what we "pretend" and what we "believe" is an ambiguous zone—where we constantly lose sight of what is authentic belief and what wears mask and disguise to cover pretense.

Another "set" with the same "aphoristic sound" consists of these sentences reflecting on Time & World:

1. We have fallen out of History and into Time. Fallen out of Time and into Space.
2. Earth is to "World" as Brain is to "Mind." This may suggest the basic relationship between realms of the "tangible-visible-expressible" and the "intangible-invisible-inexpressible"—while at the same time avoiding a "confusion of realms."

3. When the "World" is clear (or better: completely transparent), Art loses much of its reason to exist. Therefore I hand you this *Rock of Absence*; observe it *as if* the markings and the grain were visible.

Thus this brief foray into the realm of "Weights, Measures, & Affections" moves toward a conclusion. The question of Presence & Absence suggests the further realm of: Shadow & Substance. Before we go into this, the following may help "prepare the ground":

We live where *to seem* controls *to be*; where appearances, pseudo-events, dominate and replace the "true face" of reality. Philosophy presents the issue: The Way It Is/Seems to Be (Appearance & Reality). And along with this: The Way It Is/Ought to Be (Freedom/Necessity). But what we experience is: *The Way It Ifs*—may or may not be, imaginable or unimaginable juxtapositions or combinations of circumstance. (Experience also that continually confuses & surprises. Crossing the "categories of response," we find ourselves in situations where "murder can be comic and hunger can be kind.")

Metaphysics then brings "Shadow & Substance" to our attention. Antonio Porchia, in *Voices*, has some eloquent aphorisms on this: "The shadows: some hide, others reveal." "I look at myself and ask: 'What do the others say is visible?'" (translated by W. S. Merwin, *Big Table*, Chicago, 1969). My reflection on this: Language itself both conceals and reveals—is both implicit & explicit. And the tension between the extremes is what keeps it alive.

But what of the Shadows themselves—of the shadowed, the shadowing? I write this on a day suddenly grown dark. To my right, a few steps into the garden, the tree we planted a few years ago is heavy and dark with birds. Part of the light we took for granted is no longer here . . . Thus the passage of Time itself: Not yet . . . not quite . . . no longer. The dimly glimpsed "Bridge of As If" hovers between "What Is" and "What If." The "traffic" sometimes heavy, sometimes light—sometimes almost at a standstill—presents a stream of images, perceptions, thought, & feeling. We shuttle "back & forth"; chase the "not yet," have it "almost in hand," then watch it retreat, dissolve into the "no longer." The pressure on that "thin line" between "not-yet" and "no-longer" causes us to summon forth—for continuity, for a temporary stabilization—whatever may be gathered under the name: "Here & Now."

And with this we set aside—for the moment at least—what has kept us occupied with: "Weights, Measures & Affections," and turn to face directly toward the Shadows.

Glimmers Three: Mining Shadows

Everything is a little bit of darkness, even the light.
                    —Antonio Porchia

. . . like the silent interplay of shadows in a budding forest—the silence
of a thought's interacting shadows extending inside me.
                    —Vilhelm Ekelund

Start with this notation scribbled on a scrap of paper: "Closing day at exhibit of Tan-Han murals. The work of excavation. Of restoration. The semblances on the walls (have we any reason to doubt, or wish to improve upon them?) skillful copies made by contemporary Chinese painters. Photographs of the sites explored; not sure whether these are real or imagined instructions to the diggers: 'How to Enter a Tomb.' Next to this a painting entitled 'Door Attendants,' which bears the notation: 'They carried no weapons.' I feel too ignorant to know what I'm looking at: surface and depth dissolve; sensation of floating, of dreaming in a 'fluid space' . . . The dual reality of 'faces in a crowd,' of the high-pitched voices of children—and the faces on the wall (*The apparition of these faces in the crowd: / Petals on a wet, black bough.*—Ezra Pound)".

"How much do they cost?" says the child. "Priceless," says the mother. The child persists: "You mean lots and lots of money?" I walk away, diverted by the voices, and toward another exchange—this time between adults: "Give 'em credit for one thing." "What's that?" "Those Chinese sure know their horses . . ."

What then is the question of: "Mining Shadows?" It has been for me different things at different times: "the pervasive underside of experience that has not yet been revealed" (parable, "The Garden," from *The Scale of Silence; kayak,* 1970). Other reflections from about that time connected Plato's Cave with today's movie theater . . . But now an apparently unrelated thought intervenes: "It is not what we understand or know that matters—but what we embrace." For if there is something new in the atmosphere, it is that we seem ready to embrace what we formerly held at arm's length—even turned and ran from. What was then the *menace* shifts, becomes instead the *promise*: consider the Shadow as Cloud—is what we feel apprehension for the oncoming Storm—or do we anticipate the "gift of rain?"

◆

Space/Time: As Shadows
A few days ago there appeared in the paper a report of a group of scientists exploring

the ocean floor around the Galapagos Islands. One of them spoke of a million years as the "blink of an eyelid." He used a metaphor for our existence as a "butterfly dancing beside a redwood tree." What then is the scale, the scope of our imagining?

Mining Shadows—is it more than metaphor? It is if we realize that as the future of the physical world becomes more dubious, the metaphysical becomes more important. As the tangible resources—oil, coal, minerals—continue to dwindle, there is forced a greater interest in the intangible. . . .

As this points toward the future, we recall also the context of what we *inherit*—superbly said in Prospero's famous speech: "Our revels now are ended. These our actors, . . . were all spirits. . . . The cloud-capp'd towers, the gorgeous palaces / The solemn temples, the great globe itself . . . shall dissolve. . . ."

Without the sense of "rise & fall," there is what E. M. Forster wrote in *Aspects of the Novel*: "We move between two darknesses. . ." (Birth and Death). *And we lack a language to communicate with both of these primary states.* Whatever explanation or description we have to offer is from the *secondary* position, where we assume the voice of teacher, poet, priest, doctor, scientist, etc.

But what is it that characterizes the "Shadow as Source?" We might say, relating to the above, that it stems from the unresolved, the "missing dialogue" with the dead and the unborn. That the Shadow dances between What Was, What Is, and What Might Have Been. And this can be condensed into a positive/negative dialectic: *Ever Was/Never Is/Never Was/Always Is.* Our most accessible reference to this is the "Never Never Land." Good enough for children, we suppose, but what else?

Mircea Eliade refers to the universal myth of a "Golden Age"—a time that "never is," but in the racial memory persists as an "always was": *back there then.* But since it is kept alive—often out of consciousness in more sophisticated cultures—returning as dream, as psychic disturbance, it continues to direct present behavior." (In that sense, it remains an "Ever Is.")

We are in need now of some "further translation." The suggestion of the "Golden Age" brings to mind the mythic ideal of the "perfect place, perfect time." But the word *Utopia* itself carries in its root meaning what is literally "no place" and equally "no time." No wonder then that the "dissolving" pronounced by Prospero returns as a perceived world that has neither "beginning nor end" (in contrast to the particular physical entity—which of course decays, dissolves, disappears). It has occurred to me also that *timeless* and *no time* are the same words: only human desire & intention locates pathos & longing in the first, defeat and despair in the second.

———

All of this from the standpoint of what we feel, think, observe. What happens, though, if we shift from "shadow" to "substance"—attempt to approach the "thing itself?" We shall notice, almost at once, how this *approach* is already predetermined by our cultural framework:

1. Suzuki's comparison of a Basho haiku, in which the flowering plant is observed, reflected, meditated upon—and Tennyson's "Flower in the Crannied Wall," which we might seize, remove, use to "understand everything" (thus a vital difference between the Eastern & Western ways of seeing).

2. Something else appears—almost intermediate between these two—in W. C. Williams's book *Spring and All*. First, in "The Rose," in relation to the flower: "The fragility of the flower / unbruised / penetrates space." The quality and force of the thing, as I read it, "in, of and for itself." (It is not there for any human purpose: neither the "seizing" of Tennyson, nor the meditative reflection of Basho.) In the same book appears also the famous poem about the red wheelbarrow: *so much depends / upon // a red wheel / barrow // glazed with rain / water // beside the white / chickens*. As with the flower, the man-made object "stands forth" here in its "thingness," as substantial and real as the "rain water" and the "white chickens." It is this "standing forth" that is the prior condition to the reflection or "shadowing" that takes place in our mind. It is not, however, dependent on our seeing: *so much depends upon* its autonomy and independence; the world otherwise would *only* exist as an object for our contemplation (Basho) or our manipulation (Tennyson).

The ambiguity of Shadow & Substance as fundamental mystery remains— but at least the object, "in, of, and for itself," is offered Being & Presence apart from its possible role within some human "use-value" system.

We come closer now to a consideration of the part played by Image & Event. I dealt with this in the original text (March 31, 1977): "If as we said before, our perceptual system is unable to grasp the 'totality' of any moment, then a certain portion is either 'incomplete' or 'suspended.' It is the sense of these 'unrecognized,' 'unacknowledged' residues that contribute to a feeling of 'apprehension,' of 'uneasiness'—this and the 'acceleration' that so quickly turns what was 'just ahead,' to what is already 'behind' and 'beyond' us . . . ."

These lines recall a poem I wrote more than twenty years ago. The poem, "Doctor, Doctor," has a relevant epigraph from *Macbeth*: "Canst thou not minister to a mind diseased, / Pluck from the memory a rooted sorrow, / Raze out the written troubles of the brain . . ." And its opening lines re-echo the subject at hand: "If all the fall of any moment / hits us and holds us at the door / if now we turn before impending light / between the projected fault and the watched will / to any dream where symbol has passed / but dream or touch the closed address— "

In this example we pass from speculation about "Mining Shadows" to illustrate from experience what it is like *as an activity*. Also by discovering within the self how the apparently "forgotten" can suddenly reappear, we offer evidence that helps to validate a sense of continuity. (This is quite different from any "directed probe" of the unconscious—as in therapy—for as I perceive it, some relevant clue, part of the puzzle emerges: *without being summoned*. Different from dream interpretation too, because there need not be something to "translate," or to interpret.)

—

Self/Word: The Split Presence

The material in *Glimmers Three* at this point "swings away" from this direct concern with "Mining Shadows"—but not entirely: the focus is somewhat narrower here than it was in "Shadow & Substance," but basically the two are closely related. What is different is that what follows is presented in a "series" rather than a "sequence" of shorter reflections— which we hope also reflect upon each other:

—

As Myself/As The One Who

To start first with a particular situation, we offer the example of therapist and client. The presence of the therapist as him/herself, and as the "one who" is there to help. The patient/client has the same "split presence," but with the added dilemma: I am there both *as myself*, and as the "one who" is to be helped. (Note that the "search for identity" is part of the problem.) And what happens when we observe both of them, not in the abstract role, but in the more intimate context of living and loving? It would seem the residues persist, help to form invisible barriers—intrude these elements of "I-Other" even upon the "home grounds" of "I-Thou."

—

Word-Play on "World"

Our next task is to look beyond the concrete setting, the specific situation. And to avoid both cliché and archetype, try to free-associate the word: *A* is a world. *Z* is a world. The intervening space between them is "World"— sometimes thought of as "a" world, sometimes as "the" world. Reflecting on this, looking "outward," I detect its presence: "a world I never made"—in these terms I express my feeling of neutrality, of distance. With a little more negativity: "my world—and welcome to it"—the tone of irony and irreverence. It may be at this point that there arises the need to "negate the negation." And this may take the form of feeling that, after all, I am the "one who" creates the world. That part of it, at least, that lives and dies with me. In this sense then, the world is my invention: as I am myself my own invention. Somehow, though, the sense of responsibility is divided—and we set on opposing courses what comes from "out there" and what belongs "in here." We are even told there is something "characterological" or "psychological" about this: as though "introvert" and "extrovert" were, in fact, inhabitants of different worlds.

"We are all in the same city—living here or passing through—subject to certain visions, which differ according to age, language, temperament. But on those rare occasions when we get together—those who share this particular gift & burden—we somehow all 'point' in the same general direction. (Assuredly, where the 'unseeing' agree there is nothing to be seen.) And we offer each other the solace, the assurance of what we discern: 'Oh yes, certainly, right there through the mist: the towers, the steeple, the lichen-covered stones . . .'"

To paraphrase this: "Visible or invisible, 'IT' is there somewhere." What happens, though, when we take a closer look at IT itself? Already familiar is the "negative role," where IT is considered as the wall or barrier between I and Thou. To balance this, a more "positive" reflection: writing the poem, there is what I want, and what It wants to be. Being receptive to the latter, often leads more directly to "achieved form."

Another example is the role of '*It*ness' in the struggle between teacher and student for control over material and method of presentation. I once outlined contrast between "academic" and "over-subjective":
1. *What It Is* . . . for me.
2. *For Me* . . . what it is.
3. The balanced view: what it is/for me, or the reverse: for me/what it is. (On the same level, it doesn't matter which comes first.)

The World: Dream & Conscious Mind

"After a certain point," wrote Flaubert, "one is never wrong about matters of the soul." Never mind how remote this sounds, whatever it might echo of a stable, long-vanished world. Consider it instead one of those "buried residues," capable still of sending forth longing and pathos for a "higher state."

But whatever it is for the waking, conscious mind, it is something else for the "dream-mind." For the dream-mind presents us with a "symbolic reordering": transposing the literal time, name, number; often making silly "factual mistakes"; letting us know that our attachment to the "literal" or "linear" is the deeper mistake.

Pathos, longing, the symbolic reordering—in what terms can this be discussed? We know that feeling & perception work through the time-sense of "Before and Now." And we are familiar with "turning points" and "transformations." This is perceived as: "Where before there was . . . now there is . . ." On a metaphysical level:

"Where before there was nothing, now there is something." And the reverse of this: before something . . . now nothing.

Applying this to a physical structure (thinking of those caught in an academic mystique) where before there was an "empty space," now there is a collection of buildings called a "university." (A friend uses the phrase: "ivy-covered real estate.")

And what of those who enter these contexts, these suborned structures? We see how quickly this elementary matter, taking form, also takes on the "aura of authority"—the compliance and subjugation of the mind that needs the "verification" offered by these structures.

Even more serious when the "fabrication," the "fiction" is on the scale of a whole country. Joyce Cary, in *Art and Reality*, describes this in terms of the birth and death of symbols: for political reasons a treaty is negotiated, and because there is some mutual advantage for the contending parties, a section of land is set aside and given status as a "new nation." In a short while, a flag is raised, leaders take office. . . . Within weeks there are thousands, perhaps millions, ready to swear allegiance to this "fabrication." Where before there was nothing, now there is something: *to live and die for!*

Carry this over to the related: where before there was no one, now there is "someone." We need only refer to leaders and followers, the visible & the invisible. We see the dynamics of this, on occasion, with the "nameless, voiceless, faceless." This with particular poignancy in the case of the oppressed, the culturally disadvantaged. Every once in a while, one who was "wrapped in shadow" finds a voice, an audience, achieves some temporary recognition. But seldom does this "new being" find the means to effect a thorough-going transformation. More often, once the pathos & rhetoric is discharged, the light subsides. So, many then enter a limbo: unable to advance toward the completely new, unable to accept a retreat to the intolerable old. . . .

◄

Someplace/No Place

Where before there was no place, now there is *someplace*. What does this signify, and what is its importance? If we think of whole populations, having emigrated, lost touch with their origins, it would be hard to exaggerate the emotional pull of a place of origin, a place to arrive—we might say: *where to arrive is to survive*. This whole movement is, of course, filled with illusion, with a whole complex of expectations and "desires"—inherited from, or in reaction to, what is imposed or derived from existing structures.

But this is not intended as a polemic against what is "out there." For if we observe what happens at closer range, we may find an encounter between two "no-ones" (or better: "not-yet-ones"), each seeking "some one" to validate & affirm their own "some-oneness." The "uneasiness" of such an alliance, its potential for recrimination, for resentment, lies in the expectation of a "gift"—which no one has to give. (Just as I cannot create a "something" or a "somewhere" without a rare and fortunate combination of circumstance, materials, resources, so it is not in my power to produce a "someone.")

When Life speaking in its harshest voice says: "I know what you want—but what will you settle for?", we may draw back and speak more from anger than from truth. The question touches our highest anxiety, our deepest fear: that someone can be converted into "any one," something into "any thing," somewhere into "any where."

—

Self/Word/World (continued)

All this may suggest an "inevitability" that is not intended. To avoid this we return to the metaphysical base—with our focus again on: Image & Event—and this time transpose Heidegger's "Why is there something instead of nothing?" In its place we consider: "How does it happen that . . ." My purpose in substituting the "How" for the "Why" is to make more visible, in experiential terms, the possible "unfolding" of the situation in which we find—*or lose?*—ourselves.

But it is not "an answer" that I have to offer—we remember how often the attempt to find or express "first cause" ends in "wreckage" or in "infinite regress." Suppose, though, that we only "document," report, or record the outcome of an event, or series of events: "It so happens that . . ." For me this has the value that it openly expresses the limited role of the observer, that it may "slow down" the drive toward a premature interpretation or conclusion, and helps to restore what we "choose to believe"—as choice, as subjective preference. I would call this a "temporary neutralization" of the event: to set aside and help make visible "intentionality" and need for pattern and design. A subsidiary value of this is to see that the "arbitrary, random elements" do not get submerged. (Note how this appears in popular consciousness: "Well, that's how it goes." Thus the "numbed, pain-free" voice—unable to find any adequate language—as for instance in response to some "unimaginable" disaster.)

Of course a great deal is being disguised and concealed here. If we come back now and complete the phrase: "How does it happen that . . . it turned out this way instead of that way," we may be surprised to hear another voice—at the same level— offer this response: "Well, it so happens that I was there when . . ." And if we hear in this something righteous and assertive, we may be further surprised at the curious transformation of bystander or casual observer into *authoritative witness*! In other words, we have here the example of "mere presence" of a "no-one" or "not-yet-one" suddenly become a "some-one." (Fatigue as "mere repetition"—Whitehead.) But again the "double view" comes into play: if the search is for reassurance, then the "sign of Before" is essential. If it is for novelty, unique experience, then absence of precedent is to be welcomed.

But this too requires amendment: the *seeming* absence of precedent. Understood that this holds only on the level of the transitory—where fashion and small innovations predominate. On a deeper level, as indicated earlier, contact with the "totally unprecedented"—*nothing like us ever was*—brings the sense of cosmic alienation. Continuity, the need to feel connected, turns out to be more pervasive than the need for novelty. (Note: this is no argument against "radical change"—but an observation that even "radical politics," "radical metaphysics" tend to reclaim, to reinterpret what is "essentially human.")

—

The Watcher/The Performer

What happens to "continuity" with the emergence of a "media-directed conscious-ness?" If we think of the professional actor on stage, compared to those seated in the audience, the archetypes of Watcher & Performer are distinct. But on television, anonymous members of the crowd may be selected for a brief "opinion sam-pling." These anonymous persons—traditionally "watchers"—become for this brief moment "performers." It is a commonplace that technology can bring "reversals" of this kind. I mention it here—along with the presence of a third archetype, that of the "Evaluator" or "Mediator"—to get at some basic sources of confusion.

This small example is offered still within a personally experienced sense of time. What happens, though, when through the media, the scale is enlarged, altered, so that the illusion of the whole historical past being accessible becomes operative? One result might be that unconsciously we transpose this to the personal realm, so that "nothing is behind us"—whatever we may have "lived through," can be brought out of "the recesses" and "used against us."

"The whole historical past?" Occasionally in the writing of these *Glimmers*, the phrase resonates, sets off further reflections that are immediately and easily connected. At other times, however, shifts take place and something else emerges—seemingly related, but not easily traceable. This is the case of the "three-part configuration" that I offer now: first to be looked at as a series of words, representing different stages of process:

1. *Inhabit-Besiege-Absorb-Abandon*
2. *Recover-Reverse-Restore-Re-create*
3. *Translate-Transpose-Transform-Transcend*

(Using the "ed" ending, along with the imperative, what happens when we apply the personification: "Conqueror/Victim"? And related to this, as analog or metaphor: "Monuments! Ruins"?)

But this is just the beginning: still within the "historical framework," consider Caesar's "*Veni, vidi, vici*"; the Mongol horsemen; the movement of emigrants "abandoning" the old country, hoping to be "absorbed" into the new, etc. Then make the shift to "interior, personal history." It would seem the same configuration can be used with the psychological as well as the historical framework. Thus we find *symbiosis* in a love relationship, the "scapegoat" or "identified patient," "targeted victim" within the family system. We may even have here a "shorthand version" of the therapeutic process. I permit myself to wonder also how far this could be applied using the language of the physical sciences: what happens at the "molecular" or the "cellular" level?

—

Process
I have this to bring into being—this that does not yet exist. As I give the work form, it acquires presence as itself. The work completed, released, then becomes available for its own subsequent history. Thus it embodies, anticipates and shapes the future. More difficult to express, to believe, is that it does the same with the past: it changes our view of what was there; it activates and animates what was rigid and consigned.
                    (from "Soundings," *kayak* No. 11, 1967)

Still on the subject of Process, let us shift from the personal to the "collective." To evolution as process. We pick up then on the above, and suggest that imagination can be extended as far into the past as into the future. And make the discovery that the focus of our attention *until now* has been based on the *Few Existent*, not on the *Many Vanished*.

François Jacob, a cell geneticist, quotes Peter Medawar: "Scientific investigation begins by 'the invention of a possible world or of a tiny fraction of that world'" ("Evolution and Tinkering," *Science*, June 10, 1977). Jacob also refers to G. G. Simpson's estimate of 500 million species present or vanished during the history of Earth—compared to the "few million" that remain as source for all scientific generalization. Jacob's basic point, however, extends beyond "out of sight, out of mind," toward a metaphor that moves away from the long-held prevailing view of evolution. He suggests that we have accepted evolution as the work of an engineer who, to make a new product, "has at his disposal both material specially prepared to that end and machines designed solely for that task." But more true is the metaphor of the *tinkerer*, who has to work with "odds & ends," with all kinds of "leftovers"—to improvise with whatever residues are still available.

Personal Encounters (Science Division)

In the way that things happen, F. who sent me this article, arrives from the East. (About a year since his last visit.) We spend part of an afternoon talking. Interesting for me to check out some of these glimmers with him.

We talk briefly about Jacob's article, and then F. recalls an article he had sent the year before: "Paleoneurology and the Evolution of Mind," by Harry J. Jerison—*Scientific American*, January 1976. This too, from the point of view indicated by the title, stressed that we are dealing with "possible worlds"—that there are no "certain worlds." At one point in our conversation, F. described a phenomenon known as the *Error Catastrophe*—as I understood it, the "mistake" programmed by Nature in order to permit death and renewal. I could not resist then showing him my "configuration" of "Inhabit-Besiege-Absorb-Abandon," and I was pleased when he felt this could also work—up to and including "translate, transpose, transform, transcend"—on the cellular level.

A week later I talked with N., a physicist. Once more it proved possible to "translate/transpose" the view that there are only possible, and no certain, worlds. We discussed antecedents for this: from Keats's "negative capability" to Heisenberg's Uncertainty Principle. It was following this that N. remarked, concerning the nature of Matter, "We know it is there, but we don't know where *there* is." (Nice to think of Gertrude Stein eavesdropping at this point.)

Self/Word/World (continued)

Looking over the pages that immediately precede this, there is much about "Self" and "World"—almost nothing about "Word." The material for this comes not as a conscious effort to "right the balance," but arrives almost unnoticed. For there are times when a particular reflection seems so small, so unimportant, it barely misses being discarded. We might say it comes uninvited—a scruffy kid who sneaks in under the tent flap. (Who would dream that, after only a short interval, it would appear "center stage," commanding so much attention?)

Such is the case with the Glimmer on the "obliged person." It starts modestly enough (original text, Sept. 27,1977):

I can no longer pinpoint where & how this started, but note a small phrase that has continued to resonate: Who is "obliged" in what ways, what situations? How does this relate to & differ from "responsibility"? Is there such a thing as being "under-obliged," "over-obliged," even *dis-obliged*? Can the "obliged person" suddenly shift course—recognizing perhaps some danger to his own self-preservation—and with a flip-flop become "unobliged?"

I have just been reading Aileen Ward's biography of Keats. Her account shows the ambiguous acts of some of Keats' closest friends: how "obligation" and "resentment" circle each other. Sometimes this is visible, blatant, at others subtle, paradoxical—especially with Brown, Keats' closest friend, who appears as the most "giving, until the crucial time before Keats' trip to Italy. From then on he becomes the most denying and deceiving . . .

A bit more appears in an entry the following day:

> What I wrote yesterday . . . focuses on feeling "obliged" toward other people. What needs to be added is something about being obliged toward the Self: taking care, keeping things together . . . But a closer view shows: "obliged to perform at a certain level, in a certain way." I am reminded of the Little Red Hen: the super-responsible creature who will do what "needs to be done"— even when no one else will follow her example. Curious about this: it may bring the individual to leadership and power—or to self-destruction.

Reading this over, what emerges now is:

1. The "obliged person" has not an "obligation," but an *obligement*—a made-up word to suggest the *feeling* of being obliged. Note the simple sentence that puts matters where they belong: "I feel obliged—but I am not obligated."

2. The notion of "under," "over," "dis" obliged is easily illustrated: our example is that of asking directions on the street, and the responses:

    a. A wave of the hand, a few mumbled words: "It's over there" (under-obliged).

    b. A shrug, head shake, quick march off (dis-obliged).

    c. With empathy for the stranger, disrupting one's own way, taking him there (over-obliged).

(Note: Kafka's parable about the stranger asking directions of a policeman— and the shocking, incredible reply: "Give up, give up.")

As we touch here the basic question of "giving and receiving," I recall the distinction made by Erich Fromm: there are two kinds of conscience:

1. The Personal

2. The Authoritarian

The "personal" represents the inner sense of what needs to be done. The "authoritarian," whatever comes from the outside—from *any* institution, authority, religious group, etc.

Fromm says that one can only truly give out of a *surplus*. Not as a "replacement" or depletion of the necessary "self-giving," but an extension of this when it is possible. Whatever is perceived as response to an "external demand" can be damaging—an extra weight rather than the "overflow" of abundant inner feeling.

I have now to make an "experiential" rather than "theoretical" reference. Checking this out with several friends, I find that the "obliged person" sets up an "aura of expectation." This suggests that he can always be "counted upon," ready to respond, to give as much or more than is asked for. Curious that this becomes so habitual, so invisible, that the "obliged person" is made to feel he has failed, or *defaulted*, when not able to respond.

I have gone into this in some detail, partly as preparation, as background to what appears in brief form as an entry dated October 8, 1977: "Some key words: obliged/obligated, life/living, susceptible/vulnerable . . . We may have here a general proposition: it appears that sometimes there is a word next to the word we are using or looking at, which is so 'almost like' that it obscures, closes off what we most need to penetrate."

This coincides with the feeling that words have an "interior life" that we are scarcely aware of. It is a common experience that at some intense moment we suddenly "run out of language." The words or phrases we are looking for are either not available—or do not exist. At this point it occurs to us that something needs to be invented—or perhaps re-invented, re-combined, re-ordered. (Joyce, Stein, cummings, Heidegger, etc.)

As a variation on this: "There are times when the critic can only point" (Lionel Trilling on Tolstoy's *Anna Karenina*). The critic reaches a place where comment is absurd, unnecessary. He can only extend the finger: "It's right there." Note, though, that this tells us *where*—leaving us to guess: how, what, when and why. And we might also consider: "A finger pointing at the moon is not the moon" (Japanese Zen saying).

We want to say a little more about words. But nothing ponderous or difficult. Perhaps we would do better to hear from a child rather than a critic or linguist. Here is a five-year-old talking about words:

> How much space does a word take? Words are thin little things. But some of them make a big noise. You couldn't take hold of a word. What if the words were made of something? I mean if they were real, if you could touch them, if they were *things*. Then there would not be room for anything else in the world, would there? Who decides about the words? Who made them up first? Why do you use the words that somebody else decided? Why couldn't we make up some for us? ("Experience of Philosophy" by H. M. Lynd, from *Essays on Teaching*, ed. Harold Taylor, Harpers, 1950.)

◆

We have tried here making up "something for us." Not as a structure, an invention, but an attempt to follow the "winding way" (. . . *the way is only wavering*—Kafka). And it seems time now to start "winding down." For whatever has been left unsaid—and there are still a few more reflections to record—remains for future Glimmering. The Glimmer then is the smallest thing—just enough to remind us of the surrounding darkness. But it serves a purpose: appearing briefly at the periphery of attention, it marks a zone not previously noticed. It breaches the darkness enough to suggest *habitation* in areas we had considered uninhabited. (Perhaps a single campfire that might offer—not yet the possibility of rescue—but at least the warmth of human company.)

A few words, we are saying, a very few words can make a difference. Echoing the insistent questioning of the five-year-old, we wonder: How few—and which words? I had considered adding a section here to be called "The Three-Word World." This based on the "subjective span" of our feeling about the world, condensed to: Yes, No, Maybe. And to the more "objective," relating to the cosmic sense: The One/The Other/The All. But that will have to wait. For now, we will choose only one of these "possible triads," reflecting on the articulation so far of "Self, Word, and World." This is the notion that what comprises an *entity* is: Suchness-Withness-Towardness. That I am myself, with others, going toward something. (A situation I share with an amoeba, a tree, a stone.) Where human invention enters, there is added "betweenness" and "otherness." But perhaps for a tree, a stone, there is also "betweenness" and "otherness:": the flowering and the "barren" state—smoldering ash for the tree, and uprooting, displacement, and reduction to sediment for the stone.

◆

Suchness/Withness/Towardness

Refocussing on the life of the entity—wondering what makes it self-sufficient, what disturbs its equilibrium—we move in for a closer look. Note that we are not seeking pattern, or any grand design. But to make a simple statement that balances "subject" and "object": as I am Myself, so it is Itself. (This is neither to project nor introject.) Thus the mutuality of *Suchness*. As I "go toward" fulfillment on one hand, decay and dissolution on the other, *it too* partakes of the same process. Thus the mutuality of *Towardness*. (I have not forgotten the dialectic of Going Toward/Away from—but feel this is encompassed here.) Our real problem, it would seem, is with the remaining word: *Withness*. It is here that we are predisposed to think "with the Other," "with Others," and thus introduce the negative overtones of "Betweenness" and "Otherness." To overcome this I suggest—and this is in contrast with what Octavio Paz and others have called "radical solitude"—that I am *with myself*, that I have myself *for company*. This even before, but not in contradiction to, being with others. My sense of this is expressed in the poet Delmore Schwartz's phrase, quoting Whitehead: *the withness of the body*. (Also: *within-ness*.)

And perhaps after this, I may now complete the refrain: as I *am* with myself, so *it is* with Itself. Thus the mutuality of *Withness*.

The objection to this, of course, is that we have made a "construction" in an abstract realm. When it comes to the "real world" of social roles, of conflicting desires, images, ambitions, none of this will serve. But even if this is so, we may have at least shown the "seeds of conflict"—as well as a possible harmony—as being already there: not *per se* the result of the "intrusion" of "betweenness" and "otherness." Also that as a side effect of this "entity topology," there may be less need for "the language of pathology." As if to say with Whitehead: "Life itself is a disturbance in matter."

Toward a Definition of Presence

Leaving out the steps or the "trajectory" that brought us here—just to establish a context—I present these *Five Kinds of Presence*:

1. I am here—as Myself. (In, of, for and by myself: as *pure presence*.)
2. As the One Who—does and is done to. Who watches, performs, evaluates (as basic archetypes: Watcher/Performer/Evaluator).
3. The One from Whom—certain things are expected. (Note: This operates from birth. Prevents any full view of what the "natural bent," unaffected, not tampered with, might be.)
4. As More or Less than Myself: Symbolic Figure, Living Presence, Historical Being.
5. *As That Which*—in the many aspects to be discussed. (Note: The spectrum or continuum from "pure presence" to "pure function"—from the *Suchness* of "my own body" to the completely objective *As That Which*, in its aspect of "anonymous, omnipotent authority.")

As That Which (continued)

The dual aspect of "As That Which" is first as a tool or instrument to be used, manipulated—then "that which" uses tools or instruments for *its own* purposes. (Note: the impenetrable mystique of *its own*.) It would seem, at this point, that the *conversion* of subject into object is complete. But this is premature. We have still to consider residues of pathos & longing—which brings into view *The Task*, with *its* needs taking precedence over my "need to be." Also the aspect of "that which endures," presenting the paradox that it contains also "that which confers" *benefits* that range from immediate solace to "eternal life": *The Source* (original text: April 24,1977).

Also from *The Source*: "This time in the aspect of Structures *in which* we are forced to believe: Laws, Society, Institutions, Culture. The autonomy and sanctity they acquire as enduring 'Operating Principles,' i.e., As That Which 'needs to be served'" (April 26, 1977).

As That Which: *The Temple*. "The Temple as Manifest." Needs to be *preserved*. Intersection within its walls of *The Hidden and the Manifest*. (The alternation of dark recesses, spaces, objects, images that "burst forth" in radiant light.) Note that there is worship of, as well as worship in, the Temple. That as "manifest" it is matter over spirit, structure over Dream. But with the sometimes *punishing*, sometimes *redeeming* feature: it is also "physical sanctuary" offered as the embodiment of "spiritual salvation." (When Jesus says it can be torn down and rebuilt in three days—that may be an analog to indicate that *as matter* the structure itself is of no great importance.)

I have already noted the "positive" aspects of *Task* (goal, motive, direction) and of *Source* (roots, origins, spirit-giving). What has not been said, though, is that, with all this, "the machinery of Expectation" is set in motion. As expressed or concealed deep in popular consciousness, it translates into: "Why don't *They* take care of these things?" (The unconscious personification of what is often "mere machinery": *They* equals the Government, the Corporation, any governing body.)

As That Which (continued)

How far can this lead, and in what direction? We have to go beyond the usual commonplaces of frustration, resentment, corruption. For we have here, at the outer edges, the more sinister result that the "deranged" individual decides to "take care of *them*." What was the "law unto itself" translated into the "law unto himself." This suggests that when the "As That Which" is internalized, what may emerge is the *terrorist*. (That the Artist is sometimes situated in a similar—though "nonviolent" way—has been commented upon many times.)

Finally, the Word itself stands before us *As That Which* signifies, embodies, the Thing itself. And beyond this? It would be good to "round off" this reflection, but that would be artificial, a violation of what remains an active point of reference. Say then that we have "drawn the circle"—and within the circle, lines that reach from "pure presence" to "pure function." And suggested "points of intersection," the sense also of "turning points." Glimmering still in wonder at the range that extends from self-preservation to participation in a sense of "immortal allness." It would seem then that—whatever is given, whatever is taken away—all this together absorbs the name of "Circumstance." Ortega said it briefly and well: "I am myself plus my circumstance." *As That Which* then—real, invented, imagined—is the total matrix, the grid, the surroundings we know as *World*.

All very well, says the inner dissenting voice, *but you haven't heard the end of me yet*. And with this, we presume, lifts a word off the page, holds it up to the light. Assuming from past experience the negative presence, we inquire: *Is Anything Wrong?* It says nothing: merely returns the word to the page, and begins very slowly to move toward the door. To see if I can stop the retreat, the vanishing, I offer the words of others: "Glory, Jest and Riddle." No answer. I try again: "Feast, Spectacle, Predicament." Still no answer. I know what I want to say next—but I'm not sure whether to whisper or shout: "Please keep the door open when you leave."

—*L. F.*
February 1978

Notes and Further Work-Points to *The Book of Glimmers*

Glimmers One: *Unfinished Circumstance*

p. 279: *The Nature of Glimmers*: "As If . . . the bridge." There is some connection with Vaihinger's *The Philosophy of 'As If.'* As excerpted by Havelock Ellis (in *The Dance of Life*), we have a choice between "good" and "bad" fictions, and while we have no real access to "truth," we can regulate our errors. (I prefer "necessary" and "unnecessary" fictions.) Note that I have shifted the ground from what we may believe to what we may perceive.

p. 280: *On the Grounds of Being*: "Being as belonging." Some appropriate metaphors: support system, sanctuary, network. "We exist at the center of a network of responsibilities" (John Cheever). Toynbee has written that our existence is made possible within a "network situation." Also, the Zen allegory of Indra's net: "There is an endless net of threads throughout the universe." All of this suggests we are more *part of*—than *apart from*.

    Being and Having (cf. Gabriel Marcel's book of that title). To apply this to American historical experience, as it relates to "American character": "The land was ours before we were the land's. . . / Possessing what we still were unpossessed by" (Robert Frost).

p. 281: *The Who as What*: the "Imposter." Northrop Frye in *Anatomy of Criticism: Four Essays* describes the archetypes of the Alazon and the Eiron. The former inflates the Self with dreams of unlimited power; while the latter deprecates and demeans the Self. It may be difficult for the "Imposter" himself to tell which, at any given moment, is in charge. Modern literature offers an endless supply of "Imposters" and "Confidence Men" (Melville's *The Confidence-Man*, Faulkner's *The Reivers*, Mann's *Confessions of Felix Krull*.")

p. 282: *It may be useful* . . . Re What Could Be: *the primrose* (cf. *The Burning Fountain*, Philip Wheelwright, Indiana University, 1968). Without referring to Ruskin, Wheelwright quotes the description of the flower by the poet John Clare: "With its little brimming eye / and its crimp and curdled leaf." He then examines comments on this by I. A. Richards and J. M. Murry. Richards, according to Wheelwright, separates the "actual flower" from what we experience. The purpose of *What Could Be* is to unite what we see and touch with what we imagine.

p. 284: *Culture vs. Self*: The *natural bent*. Perhaps this is more visible outside our species. Watching kittens or puppies, we may observe one who hides, one who plays, one who aggresses. This suggests an effort might be made to find or design an environment suitable for the particular personality. But there is scarcely ever intention or means to apply this in a human context.(cf. W. Van Dusen, *The Natural Depth in Man*, Harper & Row, 1972).

p. 286: *Crossing Time*: Merchandising and Legendizing: The effort is also to "humanize" and "personalize" the product and the corporation.

p. 289: *Endless Reproductions*: "to make everything accessible . . ." Marshall McLuhan, in *From Cliché to Archetype* (Viking, 1970), explores the role of what he calls "memory retrieval" and "cliché probe." His emphasis is on our having reached a point where "discovery" quickly turns into cliché. "Memory retrieval" is used then to "re-present" the archetype—perhaps in some new disguise—to replace the latest cliché.

p. 290: *On Viewing & Vision*: "the judgment of the Hidden upon the Manifest" is characteristic of many religions, "esoteric" writings, the Kabbala, Sufi doctrine, etc. ("Thou shalt not make unto thee any graven image" is the most familiar.)

    I have to modify here the suggestion of what "will be, but is *not yet* manifest." With this implication of the "inevitable," I had forgotten the subtle theology of indefinite postponement. (Waiting for the Messiah—or for Godot.) Aside from this, there is something here of particular interest for writers. J. D. Crossan writing on Borges (*Raid on the Articulate*, Harper & Row, 1976) quotes the French critic Gérard Genette: "A book is . . . a reservation of forms that are waiting to have some meaning, it is the 'imminence of a revelation that is not yet produced,' and that every one of us has to produce for himself." Crossan then comments: "It is here that Borges's *permanently imminent revelation* and Jesus' *kingdom of God* intersect with one another" (p. 170).

    "The force that sustains." Dylan Thomas's line fits here: "The force that through the green fuse drives the flower / Drives my green age. . . ." Creative force, as expressed in Nature and Art, may be an *alternative* to violence (cf. my long poem: "Time to Destroy/to Discover," Panjandrum Press, 1972).

Glimmers Two: *Weights/Measures/Affections*

p. 293: *On Sacrifice & Discovery*: not only Freud, but Jung as well, experienced sacrifice in his life and work—and in the "separation" when their paths diverged (cf. *C. G. Jung*, by Anthony Storr, Modern Masters, Viking, 1973).

p. 295: *In reworking these Glimmers*: "Where is the 'You'. . . " Buber suggests somewhere that God is also seeking Man: "And where art *thou*?" But to return to the "You," there is an eloquent statement on this by Maurice Natanson: "The specification of the 'you' as a concrete individual makes it much more difficult to say with honesty and insight, 'I know that you will die.' What is intended instead is something closer to, 'You are one of those who will die.' When the 'you' is intimately known, related and loved, when the Other is addressed as 'Thou' . . . it is as difficult to say 'I know that you will die' as it is to say of oneself 'I know that I will die'" (*The Journeying Self*, Addison-Wesley, pp. 136–37).

p. 295: *Access/Refuge*: "the open door . . . the closed door." Also the perennial notion of the *Magic Key* to the *Magic Door*. The archetypal "Seekers" ready to proclaim: "*This is It*." In a short while, however, they begin looking for another *It*; and soon the previous "revelation" is not only discarded but forgotten.

p. 296: *Entrance/In Trance*: "Excessive empathy." Aileen Ward, in her Keats biography, uses "entering into" to indicate Keats's painfully close identifications with friends and with significant objects . . . Frank O'Connor made a distinction between "I am your brother" and "you are myself." The first involves a sense of solidarity; the second, which suggests "to become the other," is a risky further step few are prepared to take.

   The Necessary Angel is Wallace Stevens's study of the creative imagination. In my "Glimmering" I have located the Angel at the "Gate" in Hesiod's Theogony. Deriving from this is the view that entrance gained by such means as drug use is a violation of the "compact" one makes with the Angel. One can only approach "this far"; beyond this, the decision is "out of our hands." I even fantasize the Angel saying: "Wait here. It'll take a while to process your application."

p. 296: *Discovery: Promise & Menace*: Parody of paradigm: "existing models wear out so quickly . . ." A science-fiction film presented seriously and with much fanfare is parodied a few weeks later on television. The "lead time" before certain "works of art" are imitated or parodied is equally short. ("Acceleration" as a historical force is already observed by Henry Adams, writing in the opening years of this century: *The Education of Henry Adams*.)

   Devotion, Indulgence, and Necessity. In the original text of the *Glimmers*, a suggestion was made that the same words could be used in the parent-child relationship. The notion of the same, or similar, elements being present in the creative process and in child-rearing might stand some further exploration.

p. 297: *A Brief View of Necessity*: What *I* Want/What *it* Wants to Be. Ortega y Gasset in *Some Lessons in Metaphysics* makes the point that we are one with "Tree" and "Stone." In contrast with both the traditional "realist" position and the "idealist" position, as formulated by Descartes, Ortega finds our being with things is "interdependent and coexistent."

". . . there for us . . . just there": In line with the note here that precedes this, there is also W. C. Williams's "No ideas but in things" and Husserl's "To the things themselves." As a view of how the pendulum swings, it has occurred to me that recent "conceptual" art and photography may be saying in effect: "No things—but in ideas." (As a further *nicety*, Husserl's seminal work, first published in 1913, is entitled *Ideas* in the English edition.)

p. 298: *Another Word on Necessity*: "Does *it* have to be?" Also the comment on "problems and solutions." Margaret Mead once offered the "modest proposal" that, instead of reforming the educational system, it should be eliminated. She also said: "There are no problems, no solutions . . . but everything we have done—or failed to do—has brought us here." I see this as applying an "evolutionary" view—on a scale larger than "me and my lifetime"—which can also be read as "revolutionary." While these are traditionally "worlds apart," the poet C. Day Lewis has them neatly linked together: "Evolution is the dance; revolutions are the steps."

p. 299: *Toward a Definition of Event*: "Our need for patterns among the visible." Note the historic role of Muybridge's horse—what it meant for photography and film. The role of "slow motion," not only as technique but as metaphor: "stop-time" (the later technique of "freezing" the frame). Recently I related this to Alfred Stieglitz's statement: "To show the moment to itself is to liberate the moment." And then made the further association to W. C. Williams—the altered-time sense can be traced in American poetry through Creeley and others to the present day. (A splendid and stimulating account of Williams and Stieglitz is Bram Dijkstra's *The Hieroglyphics of a New Speech: Cubism, Steiglitz and the Early Poetry of William Carlos Williams*—Princeton, 1969.)

p. 299: *Being & Existence*: As an earlier statement on a related theme, I wrote: "*I am* and *I live*. The essential self of the *I am* is seen here in conjunction with an existential *I live* . . . I see myself in the world, moving through the scene: the 'living' image. But it is always 'that one' that I see. (There is no 'photograph' of the soul.) The *I Am* remains invisible. . . . sent on a journey, it heads inevitably toward the country of dream and fantasy" ("Concentric Propositions," *Main Currents in Modern Thought*, September–October 1969). I would have to add now: "heads toward the 'Castle'— or even toward the 'Enchanted Cottage.'"

p. 300: *On Aphorisms*: The Conspiracy to Pretend: for another view relating to this, there is Gaston Bachelard's use of "simulation" and "dissimulation" ("The

Phenomenology of the Mask," from *The Right to Dream*, Orion Press). The role of Mask and Mime in tribal cultures—particularly in rituals of "healing ceremonies"—also relates here.

p. 300: *Another "set" with the same. . .* : *The Way It Ifs*: In the original text there was the line: "Life that was hazard has become pure accident." For a long time I found useful Sartre's term "Contingency." But this no longer seems adequate: recent technology makes us so vulnerable to the random, careless act that we need the stronger term of "pure accident."

Glimmers Three: *Mining Shadows*

p. 305: *Self/Word: The Split Presence*: "series and sequence." This needs to be—as in a different form it was in the original text—the subject of a separate reflection: *Series*: a number of different views and aspects of the subject that illustrates various possibilities without being definitive. (*One follows the Other.*) *Sequence*: the subject as it unfolds, develops, moves toward an *outcome*. (*One follows* from *the Other.*) What might be applied here also is a comparison of how each deals with the "machinery of Expectation": briefly, that *Series* neglects or "puts it aside," while *Sequence* uses it to negate or affirm something that was there in the beginning, but has been altered or transformed by the end (cf. many of Shakespeare's sonnets, as examples of *Sequence*, "overthrow" or "flip-flop" the premise of their opening lines).

p. 305: *Word Play on "World"*: "WHAT IT IS . . . for me." Imagine the capitalized words a foot high and the others barely visible, to indicate the range between the "academic" and the "over-subjective."

p. 306: *The World: Dream & Conscious Mind*: "Where before there was 'empty space . . .' " The phenomenology of the "Filled" and the "Empty" has been engagingly described by Vilém Flusser (in *Main Currents in Modern Thought* magazine, circa 1972), and by Bachelard (*The Poetics of Space*, Beacon, 1969).

"One who was 'wrapped in shadow' achieves temporary recognition." A friend quotes Andy Warhol: "In the future, everyone will be world-famous for fifteen minutes."

p. 308: *Self/Word/World*: "The search for 'first cause' ends in 'Wreckage.' "(cf. John Gardner's novel *The Wreckage of Agathon*).

"The sense of cosmic alienation." The science-fiction film *Close Encounters of the Third Kind* has been promoted here with the slogan: *We Are Not Alone*. This prompts the wisecrack: "Right at a time when we seem beyond help—we are seeking help from *The Beyond*."

p. 309: *The Watcher/The Performer*: On the late, late movie, one can watch and evaluate performances by actors some of whom are alive, some dead. One wonders: What does this do to the "natural" perceptual system?

p. 312: *Reading this over* . . . "Two kinds of conscience." As to the word itself, *conscience* brings to mind the related *remorse*. In Joyce's phrase this becomes "agenbite of inwit." When we recall the Spanish *mordida* (the bribe as "bite'), we see that Joyce has indeed put "teeth" back into the dead word.

p. 313: *I have gone into this* . . . : "A finger pointing at the moon . . ." I have a childhood memory of a "retarded" child on our street: he would point at the sky and say: "The moon is to me. The moon is not to you." I see this now as a "primordial" expression of a one-to-one correspondence with what is vast and out of reach.

p. 314: *We have tried here* . . .: "Make up some for us:" A friend's four-year-old calls a hammer a "*prim, prim.*" Because, we assume, that's how it sounds to him. We also assume language as a social instrument, with approved and fixed usage—but forget those earlier private & invented words. (The *personal* language of a particular biological entity? Schizophrenics, we're told, have their own world, their own language. Is it possible to look at this as an unwillingness—or inability—to give up what was originally and rightfully theirs?)

p. 314: *Suchness/ Withness/ Towardness*: This seems to me one of the central notions in these *Glimmers*. Note that changing the order here can suggest different priorities; that the presence or role of each can be augmented or diminished—to the point where one or the other can seem to be absent or all-present. (*Suchness*: with little or no need for human company; *Withness*: in harmony with others; *Towardness*: "goal-directed.") As absolutes, these, of course, are fictions; yet there is some value in attempting to bridge the distance between the abstract quality and the concrete life of the individual. First, the sense of "blend" or "composite" that might be desired; second, although these are "awkward" terms, they are more "neutral" and "universal" than any to be found in the language of pathology. And they may also have the advantage that they call attention to what composes an entity—and in linking human life with other entities.

p. 314: *As That Which*: "The dissenting voice." This may be only part of the standard "I-Me" dialogue (a sample appears in M. Natanson, *The Journeying Self*, already cited). But also can be heard as the "detractor," or as Frye's Eiron, in response to the Alazon.

"Glory, Jest, and Riddle": from Pope's *Essay on Man*. (Where we also find the case for man's "Betweenness": "In doubt to act, or rest / In doubt to deem himself a God, or Beast . . ."

"Feast, spectacle, predicament": from one of Santayana's essays: "Life is not a feast, not a spectacle, but a predicament."

Addendum: Toward a Three-Word World:

In addition to the "Triads" offered here—and those found elsewhere in the *Glimmers*—I wish to add two more: Process/Content/Context and Situation/ Occasion/Event. At first glance, Process and Content may suggest familiar discussions in a number of fields—but the subjective experience of "Context" varies so widely from the "objective" description or explanation that they are often not to be reconciled. The sense of "Context" is also hampered by lack of perspective from always being within a situation. Never having experienced being totally "other" or totally "elsewhere," we are unprepared for the radical difference in the simplest, most familiar aspects of living (making a phone call in a foreign country; preparing food in a prison kitchen). "Glimmering" presents no end of surprises. Just before writing this, my "mind-set" was to relate Process/Content/Context with Suchness/ Withness/Towardness. (More serious thought, further reflection would probably—in my own mind at least—vindicate this.) Instead, I seem to have set up—by relating "Context" and "Situation"—a possible "configuration" linking those six words. Thus the "random" intercession may have its own validity. *And so it comes. And so it goes . . .*

Afterword to *The Book of Glimmers*

This book is the outcome of a process: it has both direct and indirect antecedents. I trace the "indirect" through decades of reflection; the "direct" to a specific date, February 1976, when I wrote to Don Cushman of Cloud Marauder Press. My original suggestion was to extend, through correspondence, things we had talked about over the years. When it became clear his editorial duties would not leave enough time, I continued on my own, setting down various notions, gathering material from past notebooks.

In April of that year, I wrote Anthony Rudolf, publisher of Menard Press, asking if I could send this material. He responded favorably, urging me to continue, and kept encouraging me as one "installment" followed another. By January 1978, I had accumulated and mailed over three hundred pages: the *original text* from which this derives.

The present text, in turn, is linked also to reflections that remain ongoing. This suggests again that, more than the specific content, we have here an illustration of process. (As of this writing, I have accumulated another hundred pages that extend and change what is presented here.)

The "Notes and Work-Points" are, in this same spirit, intended to open avenues toward further exploration.

—L. F.
June 1979

from
Unlawful Assembly:
A Gathering of Poems,
1940-1992

(1994)

for and with Justine
and with the memory of Ruth Witt-Diamant
and Édouard Roditi

Letter to a Friend, 1941

Finally the news came this morning
And it seemed the day grew short
And all at once lateness came into the air
And I wondered what had happened to the day.
Now suddenly there were things to tell
There were the minutes running through my fingers
While I tried to put into words what was not really words,
And the telling was not to be easy, even with you, listener.
That is because failure is not easy, and retreat is not.

There is no way of saying this is what it means, or I have lived that.
Not long ago it seemed the mark was clear, the sight telescoped, the range sure.
Then the target was vague, the aim unsteady, the brush near.
Time passed, hunger grew, and we were the hunted.
Not long ago there was a classbook promise in the afternoon,
A voice calling us to be career-bound, the way was known.
Then it was a strange land, and the passports canceled.

Time passed, we strayed and wandered
From the city to where the forest loomed ahead—
Remember: Standing there among the watchful trees:
The alien wind stirred our hair and fingers—
How those birds flew shrieking from the branches?

In That Which Passes

Looking Backward

Who lived here then? The name should reach
to gather the filings, hold fast, protect
the thread of vision—yet where is one
to believe and revere? Former tenants
supply stories of this house:

Some went this way: the view of machines
held attention for days: the carousel
and the cyclotron turning . . .

Some went down in the strangeness
of valleys   others to die on the acreage
where they were born. I recall passion vines
in the garden. The steady work of shears
kept nerves from tangling. Children full of guile
peered through the windows. Priests & neighbors
took sides in the quarrels. A few made appeal
to a higher court: their claim for damages
suffered in the course of aborted careers.

But choose no resemblance: as it quickens
let it fall: let memory create the country,
laws that serve the season of endurance.

1969

Looking Toward

Neither the high temple, nor the narrow house
washed into the sea; neither the recovery
of what was lost, nor the will to imagine
what might be done. A time of demons
for the unsuspecting; a game for children
left on the crystal-white sands: the legacy
of uncoiled wire rusting, mines buried on the dunes.

I view it often: sleep sends the current:
waist-high in the water, the whine of wings,
bathers running faster than the clouds—
Time spurts past the play of shadows:
those beaches where the years went down
signed and delivered: a fountain of gunfire
where swimmers dived to the nearest death.

Each time the chalk cliffs are assaulted
faces harden toward tomorrow   each time
the house sways   the seawind rises   children disappear.
Where are the features   of things to be done
the death of warfare   the worlds unsigned?
Here at the flood of voices—even as tides trend—
speech breaks light forth: saying again.

1969

Landing in Idaho

1.

Seated close to the visible pilot we look
past the directional voices toward a range
of hills that astonish: snow islands and the white
encore of clouds—*a loved whiteness*—dropping down
to vertical stones and trees we cannot name—
diverted then by our uncommon breathing
we cannot stabilize what is ray or radium
within the fractured circle of our drifting glance.

2.

Emerging into the real afternoon we take
our first wavering steps: testing the weighted ground
of a small-town airport—whose name we are
not yet ready to remember. Our friends greeting
and having luggage to seize and identify
helps clarify our role—at least as entities.

3.

Days later we acquire the aspect of visitors
present for obvious and reasonable reasons:
we shop and sample the local restaurants—
the daily special of *trout* from the nearby rivers—
and even register that the town—*Ketchum*—is named
for someone's great-grandfather. That it has a library
and that Hemingway—beside three pines—is buried here.

4.
Getting ready to return we wonder about
the contradiction of choice scenery for sale
and a clarified sky that promises a place
we could occupy and claim signifying more than
climbers skiers or real estate agents could define.

I try to remember that the airport is actually
in the adjoining town *Hailey*—where Pound was born.

1979

Riding the Bus in Sicily

Time faces this way
whenever we are called upon
between evening and the dark voices
to fulfill or violate the fading hour. . . .

Driving past towns where sleep
and waking flow through winding streets
where notices tacked on warped doors
border in black the short simple names—

The driver never turns his head
while the clenched hands and gnarled faces
tense toward the horizon: the archaic horsemen
shadowed by boulders and violent dreams . . .

Turning on blind curves
we watch gray trees and yellow dust
assemble that island where silence
is honored: learn once as always
we cannot choose the country
nor dissipate the faces staring
into space beside the scarred doorways. . . .

1977

Italy, 1978

Whether it was the garlanded corpse
we saw floating in the carved gondola
or between dark pines the falcon descending
straight to the bent arm of the falconer—
We came to believe in the uncommon encounter
that verifies flesh in its hour of transformation:
moving with the crowd toward the circular light
that enclosed the form of David: just when he moved
and the ambiguous tourists became more nearly stone—

All this dissolving now upon the screen
projecting images that certify an intolerable view
of the occupied country: under the strained light
of uncivil warfare that amplifies each gesture
and truant whisper to identify the moving target
from among the random & unaligned figures
following the measurable ways of ordinary living—

We shift allegiance to those seeking release
from the night of killing games: those who leave
no inscriptions carved upon the triumphal arch—
but follow always the same disarmed longing
to carry them past the ruined circus & the horseman
cast in bronze—we offer them our useless affection
for temperate weather: the warm intrigue of memory
trailing daylight through the splintered stones

1978

On the Death of Aldo Moro (Rome, May 9, 1978)

1.
Before our minds are mobilized
to meet the next disaster—and this particular agony
fades into something vague as rainfall
in the downpour of besieging images
that present the whole spectrum of affliction
parading on glass on the evening news—

We reach for the living presence: whoever was there
feeling real in the aroma & idiom of his body
before the shootout & abduction turned flesh
into facsimile: the figure outlined in a dark suit
retrieved from the steel floor of a stolen car . . .

As we sift through the ambiguous evidence
that includes the complex pleading messages
and the simple farewell: "I kiss you. Kiss the children"
we find clues that restore the human semblance
in the decision to reject the raucous funeral
spectacle for the needs of the temporal state:
"The family closes itself in silence."

But then there intrudes the melancholy face
some remember as the professor of criminal law
at home in the labyrinth of qualifying clauses—
and the legend already growing postmortem
deep in resonant cathedrals & high in exterior walls
slashed with words that compress rage & mourning. . . .

2.

Buried now outside a village whose name
we need not bother to remember
he is gathered deep in the unforgetting skin
of those who dream for themselves   the rounded stone
lowered to the ground   and the long slow walk
of abandoned mortality: from there we imagine

He leaves the fact-world—in which he was vulnerable—
to enter a dream scenario: where the light-filled flesh
narrows the range between the silenced living
and the silent dead—until something appears
more than a puzzle for sculptors: perhaps an emblem
                    for our always groping fingers.

1978

Year of the Bloodhound

Year of the bloodhound: of the foremost nose
that follows the concept back to the flesh:
the trail with wheat stalks, asphalt, and a kiss;
in the beast's brain is a memory of treason:
in the flight toward corners of the calendar
over blossoms and ice, the verdict of baying.

Year of the honored ear that lived on wire
and guilt shrilled in a voice of neighbors—
the finger endowed from the witness stand
points to the downed one in a winter of weeds,
and the fable formed in the amateur mouth
spreads on the shrinking city like moss.

Year of the queer, legal hunters: of the twelve
who appear in the posse: with the season open
on john-the-doe: with the no-limit flesh
circled in the cross—death is not the falter
and the failing, but in the fanged now
as steel measures to the bending bone—

But who in the chase wears the dry throat,
crying ho for the fox of the future—
far from rifle and gavel, aloft in the fields?
Who fills the tracks with the size of his shoes
and as the punctured image forgets to fall,
learns to travel apart from the stalked name?

1952

Song for the Ending of the Year

One by one the subjects disappear:
The gift of speech is going with the year,
In company with silence and with fear.

The package on the table waits to be untied.
The Child, the Tree are left inside
The House—no message from the crucified.

We ride the painted hobby-horse of days,
Or stand aside, or join the latest craze—
Next year's another box, another maze.

1966

Studying the Season

More than ever
what's left of their voices
is distributed among wandering children
and men locked inside themselves.

The sound is errant and deformed:
the scream of one is silence to another:
the coming together and the giving way
represented by a single word.

The time becomes attuned
to the calm, slow death of strangers:
the procession down one street, up another—
no one knows the music: the horses hunger.

1967

Speech to the Sentries

This year the imposter, bolder than ever,
may appear at the gates without a disguise,
and offer a passport retouched by forgers—
How clever the face he presents, the shape
he inhabits, the style of his clothing!
You may feel forced to accept the performance,
to believe that this one using the name
must be the genuine person, the original man.

How then to detect the counterfeit, the intruder,
among the crowds that clamor for entrance?
Passwords sound in one mouth as another,
and fathers are known to have claimed false sons.
Yet with the trained ear, you may notice
something out of place, the wrong word stressed—
the same conviction in the same voice before:
last year it was urgent for his leaving.

1967

News the Body Brings

Beginning

1.

When I felt the deep pump throbbing
chest-bone and ribs pushed against the knot:
the man I was   alone in that room
space & shape   and everything else lost
in the rise & fall of silence—
It was a strange thing to be processed
delivered into the strict fold
of flat white sheets   to become the man
defined by glass tubes dangling in the air.

2.

Having been there & having returned
the experience of being cased by doctors
turns years of earning and learning
into an instant of casual presence.

3.

This morning of beginning
I turn on a bed that I remember
and suddenly what was narrow is enlarged
by the dream of all those worlds
one man was never meant to enter
Now I forget to listen as the pump performs

and silence settles on my veins.
The man I am: space & shape & the body
in which I awaken: confirmed where I am confined
by a loss that need never be redeemed.

1970

Breathing Lessons

1.

Night tests the proposition:

                    at this altitude

and in this season   a certain way to live.

For a while the world

               withholds the edge of cruelty.

But without notice

               fire drills down the sky—

fateful & strict for reasons

               I hold the weather enemy

               that seals me in this room.

2.

Night stings this throat.

In sleep I walk the measured mile.

Dream sends out the searching party—

                  somewhere among the missing . . .

And what of the liquid tongue? What secrets lost

when dried into wakefulness?

3.

Rising in that interlude

               before the sun appears

the waking sky colors

               forms of all beginning.

Stepping lightly not to disturb

               hostile forces of a presence

               no sane man can tolerate.

               What was there

so nearly in my hands   that given its right name

might find the perfect crime   a full confession

eligible for special amnesty . . .
One side of the missing face
one letter of the word needed
to decipher the whole code of deception.

                              For lack of this
the drying mouth   night-climber   begins again.

4.
                    First breath is arduous.
Voice is companion
                        only on those mornings
                            when silence is ominous.
Out there is empty
                        not yet filled in—
                        eyes trouble to remember
                        what looms around the corner . . .
Stepping out of space
                        I gather shreds to restore
                        enough form to believe
the speaker is alive.   Given unto these hours
I make the human moves:
                        counting that even intake
                        outflow of breath
blood rises to refresh the stem.   Another day
opens the curved fist of petals.   Where the world swings
I flutter in the wind.

1959

Coming to This Place

Arriving first as visitors
where white uniforms confirm
the gleam of corridors   the formal logic
that charts the iron bed: time of departure
and of return to the "normal" and the "sane"—
We suddenly find ourselves
fair game for the guardians   who offer
the strict regime of pills & needles
the shapeless robe   that needs no laundering . . .
We protest: this single-minded realm leave
no room for the "special grace" of being—
then read the schedule   all exact numbers

arranged for the convenience   of those whose skill
with serving spoon & knife   validates the course
of treatment—however long it takes.

Coming to this place   reserved for us
by pure rotation confined under the light
that leaves no room to wander in
we watch the gestures   of ritualized actors
who perform as if   there is no breathing space
                    beyond the shadows.

1976

Doctor, Doctor

Canst thou not minister to a mind diseased,
Pluck from the memory a rooted sorrow,
Raze out the written troubles of the brain . . .?
. . . If thou couldst, doctor, cast
The water of my land, find her disease
And purge it to a sound and pristine health,
I would applaud thee to the very echo. . . .
                              —Macbeth

1.
If all the fall of any moment
hits us and holds us at the door
if now we turn before impending light
between the projected fault and the watched will
to any dream where symbol has passed
but dream or touch the closed address—

But if there is a way
that turns toward any sound in time
and we can walk where shapes
are something for the fingers
and if there is a place
and one goes there and awakens

tell us the name and how we can live there
        that light again   that wind again
and bone is free from danger of edges—

show us the dream has a door.

2.

In a corridor, the rooms as trenches:
friends were always falling
before they touched the ground
names slipped past the mind
                    —and in that year
changing the initials on our cases
we entered the rented oblivion
(how many aliases make a summer?).

Outside the corridor
the view left little for the lungs:
weaving in and out of business
wearing our last year's illness
fathers patrol the beat of childhood
(how transfer out of neighborhood?)
                    —and in that year
footstep like investigation on the stair
                    other voices telling
light negatives   images of striking air
                    dramas of our falling.

3.

If the return does not resolve
but a pinwheel version of those evenings
moves the celluloid season in the mind
that wind again   that stirring blur
if the door does not revolve
but the divided clue-ring of the present
presents the alternatives of metal—

we may be well enough for knobs
and stairs that shrink as we go down:
find relatives not more than human size
and passing voices that were almost ours
pass brothers in the hall
when with awareness of the total address
we furnish this interior:
with all that we acquire as we are.

On the slick disordered streets
in the name of the symptom
              learning to measure
discover the face of the source
              if not to admire . . .

Doctor,
as wish outgrows the need of plague of time
Doctor,
our sleep takes down the sign of quarantine.

1958

Digging In

Winter: I remember the season:
the cold stops everything.
In a separate shelter
the body unfolds: let the fire decide . . .

I should be somewhere in the mountains
among those lavish distances
not needing to measure anything
listening for the fall of footsteps

                                   the snapping twig:
one sound is the self: composed as one.

But this hour is between walls: cannot remember
what's to be earned staying alive
cannot tell the promise from the dream . . .

Yet whispers in the blood:

                         here or somewhere else

there must have been   "white and blessed evenings"
signs among the stars

                         and the affected breathing.

1970

On a Recent Suicide (G.A., June 1973)

1.

How song in one hand

    scalpel in the other

Could he conduct that music

      to heal & revive

While mocking in his head

     were those silly jingles

      that accompany the act

       of juggler and clown?

2.

Death in retrospect

    gives clues to the performance

    the living cannot applaud:

Quixote we say—thirsting & stumbling

     across the dry plain—

And Hamlet takes his fall

    to leave some blonde Ophelia

    with flowers floating

     in her hair . . .

3.

Gone from our imagining

     is that legendary child

Who would embarrass

     friend & multitude

      to spy the nakedness

    as the one garment

     we all must wear.

Not enough to cry out

>and take his punishment
>>he must go further:
>crossing over in his pride
>to claim that wreath of bones.

1973

Figure into Form

However we appear
to the informing eye: face neck shoulders
draped or uncovered   torso of the vertical Adam
the rounded Eve—full-blown or shade
by the wandering line   whatever image
our presence utters—

Whether we intend to hide the fact
of loss or suffering   or to proclaim
we are indeed what we display: shining forth
to figure in the name of love
all we may grow and guard within:
                the ghost of yesterday
the spider's dance across tomorrow's mirror—

Let it be known   through the whole array
of mask & costume there is no departure
from what we seem but poured into this form
as much the water & the wine
as the knife the voice   we wield upon
each other's circumstance—

Not yet awake to the mist
we soon become   we still perform
as if allure   illumines   every where & when:
As if these bones   arrange to encore
                in bright response
to whistling fingers of the wind.

1976

Rising

Speech is companion
                only on those mornings
                    when silence is ominous.

Out there is empty
                not yet filled in—
                eyes trouble to remember
                what looms around the corner . . .

Stepping out of space
                I gather time to restore
                forms to believe in.

The speaker is alive.   Given unto these hours

I make the human moves: counting this even intake
                and outflow of breath

blood rises to restore   the stem extends another day

opening a curved fist of petals.   Where the world swings

I flicker in the wind . . .

1962

Sixty She Says

Sixty she says: wondering how it arrives
unnoticed already here under her fingers
already taking the shape of a question:
the decidedly different—or more of the same?
Sixty she says: tasting the word the number
it's no ordinary April   bringing tulips & lilacs
out of the backyard garden   onto the kitchen table
but rare as a kiwi or mango   deep orange shading into green:
the face of absence   within the food of presence—

It's time she says   like a book put down somewhere:
guess, guess and keep on guessing—it's time wearing
the disguise: the child dressed in her mother's clothing:
lipstick tasted   high heels *klop, klop* on the floor—

For this you keep reaching   for the undeniable image
as if you could hear   what the photograph said to the mirror—
Faces there that dance away the numbering hours
and yet these friends who put the candle on the table
intend that number can be—now as well as then—
more gift more choice than burden

1978

Left Hand/Right Hand

What brings it to the falling apart
is the left hand, unreliable, seized with the whim,
not watching which way the fingers move
not wanting to know; pressing the pulse
under the wrist of words, inordinate probing:
That kind of shaper   ready to follow & fondle
what may or may not be there
leading the mind to dance in throngs
of the ungathered, winding threads of the invisible
through loops & corners of improvable dream;

While the right hand
strains to take hold, to convert the shape
into what can be touched   fitting all to the frame
playing house with the walls
and host to the concept: brick upon brick
filling the cracks of ceilings & cellars—
that kind of shaper   that fact-finding mason
who molds & delivers what has to be there.

Asked to march between the span of fingers
the mind twists and twines the cords of confusion
begins to coil what it has uncoiled: forgetting
the idea, the motion, of hand feeding hand

1969

Water, Sky, and Unmarked Time

Northpoint

1.
Hour of light and landfall
the going down of unmeasured suns
the leaves of being scattered . . .

We are again called upon
to discover which one
lives in the thicket, which horns
are buried in the flesh.

We move again in provinces
never knowing what the sky intends—
the tree visible as a question.

2.
One must provide work
for idle hands: curious seasons
to be sifted, parking space behind the sea.

One must again arrange
the spaces: between the mythic forest
and the actual leaves of morning.

3.
Long as the path of arrival
it is again: washed up on the shore
feathers and skin that become
entrails spread across the sand.

Time then to assemble image
and the wandering word: to follow wind
that shakes the flowering tree—
enter waters homing toward the sea.

1970/1984

As Helmsman

As helmsman
asked to perform in time of war
beyond my skill and nerves—
I recall that moment;
the gray steel ship entering
the dynastic waters of the Nile . . .

The Pilot noted
tense hands gripping the spokes
the wheel the body slow to respond—
called for a replacement . . .

Twenty years later
I review the serious failure:
beyond my fear and the Pilot's concern
for the safety of the ship . . .

What enters now is the river
and all that lives and dies
along its shores: moonlight and fragile sails
wavering shadows of Isis and Tutankhamen
scurrying past the steel prow
probing through the floating minefields . . .

At this distance
            the command is choice.

1970

Elsewhere Then It Happens

Having mistaken the clues stored
in the earth misplaced the evidence of stone—
we select to remember   only the flowering meadow
where wind or war cannot disturb—
Time then is useful to forget
the forest the intricate swamp   from which we have emerged
and to which we may retreat
                              in the dangerous season . . .

Return then to the elaborate & dense waterways
where the narrow boat can drift   past trailing moss
and we may watch bright fish   leap out & upward
watch leaf-green and breathing gills
propose the silver dawn—creatures like these
who cannot tell   what is destroyed   or begins again
when water sky & painted flesh
                              slowly and equally burn . . .

1975/1982

Encounters on the River

1.

Evening trails across the water
glow & afterglow   evokes the promised delta
small bay of repose   where crickets sign
the vast accord: all creatures haven here . . .

2.

The leap that breaks the surface
where frantic wings stain the light
spreads the wounded water . . . another broken treaty
lies shattered on the rocks.

3.

Beyond the twisted vines   spindrift unveils
dwellings of tin & straw   abandoned trading posts
remains of the Fallen Kingdom   the burned-out space
the darkest heart   in its darkest place.

4.

Encounters in the mind? Or the actual river
rising to witness: from that trickle in the rocks
to the whole descent of waters
swirling past the hemmed-in shores . . .

5.

And have we come this far   clinging
to the simple craft   that flesh & faith
carved from the chest of expendable trees?

6.

Sailing eyeless into distances
where water derived from snow   contends with
incoming tides of salt   we enter the sounding surf
and become the deafened dream . . .

1977

Entering Waters

1.

Whatever wave it was   came crashing down
to send forth upon the shore
the dubious amphibian   who would have to learn
another kind of breathing   a different way to move—
We reverse this day   entering here to end
at last the landfall: exile returning home . . .
In buoyant waters   we begin the downward plunge
where luminous shapes   pulse with the color
of streaks that survive   by quick inversion:
blending into tendrils   of iridescent flora
light could feed & feed upon

2.

Coming to this depth   where glitter seek & hide
is the game played   by wavering darts
by stripes that inhale   the pores of light
We try to separate   fear-giving shapes
from what is neutral   to the invading presence—
All this motion stirs forms that spawn
somewhere back of memory: *as once we were . . .*

3.

Passing through the unmanned gate
where dog-swimming stars   enter the flow of fluid light
we scan that deeper place: where eyes of coral sleep
and all that moves is harvest   to the harvester—
from rays that sting   to almost grain and flower—
food of the swaying chain   that welds the dream of being
to seamless hulls: the altogether vertical   to universal bones.

1976

Evolution

We have misread the rocks

    the slow burning

       choose to remember

    only the meadow

       long flowering

from which we create

    parks & gardens

       pastures of peace

       where no blood flows—

Time then is useful to forget

    sticky mud the slime

       of that gorgeous swamp

    which does not die

       with our desertion.

Often in the long nights

    I drift through intricate

       & dense waterways

where even now bright fish

    leap up and outward—

    how high I cannot guess—

but I see scales flash

    on topmost branches

    leaf-green and breathing gills together

    each early silver dawn

      water, sky, and branded flesh

      slowly & equally burn.

1968

By God and by Guess

By brass spokes, circle of the fluid arm,
needle's quiver in the floating bowl,
that worm of light charted in the sky—
Survival hung on precision instruments
sworn to produce that flake of land:
shape darker than any yield of dream
rising to witness what the bells foretold.

I watched the distance dissolve
churning waters wide enough to deceive
the triad of time: birds following
the wake at sunrise, the foam of evening . . .
and there it was: the chartered island
looming above the prow: sheer rock-face
of downgraded farms and salt-filled seasons
brittle acres deserted by the wind—

Departure broke the spell: waters evolve
across the turning wheel of forenoons—
belled into sleep I swam the shifting night
with lost meridians chiming in my ears . . .
Worlds later I navigate the course
that no weave of water ever alters:
here the black arrows of direction,
salt stained on brass, invert the stars—
Those islands shift in streams of time,
but one horizon bowls the numbered glass.

1972

The Color of the Sky

None of them knew the color of the sky.
            —Stephen Crane

So intent were they upon the possibilities of being saved that they had
no time, interest, or impulse for seeing the color of the sky above them.
                        —Irwin Edman

1.
Deep in a distance spread through attacking noons,
that bone outline of rib-spread drifting on a spine,
that wood welding one and all the glassed-in ages,
they found the size of a stuffed boat, a season's size.

Alone with their features and linear eyes following
that green edged with reminders, that literal return,
sent a passing word for funnels; but a present oar
and the wave of message furthered the past and lost.

The sky was there: bird steered in the instinct color
time-aimed its need for weathers and survival;
but when meridians met them, they and the needles
danced wind-in-a-wire—that law went star-wise.

2.
Light, as quadrant tells the single place of presence,
Distance, they raised your blind.
Direction, it is not the hours down or miles across
they fitted empty spaces to their puzzle.
But Sky, report their position made obscure by their code.

And they cried:
"Latitude of a family of latitudes,
we too have sisters!"

3.
But as the miles went down, days and waters merging,
that cry reversed on the arc of its utterance
drowned on the tongue   the unheard-of sky
painted all in thunders and salvations after rain.

O they knew the time to be potent and plucked,
but when a flare dropped fear to size horizons,
sought their weather in the magnet of hulls:
the gift of a rusted deliverance.

O they knew the small acceptance as daily death,
but could not spill the rationed hour for vision,
but felt the bulwarks, touch-wood for dimension,
and derelict themselves, between oar and evening
                              offered motion to the night . . .

4.
If any among them, light voice lined with surprise,
crying high as the prime bird far from the decoy,
clearing its throat before the cued-in season,
soloed information of land and future to survive,
they found a way to double exile: daring direction.

O if they were not sighted on the water
                    when they still had water
                              forgive them their location . . .
Did dividers leave them intact, the charted hairs
                              far from their heads?

Present in the color of their death, the sky

                              where it had been,

horizon of kaleidoscopic birds   the glazed afternoon

the floating element   seen   where it could not see.

1954

Present Shores

1.

Letting go of distance

           the protective situation

           "the water is never warm enough."

Entering at last

        a further realm   naked in this moment

       before the visitors arrive.

           Wonder at the vessel

           that steers without effort

through this shifting space.

2.

Above me the shore   the island   time has a name

But down here I perform

           as if to outwit

the watcher who spies:

           "A body in the water!"

Trailing that line

           past all those shapes and colors

that flicker to invite

           or deceive   destroy

seeking that level where water

           astonishes no one.

Presence in no way alters

           the suggestion of silence.

3.

I cannot dream that dream

           having arrived too late

rumors reach me   the self that floats

remembers its own weight kicking the rubber toes

to expel the lightness that cannot be believed

4.

And return to sand:

        white on whiteness

streaming salt to ask forgiveness of the sun—

And what is down there

       after all unanswerable

hulls flowering castle of bones stolen brass

5.

Before the Visitors arrive

         I dress & return.

I have been here long enough

       not to be shocked

       at the clock on the wall.

1966

Slipping Away

After the long holding pattern
of strict nights & dry solitudes
it happens as if without effort
we lift the dripping rop
from weathered iron on the dock

and feel that easing   as the hull travels:
first the smooth drift   then the cough
the throb the shudder—and all at once
insistent white churns through
the blue-green channel   we move farther faster
from the fading city   steering toward the unclogged sky . . .

Distances we want to say:
how much longer can we preserve
the salt of presence? Caught in the tide
the flow can we believe the precise island
exists somewhere   between the darker waters
and the clarified sky?

Tied for so long to this street
this continent this bounded sphere
we prepare to enter—not another port of call—
but a greater space:
               the geography of dream . . .

1978

The Stranger: As Balloonist

"Then what do you love, extraordinary stranger?"
"I love the clouds . . . the clouds that pass . . . up there. . . ."
                              —Charles Baudelaire

Who was the Stranger? Was he the first
to transfer affection from this planet
of leopards, swans, and men? Read that airy, bitter
dialogue in which—in a single paragraph—
Baudelaire throws overboard: personal love,
family love—then links the love of God & gold—
Begin to wonder: did he rise higher then
swaying in the gondola   of self-esteem
to embrace those drifting shapes?

Dream along on that unfettered wind
and find ourselves among blue-white islands
on voyages where we descend   soft as feathers
on the painted garden   the flowerbeds of choice . . .

But waking in a different century
we breathe the weighted air   that clouds our love
with deadly shapes: cosmic creations
of particle-hunters   big-bang theorists
exploding worlds too small to classify . . .
Clouds we might dream   to love again
in some other galaxy   some other time.

1977

Echoes and Entrances

The Identity of an Hour

Whether the scene opens with a feather
on nerve end—and recall bristles our cat fur—
or with a small smell of afternoon
and the flashing streets revealed in Braille:
pause, puzzle, poised for step at curbstone
while instants of before arrive: rehearsed.

So an image returns to cross a soft frontier
and a generation is marked in scale between towns . . .
We enter a theater of continuous performance
where an invented voice speaks the immaculate lines—
But it's not opening night when memory attends:
with the star gone, we follow the stand-in hour.

And learn that the hour gone, is missing.
We work backward from a fingerprint and desire,
send notice to all stations where we stopped:
look where the register was signed—
but the swiveled clerks refuse to recall:
no one of this face . . . no clock will take our check.

1952

Take This City Now

What is it: here are the fields, now you see it,
the grass is green on and on, now you don't,
the road pours into a puddle of distance,
then . . . solid and hard in space, there it is,
shut tight like a fist; then closer and closer
and it softens in the eyes, opens its spreading fingers
into the suburbs, in a welcome; then, it is past:
and again into distance again the road pours . . .

But down from the hanging hills, eyes make a space-descent on it,
and it fits in a setting, seems cut in the rock, seems
to be lasting.

It is stone on stone, wood on brick, and on top of that
it is glass, so much, so many, listed on this map,
according to a graph, according to a census,
but it is more . . .

It is all the people living here, surprised to be alive
and surprised to be living here, because first there was
only light, only sound, only smell,
a doughy mass with no form, a hand pointed a certain way,
a foot raised and put down, then it was words,
and that too was a wonder,
then it was a girl surprised at the change,
and a boy waking up in the morning different, then it was
a long aisle and long white candles and a girl in white dress:
How did it happen, when did it happen, why did it happen:
birth was a point and death was a point,

and life being short was a straight line—
but here was rent a twist, and taxes a turn, and food a spiral,
and war a sharp intersection:
and here was the whore . . . nobody else but you,
and the politician was nobody else,
and the stew-bum stared at you from the glass,
and somehow there was no getting away from it—
the thing hidden from all the others—
you were crooked as the streets of this city.

Who is this man wiping a machine a certain way,
in a way that says no other machine is quite like it,
and no one else really knows how to run it;

Who is this woman, pinning back a colorless strand of hair,
lifting the stale smell of sheets out of the window,
putting the slicing bacon coffee odor in its place;

Who are they with the black box in one hand, morning paper in the other,
eyes not looking at the sun, the words not being spoken;

Or in the exact room, with the floors and walls neat, the desk tidy,
the greeting precise, and at the set time the forms
to be sent out, and the margins to be put on the letters;
how did they come to this air-spiking shout, this swift but final act,
to the change in the body in the mind in the single change
from a walking step to a marching step;
and somehow feel the moment feel the pulse race then rest
and then cut deep; there is a thin vein here,
a thick blood flow, a continuous battle in the cells,
a meaning to each of the parts, a large relation between the parts.

Here is one from somewhere out of it coming into it,
and the crossing is a road mark that is soon the past,
saying what will it bring, will what I bring belong,
add to gain or loss;

Here is one from within it going out
saying to this window on this street goodbye,
last step in this hall and on this stair,
down this long unending drive, past the school and the church
and the hospital and the department store:
a lost beginning:
each thing stands apart from the rest in a way it never did before,
and each stands for some moment that belongs to your true self;

And here is one stands still lost sunning in the open square
not taking a step, not knowing how why where to go,
lies late in a stale room face flat as the walls
face uncolored as the floor,
sleeps eyes open or closed body moved but mind sealed in sleep.

Take this city now: out of the trail of smoke, move quick,
but cautious at crossing,
while buildings press together and people press;
read it on their faces before it changes
one elevator goes up and the other speeds down
the phone is picked up . . . the busy signals ring
the letters slide into the slot:
and now it is this curious home-hunt fever;
and now it is nearly neon time:
But between the light rising on the one hand
and the light falling on the other
Between the cars going one way at that set hour
and the cars returning at this set hour:

Here being rolled upon the presses is the headline,
and here between editions is your life.

While the hour hand turns, and turning, lifts wheat out of the field,
Sends the heavy ships home, spans the swift streak on a slow sky
Pulls the old oak upward, and once again the barn needs painting,

and the colt stands ready for the saddle
and the kids asking things—

Take this city now: here are the nine-count losers
Coming up for the next round, not waiting for a decision,
Somehow rising to their feet: being more than the blows,
Standing there for some reason taller than before—

Take this city now: seems cut in the rock, seems to be lasting:
It is only the men and women asking, where do we go from here?

1940

All at Once

Awakening to the sight of the same walls
in the same house in the same city
the furniture in the same order as before,
we surrendered to the imperative of dream—
Now is the time we tell ourselves
and here is the place—or is it or was it
ever any different walking beside the river
as it appeared that afternoon in new light after rain . . .

So mind questions the eye untaught
unpracticed at this level where questions
descend from a realm we have yet to enter—
We sift through memory for precedent,
are forced to wonder: what if it falls apart
in translation and this no more arrival
than any previous place we stopped and waited?

If only language could spell the world
sounding order: this is noise/that is music
we might forget the intake of whole light
in the dream that confirms the substantial birth—
that cognitive wedding of where and when—
we might awaken among the waiting messiahs—
not knowing what it means to be ignored or chosen:
but persuaded that to be here is enough.

1977/1985/1986

City Between the Lines

—For E. G., on receiving her card from Rome

Those who from that city
Reached out of stone: the living hand
Strong as sculpture
Touched our lives.

They will again gather
Beside the bronze horseman
Presenting faces
Among the monuments: heads to remember.

(White lines wheel in that space
Where he, Aurelius, is centered;
And the city revolves: faces forming
And being expelled from the circle.)

Remembering: time upon time
The mind circles upon grave voices;
The same speech resounds, bringing
Martyrs and flowers to the perfect squares,
Fullness to the round fountains.

Here in your living hand
Loss is written on this card:
The verbs of absence
Weigh upon the scale of seasons.

If only, says the mind,
We could have walked
Beside the unused river . . .

1969

Dreaming Gardens

There is a war

>> and children playing tennis
>> and a ladder for the lover—

the scene shifts—

>> an invitation to view
>>> the formal flowers . . .

Once past the wall

>> dream of revolutions:
>> the once-proud owners

clad in their own kind of innocence
caught fleeing in the night

1969/1973

The Fool Not Yet Complete

The fool not yet complete stands
under a diffused light in a recording studio
listening to his voice on a multiple soundtrack
singing without music or libretto—somehow my mind
jumps the track and I translate "sounds" into "wounds"
and I remember being told that in the Philippines
there are these healers who can remove an organ
with their own hands—I forget the point of the story—
but recognize that in the "music room"
the subject must be convinced the "cure" is listening to himself.

1982

The Survivors: A Legend

I hear those spectral voices
spinning through dream   the liar's landscape
tongues clacking wind among their bones:

this continent waited
with open arms to receive the intrepid
hand that handled gun and axe—
great names we might retrieve
to spell on bronze   dazzle the awed children
where birds encircle the falling noons . . .

For the birds then:
        "Such men we were
in those dusty places   forced to take shelter
in the shade of boulders   pressing forward
against the Savage   to found the City-State."

That tongue is image: the yellow teeth
clamped on the sun streaming bright
upon the painted bodies of the slain.

And the true history? Not said or written
but reflected as in the lizard's eye
the refracted image of mirage or hallucination
dispersed as the quick tail scatters
the loose pebbles . . . I guess the wind rising
under a neutral sky   the dust as evidence
of a small disturbance   before the desert world
turns into the void of unscripted sand.

1973

Return to the Air

Return to the air
                what belongs to the air
                        nor is there need for sky
horizons   only confuse the issue—
begin the sifting   to be learned
                        in perfect innocence—
All power to the Weather-Makers!
                        (God-handed, the cave children
are pierced with confusion.   Go there and return—unchanged!
Simple-minded meat-eaters loaded down with orange
rocks—the very hot stuff itself!
Meanwhile over a small country
                        the profit-sharing bombers . . .)
Return to
          those dark faces at that altitude
where bleakness burns
           temple stones   ornate hangings
jeweled fabric   perfumed with worship—(is it
possible to learn to read again the Book of the Dead?)
I cannot tell. The split century of my years
does not reach far enough. But those climbers—what
of them? West-face for the professionals. Equipment
checked. A flag to implant . . . I cannot read their lips
but rising through the dream
                    wailing flutes
                    flutter of white rags
speechless eyes question the future
                    the voiceless air.

1960

Echoes and Entrances

1. The City/The Legend

Here it happens   as the bright brief question
flares between opposing poles of light   the sleeper turns
to mark this day   as when the vision finally arrives:
somewhere in the distance   he is suddenly aware
of mythologies that bring into view the towering city:
spreading white lines   in a space designed by Michelangelo
watches them converge upon a sculpted horse and rider
remembers the legend that if the bronze turns green
the city must prepare for its ultimate downfall . . .

Within the same hour   we identify the sleeper
as ourselves: the dream departs replaced by this narrow room
where bed chairs table leave little space
for the mind to maneuver   or widen the scope of passage—
Left with these changing up-and-down-sized worlds
we discover we are   more than we seem   less than we imagine:
one moment nameless among the named   and the next
the ripest fruit of legend: this pulp of crushed
stained flesh spread upon the ground   where the Serpent
invited the temptation   we have not forgotten or forgiven.

2. The Forest/The Park

Long after this we set aside   what was once a forest
and called it a park: a place we may enter with the delight
of tourists: a place to picnic and watch the children
and the dogs running on the grass—but even here the scene
may change as a leaf descends   as the wind stirs shapes
and shadows of unknown intention among the flickering trees—

We are reminded then   of the forest as the original home
of prey and predator   and how we were named the beast who dreams.

3. The Forest/The Film

Something in this emerges as a theme
sets in motion a cinematic memory   that converts
the forest into film: mind moves east to project
the title *Rashomon* upon the lighted screen:

Once more we follow the slow walk
of the burdened horse carrying the veiled bride
wrapped in custom and brocade   her lord and master
walking stiffly alongside the swaying silken canopy.
Already we sense the impending menace in the light
that flickers across the foliage leaves and bark
and it is not long   before our unease is confirmed
when the shrewd greedy bandit dances into the scene—
How swiftly the mood changes   the forest is transformed
as the scenario of arrogance lust and death unfolds . . .

Begins then the contest for the sensual prize:
clumsy circling the absurd sword-play advance and retreat
the heavy blades striking air   first one falls down
then the other: both parody the archetype of hero warrior . . .
We move the action fast forward toward the aftermath:
harsh breathing   dishonored voices   as each witness
recounts their own self-serving version of the truth:
each a mixture of banality and evil—which only confirms
how it all must end: *in silence*—while the dark heavy rain
falls out of the film and into our lives . . .
Leaving the theater we emerge   taking with us the sight
of a life spared or thrown away we join the violator

and the violated in the light of a tarnished afternoon
where fear shows everything we pretend is theater—
Out of all this we take with us the single image
of the abandoned child   image of the monk imploring
an empty sky—while the enormous bronze bell continues
to toll the bright brief question   we are left to wonder
what even now flares   between opposing poles of light . . .

4. The Room/The Mountain

Returning to the smaller space and circumstance
we turn our scrutiny   upon such objects as a straw madonna
a wooden lion: low-cost reminders that we have been
where we have been: light of that time that place
appears once more in the gaudy shop windows
that appeal to the customers of make-believe lives—
While we await the arrival of the one who signifies
we order the exact moment to appear again   to restore
whatever dream was lost in the orange light
that surrounds the manifest mountain   standing where
we thought the sight of hopeful hills and unscarred sky
might instigate our first true dialogue with wind.

5. The Voice/The Witness

Besieged by small attractions   we forget what was
revealed along that slope: *there was a voice* we say
that told of mountains   the witness now is silent
or speaks another dialect   we live where light unveils
reduced and harmless details: the cat in the garden
coexistent with the fuchsia and the hummingbird . . .
There was a voice we try again   that told of rockets
reaching stars that sing salvation; the last best chance

to board the vessel   outward bound   rounding the curve
of inviting distances—*tell us* we persist
if it is time to transfer our affection
to another earth ready to begin at the beginning . . .

6. The Song/The Story

Reprise the song. How it was and is. Using the voice
of legend to confirm the seed within the stone:
remember then a file of silent walkers   descending
from the mountain: beaked straw hats darkened eyes
damp wool blankets draped across their shoulders
moving through the mist   and tell it as history intoned
putting aside the question   of what is real or apparition—

—"These were the last of the lost tribe
coming down the road   entering time & history
just at that moment   when you and I leaving
the electrified city were seeking timelessness—
speak of it now without echoes or the resonant name
but as the story of how we ourselves came to be here:
recall how we were stranded on that ledge
of sharpened stone and the outstretched hand
that lifted us to safety—and later that morning
we joined the procession   raising our voices in joyful song:
'Welcome now to all who have traveled this way
to all who have been to that place where we saw
plants like elephant ears and in a flashing ligh
the sun turn green—we do not know how we survived
but remember waking later in the deep restoring shade.' "

1976/1977/1980/1992

Beyond the Name and Number

What the Wastebasket Tells

What the wastebasket tells and not the printed page
What the flesh feels in the night
What the mind reels from this day on any street corner
Or in the advertised sun beside a park bench—

Is the document of a man lying nameless somewhere
The index of hours spent in bug-ridden beds
The entries in the diary of a corpse.

This is the something polite words will not report,
This is the actual guts being spilled in an open field,
This is not on paper or a thin flash on a fading screen,
This is the time you face truth and you answer alone,
This is the tide that makes of you a drifting thing—

When the bought voice befouls the air asking for trust,
And the talking of the tailored man to a moneyed meeting:
Thinking of initials on the silver, or a butler in the lobby,
A weekend in the hills and a summer home—

Look closer, for this is the dream you awake to find:
The mother home from the hospital sees the waiting mouths,
While the miner turns to the shaft for what is perhaps the last time,
And that night the bookkeeper returns from the office and has a breakdown,
Later the soldier looks at his hands and is silent,
Still later the refugee blinks at the sun and the road is dark—

Here you are with short pants and a shining face.
Then it is not you and not the present but a printed page.

Here are your years is what the wastebasket tells . . .

1940

Notes on a Doppelganger

Mister it was you
whose face stalked through endless windows
in the city of bronze horsemen:
white hands and bony head
the gift of race and culture:
that privileged intensity
at home among the books—
while I ate bitter bread on dusty stairs.

1966

Guesswork

—for Nanos Valaoritis

1.

I know you are there
hiding behind Homer: wars one might believe
and die in.   Ships that enter & depart
when the gods are favorable.

      But what to do with
"such stuff as dreams are made on"?
Tenuous I say   although the thread
      makes it through the maze—

What worries me is the piling-up of detail:
      cripples in black overcoats
clumping up the red staircase
      that leads nowhere.

2.

      Is love Lilith
          the wind herself:
balm for the rasping soul?
      I guess—holding the short straw—
at times secure in madness:
      at times   wielding the whip
that cuts the plunge of bats' wings—

Yet somehow in Greek light   you waken
stillness weigh the empty dawn
the metal promise   slowly   lift the hammer—

I witness oil lamps   worked bronze   minted profiles.
Your hand   confirms the report:
     there are temples
               blue waters   a hill to ascend.

1972

Equations

If there is to here as then is to now
and tree is to forest as star is to galaxy—
more we might wish to describe and explain
but the words the numbers fall short—
And there is no provision for the errant outcome
the unasked-for dying under the random sign
the peculiar hour of the undistinguished day.

We strive to correct the small or influential error
but wherever we travel: in bright or darkling worlds
discover too late we cannot follow
those vague instructions: "Somewhere south of infinity . . ."

Nevertheless we prepare once more
to test the limits of this human clothing—
and when we fall retreat and try again
One foot up and one foot down—it is practical
and sensible to learn the way: as one was

one is   going   sooner or later   completely   to become . . .

1977

Born Unattended

Born unattended these starlings sing
unknown melody: neither anthem nor emblem.

Hidden deep in their own colonies
to be guessed at: music out of season.

Attentive eye and ear catches only
their sparkle: living and mating

beyond the cage of reason. Privileged once
to hear that song gathering

nests extend our borders—I praise
the name and canvas of: *Paul Klee.*

1974

The Apex Travel Service

Go where there are faces
The bandits will kill you
The shepherds beg blankets
The women, bending, steal herbs
                    from the field—

I know that place exists
It is on that island
                    or in that city
Where the *Art of Falconry*
                    is required reading.

1967

Therefore

Therefore what is needed
                            is one voice or another
breathing into sound   forms that break step
with knowing: the yellow leaf stirred   by the wind
water creased on a pond:
                                    evidence mute and mutely given.
What world is   is not   to be foreclosed:
dream is wilderness   no glass name destroys.

Therefore I suggest: somewhere in the distance
                              prepare the clearinghouse
toward which   new walker   set forth tomorrow.

Therefore foretell the dazed historian:
                    "From that time on—we must record—
love's energy poured forth
                    in ways we could not guess or hope" . . .

Therefore offer to breathe   that not-yet wind
of worlds to come: home at any distance
                    anywhere on the horizon—
to follow the vagrant emblems
                    where stars & clouds   permeate with music
                    the dreaming air.

1973/1976

Unsaying

Refusing the demand   for the inflated name
the tabloid interview   products of the factory
of media invention   that have given us
instant artists: the trumpet without the ear—

We draw in pencil   what we may remember
of the violet flower   the incredible raindrop
locked mouth   of the shining world—

to keep secret   what is left of silence
light as the wave   that follows the flesh
where any insect voice   enters the cloud the wind
with shapes that trill

        the harp & spine of leaves
beyond the printed word—the guns of morning.

1977

The Unnamed

Faces bending toward the light
the loose-limbed women bequeath
a sense of motion we have not known before.

What we expect or experience is water
flesh that imitates the flow the light
that convinces us it can happen

as it happened before—but the women disappear
and we are left wondering: What is there
to be bequeathed: the awkward walk on stone?

1970/1985

Something That the Name Gathers

If every event which occurred could be given a name, there would be no need for stories.

—John Berger

1.

To help persuade us of the real. We begin our search in
separate rooms of need and desire. And call for walls and
mirrors that can summon the fragrant object/the very being
our flesh fears and welcomes/assembled from the fragments
of a once-heard conversation/someone we reach out to embrace/
who seeks another home in absence. Remember how our arms closed
on air that promised touching/but what was gift turned into
burden/with the abrupt departure of the fictional self/
entering the traffic of a fictional world?

2.

Something that the name gathers/that could hold us here/
long enough to be persuaded/we are indeed the ones/
who inhabit this house of breath/and pay the tax of circumstance . . .
What then can give encounter the status of event?
Study the light that spreads across the incised stone.
Light we wake to witness/the eye of conscience may now
proceed to identify: twin spires of the Cathedral
rising in the east/and those painted towers pointing north/
witness the surround of water/fog-stained vision of white sails/
wind-harp of a bridge to dream/a bridge to remember . . .

3.

Sorting through such items as find their place
within this text of time/we seek an occasion to make memorable
this house upon that street/but the blur of name converted
into number presents a scattering of syllables—the view contracts

from panorama to the precise scene/from skyscraper to the
fragile mode of three yellow roses   in your own backyard
witness the rise and fall   that in his head   and in her heart
will be their history—all this works its way through the mind
while sluggish in the morning light   the stranded cars
are filled with frantic beating wings . . .

4.

And now to admit what we must admit: all this under the sign
of before. Manifold meanings escape the net of words. Thought
cannot rise to meet the level of intention. Word again gives
way to a scattering of syllables . . . The number we dial fails
to provide the one face we count upon to respond . . . No longer
able to gather under the sign of "what is" we move now
where hieroglyphs incised on polished stone
are assembled courtesy of architect and day laborer
(await their testimony to provide an accurate translation
of monument and amulet) the proverbs the myths the shortest
distance between tower and abyss—and all this taking place
while we are moved to consider the rise and fall
as nothing more than the story of a faltering star
without horizon or event/the muted future of the grass . . .

5.

Early or late there may be song or story. It may sound like this:
there is a stillness to be sought. Stillness in and of the water.
This morning we woke before the city stirred. The houses were
still dark. The sky presented a small show of glory—but no one
paid attention. It would be warm this day. Warm and very clear.
We would watch birds looping through space. Crisscross patterns.
Motion that infers both madness/and the serene being of the
"natural order" . . . Above and beyond all this light moving
toward the other shore. What becomes clear is that if we
are not chosen surely another will be witness.

6.

Glory and grace the continent ends here. On these streets
the story of an absence. Time and no-time. He stands in front
of a door. Searches for the key. What keeps him here keeps
him going is a name a face a voice. Composed and created
as the "ultimate composite" rearranged to become *this one.*
What the witness sees the image fails to confirm.
Love the long voyage moves apart/separate from the voyager.
He turns and turns upon the turning. Still there is no amulet
to exorcise the spell.   Thirty years later he remembers
writing this: *if there is a place / and one goes there
and awakens / tell us the name and how we can live there /
that light again / that wind again / and bone is free from
the danger of edges . . .*

7.

Turns the city and himself into time. The fragrant air hovers
between the radiant and the begrimed face. And who will sleep
tonight between the cracks of corrugated cartons—and turn
another way upon the rumpled bed/between the perfumed walls?
Trying to remember what the voices said. And what they meant.
Spectrum of towers and roses. All those colors merged.
And now that exile music spreads its warning notes—
he can no longer imagine whether he is all or none
of what we are meant to be—*something in abeyance
yet to be discerned*—is happening here or elsewhere
in the awkward continuing dream   and it begins again:
we join and rejoin the procession   we enter and depart
where we were told—but cannot remember—the believable name.

1988/1991

Afterword to *Unlawful Assembly:* A Time to Gather

I have chosen to call this a "Gathering," rather than the more usual "Selected Poems." And I have underlined the distinction with the title *Unlawful Assembly.* This was not just a matter of choosing one name, one arrangement over another. I meant it rather to set aside any notion that only the "best" was included here, in a "definitive" presentation. And to indicate a departure from what is often taken for granted: that a finished manuscript was delivered to the publisher to accept or reject.

Other considerations were that—over this long span of time—I could not find a distinct style, or any fixed view of what a poem should express. What came to light instead was an evolving consciousness, a continual search for a language, and subjects, relevant to an ever-changing world.

The work of "gathering'" then required a search—sometimes through pages turned brown and brittle—to find poems that would span half a century and still be of interest to today's reader. As it turned out, this whole process was aided by the fortunate circumstance that it took place while I was carrying on a correspondence with Michael Thorp.

It happened naturally then that I wrote him about what I was doing. He wrote back that he would indeed like to do a book of my poems. What gradually became *this book* emerged from a further series of letters that followed. So that the "field of vision" was enlarged for both of us in a kind of continuous interaction.

—

The book you have here has all these "collaborative" aspects. It stops short, however, of an actual collaboration—because the poet must retain ultimate responsibility. The key thing for me was that the poems included would have to reflect the radical shifts in perspective from one decade to another. This might have indicated a chronological, or even thematic, arrangement. I chose instead to seek a kind of symmetry that would reflect both a spectrum and a continuum. After some initial difficulty, I found a "solution" in dividing the book into named sections. This happened, as it turned out, from what I was able to learn from the poems themselves, as they made known the "affinities" that would group them together.

—

What I have written so far is to indicate what was included. I have not touched upon, except in general, what was excluded. Yet process, as we know, consists of both. I would now ask the reader's indulgence as I take the unusual step of adding here two poems that were considered and, after consultation, discarded. This in the hope that it might illustrate the somewhat arbitrary decisions that occasionally have to be made. It may be also, in this case, that the titles of these poems helped to "invite" them back in: "Among the Missing," and "Another Time, Another Voyage." Whether this "second choice" appearance here is justified is of course for the reader to decide.

—*L. F.*
January 1994

Among the Missing

Symptom or copy-cause of the original
he invents a scenario in which his body lingers
on the creased green water: the searching party
finding him there shocked by the resemblance
to some forever person cast in stone
playing his flute among the competing frogs . . .
Watching from behind a tree he saw the bird
diving for a fish shatter his once-only totally
achieved form: the fragrant wind whispered:
once is enough: at least it was evidence
some time some place could come together
to give a perfect reading for his name . . .
Was he left then with only phantom of his feeling?
He might declare now his hour of return
in this revised version stretched upon
the mitered corners of the wooden frame:
the canvas prepared and ready for the brush
waiting for the colors to amplify the image—
something to show his friends: a kind of likeness—or even better:
Nemesis facing Echo: a "double delight."

1980/1984

Another Time, Another Voyage

1.
Nothing seems to hold them—
neither their fathers nor guardians—
forbidden to move or to name
                    the color of their victims
they seek the air their bodies cannot enter:
we are forced to imagine:
                    the secret capsule, the launching,
                    missions urgent but unnamed.

2.
Reported among the missing
they may appear this morning
in the same parcel of flesh
ready to answer as this one, that one,
to the convenient name—
But body in one place, mind in the other,
their feet tread upon the ground:
                    here on the private grass
they distill the fumes of their imagining—
                    They must assume
the glass can be entered
                    and what they name believed.

3.
We have seen only the glassed look
suppose they project themselves beyond
and by miracle or by luck
                    survive the crossing:
how can we tell   not having been there
what worlds flourish beyond our hands?

4.

Have we forgotten noons of glass melting,
the hospital invaded, turned upside down,
survivors shooting splinters from their hair?

These were born and wholly lived in that time
when the small compact container released
the force that sent flowers shooting
giving the grotesque the whole sky to flower in—

No need to ask then   what brings them to lie down
with folded hands and vacant eyes
what rituals or music they must perform.

5.

In sight of this two-headed world
we study the mirrors: the silver coating
leaves dream on one side, living on the other.

Yet they claim special devices
                              thrust them into space
thickness of glass irrelevant
                              moving through as light does
in the pores of prisms   the end of prisons
and passage at will—

We hold to the world we know
                              waiting for the image
to reveal the stark day   the structure of the law.

As we were born and defined
they must be: one continuous horizon
                        blends our beginnings
separates the night from these distorted suns.

1970

Lost Subjects/Found Objects

(1998)

Foreword to Lost Subjects/Found Objects

As the title suggests, these poems were not, in the usual sense, selected with publication in mind. I had already made such a selection in 1994 in the book *Unlawful Assembly: A Gathering of Poems, 1940–1992* (Cloudforms, England). This book included only fifty poems, written over fifty years.

Obviously there was more, in file drawers and countless notebooks, that might interest some readers. I was already looking through these notebooks, considering what among my writings belonged in the archive I was preparing to send—at the appropriate time—to the Bancroft Library.

While not totally out of reach, this felt like a projected "out of sight, out of mind" situation. I cannot describe in detail the hesitations, the mind changes, that followed. All I can say is that the poems included here refused to go quietly into that "dark space," as it were.

I then looked at them more closely, exploring their affinities, considering the possibility of their appearing in a limited context. What seemed to work best was a three-part arrangement. The first would be those that came across, as the shorter poems, in a kind of "lyric" mode. The second was an easier choice: it would include only the two longer poems: "Assault on the White Frame House" and "Schliemann at Mycenae."

The third part would include poems that expressed homage—a kind of "portrait poem"—to writers and a poetry teacher I admired. And because they shared this also, a sense of commitment to the poetic community and the world.

—L. F.
1998

Part One

Rope Song

Light thrums the chords:
                            the blind true guitarist
labors first to tie   then to untie the dreaming word.
Music is more than   the spell of numbers
                                 printed on the scale:
wind that sways   the twisted vines   voicing
                 rites of alphabet.
How far have we come   gathering notes
                 to remind the listener
what hangs upon the flickering song?
Light twangs the tune:
                         enter children   chanting rhymes
jumping squares small feet perform
to illustrate the leap—*how high is up?*—in the musical air.

Farther across the fields
                        the darkening call
comes from the swaying tower: listen
as bronze tolls the range of evening . . .
as pilgrim sound   draws forth together   from wandering ways
one of a kind   at home with the fish the bird the river—
Music twines the hemp   the weave of dream
to snare the listener   with light-touched song.

1976

Dreaming the Figure

Dreaming the figure we may fashion
when sleep brings us into drifting
passage through the insulated wall:
the very one to act as gifted double
to plead our awkward case: one moment
the loving witness—the next accusing
voice and image ready to introduce
testimony of the shattered mirror—

We summon in defense this other being
to restore the apostle or the guardian . . .

Morning With/Without Love

Love the great noticing of the small:
leaf—stir and harp—sound the brown finch
shaking water from its wings . . .
But the tower looms across
the waking flesh the gate opens upon
full attention to the need of being—
How slow we are   to be astonished
at dancing colors   in stray forbidding shapes—
Silent now or shocked to question:
How long have we been strangers here?

1976

The Sleep, the Waking

By order, by invitation, fingers on the knife,
ready to spread the weight of plaster
upon knotted wire that bends to the touch
to launch the bronze wings out of dust—

But before the fingers move, the spent bird
crashes to the floor; voices from the street
denounce the false angel: the eye deceived
under white light in a borrowed room . . .

That charge I have to remember, to consider fingers
not prime enough for the task: too many fools
carving the wings that fold before they fly—
facsimiles sold before the end of the season.

Under the white, borrowed voices
dance in my head: Rilke and his Baroness,
Blake's mewing angels: the whole crew radiant
from real voltage stored beneath the skin—

Who let me in? Even to breathe those names
I inhale more than I might remember:
feet muddy from the street, white dust rising
to clog the lungs: here the knife, there the broom.

1969

Chopin in Alaska

They are waiting, Chopin, for the concert to begin.
You are startled? This room log-built, and the benches,
and this stovepipe sticking in the air
They enter, kicking the wet snow from the mukluks,

Inside the parkas, eyes darting through the hood,
they are watching you.

Who are these people: hair back straight
and black, a touch of yellow in the skin,
and the cheeks high. Do you smell fish?
Taste the strong taste of reindeer?

You are thinking: what am I doing
in this forgotten place, terribly alone;
if I must play again, to Warsaw as it was,
Berlin, and glorious Paris, then restored
it puzzles you; but at least you're not bored.

Why you? Why not the stark Russian, more akin,
the sweep of the steppes, or the brooding Finn?

Shall we tell you how the day ends here,
and the night moves slowly, a glacier,
how the drifts close behind the man
behind the footprints in the snow . . .

Why you? It seems men have a longing
for what they cannot have.
In this case, if you please, something refined.
This world culture, they want defined

as you have in this melody—is it fir
poured on ice: what is subtle about desire?

Do you feel your fingers warming?
It's been a long time since the last polonaise.
Will you try another étude?
Of course the audience is crude,
but the encores have never fallen on a purer air . . .

It's been a most unusual evening.
For once you play without a reputation.
They'll probably call you the "piano-playing man,"
And back in Metlakatla, Umniak, and Ketchikan,
they'll never know you for an egotist:
they never heard of Balzac, Lizst.

Thanks for the concert. Is it cold too
where you're going? We're moving into the night again.
A most unusual evening . . .
You have learned about music,
and we have learned about men.

1944–45

Ghost Farm

Somewhere north of here—the rumor goes—
a man is raising ghostly chickens spectral goats
transcendental cows with astral bodies;
vegetable and plants—they say—cast their shadows
over enchanted ground.
Unable to confirm   we're forced to guess:
he must be versed   in tides and moonfall
or else with hired witches   casting spells
across the fields   able to persuade

                          vines in silhouette
to perform the dance of wicked nights.

But still we have   the skeptic question:
How at the source   of mundane daily labor
could there be black magic   working forbidden ways
      among the artichokes   cabbages and beans?

Somewhere south of here another rumor has begun:
a ghost is raising men! For what purpose and what buyers
no one seems to know.
                 North and South   East and West
through higher and lower regions   intimations
                       of Heaven and/or Hell:
winds may bring us odors   to help us to decide—
or perhaps send for *soil samples*

                 before we curse the Garden
for what tends to grow   beyond intention
toward all the weird and twisted shapes:
        calling the snake who glides there
        the devil of our dreams.

1976

The Torturer's Horse

The torturer's horse scratches its innocent behind on a tree.
                    —W. H. Auden

Meanwhile back at the ranch the rider dozes
through a dream of chemical invention   the glory
of roseate days the defoliant war captured
with one throw of the lariat: comic opera presents
the film star as Colonel Bird seizing power from General Worm—

His chief of staff withholds the latest news from Brazil
all those cheap shoes and martyred priests attract
Exxon and the slide-rule engineers to the town
deep in the jungle where the natives hide in trees—

He returns to sleep assured that the cinema world
offers a scenario of miracles to soothe the consumer . . .
Meanwhile the torturer's horse—somewhere off camera—
dreams of the universal grass: north or south or east or west:
grazing in all those fields: the dream too commonplace for words.

1977/1985

Part Two

Assault on the White Frame House

1.
In the area circled, using a pointed stick,
we indicate, precise as divots, the target ground . . .

Here rooted in its postal zone, the dead-end door
leased from the mortgaged street,
where taxes loosened the nails and broadcasts
                                        warped the boards,
the forever mood of chintz falls over the benchmark,
and even a funeral of flies held on the porchlight
helps to preserve the camouflage of quiet.

But inside the arena of its usual location,
observe the sleeper awake from a mouse-colored chair,
his needle swinging wildly, his optics efficient,
and suddenly out of wherever, the late-model children,
with features not on our blueprint, have appeared.
And beware the scooter across the flagstones,
the roller skate sly under the final stair.

                    We have ordered, therefore,
                    the target secured,
                    the wallpaper decoded,
                    the brain cells exploded,
                    with victims a victory insured.

2.
We precisely entered the street
at zero hundred hundred hours hours . . .

The crack newsboy division commanded by
inhale, exhale,
reports the enemy deployed at
the fence that needs painting.

Patrols must set the table:
the achievement of identical eggs,
the self-watching, tick-tock conversation,
is their limited objective.

FIRE HEADLINE ONE!

Operation Foot in the Door means
the sale of one pink silk souvenir
of Hawaii, and early American
god bless needlework

On behalf of 51 percent
of all widows and orphans
the general staff decided
one in every living room.

FIRE HEADLINE TWO!

For bravery beyond the call of
mom's hot apple pie
mad antenna sprawled on the scenery
darling-i-love-you uses this product.

3.
When the head is a geranium plant,
and needs to be watered once a day—
lips are the shutters never opened;

When the blood swims in a pipeline,
and interior wiring guides the veins
into a smooth and cheated flow of impulse;

When the day is fixed as teeth or walls,
and the walked-on flesh stretches into corners
of toes and fingers its carpet of identity;

Then the mind enmeshed in its furniture
stores in a vacuum closet its idiot umbrellas,
and like these curtains, fades dull, accepting light.

4.
Inside the sleeper, the cubic dream grows ranch-sized
and the room, shaken alive, quivers with dimension.
The mahogany stain spreads, deepens into
                                    a Lincoln legend,
the chandelier whirls into a shaft, lightning
                                    a surgeon's mask,
and the body bends like glass, passing a sonic barrier;
but the forbidden match of his childhood
                                    strikes this helium,
and back to the jungle of flat and high goes
                                    a shrunken head.

Inside the sleeper, codes conceal the treaty of his birth,
wanders into the wallpaper garden,
and ponders, squaring the circle with his feet.

5.
Within the waking hour, a message from reality:
an electrical proof: all channels equally infected.

Because it is written, the impartial veins bless
the test tube gift and the drugged romance.

     because you have listened
     because you have listened
     because you have listened
It might be fun to throw the huge child
back and forth between ourselves—
but then, I get tired so easily!
Or let's play that symbol game
where you hide beneath your skin,
then marry anonymous, who signed
the necessary forms, and thank god
for the birthmark—
You never suggest anything
all you do
is count your blessings
inside the womb.

6.
We sent a small force to isolate the garage
and reduce the strongpoint of their sandbox;
then with gophers encircled, we began
the frontal din of our synchronized watches.

In order to spare the mail-order treasures,
the living room was declared out of bounds.
As the day ended, we occupied their porch swing . . .

With the fall of the white frame house,
proceed to the tank path inside the playground.

With the tenant machine installed,
begin to dial numbers for a nation.

1954

Schliemann at Mycenae

1.
Consider him first in the favorable light
of passion pursued and rewarded: the single-minded
effort that would not be denied—aside from talent
or knowledge that later years and more precise
instruments would tend to disqualify: *in situ*
on the rocky ground beside the sweating dark-faced men
through those tedious Greek summers shifting rock
from rock from clay from bone—his own face lightened
as the first artifacts appeared—even more when
the unrelenting light was softened by the form
of Sophia the Greek bride (*sophia*: combining poetry
and wisdom)—Schliemann in person directing the probe
of a hundred English shovels—important to have the
quality of English steel—and we may put aside
the downgrading names that followed him: *rich amateur*
he was called by the official scientists in Germany
slow to follow the acclaim he finally found in England.

2.
Observe him then digging to find Troy
just where Homer told him to—yet they say
he never noticed where he was: incredible
unless we consider the excitement of being
there at last: how long he had pursued the dream
that glittered among these stones—
imagine the German boy at twelve reciting
from memory whole passages of the *Iliad*:
giving voice to syllables that raised into
sight encounters on the damp beaches and bronzed
the shields of the god-obeying warriors . . .

3.

He'd come so far from Mecklenburg and from Minna
who loved him most when buried treasure
was the favorite childhood game—left her
and the town behind when he began accumulating marks
and francs and dollars: so intense the dream
his wanderings followed a straight line
leading to that moment when he arrived at Mycenae
ready for epiphany—only to be confronted by
greedy bureaucrats and dubious experts who scoffed
at his careless procedures: "*more passion than science . . .*"

4.

More than a century later we wonder also
what Sophia thought: married to this almost ungainly
foreigner—not to say *father figure*—as they tracked
the silent ancestor fleshed out by dream: her own
and his borrowed inheritance soon to be revealed
in the widening circle of the assembled stones . . .
Wonder heightens into awe as we recall that olive-dark
morning when Sophia noticed something glinting there
among the crevices—as she signaled Heinrich and when
he glanced there he sent away the workmen: that evening
in their tent in a gesture of solemnity and love
he fitted to her chest and throat the golden diadem . . .

5.

What more remained? Years of love and digging
and the active voice of Homer persuading
him that he would look upon the face—
chiseled into gold—that was surely Agamemnon—
even overhear the most moving conversation
ever spoken: Achilles touched by Priam's tears,

both weeping then for Patroclus and Hector's hacked body . . .
That was his special hour in the citadel
of the Atridae—soon after, as we said,
professionals of the new sciences he helped
bring into being would dislodge his evidence
and put into another plane and time artifacts
he had misgauged by more than a thousand years . . .

6.
We listen closer, though, when the testimony
of the spade is joined with twilight striking
a landscape that verifies what Schliemann guessed:
what the poet told was tenacious and literal truth:
that beings silenced by time have shared
the shrill desires that gods or demons choose
to hook or hang upon the human frame . . .
For whatever the exact location of the altars
and samples he uncovered there, we now observe
the lithe and gifted chorus swaying on these stones.

1978

Part Three

One of a Kind

Dreaming he is the unafflicted man
who rises to discard this single garment
of vulnerable flesh—setting forth at last
from the constricted shape to wander
for a while liquid as the river: the flow is freedom
that says goodbye to arrival or return
yet stays in sight of the flowering shore . . .

For somewhere is the very one he summons
memory to retrieve: most likely to be loved:
the cleverest monkey on the ladder climbing
the rungs of his own identity; glory and jest
converge in this strange motley uniform—

Here Janus assumes the double face and mask
looking forward and back at the same time—
and there is Thespis weeping for the clown
who with better luck or in a more serious time
might have been martyred and preserved:
worshipped as artifact in a treasured jar.

1978/1986

Lines in Praise of an American Novelist

—*for Nelson Algren*

He works in that considerable summer,
in the stockyard city, in the city of confinement,
in the fevered season, in the bright endemic hour,
when each one shared his body heat with strangers—
one street of walls contained them: one geography of contagion.

He walks through tension and the electric hours,
through the electric streets, the breeding ground,
the lost smell of hallways, through voices rising
where the human step, confined to stairs, repeats
and moves between collected doors before the name is nailed.

He moved into light at the unmentioned table,
into the cinematic circle: light on the centered heads
cut down by night-shade green, light on the foretold fingers
dealing the shuffled kings—all darken with the gift
                              of eyes exchanged—
and the morning of the child begins: in the night
                              of killing games.

And we are one and many in a calculated line
where among the lighted faces, the simple face is chosen:
and we enter the vast night court, shuffling inside
                              between the bailiff's arms—
Our evenings in this world obsessed
                              with the realism of the police,
we come to trial defended by our luck—our sentence
                              is dark and suspended.

1958

George Oppen: 1908–1984

Somewhere in his skin he was becoming
the poem of his disappearance: words within
the man becoming the man within the words—
going or gone into a different space
his mind moving through doors or windows
seeking a face a name   lost in corridors   in empty rooms
memory wandering wild the shifting light over water . . .

Holding here and now a book a photograph
a poem to study among shell fragments and pebbles
on the beach—here as elsewhere/then as now
we believe and testify there is no departure
but entrance into a widening space   the boat sailing
toward the island where trees are named for children . . .

And still we cannot solve the paradox of speech
through silence or the love for one person
converted into the implicit politics of witness,
love enlarged to share the "bitter bread of exile"—
bridge across the void: here or elsewhere as the wind
or light indicates: the shadowed stone/the almost silence
through which we hear a steady ticking in the grass.

Memory reverses to return to the river in his voice.
The mariner in his skin   patrols the grieving light.
The words he taught to navigate   pilot the harboring dream.

1984

An Afternoon in Athens

—In Memory of R.W.D.

Handing the tea cups across the table
the years went spinning back to that afternoon
when she climbed the steps toward the white temple—
memory made it white although the exact color
might have mixed earth and a thousand years
of bright and fading suns that shined
a complicated grandeur then in her young eyes—
She leaned now on the wooden cane
feeling the weight of all that time,
could not remember what she was going toward
or what followed after—what was the thought
the thread of which had fallen from her hands?
Her fingers tightened on the handle of the cup
not shadows but the living presence of the young
dark hair and loving voices: the light that shone
through all those streets and all those stones—

She looked at them and saw that they were listening—
waiting for what had touched her to touch them
through her words—said something in a low voice
they couldn't quite hear: did she want to remind them
of that other time when she thought: *Homer was there.*
Her lips moved but she could not form the words:
"Young as they are now I was then."

1980

Seekers Awake

It is strange to be in motion, without direction or distinction. One is conscious only of roads opening and closing, the rise and fall of light, the darting birds. No name for this landscape; the fugitive images flicker. All we can hope for is that it is—or soon will be—more one place than another.

At a time like this, I have only to extend my hand and believe that something or other will fall into it. . . . Making the experiment, this is what happens: I find myself holding a book. The cover shows a traveler resting in deep, stiff grass. In his right hand is a staff; he is leaning forward, making an effort to rise. I look again at the picture, and this time observe a small turtle just beside him on the grass. Its mouth is close to his ear: as if whispering some message. (How absurd this all sounds.)

I wonder why this image should appear now, while I am still meditating on the relative merits of real or imagined landscapes. . . . And for some reason my mind turns toward the more familiar sight: the backyard of a house where I once lived. A small space with a few trees, a little patch of dried grass. And just at this moment, in some unexplained way, there is a kind of crisscrossing of images. There is a sudden insight, a vision that brings an absurd, unanswerable question: "How does the tree—or the traveler—look to the turtle?"

1970/1998

Conversations About a City

Different voices coming from different directions. And just at this moment when you already feel the subject has been discussed from every conceivable point of view. But it keeps coming back, doesn't it, making the case either for your remaining here, or to consider leaving, finding other alternatives.

And it is just at this point when, without further notice, you hear a kind of disembodied voice coming through the air: "Well, go ahead, leave if you want to." And as you look around, not really expecting anyone to be there, the voice continues: "Of course there are other places, which conceivably might have more to offer." There is a slight pause and then: "Is this what you have in mind?" There is no mistaking the mocking tone.

Well, you get the message. You know how easy it is to succumb, to be rocked to sleep by the cooling mist, the invitational air. And just then, out of the past, the words you once wrote suddenly appear: *seems cut in the rock, seems to be lasting . . .* Then you remember how important was the presence of the surrounding sea. Remember the return, after a considerable absence, standing on the deck, watching the land harden and darken in the distance. A return that was also somehow a farewell, unexpected and yet inevitable, not only to this, but to all cities everywhere.

1971

from

All This Is Here

(2003)

Ritual of Return

Entering the ambiguous forest
we stumble through the ritual
of return: studying the trail where
every branch sways ripe with intimation:
here rider & horse went down—
there the terrified bison fell
into crevices: creatures whom love
and chemistry abandoned: gone gone
into thickening twilight   dropped by gun or knife
the blind hand of unknown circumstance—
As if by going back we could retrace
the course   retrieve that moment when
touched by the wind   we might have made
a different choice—as if this time
we could avoid the dark betrayal—
resist the beguiling image that stirs
the forgotten ancestor in our flesh:
even now we feel it beckon through the leaves:
the light of all we were—and might have been . . .

1979

The One-Sided Conversation

"What took you so long? Who sent for you?"

Remember: it's not your story, but the conversation between the Geologist and the Astronomer. This sounding as you sift through the fictive baggage of the mind. Consider using the first person tense/intense that brings the obsessive scrutiny of every word and image.

What slows you down is the aging flesh—along with the heavy fictive baggage of the mind. Each time you leave to go somewhere, you face the prolonged departure and the disputed arrival. I suggest you might then find yourself elsewhere from your stated destination. You know it often happens that the map and territory so seldom coincide. You might consider this as a little more to remember, a little less to anticipate.

It's as if the name and number passed in review as different beings or even former lives—carried as contraband smuggled in snug containers. As if the truth needed to be concealed from some Customs Inspector who opens and stares at everything, looking for the essential clue that will alert and win the admiration of his superiors and eventually guarantee him fame and promotion . . .

Light When It Moves

Light when it moves across steel towers
the imprint of gargoyle faces on storage tanks—
the city is suddenly there as sculpture—
not mere geometry or urban madness but metal
and stone molded to function—the here and now
of traffic the noise that turns loose a giddy
partygoer's vision of tomorrow (we are not invited)
when we may be launched within a capsule
zooming off to escape the normal mind's
nesting with inference: home the divided/uncertain spaces.

1970/1987

Directed by a Clown, the Cats Perform

Playing with the cat, how can I tell she is not amusing herself with me?
— Michel de Montaigne

. . . Not perhaps a serious question. Does it really matter who provides and who receives the pleasure of these moments? I bring it up here simply because it came to mind recently at the end of a broadcast of the evening news. It was the closing item, offered as a "lighter touch" to what had gone before. Briefly, what was shown took place in a theater in Moscow that presents a troupe of performing cats directed by a clown. Also shown, as the cats went through their paces, was the entranced faces of their audience, mostly children. As for the clown himself (I believe the name was Yuri), he is a long-time professional, someone at the top of his profession. This because he had to obtain permission to restore and refurbish the theater that had long been standing empty. And success was apparently immediate, for the performances took place before packed houses. . . .

. . . Now comes a more serious question, one I'm sure the reader has already thought to ask: how were these cats persuaded to perform? I have heard the usual grim stories about trainers using "induced helplessness" and something else called "aversion therapy." But if I ever knew the details of what these terms include, I seem to have forgotten them. Without thinking much about all this, I have shared the general belief that cats are traditionally immune—a case apart—with their trademark of individual personality and independence. But I really don't know any more about them than anyone else who has shared living space with a succession of cats over the years.

. . . I had not intended to parade my ignorance here. I had hoped only to say what I had seen—and let it go at that. But I have to go further and confess that, as a child, and even later, I could never quite believe what I saw at the Circus. Not in the Tiger jumping through a hoop ringed with fire. Not in a troupe of Elephants in a prancing procession. This is not to say that I could not appreciate the wonder of what seemed to be happening—without having to admit that it was as real as things were in the real world. . . . I can hear the voice that says: "Isn't this the path to denial?" And I do admit this now: thinking back to the entranced faces of those children. For them, there is as yet no urgent question of surrender and accommodation. They can still enter the realm of wonder without question. A realm where the Clowns and the Cats together give us those amusing moments that make our lives tolerable.

Credo

A cigarette lingering in a porcelain bowl,
A half-filled cup (yes, I'm an optimist) on
The Indian taboret, the phone off its hook
Murmuring *Credo, credo* like a true believer
Perish in the weak October light among
Rose-plush ottomans and buhl cabinets.
The paintings have witnessed more than age.
There is a book laid by, an eye closed forever.
Outside, the leaves drift across the terrace.

The mailman won't ring this bell today,
And not because of snow piled against the door
Or hail or the mad dogs in the front yard.
He too is footsore and weary. He looks sad.
But what could the letter say? you asked,
As well you might   as if a pen could mouth
That formula which claps a lock on night
Or kills the muzzled terrors in our way.

Nothing, I answer. What do the words matter?
Even theories of silence burn to an ash.
The cup that runs over pours out false names.
And voices from some rejected telephone
Murmur *Credo, credo*—to an ear of stone.

1975

In Distaste

Distaste which takes no credit to itself is best.
                              —Marianne Moore

When I believed it, before there were retakes,
death was preferred to a dirty uniform.
One crooked arm up out of the snow
pointed toward the trenches—or even earlier:
"I turned around, and there was a flame
in the place of his head . . ."

But now there's a pause: the Director calls
a break for lunch; these lovely children
make the best soldiers (swathed in cream oil)—
Not to be bitter about what passes for Art:
the game implies the gamester—mind travels
toward the gimp and the gamey: hold there.

Nothing to be done when the shadow
grows lean and lengthens: in the breach
as in the observance, one is watched and forgotten;
when love's reversed, will hate return the wheel?
Enter a late listing for the as yet unsolved.

1979

Meditation on a Stuffed Owl

1. Why an owl? Why not a rabbit—a hawk—a field mouse?

2. The fool is at it again: as if the question provides the answer.

3. The search for: "prima materia." The child on seeing ice cubes melting: "Will I melt too?"

4. Landing on the island one foggy morning (could they believe what they saw?), strands of light drifting through the ruins, the temple of Venus . . . Who were the builders? Staring at the green lichen imprinted on the gray stones, they wondered: What is it that echoes down the corridors?

5. But on the desert they stood in different relation to a different space. It was the voice of the Lecturer that returned them to themselves: "Base wider than seven football fields . . ." And as they stared, the voice continued: "When Kings were suns, stones of any size could be moved . . . Since then, we have worshipped emblems of light—not Light itself . . ."

6. Is the Sphinx mute—or the Travelers deaf? We follow the voice in the wind: If not in the stone—then where? A few ambitious dreamers offer alternatives: in the sea—in the sky—in the stars?

7. Fish-talk. Wolf howls. Whale songs. Stones wince at the hammering . . .

8. To refuse radiance? We are still at this moment

　　　　　　　riding a raft of names and words

　　　　　　　into unknown waters . . .

1975/1985/2000

Time to Destroy/to Discover

(1972)

Time to Destroy/to Discover

In my case a picture is a sum of destructions. I do a picture—
then I destroy it. In the end, though, nothing is lost. . . .
                          —Picasso

1.
                    Relics, the rich hobby of collectors—
                    Or membership in the bomb squad?
Entering the villa of investors
                    light spreads across the window
                    a private view of the sea
The conversation turns   to the latest offering
          in Swiss banks   the name invoked
          performs well   in a falling market
It is agreed at the highest levels:
          work of this kind belongs to the Republic—
But locked in the vault
                          of his own house
the currency of the flesh
                          faces devaluation. . . .
Standing here in khaki shorts
                    and dark sandals
          wheel of color   trailing odors   filling the mind

It goes back   as it goes forward
          long lines of weather   stretched across the landscape
The extended definition   of those unquiet places
          field marshal of time   and booted foot-soldier
nightfall in city and garden
                                invokes the distant caves
bringing memory into the face of light. . . .

So much has scattered   lives that ask and disappear
faces turning into pages
                         of illuminated manuscript
a horde of scholars   waiting to descend
                         displaced names   lost in the flood
of museums   smell of burning   fills the room—

continues where it begins
                         through the nostrils, the fingertips—
The question never ends:
                         what does it take
                                 to move this morning?

2.

Light spreads across the porcelain:
                                         colors turn
          we are plunged into   the face of mornings
          waiting for the wind   eye of travelers
          neither meeting nor mating   feathers of stranded birds
          neither message nor air   all flights canceled
          smell of veined leaves burning—

We are again in the presence
          of the sick rose, fearful lizard, bleeding frog
                 despairing rocks await erosion . . .
Needle quivers   tremors in the tree   another season
     It begins   as it continues   from the static
     to the extreme possibility: infinite regress
                                     decapitation
While in the same hour   unannounced
                 the delicate object   waiting to be born . . .

3.

      Standing at a distance:

    watching the crow circle   the clouds perform

taking a few steps   nodding to a friend   testing the air—

signs seem favorable   no better hour   no better day

—they wait—   hands tighten on the handles

arm raised for the signal   and down, down, down

greased plungers   slide into the slot

            The moment expands

                force accumulates

                   inside the head

Going, Going   all at once

          tides of concussion

            another ocean breaking there . . .

Waiting for the earth to recover:

    the ground settles   the crow circles

        It is the same morning

here are the same faces   it had to be done   ears singing

    white dust rising . . .

          Here are the twisted chairs

    see-through walls   guts of debris   nightmare wiring

Workmen are waiting   wanting to know

    what's to be done

Step forward in full view   inspect the fragments

    the house is matter   they can see that now:

    owner's rubble: dream loves: money's mother

    lace shreds glass wire shapes

    gargoyles among the plumbing—

Tonight we will sleep on the ground.

4.

It is not necessary to paint a man
with a gun—an apple can be just as
revolutionary.

The rose of war   a young man's dream

                                      petals of explosion

open the city's core   and from this follows—

the green hand   the poisoned growth   year after year until—

stroke and counter-stroke—

                               the years revert

Light spreads across the stone   another set of walls:

once more dark vaults   where objects can be stored

in that sense: accumulation   deep out of sight

webbed indifference   and when it is indicated

       bringing forth into light   stuffed owls

       the crackling skin of serpents—

It continues as it evolves   even the cult of violence

       evolves   destruction takes place   and is replaced

It remains important   to create the occasion

          to keep the seeing alive

      while friends lovers canvasses

         appear and disappear:

Departure turns into arrival   at a moment

and through a door   where no one thinks to look

      no need to ask what remains   something is left over—

      What name What face The Critics clamor

             and so we explain:

        Left over are: Egypt and embryos

           clowns bulls warriors owls and children

cones circles squares cubes and triangles
and for that incredulous stare   we add:
These are details that can be observed!

5.

And all this time
through the closed circle   light seeks an opening
a child can understand   time to destroy to discover
(a small thing can be decisive)   to pass through
the guiding and guarding

encore l'audace

the maker's hand strays on purpose
the nature of advance   is to retreat   before the shadow
of completion—
Mornings turn into years   and all this time
the body needs attention: catch as catch can
early rising energetic gardener—
(When it is hard to rise, when there are no reasons,
put your head on her breast—and let the milk
of mornings flow)
And there it is! :   That Bursting Time
When supple fingers ripple across the
strings and the torso trembles—(to plow those fields with
fertile language)—swaying where he stands the easel
dances: Feet planted sword sighted rises to the occasion
The tattered matador never retreats—capework not always
perfect—an occasional goring condition of the trade . . .

It swells and departs on desperate and comic afternoons
(shrivels to the size of his finger)   But he returns
with serious work to be done: When the beast in man
is target the experienced hand   works with perfect timing:

spear-point enters   know exactly when   to pull it out

to assign with assurance   handle of bone

red-tipped axe   their place among the artifacts

6.

Clowns into bulls   warriors into women   owls into children

in the evolution of form   there is no perfect weather

exact placing of the seed   only confirms the limitation

dialectic of need and will   shallow as assertion

dread war of object and eye   leaves but one question:

What does it mean *to move* this morning?

7.

And then come to a place   where it is necessary to descend

        because the caves cannot be reached

                consult with the geologist

                        these layers must not be disturbed . . .

Finally entering that space

                where man in retreat worshipped bats and bears

in the light of that time which never darkens never ends

            staring at the source   tracing from cave to cathedral

                returning as himself   ready at last to begin

                    "the archaeology of the imagination"

8.

Restored to light: eye awakens: echo hides the fallen

guess or memory   —What remains of the nearby mountain?—

Early or late   expect the smell of goats   bones into milk

into leather   spaced across these stones there bursts

the glow of grass . . .

At last descending to the small sandy beach here are the waves

for which we have been waiting   children and dogs the tracing

of other shores   So long So long   stand and listen   until
there is an ear under the rib of Death   *More Is Needed*

The light of years filtered across space
throwing into the gap and crevices
all one can metamorphosize   and steal: the eternal junk-
dealer sorting with his fingers   taking and giving away
becomes the geometer   who exceeds geometry
walks without weight   moves beyond equation
to become   the astronomic gardener:
              Out there color is sound!

9.
Clowns grow old   The tattered matador
shipped to a small town   performs for jeering children
the guitarists falter   women change their names . . .

Time mounted on a stand
                              swivels at the touch
move back a step   perhaps the light hard to decipher
                    even here space is deceitful
One morning like another   having traveled this far
leaving the villa of investors
                    entering Goya's House of the Real Man
Forget yesterday and tomorrow
                    one more degree of attention
can make the difference watch closely: wind touching
the fingertips   something not here before
        wait—not yet—these fish require patience
              only when they are ready
it comes yes it comes   why not, why not indeed?
The eye between the shoulder blades!

Uncollected Works

The Conspirators

1.

. . . What are they up to now? More of the same it appears: weaving their way in, through, around the obvious, accepted places. Their movements protected, as though with a cloak of invisibility. And all this while, I suppose, gathering evidence to incriminate or intimidate their chosen targets. We have tried to prepare ourselves, to be on guard—but all we have to go on, at least for the present, are certain gestures, an unexpected emphasis on an unimportant word.

2.

. . . Is this any more than the vaguest of suspicions? Just a response to certain unexplained comings and goings? For they do seem to arrive at a time of their own choosing: and depart whenever it suits them. If indeed we can call it a "departure." It might be more accurate to say they simply appear, disappear, and after some ambiguous interval, reappear. We are left then with the sense of an unstable presence, as they seem ready, at any moment, to move back to their "true home" among the shadows.

3.

. . . I seem to be getting it all wrong. Making the familiar mistake of equating the unexplained with a foreboding that something evil or dangerous is about to take place. Perhaps I ought to admit that I have little to offer in the way of any genuine "disclosure." And leave this to those who have made careers out of naming names, telling what goes on behind closed doors. Whereas all I can do is suggest what may be taking place in plain sight, but has not yet been noticed.

4.

. . . Is this then the voice of reason or of some deep-rooted fear? It has even occurred to me that my real alternatives are to approach them, offering some substantial bribe—or to distance myself from this whole scene. (I have not mentioned the possibility of reporting them to the proper authorities, but the absence of any "braver self," I admit, puts this out of reach.)

5.

. . . I have decided my best course of action is to discuss this with a close, trusted friend. One who in the past has proven helpful on a number of occasions . . . His advice, it turns out, is simply to forget about all this. Anything else, he says, is innocence and naiveté, opening the door to a possibly dangerous obsession. "Hasn't it occurred to you that this is something that we have always known: *That we are them. And they are us.*"

See It, Believe It, and It Happens

1.
. . . Shown once and shown again—and again—as if we cannot see it often enough. The scene, the image, the brief sequence, the fascination with what we had not expected to see—and still have trouble believing—this is indeed what we are seeing. We try telling ourselves it happened this way for this reason. But another part of the mind reminds us how, like a disaster, it arrives in its own way, its own time.

2.
. . . Filmed by an amateur, whom no one has hired, summoned, or instructed, the camera shows what it shows. The figures seen but hard to focus. In the murky light, a kind of fog, an unexplained conjunction of black and white. A kind of dance; a ritual of power exploding upon the powerless. The arms are raised; the arms descend. It is retribution; it is justice. . . .

3.
. . . Another film plays and replays in the mind. It offers a "theorem," in which the scene is "witnessed," but with a different focus. This time with an added distancing, the event-as-perceived has become so familiar that we are prepared to discuss the precise details. Prepared to take sides, make judgments—as when fear and hope collide—thankful also that the battered head is not our own. Now the color of the body on the ground is seen as a cause, a motivating factor. We have reason now to widen the context, to examine the aftermath, to say what is wrong in *the city of angels*. . . .

4.
. . . The blows have been delivered. A point has been reached where there is no inhibition, no prohibition. In the name of the law, men in uniform have taken the law into their own hands. The sound of iron encased in wood falls upon the hollowed skull. A sound that even now claims a place for itself, a secret place.
. . . A strange thought makes its way through unknown crevices in the mind. It occurs to us that we have experienced a kind of "revelation." We have learned that no inhibition, no prohibition is also the "shadowed name" of freedom. There is a "victim song," a "victim story" that takes possession of our eyes and ears. We see it and we hear it coming through the night air. It arrives along with the music of love, the scent of blossoms. It instills a fragrance that reaches into and permeates memory and dream: a fragrance that haunts us, long after the smell of burning departs from the city.

Goodbye Home. Hello Somewhere.

1.

. . . A time neither one is prepared for. The words have been spoken, and there is nothing more to be said. They have arrived at a place where what is broken cannot be repaired; where what is lost cannot be retrieved. . . . The loss can be summarized in a word that constellates into a range of meanings: "home." As though standing there, they could watch it change, become abstract, *untenanted*. As though in its place the word *house* has appeared. And they can only stare at the alien letters, unsure of its spelling. Stare with growing apprehension, wondering what it could mean. And perhaps even further, more remote, more menacing—intimations of the unthinkable—if the word *shelter* should then occur to them. For once this arrives, even if it is still only peripheral, in the remote precincts of the mind, then the world, *their world*, can no longer be considered theirs.

2.

. . . And how long before the arrival of increasingly separate, uncontrolled dreams? How long before they begin to receive news from a fractured world? A world that sends their way a procession, a "carnival" of masked, hooded figures. The loved one at last unmasked, revealed to be "demon" or "monster". . . But it is not only the hostile, wearying nights that have to be dealt with. There is also a succession of days into which various "intruders" may appear. Just there, on the familiar streets, a single, emblematic figure may confront them. It may be one who appears huddled and diminished against a blank, unforgiving wall. And this figure, as now seen, does not merely stand there, but makes a significant gesture: thrusting forward a bent, smudged white paper cup. A gesture that is both imploring and aggressive. And at this very moment the word *shelter* has advanced, adopting this specific form. It repeats, this time with a smeared but believable human face.

3.

. . . Moving now in separate orbits, each may enter their his own version of an intolerable space, their his own kind of "exile." Where there was "he and she," "you and I," now there is the one who does and the one who is done to. She, for instance, may begin studying the mirror, seeing there a face that reads: *the face of absence.* She may witness the transition from "home" to "house." Witness how a chair, a table, a lamp, can be stripped of its past, deprived of any future. And what of him? What reaches him as the separation unfolds? He too, it seems, has entered a "questionable space." He finds himself reading into papers on a desk smiles and whispers of those he thought he knew, now suspect, possible conspirators.

4.

. . . The terms of speech are now the terms of loss. It is a time of not-quite grief, not-quite anger. But with elements of both. All the familiar emotions may still be present, but somehow acquire different names. There may be a choice that involves merely changing partners. Or the beginning of a kind of "transformation." One or the other may ask: "Are we more visible when we have learned to see ourselves—one as each one, apart from the other? Parting one from the other, do we depart also from our reliance upon the mirror, the photograph?"

5.

. . . After all this, after the goodbyes have been spoken, can another self, other selves, emerge? One that is prepared to say—even with a still tentative voice—"Hello, somewhere?" Strange things affect the outcome. Forgotten things from yesterday, and from the earliest years. An inclination, a tendency, a predisposition, may turn out to be decisive. . . . The man may now feel himself drawn to a place dreamed about but never entered. Perhaps a small, single house on the edge of a forest . . . The woman may find herself one morning standing before the figure huddled beside the wall. She may not know even a moment before what she really intends. She may be quite surprised, a few moments later, at why she reached into her purse, and placed whatever money her hand held into the white cup that was thrust forward toward her. . . .

The Lecture

1.

I wish first to thank those in charge for giving me the opportunity. I trust none of these remarks will in any way abuse the privilege. Even as I say this, however, the clock is ticking away—an immediate reminder that there are tyrannies beyond our control.

Today, as many times before, I will try to define the various kinds of restrictions, to separate the imposed from the self-imposed. Not in any strict sense, for that seems impossible, but simply to delineate the apparent boundaries. Within this limited objective, I hope, however, some light may be shed: not without value for those directly concerned.

I begin then with the simple, the obvious—merely to peel away what does not belong to this discussion. I refer to those minor afflictions, too small and too arbitrary to be considered genuine burdens. The cat, for instance, is part of my existence; at times he makes claims, impinges on my way of life. But there is no question here, on either side, of enslavement.

To go a short step further, I call attention to those figures with whom one is in contact as part of the ordinary business of living. Here one has to grant the accountant, the lawyer, the insurance salesman are not instruments of bondage. No matter how irritating to make appointments, prepare the necessary forms, respond to constant reminders.

I have found it easier, in any case, to remind myself that I am not their target. Of course I too have had moments of unthinking rage: dreamed of burning letters, emptying contents of files, scattering documents from the nearest window. But in calmer times it is clear nothing would be solved, nothing gained.

For the wheels continue to turn, obligations to appear on all sorts of occasions. While I may feel singled out, imposed upon, serious reflection shows this is not the case. One can argue, no doubt, that burdens are unfair, unevenly distributed; one can then propose remedies, suggest solutions. But even this, as we know, does little to alleviate or change the feeling—that of stress, of being weighed down, preyed upon.

And as the feeling grows—to the point where things seem intolerable—there comes an impulse toward flight, toward a change of scene. As many of you, I have also been subject to this: dreamed of broader vistas, uncluttered hours. I too have yearned for the soft wind, the light step across shelves of snow, the mothering murmur of the sea.

But it is clear that, aside from a few brief interludes, I can only move within these spaces, listening and being listened to, observing and being observed. On occasion I may have worthwhile companions, bracing adventures, inspiring thoughts. That still does not secure for me a place among the children of light. . . .

2.

We have now, I think, a better view of the essential distinctions. We could go on, making further, sharper differentiations. But at this point I propose we move into a wider context. For I can already hear those voices that say: of what use is all this rhetoric? What does it tell us of a world in which millions go hungry, sleep on wet streets, lack shelter from menacing skies?

I would agree that we cannot escape these questions. That what we feel as burdens, as restrictions, may indeed be merely the irritation of the over-privileged. For example, I refer to a report published recently in the foreign press. This incident took place in one of the small, almost forgotten countries: a grenade thrown by some terrorists exploded in the marketplace. In the excitement, a number of children disappeared. That is, their bodies were never found. Assuming at least some survived, where are those children today? I have heard it said that their parents know, but are too terrified to complain. One may imagine the child carried off by hooded men, forced into servitude, perhaps worse. We may feel this belongs to fiction, to the remote past. Yet documents are available—from several international agencies—that show this is no exaggeration.

But one need not strain the mind toward the exotic, the unusual. For it is a commonplace that, in any number of places, bodies still bend close to the terraced earth. And it is from these, voiceless and remote, that much of the food we eat, the clothes we wear, still derives. Such instruments as whips and chains are less in evidence, and perhaps torture is more reserved for special occasions. . . .

. . . This note I have just been handed—*unsigned of course*—says I have only a few minutes left. It also asks me to identify those who have endorsed my position. This of course I decline to do. By my own choice, though, I will conclude soon. For those who wish to learn more of my views, there is what I have written over the years. I am sorry most of it remains inaccessible, out of circulation; I would challenge those responsible: either make these available, or make a public bonfire of their contents. . . . I have considered going on—shouting past the dead microphones—but recognize this would be self-defeating. I yield instead, as an act of good faith, to those who claim the discussion should proceed behind closed doors. I have their assurance that, with secrecy guaranteed, fruitful negotiations can take place.

For a while then it seems necessary that members of the press, the general public be barred. I have been asked to announce that, for the next session, those with the proper credentials will be notified.

1993

Making the Claim

1.

It seems only fair to say I have done everything possible: filled out the forms, gone through the whole procedure exactly as prescribed. And so far all I have to show for my efforts are a few printed memos—the same no doubt sent to all claimants. I have of course read them over carefully, and there is nothing that sheds the least light on the particulars of my own case. At this point I have to wonder if it is worthwhile to continue, eventually reach the appropriate authorities. . . .

2.

. . . More than a month and no further word. Still, I am resolved not to lose patience. There may be some reason for the delay that I have not yet thought of. I suppose that the documents submitted have to be carefully scrutinized. Which may require the informed judgment of more than one specialist. I must also take into account that each item must travel from office to office, desk to desk. And each will have to be stamped and initialed, processed, then sent on to the proper eventual destination.

3.

. . . At last, it appears I have exactly what I have been waiting for: a letter addressed to me personally from the Office of Individual Complaints. My case, it seems, has been mislaid in the files; there is an acknowledgment that an "error" has been made. Fortunately it has come to the attention of "the undersigned" that the material I sent was assigned an incorrect number and sent to the wrong office. All that remains now is to call the number indicated and make an appointment. Once this procedure is followed, there should be no further difficulty. But it is of the utmost importance that I should appear there *in person*, without further delay. . . .

4.

. . . Having all this in mind now, telling myself I am close now to a resolution of the case. And yet as I move toward the phone, something holds me back. . . . I can see myself being given a number, taking my place in line. As the time passes and the line moves slowly forward, I would try to be pleasant, even affable, to those beside me. Waiting my turn, I might remark on the weather, making casual, expected small talk. . . . I am trying hard not to deceive myself. For it is one thing to contemplate this scene, and another to actually go there.

I have to ask myself: isn't it better to keep this as a possible course of action, rather than rush into things? For after all, although it would mean a tighter budget,

I can get by without the remuneration that satisfaction of my claim might bring. And yet, and yet, there is another kind of "satisfaction" that a favorable outcome of the case would give me. It would show, once and for all, that the authorities—*whoever they might be*—would have realized that I cannot be ignored. And that no matter how badly or carelessly they may have handled—or rather *mishandled*—the entire matter, mine was a name they would have to remember.

1969/1993

Concentric Propositions

It is, therefore, necessary to develop a new kind of thinking, free from the dogmatism of our self-created laws which—though being useful and justified in a world of concrete objects and concepts—are not compatible with the laws of a universe that goes far beyond our sense-experience and thought-forms. . . . By moving in ever decreasing circles toward the object, a many-sided, i.e. multi-dimensional, impression [is] formed from the sum-total or the integrating superimposition of single impressions from different points of view.

    —Lama Anagarika Govinda, *Main Currents in Modern Thought*, 25:3

1.

Sartre says somewhere that we have to improve the biography of man. The statement is appealing as a broader view than that offered by psychology. Psychological questions stem from the life we have lived, out of the life that is *available* to us. But the question of extending and improving life—individually and collectively—forces us to project beyond this, to consider what is *not yet* available.

    On the large scale, this means the encounter of history; on a personal level, the opening of new horizons. Psychology then can take its rightful place as the effort to supply the means that relate to these larger ends.

2.

The Impossible Dialogue: Between one who sees what he cannot tell, the other who tells what he cannot see. Between the mind that has not yet arrived—and the other that has already departed. Between the one who is deaf—and the other who is in jail.

3.

Add Aphorisms: It is because we make so much of ourselves that so little can be made of us. We become what we study—let us study what we become.

4.

The Companions: One is never alone. At the very least there is this steady, faithful, unobtrusive pair—who appear and reappear under different names. Sometimes there are more: four, five, even six at a time. And this is just as well: simply there is too much "ground" for one man to cover. . . .

5.

The Secret Life: Deciphering one code, inventing another. Reaching for the beyond—and being terrified it might be reached.

6.

The Flickering Light: Different ways of dealing with the intolerable: culture as the filter for consciousness: a "light" filter. Consider also the situation in the "dark-room," the light that ruins the negative.

7.

History: The period with no sentence. The sentence with no period.

8.

Coastlines: There is no way to tell what these moments mean. It comes back in shards, in fragments—not even a memory. And who can say they are done with these things? The dog runs along the wide expanse of sand; the child watches and waits. The sea circles, pounds the black rocks; spray dances in the air. . . .

9.

Self and Soul: Talk of these things is inevitably embarrassing: it is doubtful whether one clarifies anything, or adds to the confusion. But here goes . . . *I am* and *I live*. The essential self of the *I am* is seen here in conjunction with an existential *I live*. The relation between them can be described as that of an internal "I-Thou." I see myself in the world, moving through the scene: the "living" image. But it is always "that one" that I see. (There is no photograph of the soul.)

The *I am* remains invisible, concerned with other matters: the intangible, invisible, inexpressible. Sent on a journey, this *I am* inevitably heads toward the country of dream and fantasy. . . .

10.

Eye into Thou: And what of love in all this? Having posited both an integral I-Thou (the self in harmony) and an I-Other (self-estranged, in conflict) and an external, I now define the love relationship: My I-Thou loves your I-Thou. It is not simply I and Thou. Nor is it Thou and Thou. For you have your life and I have mine. As I make the clear distinction: I am and I live; you too are in the same situation.

11.

Interludes in Limbo: Another of those gray afternoons. How to resolve: a book, a movie, a play? The usually desired aloneness cannot sustain; the present dissolves. We begin searching for the newspaper—always misplaced at these times. And the absurd conversation starts: someone has said something about this or that film, the director, the star . . . At last: the choice. Not that much is expected. But it does get us out of the house, out of ourselves. On the way, further silly talk about the time "it" begins—can we even agree at which theater "it" is playing?

12.

Reader's Progress: Not too seriously, but thinking about it in terms of steps taken, where the writer attempts the invitation: (a) Credibility; (b) Acceptance; (c) Involvement; (d) Participation; (e) Commitment. Thus reading as an *activity*: the progress from Spectator to Partisan.

13.

Against Entropy: "We seem to be moving toward no enchanted future, but toward a darkness from which comes no morning. Entropy is evolution in reverse." This is the feeling with which we are all familiar, well expressed by Wylie Sypher in *Loss of the Self in Modern Literature and Art*: Destruction hangs over our world; tomorrow is more perishable than ever. It is interesting, however, that Sypher also says: "Age itself is entropy, and life is a form of negative entropy: a living organism wins its individuality by resisting a tendency to fade back into the stuff of dreams from which we are made. . . ." It would seem then that, whatever the odds or circumstances, the fading, the dissolving, has to be resisted.

14.

Light and Sound: There are images that generate images, and those that have the opposite effect. As the present saying has it: something is "turned on" or "turned off." One could go on with this, noticing how the metaphor expands: to make contact, the necessary "connections," etc.

15.

In going through one's notes, one finds various "speeches" and "declarations" for no-longer-remembered occasions. Here is one inspired by a forgotten "departure": "It is of course possible that we shall meet again. But better if we accept that there might not be another chance. We should try to say what has to be said; not get mired on the surface, with the usual trivialities. . . ."

16.

The Burden of Uniqueness: For the individual: nothing like *me* ever was. For the generation: nothing like *us* ever was. But under the pressure of isolation, it changes: *Something* like us always was. . . .

17.

Expanding Consciousness: It is interesting that a quantitative standard is implied here: more is better. The qualitative word would be *deepening*—which could also suggest a "narrowing" rather than a "widening." Thus what is also concealed here is a possible conflict between the horizontal and the vertical.

18.

Hesse as a phenomenon: The exhilaration felt by the uninitiated in their first contact with metaphysics is often accompanied by a dangerous letdown. This seems to be already happening with some of the young readers of Hesse. The question of what the world *is*—no matter how dangerous and uninviting—remains after all these forays, excursions toward transcendence. Hesse himself must have known of this: cf. the ending of *Magister Ludi*.

19.

Identity Crisis, Alienation, etc.: The terms are one thing as expressed in various textbooks and clinical reports—something else as felt by the individual. It seems that one could only get to the source through an expression of feeling by the individual. One feels lost, disoriented, separated from, fragmented. Any one of these brings up its own associations, images, occasions.

20.

More of the Same: Identity: The search for "who I am" is bound up with the questions of "what I am" and "that I am." What does it mean to be human: and what does it mean to be in the world? These remain the great open-ended questions—one arrives at answers by various choices and experiences and decisions. A primary, "neutral" answer would be: it so happens that I am; it so happens that there is a world. We might say then of this often agonizing quest: out of two mysteries, we try to form one certainty.

21.

Old Mortality: Jung says the first half of life is a preparation for life; the second half, a preparation for death. But how, in fact, does one "prepare"? After fifty, one experiences the "sea change"—but again how can that be described? There is the sense of all that life lived, none of it to be recaptured. There is a certain alertness, paying attention to the day; there is less expectation, a greater acceptance. And still that says very little.

22.

Poets & Conspirators: "I am Cinna the poet. . . . not Cinna the conspirator." Voice from the crowd: "Tear him for his bad verses!" This from Shakespeare's *Julius Caesar*. Lenin said: "Every cook must learn to run the government." But the Poet whispered an aside: "Cooks may be fat—and yet their soup be thin."

23.

Art & Politics: "Politics is the art of the possible." Turn it around: "Art is the politics of the possible." Is this merely playing with words? Try to look at it seriously: the Artist takes something from the actual, turns it into the possible. (Because it is, by itself, often boring, deadly, inert.) He brings together shadow, act, gesture, form and feeling. *This converts what* is *into what might be.* Politics in its own realm is faced with the same task.

24.
Fire Without Ice: (a) Could Prometheus be persuaded to return what he stole? (b) If somehow the fire could be confined to the stove, the "roast pig" of yesterday could be the "haute cuisine" of tomorrow.

25.
Man and Crisis: The intensity of the present crisis is due, at least partly, to the uncertainty about tomorrow—not to mention next month and next year. Difficult as it is, we have to act "as if" there is a future. And do what we can to make it possible . . . It seems, though, that the pressure would not be nearly as great if our sense of the past were not also being undermined. Here at least something can be done: once viable images are found, connections and continuity can be restored. What stands in the way now is that the "data of the antecedent world" has been permitted to obstruct and prejudge the present and the future (cf. Whitehead).

26.
Ideas & Things: "No ideas but in things" (W. C. Williams). ". . . go back to the things themselves" (Husserl). If there were time, one could spin off on this, turn it in all directions. What interests me here is a possible definition of Man: "Man is an Idea—capable of being turned into a Thing." As a slave, as a commodity, at the service of the State or of a Machine. The Idea then can be distorted, suppressed, made to disappear—but not entirely and forever. . . . This is an aspect that remains, with the current discussion centering on man's animal nature and instincts, largely unexplored.

27.
On Experimentation: What can one say about the ethics of the experimenters? Up till now it has seemed as though the race for results would consume all human values. There is, however, some revaluation going on. Suggestions: to reject *any objective* that depends on turning subject into object: person into thing.

The Smile at the Foot of the Ladder

If there's one among you, or among you one, who climbed the ladder of his own identity,
he shook the hand of Mister Agony.. . . .

—A. T. Rosen

1.
. . . The painful ascent: hands gripping the sides, step after step, not knowing how much further we can go. As if it were indeed some risky venture, on a sheer rock face, that we have foolishly undertaken—perhaps to prove something, or answer someone else's challenge . . . But this is just one reading of the poet's words. Better perhaps to set aside the warning, the cautionary note, the metaphor itself, and return to the literal, familiar object. Precisely what you can see for yourself: stored in the garage, or propped against a wall that needs cleaning or painting . . .

2.
. . . Have we moved too quickly here, or in the wrong direction? Perhaps even more than either image or metaphor, our real need is for a concept that the ladder itself involves both the horizontal and the vertical. Something designed a long time ago by someone with a direct, useful task to perform. One that involves both ascending and descending . . .

3.
. . . But of course we have left out something. We have forgotten that we still have a story to tell. One that we have heard, read, or invented, imagined . . . Ladder in a romantic novel. He finds one conveniently placed beside the house. And there he goes: in moonlight, or hidden among the dark shadows, up, up, toward the arms of his beloved. . . . Or more seriously, in desperate circumstance, the last chance for escape of the men trapped in the mine . . .

4.
. . . And where out of all this comes the notion of standing at the foot of the ladder, with no inclination, no desire, to ascend? Even if it is only that "one among you" for whom it is enough to feel the earth under his feet . . . True, he has missed the heights, the excitement of the ascent, the panoramic view of peaks and valleys. . . . He feels ready to move on, for he has witnessed enough to let him know he has found his rightful place. This must be one of those moments, he tells himself, when one can simply walk past, praising the small beauties of the small world. . . .

In the Land of Un. In the Land of Dis.

And now comes one. . . . that shall unbar to us the gates of Dis.
                                        —Dante

To extricate oneself from the world—what a labor of abolition!
                                        —E. M. Cioran

I found myself far off from you in the land of unlikeness.
                                        —St. Augustine

1.
We offer our presence, in the hope that our absence will be noticed.

To be included, but not enclosed, is a condition of our freedom.

Each word carries within itself the weight and history of the language.

In the evolution of form, there is no perfect weather.

. . . A short stroll along the Via Negativa. We already know we will not go far without having to employ the telling prefixes: *de* as down; *dis* as separate, apart from; *un* as not. What can we find along this path of denial? What obstacles stand in our way that need to be cleared, set aside, before anything can be said? Remember that we have traveled this route many times before: wading, climbing, crawling, yet somehow found ourselves at some kind of destination. Thus we call upon dream, memory, to come to our aid: so many unpromising beginnings that have somehow been resolved . . . Our aim then, it would seem, is not sanctuary or absolution, but the more modest idea of temporary shelter. A text we can inhabit: walls, mirrors, window, a floor, a ceiling. We have done it before, and can do it again. Yes, even without a theme, without assumptions, without an agenda . . .

2. "Nothing Left to Tell"
Even where there is "nothing left to tell," there may still be something left to say. The distinction offered here is that, in a participatory mode, "speaker" and "listener" may alternate, unlike the usual relation between reader and writer: that of transmitter/receiver. ("'Mankind' is a conversation": George Oppen.) For whatever is said or written is modified in time by other words, images, concepts. All of this then represents an "effort to say," which is part of a shared "global" ignorance.

3. Going Toward/Away From

The traditional questions—"where to, what next?"—are joined at times by the more fundamental: "who are we, what are we?" Questions that confuse and immobilize— precisely at a moment when the imperative is toward motion: of any kind, in any direction. Not to resolve anything, but to broaden the base of our questioning, we may see this in the context of "the dynamics of Time": *Coming From/Going Toward, Going Toward/Away From. Closing Here/Opening There.* Perhaps this brings us closer to a view that is more "part of" than "apart from," the individual life seen as embedded within the life of the species. For however one views one's place in time, there seems to be both a turning away from and a turning toward history and memory.

4. The Threshold Situation

The sense of the unprecedented, of a convergence of disaster and discovery on a global scale. (Utopia and/or Apocalypse?) Within this ambiguity of promise and threat, there is a mounting confusion over beginnings and endings. Are there borders to be crossed—or boundaries to be maintained? On one hand there are parameters, made visible on the map of the known. On the other, shifting lines indicate the territory of the unmapped, unknown . . . A parade of faces, emblems, generations, appear and disappear. The numbers click and turn—the impending two and three zeroes—*the fateful year* comes ever closer. . . .

5. Possibility/Necessity: Toward the Extremes

The same convergence intensifies the sense of facing the void. It is necessity as an absolute—"negentropy"—that places the void on the horizon. And possibility as an absolute—unlimited and uncontrolled—that can bring a sense of "chaos." Thus the conjunction can project a "dead-end" feeling, as elevation and downfall appear— almost in the same moment. . . .

6. Evidential Being

We are witness to a series of confrontations between an "emerging" and a "disappearing" world. The conflicts center on different sets of values, goals, moral imperatives. As mentioned earlier, the "who are we/what are we" questions predominate. . . . This occurs not only between generations, but within each generation. From one side, there is a "throwback" to more traditional modes. From the other, a "throw forward" to a bewildering variety of transitional modes. Evolving from and through this— experimenting with mask, costume, and "lifestyle"—there emerges the *evidential being*. Already remote is the Heideggerian/Sartrean being, the Dasein, "for whom being is a question." In its place are those for whom being is improvisation: we are what we do and, especially, *what we have*.

7. Knowing/Understanding/Meaning

Knowing is a journey that seeks *arrival.* Understanding is a journey in which every stop is a stop "along the way." Meaning is a view through a window above the city, observing various forms of motion: motion without apparent reason or direction. . . . Knowing starts with one, fulfills itself with an increase of numbers. Meaning starts with zero, maintains itself by fidelity to the same point of reference ("zero at the bone"—Emily Dickinson).

8. Thinking Past Words

This comes to mind with the thought of a poet who, after his death, is still "present in absence." To say that he found a way—after a long silent period—of "thinking past words" is to refer to a realm others have encountered but few expressed. That realm in which *acts* are committed—"unspeakable acts"—that have yet to be spoken of, to be dealt with . . . The importance of this kind of expression, no matter how elusive or "difficult," is that it reminds us that a once-lost world, through dream, therapy, and poetic process, can be restored, recovered, *reactualized.*

9. Words/Again Words

Words that appear, with equal facility, on paper, on glass, or floating through the air. Now, all of this, given the "generic" name of "information," is asserted, even valorized—but then, just as easily, as quickly, is discarded, canceled. As for *memorable,* I'm sure it appears somewhere in the dictionary.

10. Some Easy Saying

I find it easier to say: "This bird is a student," than to say: "This student is a bird." Easier to say also: "This poem is a city," than to say: "This city is a poem."

11.

If the *ding an sich* and the *sine qua non* were to join in a dance, who would supply the music?

12. As the Mind Travels

We try to compensate for the loss of a sense of place by dreaming, even arranging for "travels through time." For a loss of the sense of time, by "travels through space . . ." We seek *compensation* for what is denied, taken away. But how is it that, in this pursuit, our basic strategies are so often *counterphobic*?

13. The Traveler/The Travelers

The traveler, alone by choice, can go just so far without meeting others. Having passed through the forest, ascended and descended the mountain, he comes to a sandy beach fronting the ocean. There, in various prone positions—apparitions of a civilization he has longed to escape—are a group of sun-worshippers. Unsure whether or not to give up, to join them, he wonders: "How long before the sun goes out of style?"

14. The Habitual/The Obsessional
Obsession is the "habitual" turned against itself. As the "habitual" reinforces, reassures, the "obsessional" invokes its opposite. ("The familiar / becomes extreme"— George Oppen). The intensity of the "obsessional" is that it is located, articulated as a *single locus*, where it gains force through repetition, through a single image, concept, metaphor. We see here the unyielding, unalterable point of reference of the "fanatic," the "true believer." (Kafka often reflects and makes use of the tension involved here.)

15. The History of Religion: What starts in an impulse ends in a *shrine*. What starts in a shrine ends in a *schism*.

16. Two Heretical Views
a. The "gift" that disqualifies.
b. The attempt to prove, to enlighten, *debased* by example.

17. The poet has opinions—just like everybody else.

18. Un and Dis: Concluded but Not Completed
Without a theme, without an agenda, the words gather, take their place on the page. We are reminded that the Celtic god of the *Un*derworld was named Dis (Pluto in another version). The opening toward Myth is itself a reminder: that the "chapter" we have yet to write, to experience, may resemble one that we have overlooked or forgotten. . . .

A Horse Called Burden, A Horse Called Venture

To live is to live like two horses standing together in opposite directions, tails flicking flies from each other's eyes

—Jim Johnson

1.

. . . Still trying to figure this out. At first I thought: it's just an interesting image—that may or may not mean something. Perhaps intended to suggest that we are called upon, more often than we imagine, to face in "opposite directions." (As for instance where we have been, as distinguished from where we might be going.) Difficult to visualize, because he has explicitly stated they are "standing together," as in a pasture or a meadow. The key thing, though, is that they are *positioned* in such a way that they can keep "flicking flies" from each other's eyes.

2.

. . . Notice that everything depends upon there being *two* horses. This places us in a different realm from the usual conjunction of the *single horse*—real and/or symbolic—at some intersection of history or memory. A procession of *winners* and *losers* passes quickly through the mind. And an old maxim we have not thought of for many years: *horses for courses* and *courses for horses*. A totally different scene from what we have just located in pasture and meadow . . .

3.

. . . I see now what has been left out by the writer. He has compounded our problem by failing to name his horses. And not only has he left them *nameless*, but failed completely to distinguish one from the other. . . . Should we ourselves then assume the burden of supplying these missing names? If so, why not call the first horse Burden? And the second, for somewhat obvious reasons, Venture. Consider, for instance, that one horse is born to "pull a load," while the other is—being bred for this purpose—"born to run." Put them in tandem pulling a cart, and one will be at ease, doing what comes naturally, while the other will be stressed, perhaps even to the point of madness. The same thing if we reverse the process, entering them on the track in the same race . . . Where does our confusion start, and where does it end?

When we are next called upon, will it be to carry the known weight to the known destination, or will it be to run—not on any track, for that too is a burden—but to move freely at our own pace, in any direction we have ourselves chosen?

Soundings

Few questions, fewer answers, says the voice. A voice close to silence. I look out, though, across red and black rooftops, farther a row of trees, and then the bare hills. Later, perhaps, I shall have something to say. For now, though, as I listen to the muted distant traffic, there is only one question: What is today?

◆

One asks: Where do I stand? In the light of this, we review all the confusion amid difficulty of being-in-the-world. But there is a parallel question, which perhaps needs to be expressed: Where does the "I" stand? (The image is of a constellation of selves.) And to this we reply: Inside at the Outside. Outside at the Inside.

◆

What happened to all those words? They were here only a moment ago: statements, claims, proofs, concepts. The shelves full of notebooks—dreams, abandoned projects. More and more the whole process seems to depend on the ability to swim under water. The clever, up-to-date thing then would be to go out and buy the rubber suit, the mask with the glass screen, the artificial lungs.

◆

On Systems and Philosophies: Walk up and down these streets; look at all the houses and apartments for rent. Listen to what the landlords have to say: how convincing they sound! Yet later on, we discover a strange thing: none of them live here.

◆

On selling potatoes: A. offers the small, shiny red ones; B. suggests the knobby brown ones with the thick skins. C. points out that, while his competitors' wares are attractive enough on the outside, they are dull and pale on the inside. His own are another matter; he splits open some samples: one is a bright yellow, the other a creamy orange.

Are we buying out of a real need, or out of habit? We ourselves take turns, being at different times both buyer and seller. This is clear enough. When it gets confusing is when D. says: I myself am in the business of *not* selling potatoes. Try his non-potato, his anti-potato.

◆

What starts in the need to be more than human ends in a performance that is less than human.

◆

Process: I have this to bring into being—this that does not yet exist. As I give the work form, it acquires presence as itself. The work completed, released, then becomes available for its own subsequent history. Thus it embodies, anticipates and shapes the future. More difficult to express, to believe, is that it does the same with the past: it changes our view of what was there; it activates and animates what was rigid and consigned.

◆

Images flicker in the mind, words disappear. At the moment one sentence remains, commands my respect and affection: "Playing with the cat," says Montaigne, "how can I tell she is not amusing herself with me?"

◆

Ghosts: How easy it is to get "spooked" these days! A message arrives from nowhere, unannounced. The phone rings at four in the morning. A stranger follows when you descend from the bus. The irrational rises like a tide, threatens to engulf us . . .

◆

The fault, dear Brutus, lies not in ourselves, but in our starlessness. Talking to the man in the small boat, about to set out alone for unknown waters, I learn something about navigation: all calculations rest on the—ultimately unprovable— *assumed position.*

◆

An Unwritten Story: The call comes from the airport. Hearing his voice, I assume the familiar message: between planes—an hour or two—just to say hello. But no, this time he's going to come over. Face to face—how long has it been? Anyhow, we'll find out whether we have anything to say to each other. . . .

◆

Humiliation is the Teacher. Surveying the wreckage, betrayal rises in our throats. The whole vast panorama of deception comes into view. . . . Now that we know its name, we are ready to attempt a definition: humiliation is the debt we pay the Other for recognizing our existence.

◆

To place man on the cross is to locate him at the point of intersection between the horizontal and the vertical.

From time to time we feel the need to be "cured of words." Silence works for a while. And music can be helpful. Then the color and movement of dance, painting, sculpture. I have this fantasy in which the other arts were invented for precisely this purpose.

Generations: Every time you turn your head, here comes another! Suggestion: bolt the doors, bar the windows—get out of the china business.

The Reading: Here are all these people listening. The Poet says something about the expense of the Spirit. This time I believe him. Among those present there are other poets—if called upon, wouldn't they, each in his own words, have a similar story to tell? More than this, it suddenly becomes clear that everyone here has at some time sought "the still point" of the turning world. Everyone has tested the ground beneath his feet—felt it sliding this way, that way. . . . We have come a long way, through griefs and disasters confined—as we thought—to one room at a time. And it is finally before us that we are not alone.

On Ignorance: Can one get attached to it, develop an affection for it? I seem to have. Blindness close to radiance. Think of it as a reservoir, water stored against the dry season.

The Shield: An Inheritance

. . . Standing in front of a whitewashed wall in the open square. A short distance away, a few dozen men are gathered. As his presence is noticed, one and then another wave and nod in his direction. Perhaps some of them have heard the story: how he came forward at a critical moment in the battle, shield raised, while those around him were beginning to scatter in retreat. . . . And what was it that had kept him going—was it any more than sheer momentum? Surely he was as much concerned with survival as any of the others. (If the order had been given to retreat, he would have followed it gladly.) Perhaps what carried him forward—if it was more than impulse—was the sight of those dropping their shields, their swords. Perhaps the sheer *chaos* of their actions . . .

—

. . . One of the men appeared, heading in his direction. He waved him off and started moving toward the far end of the square. Reaching there, he sat down at a café table and ordered something to drink. After a while, he closed his eyes. In reverie and close to dream, scenes of the battle returned. But it came to him in a softened, more gentle version. As though those who staggered and fell had felt no pain. And even those who died did not suffer. As though they accepted that what happened to them was ordained, inevitable. The thought surprised him: wasn't this to suggest they had been *chosen* to end their lives at this time, and in this particular way?

—

. . . The voices in the square were quieter now. One and then another had departed. It was just as well, he thought, for there was nothing he wanted to say to them. . . . And now, a curious thing happened: his mind went back further, entering the precincts of memory. Went back to that moment when, as a boy, he had found the shield on an old, deserted battlefield. Later, he learned that it had belonged to one whose name he was to hear over and over again in the years that followed. And once he was shown a book in which the name was recorded. A book that could be touched, handled, given the rich, full name of *History* and of *Legend* . . . And he had taken up that shield— barely lifting it at first—feeling that once it had come into his hands his real life had begun. A life where he had a mission, and—how could he put this into words?—to keep the shield from falling into "the wrong hands." And this was not for the pursuit of glory, but to preserve his own life while doing what he could to preserve the life of others . . . Falling asleep, he went on then to dream of other things.

1967/1993

The Listener

. . . Voices in a room. The sense of being there, moving among them, trying to sort out what they were saying. One in particular, who took him aside, spoke to him with some urgency, asking to be understood, agreed with. . . . If only he could remember the time, the place, the occasion. All he could tell now was that it was a gathering of some kind. A minor occasion; a get-together of more than strangers, less than friends. And still, something was said there that memory—called upon for some reason—could neither summon nor dismiss. . . .

—

This comes to him now while seated on a bench in the park. Part of his mind remains occupied with what he is trying to remember. Another part registers his presence in this sun-filled space bordered by trees. Light on the leaves, on his eyelids. Something else enters his mind as a diversion, a distraction. Instead of the words he has been listening for, suddenly, as if stepping forth into the light, there emerges the figure of an old man. Not anyone he has met or known—but perhaps read or heard about. He shakes his head, as he tries to sort out the double confusion of a faulty memory and an imagination that is presenting him with a mystery . . .

—

. . . On that very evening, his work done, the "old man" is escorted into the theater. He is an honored guest at the premiere of a new production, a musical, written by one of his young friends. The plot is of no interest, but the dances, the costumes, the songs are delightful. . . . The man beside him, who has brought him here, asks if he is tired. He smiles and shakes his head—and as it turns out, he remains for the entire performance. . . . As it concludes and the applause dies down, one of the actors comes forward and asks the Author to take a bow. The Author then mentions his name and asks him to rise and be acknowledged. As he rises to his feet, he says to himself: "Yes, that's what I'm here for: to watch and to listen."

1970/1993

Reflections on a Drowned City

1.

We are given that task: not once but many times: to restore, to recover. And we know—or learn—as those before us: that we are bound to fail. Yet as Z. said once, smiling, standing there in his cold studio surrounded by dark wax figures, white plaster dust: there are occasions when one can only "fail nobly." And it seems right that this occurs to us, right at the outset, for he was referring to his commission to provide drawings for a new edition of *The Inferno*.

We could go on from here, introducing some appropriate remarks about Dante and Beatrice, the old bridge, etc. But we are not moved, at this moment, either by the love of history or the history of love. We recognize only, at this point, that we have to pick up a thread or two, find where it leads. Cold fingers on the cold keys, trying to strike the warm chord of memory—as brief, as imperfect, as any other event that travels quickly through the mind, and as quickly disappears.

We are not ready yet even for an overture, a prelude. Our fingers are still moving toward the point where we are forced to say: seven days or seven centuries, what's gone is out of sight—and hope for some limits on the tedious work of recall.

2.

There are cities—and cities. The visible, the dreamed, the unfathomable: all present in one form or another. And there are the endless words that describe them. Of this city, I chose only the words that come first, most easily to mind. *This is what can happen when a city trusts its artists. No other place affects me this way. I stand on the old bridge, and tears come to my eyes.* The woman who spoke these words—now quite old—has no particular place in what follows. But it is worth noting that she is not easily moved; rather more inclined to be skeptical, to look beneath the surface—there is even something hard-edged about her.

3.

We seek that garden, the moonlight, the house. *Galileo's house!* And still on the same grounds, library, the observatory. And would want to know the occasion—for without that, what can be said? But none of this returns; it remains where it was: shadowed between what might have been, never was. As time passes, we understand even less of the sense of urgency. Surely something transpired that must have made a difference.

We summon a face—and one appears—not in sufficient detail, clarity of features—but enough for us to examine, and hesitate. Is this indeed the one we believed in—back then, back there? We cannot be sure. . . . Mind circles around moonlight: around faces that do not emerge, cannot be named. We try to bring back something that was said in that room. . . . But it is too soon to hear the voices. First, we must set apart the time, the space. How long has it been: ten years, twelve years? We have returned since—several times, in fact—*after the flood, after the restoration*—and of those visits there seems hardly anything to tell.

Mind circles, and slowly, slowly the space narrows, takes shape and form. *A soft, mild evening in October.* We begin now almost to believe that we were in fact present. That we spent a few hours in rather ordinary conversation—partly in English, partly in Italian. *Question: How many were there? Five, six, perhaps eight.* And just at this moment, something pops into mind: *the Astronomer least lost.* And just as quickly, the story told—later that evening, or the following day—of the illness, the long painful illness of the Astronomer's wife.

—So much wasted motion, I begin to despair; even before we start, the task seems hopeless. The fragments are too scattered, meaningless; too much time has passed, we are now in a totally different space . . . I try once more, this time with a bit of the voices:

—How politely they treat their guests, the foreigners—see them take the bottle from the shelf: Johnny Walker Red Label. Fair enough. Don't think because he works for the government—not on his salary—but there are undoubtedly other sources.

—Astrophysics, indeed. But just think: they're actually living in this house. Why not? Personally, I tend to be matter-of-fact about the whole thing. So *Galileo* actually lived here? So it seems. And the house has been converted—and is used as the home of the present—what shall we call him: *Astronomer-in-Residence?* Why not? Highly symbolic, wouldn't you say? If you like—but why not: highly practical.

—Do you recall now a bit more of the events of that evening? I believe I do. What, in particular? Well, don't be disturbed, but I have to tell you of an absurd impulse. What was that? Wanting to piss in that garden. A childish gesture. I agree. . . . Can you think now of something else—perhaps a bit more significant?

Yes: the difficulty about finding the key to the observatory.

—I should like to hear more about that. But first, in order to help me visualize: how far from the house to the observatory? A hundred, hundred-fifty feet. And about the weather? A clear, cold night. Very well; go ahead now with whatever comes to mind. . . .

—Waiting there until the Astronomer returned. The thick green grass, the noble winding trunks of the trees—the garden more like a small park, as I think of it now . . . Well, we were already in high spirits: adults involved in some marvelous, magical game. And suddenly there he was, a slight, sprightly man, an Italian in English tweeds, smoking a pipe. Impossible to say whether he was already in a good mood, or whether he absorbed and responded to what was already in the air—at any rate, I recall we went gaily down the path, following the leader, the noted, distinguished scientist. It was understood, of course—the counterpoint to our gaiety—that we were completely in his hands. Looking forward to the moment when the door opens and we stand inside. (No fanfare, please, and no hushed reverence either.) But no longer giddy either: the serious undercurrent coming slowly to the surface . . .

—I see you have introduced a note of anticipation of what is going-to-be. Doesn't this disturb the course of memory: the essential looking-backward that it entails? If you'll allow me this small projection, I'll proceed to that moment when the door opens and we stand inside. Wonder as we wander among the delicate instruments—shining glass, gleaming wood, polished brass—*the delicate instruments*—in which of course we trust implicitly (what else, in our state of ignorance?). And that cultured, refined, gracious man responding quietly, thoughtfully to our questions. In tune then with the stars, the heavens above, and with the successive generations, all that accumulation of knowledge, coming to this point . . . And now hear this: are you listening? *(I'm listening.)* He reaches confidently into the pocket of the tweed jacket—one and then the other, searches his pants pockets. *No key.* A shrug of the shoulders, embarrassed cough. Low voice, almost impossible to hear. *I'll be right back.* . . . Standing there, waiting for him to return. Record the quick shift of mood; the gaiety replaced by something more subdued—not quite uneasiness—*the threshold situation*—that's what it was. Strange, isn't it—how we think more of highs and lows than what goes on within the moment?

—Standing there, waiting for the door to be unlocked. It was cold, damned cold. Why do you keep saying that? Because we were so unprepared—expecting a mild, pleasant evening. And as a matter of fact, if I recall, you were wearing that yellow dress, the shaped knit—a little long for the fashion.

4.

The Astronomer least lost. Returned, as promised, a short while later, and we entered, were given a quick tour of the premises; read the inscriptions on the brass, bent down and squinted through the lens. Somehow, all quite unexciting—if there is a mystery here, it is how we could be so unaffected by the experience. . . . *Least lost:* at home in those distances. *To measure is to know:* the certainty of that world. Yet when the Observer is observed, the Watcher watched, the question is: *who measures him?* Seated across from him, after we returned to the house, he appeared at home within those rooms and within himself.

Our feeling was one of unstrained competence; things after all were in good hands. Talking of the new science, the new equipment, he seemed to know precisely what could and could not be said. Doing his job as well as he could—and if in the course of it, he had to learn another language: no need for pride or annoyance.

—

—Excuse the interruption, but much as I appreciate the resonance of meaning . . . it is hard for me to get out of the present. The paper in my hand, for instance, tells of a planet moving closer to the earth. Some among us are ready to abandon this one; seeking a cleaner, freer space. We are not now—and perhaps never were—far from the Chicken Little mind. Wars and the rumors of wars. Worlds in collision. The name of that other, dreamed-upon planet, let us say, is *Icarus*. But once we invite the symbol, we trail a swirling mass and vapors in its wake. Entering the mythic dimension, we may choose what names, what shapes we will—lacking only the force of a belief that survives the cold wind of disillusion.

—You see then how hard it is to change direction, to get out of the present. We could, for instance, go this very afternoon to the local observatory. There, we could watch the sky turn, expand and contract; we could try to follow and decipher ironic points of light concealed in the ceiling. But of course you will say: up there—out there—there is no ceiling. And I respond: very well, but for just this once could you suspend your disbelief?

—The show begins precisely on the hour. Leaning back in the metal chairs, watch the lights, the moving arrow; they portray the season of the year, the stars in their courses—all this against the toy silhouette of the city. When the lights go on, watch the unbelieving faces—how easily these judgments are made!—step out into the same ambiguous day from which you make these small departures.

Can we go forward without going back? I doubt it; as far as I'm concerned, we're still in that house. We have never left those rooms. . . . I would say rather that time is a fiction; that in a sense we have only "*theaters to believe.*" So if you want something to remember, why not the play? What play, what are you talking about? Brecht's *Galileo*. Why bring that up? Because of the occasion, the analog . . .

5.

—Here we are, seated in the balcony: a full house, waiting for the action to begin. Look at who is seated next to you: the "accountant" trying to impress the "secretary" on his left. You imagine, fantasize: both of them more at home with neat piles of folders; a guarded, wet-lipped smile as he hands her the latest figures: all divisions showing increased profit over last year. . . .

—Meanwhile, smoke rises from the stage. Children, clowns, tumblers; all color and movement: a stylized unfolding. Spectacle, yes, but the sense of an impending event, a significant turning point.

We are in the presence of one of those—how to say it?—moments when we are about to enter a different world. Inside each man, woman, and child begins the terrible flowering. No one wants it to be now—now that it is here—but there is no turning back. . . . The actors move through the scene: not the active, involved performers we expect—but as though drugged, tranced: knowing they too are subject to the winds of memory, man and stone whirling together—where and when will it ever stop?

—

Still within the play: in the kitchen, Galileo, in conversation with the Apprentice. But no, this is all fakery, witchcraft. For centuries they labored to produce *the Stone.* All systems go. *What Stone, what are you talking about? What happened to the play?* Forgive me, my mind wanders all over the place. I started thinking about the Philosopher's Stone, about the alchemists—Confusing the scientist and the alchemist? I'm not quite sure: the scientist or the playwright. Can we get back to the play? Please do.

—Yes: consider that this performance was taking place in the "eternal city," and you see there was the built-in drama already there— Another detour?— No, just to explain why I turn now to the famous "disrobing scene." The transformation takes place before your eyes: you watch it as he changes from the man—piece by glittering piece, he achieves radiance—until he stands there twenty pounds heavier in the best brocade, all-dazzling, and lifts high the symbol of his office, then slowly turns full face to bless his subject audience. . . .

—

At intermission, the full volume of their voices. Released from captivity, the fluttering starts. Waiters in white jackets move deftly around the oval-shaped bar. Head turns to head; noses sniff the perfumed air. (Words that betroth and betray.) A small thing if he sleeps with her tonight; he could, you know, and would if it seemed worth the effort. *Less than real, neither the perfume, nor the sound of their voices . . .* I say to you what I have said before: what is real is what happens inside: when that "fat man" insists on measuring man and his earth—testimony of the trained eye—and the world changes. You see perhaps now the reason for the long detour. We had to enter the theater in order to begin to understand where we were when we entered the house. And so we do: *enter the house. There is nowhere else to go.*

6.
But of course I forget the main thing: the city itself. The drowned city. The event that touched us one and all: so deeply it seemed we would never forget . . . *Florence, Firenze,* all that circles around the name. The raft, the stone, the hanging man.

The manuscript taken from the vault . . . It comes back then with a view of the Cathedral. Moving closer, your fingers touch the bronze doors. There was a competition, remember that, and this was the prize-winning sketch. *Ghiberti.* Much more to the story, but all I care to remember . . . the Baptistery of San Lorenzo—

—Shining cars in sunlight. A child squinting, the camera aimed at his face. Step inside if you will; here it is damp and dark—*the Baptistery*—incredible cone-shaped symmetry. Now in the present, you are in the presence of *that time.* Do not stay long, though, for the image of all that martyrdom is oppressive. In dark recesses, the white candles, women kneeling, the subtle voice intones. We need not interrupt the service but observe: tourist and worshipper sniff each other: one smells greed and the other smells death. And as for us? We exempt each other: being here only because of the stained glass, the altarpiece.

—You present the making of memory as if it were to return—even *to restore* what happened. Perhaps I do; but if you feel this is false, imagine the voice of the scribe, the chronicler. And yourself as the reader or listener. The manuscript then is in your hands. . . . Very well, then, if I have the option, I do not intend to open these pages. Not that I am afraid of what is contained here—even if the sonofabitch used the occasion, exploited his friends—and a disguised version of myself appears there—under whatever name. And yet I am afraid; for who knows what use he has made of our lives—how shallow and deceitful he makes us seem. . . .

—Let me suggest an alternative: looking at what is written on the page, can we also look through it? Is there a vision that holds what the words cannot contain? I cannot tell; I know only that this city exists: that, whether seen from this hill or that, there are towers and steeples.

—You choose these instead?

—Within limits. I realize that one must not believe too much in these things, either—no matter how gifted the architect, how intriguing, beguiling the shapes; for they too are only arbitrary arrangements.

7.

Let us return now to voices, to the remembered act, to the men and women who lived here in those years of intensity, of dream, of commitment.

—Pardon me, do you prefer tea or whiskey? Tea. And tell me, where are you staying? At the Brand. The Grand? No, the Brand. That's funny, I'm staying at the Strand. A view of the river? No, I'm afraid not. How is it there? It's fantastic. Did you know: the hotel has been declared a national monument—*the hotel itself!*—which means that it has to be preserved intact. Is your friend Moss staying with you? No, he's rented a villa—a fantastic place, a few miles outside the city; living there with stuffed monkeys, porcelain, cannonballs, illuminated manuscripts . . . And what happened to the woman, the one who meant so much to you? Remember you said you could never keep up with her: the way she went striding through the city. . . .

—She came back—as she would again and again over the years. And each time, the sight of the river, the bridges, the churches, the statues, brought tears to her eyes. . . . This time, it was arranged: she would meet him at four and they would go hand-in-hand through the narrow streets, past the carts laden with fruit, vegetables, art books, leather wallets. And they would be looking for something—for what? For a room with a view. And then—ah! the slow crossing of the bridge; the feeling that their bodies added to the weight of all the others who had ever walked here—in sunlight and in mist. The glare from the windows displaying diamonds and jewels, sending out rays of brilliance, which in turn reflected from the river.

But of course, much as it meant to him, he understood that for her it was something else. For although he nodded and smiled as her finger swung the gold earring, she saw that he felt caught between her devotion and wariness at her self-indulgence; his own survival required something else: the strict exercise of patience and forbearance. . . . Meanwhile, the river passed below; and years later, they would come back under other circumstances—she would have to endure that winter when he had trouble with his eyes, and it was strange to see him about the house with those wide-rimmed dark glasses—almost never took them off; still, she had to believe it was a temporary thing. She was to recall then that it was at that very time that he first began to speak about perception—sensory and extrasensory—notice he said how we confuse the senses: *I hear* what you're saying, but *I don't see* what you mean. And he made much of a news item that told of some blind woman who could tell color through her fingertips.

. . . She would leave him right after lunch and go wandering through the city. He remembered her saying: this is one of the few places in the world where *just to be* is enough. Strange, he thought, she seems so restless, so occupied. . . . Wherever there was a flight of stairs, she would dash madly to the top—something she could never resist, never explain—and then after a short while, slowly, languorously, down again.

. . . And at other times: she would be at the desk talking to the clerk and someone would come in—the fact was, she would explain later, that you spoke the same language—and it would go on from there: not to anything serious, but perhaps a drink at the bar. . . .

—Sitting there in the darkened room, he tried to imagine where she had been by the force of the softness of her entrances and exits. There remained for him the reflected flurry and radiance that would go with her wherever she went: after a full day of wandering, she would wind up in the restaurant a few doors from the hotel. Something about the place: the glossy white paint, the curved glass shades, the thick white tablecloths, that always soothed and sustained her.

She spoke of that sometimes, and of another favorite: the staircase of the Library; how she loved *the feel* of the polished brown wood under her hand. But most of all, at the top of the stairs, the anticipation of opening the door into that incredible room; how she felt bathed and laved in light the moment she entered; how it stayed and glowed within her: her head bent over the illuminated manuscripts. She told him once, in rather halting speech, something of what it meant: at that moment *she was everyone*—inside and outside the room—*and no one* at the same time—rejoicing and being afraid—her whole being focused on the hand turning the pages.

8.

I wish I knew where we were going. And I do, too. There is nothing more difficult than this feeling of merely floating upon the tide. But that is so often the case, I would not want to deceive . . . Well, I would rather go somewhere than remain endlessly circling. That is why they have guides, to help us get from here to there. And besides, we simply do not have that much time.

—I know that. But you must admit that *the death of the Guide* makes it more difficult, and that we must enter these various levels—each with its own glories and torments—these various circles to experience along with whatever they contain. . . . But for your sake, I will try once more to summon the faces. . . . Woman of dark skin, noble daughter of a noble house . . . Nothing happens: although for one last moment I see her standing on a hill, looking down across the rooftops, watching the water rise. . . .

—Let me ask then the practical question: how far from the house to the city? Study the map and find out. This sort of information is always available; but although the mind, like a bird circling the dry landscape, will gladly settle for this, we have here a more strenuous task.

. . . The ghost of that afternoon passes quickly over the unmarked ground. A child runs across the steps of the old fort—what war, what soldiers? We have serious business to attend to: the drowning and death of this city. *Speaking now, after the event?* Yes, the news comes to each of us in strange places, strange times. For me, it was that afternoon, almost five years later, when I picked up the picture magazine and saw the tides of mud, the blackened houses, stunned faces. And I thought: so this is what they have made of it—*into our hands it was given*—the warnings buried somewhere under a pile of old documents, the mayor, the engineer, the clerk asleep, dreaming of promotions. . . .

—I see now that you are deadly serious. That you have more to say in the same portentous, even apocalyptic vein.

—When I think of how we have conspired to promote these disasters, I can do nothing else. For it is no great mystery that—now as always—our appetites are larger than our eyes. And for this, and this only, the system of the word fails. Along with the system of the world. How then to apprehend the system of the Universe? My heart beats faster. I cannot live with the thought. Let the Astronomer and the Physicist speak confidently of quasars and light years, of horizons beyond horizons. I must still react, on the small personal scale, with panic and dread.

—Well, if you must. But frankly I am more interested in our mundane sources—so if you'll just hand me that clay tablet, hammer, and chisel, I'll see if I can inscribe a few hieroglyphs. . . .

—Within the system of the world. That afternoon in the beach house, Mark told us how it was at the landing: knee-deep in the water, and just at that moment the loudspeaker blaring out the names and ranks of the advancing soldiers . . . Charred logs on the beach. Lying on my back in the water, I dream of floating mine-fields. Salt on my eyelids, imprisoned in the house of flesh, what else is there to do? Must we then love or hate or ignore victims and killers with the same understand-ing, the same devotion?

—But I am not sure I care to remain under these conditions. It seems to me there are certain minimums—and if these are not met . . .

—If you do not care, I do not care. But see how it works: we collaborate to overcome the intolerable—holding up a shield, or hiding behind a veil—and if we play it that way, it comes out: if you make the slightest sign, the smallest commit-ment, to extend your hand toward mine, I too am obliged. But if this is not done, then we can only say: sorry we missed it, better luck next time. And there is in this a crucial turning away that says in effect: I would rather not depend on or be made responsible for your caring or not caring. But only to follow the river, the stream of images. For whatever the mind intends, the eye wanders. Concealed in this we are as we were at the beginning: both nomad and settler. And if the soul must have a country, the spirit has an equal claim: to wander where and when it chooses. . . . So it is with the claim, the obligation. In love or in hate, acceptance or denial. —Do you think I give a damn? I do not. —But they are showing the face of the victim. Same response. Face of the Assassin. Ditto . . .

—

Down, down from the hills, they returned to find what was left of the city. But when I was there it was dusk: sound of music, red banners, gold lettering. Strange to be confronted thus with spectacle and celebration, not knowing the cause; strange too that for you it is a moment of fatigue, of vagueness, of caution—while for others— perhaps those who have taken a different path—there is the excitement of what lies just ahead: the sudden burst, efflorescence of color, fountains opening, transforming night into an endless source of wonder.

—

What do we see in this then; what can be learned? How often it is that image follows image; yet in this proliferation, there is no vision. To express the vision, the ancients said, there is recourse to the secret language. Of this no more can or need be said. Going back to that noise before the word: sound of heavy breathing shared by both pursuers and pursued.

—But what about the transformation, the "endless wonder"?

—Sometimes these transformations appear to be genuine; more often they fall apart, showing the elaborate costumes of self-deception. We work blindly then to pull these shapes and forms out of the darkness. It is still a question for me whether we create—or release—the figure in the stone.

—But you see *David* standing there, don't you?

—I see *two Davids* from the same hand: one is real and the other a copy— which? Bells ring in the square towards evening. The crowds move toward both with equal fervor.

9.

Shall we begin then? It would be well if we could—but I fear the intrusions. Nothing for it, I suppose, but to deal with them as they arise, to handle whatever comes our way. For even as we approach that other present—which for convenience's sake, we call the past—this present present presents itself. Plunged at once into *this city*—the gray morning, mist that encircles garden, wall and house. We have come to respect these structures, with all their fallibility, rusted-locked, secret places of decay. In the morning, I scrape dead leaves off the walk; in the afternoon, fill in the cracks where moisture has gathered; in the evening, if it is not too warm, burn whatever loose paper has been left lying around.

—So the hours pass into days, the days into years. All so fleeting, we are forced to inquire: and beyond this? And here our friend the biologist, archaeologist, raises his voice, along with the voices already heard of the physicist and astronomer: in the end is our beginning. This we must not forget in assessing where we have arrived. In water we began. In water we begin again. So that there is a cycle and it does work this way . . . Standing before the glass wall that stretches some twenty feet to the ceiling: water sloshes in the blue-tinted tank. Watching the dolphin perform, we go so far in imagination that we begin to think: how pleasant it is to turn and turn again, to dive and feed in this way.

10.

But in the drowned city, time is measured by the flood: before and after. I sit here turning the pages of a magazine called *Life.* (Itself now only a memory.) And as my hand flips the glossy paper, pictures rise from the page. Names echo, faces flicker. Before my eyes, the river rises. I see the city trapped in the tide of mud, walls covered with the thick, dark ooze of petroleum. I try but cannot read the text; but before my eyes the images emerge. . . . Volunteers stream into the city. A voice shouts: over here, we need help over here! There is an immense frantic scurrying in all directions. Armbands and intelligences—trying desperately to overcome the walls of language, the shortage of resources—directing the work. The problem of art, of history, swirls in these waters, turns into a medical problem: pictures to be saved, along with lives to be saved. Is there enough serum? *Make sure the needle is clean!*

—And in the days following, the living artist surveys what is left of his studio. While the restorers are already at work: you see, this is the drying process; we take one leaf at a time, one page at a time. And then, in the months and years to come: one brushstroke after another—squinting at the light—a glass of wine—a cigarette—back to work. And the churches, the cathedrals, open their doors again to the faithful: mostly old women at first; you see them in black shawls, flat-heeled shoes, nodding and crossing themselves.

—Is it for these then, that all this must be done? A strange question. Let me rephrase it: you see how few worshippers are left—how few in contrast to those who come to stare in wonder at the skill, the art, the magnificence of *what was there.* Now look at the men on the scaffolds, their hands carefully touching the surface of the wall. From this will come what in time will again appear: light on the enraptured face, the glowing bones, the dark red spot where the arrows point between the ribs . . .

—So that we may worship the dedication, the sense of what lives on, no matter how bloody or cruel the history? Yes: the effort, the energy is the essential evidence, even if what is restored is only a reasonable facsimile. But I insist on the distinction: the custodians are not the guardians. Sanctuary is not absolution. After the flood, we return to our houses, to our places of worship—and of amusement— altered perhaps by the experience: enhanced by the sight of what was freely given in love and reverence—and yet depressed by how the course of greed follows the course of rivers that pass through these unfolding scenes, city after city, century after century, and we stand open-mouthed before the rise and fall of monuments and ruins—never knowing what we perpetuate, what we unveil and conceal.

11.

Are you still here? Yes, I am; but I find it hard to concentrate, hard to listen. I'd like to make it easier—but it is very elusive. That's what you said before. All right then, think of it this way: you enter the city on a certain evening, say in August or September. Your arrival means nothing to the city itself, to the people entering the shops or the churches, the children playing in the street. Whatever meaning this city has is already established for the inhabitants. . . . You're laboring the point. I know. I know that: but you see it is difficult to summon the images—whatever the season—even if one refers to processions, to spectacles, to pilgrimages.

◆

They are coming in now: coming in from all over. With the waters rising, there is work to be done. Eager faces, strong bodies, the sense of mission, of crusade. And beside them, the older ones, those who remember the war: the last time they experienced this sense of urgency: the tense days, the iron helmets, the booted soldiers . . . We sat up all night figuring a way to save the city. Bottle of wine on the table, map of the city spread beside the glasses. So much to say, so much to consider. And in our minds: this to be saved: most precious, this chapel, this bridge, these houses, these memories . . .

    —Look up, now: they are coming in: those born in the years before and after that very war. Look: the legs are so long, the teeth so straight. How is it that they resemble each other so closely: no matter whether their hair is yellow or black, shape of their faces, color of eyes. Who are these delegates from the country of the young? Here to make the old new; to restore, to regenerate images and icons they do not seem even to believe in. —But not all are pleased, not all—even in this desperate moment— welcome them: You see what has happened to my shop? Here, wipe the salt off the leather; see how the white line remains. Who cares for this, for the life of the shop-keeper, the housewife—no, all they care for are the monuments and the ruins. . . .

◆

In the drowned city, there are voices to be heard. In the city of silence, flowers to be listened to. And now that we have listened, still unsatisfied, we ask: where is the pattern, the design? It can be drawn on the graph; we can watch or trace the jagged line—but as for what it means, we have only names and numbers. And even this is perhaps visible only on clear days. Yet when I close my eyes, I see many worthy to be loved. And as the dark approaches, before the voices turn to stone, I would say: let life and the living proceed.

    —Is that all? No signature, no meaning? Only this blind pursuit in which we end walking through our own life toward our own death—in the manner of light through a wall? In any case, this form or shape is no more than an aggregate of matter—molecules with less pattern than those within the crystal.

◆

We came to the drowned city. A moment brought us together—for what purpose, neither knew—and another moment saw us separate, going in different directions. . . . Standing there, watching the train pull away into the darkness, we knew that whatever brought us together was already behind us. That whatever arrangements were made, we could not know if and when we would again meet . . . It occurred to him then that, even on arrival, taking the taxi to the hotel, she was already looking out of one window, while he looked out of the other. And he thought: surely the sight of all that was achieved here must have reached us. For think of it: there we were in this city where the towers rise, and the bells sound their summons, and the shadows fall on the slow-moving water. . . . Not so slow-moving, after all, not at all what the dream invited—rather the angry waters, rising in wrath for all the neglect, the deceit, the careless use and waste of the living.

—

And what now do you remember? I remember the arrogance of the wound. Those who walked where none invited, proud to exhibit their scars. I remember staggering through sunlight the birds that rise and depart. The wind that blows between the stones . . .

   —The house stands in the drowned city, a short distance apart on a small rise of ground—far enough away, high enough to be spared by the raging waters. And there the Astronomer—after this small interlude of flood and restoration—is again at work. Yes, I can see him now: this very evening, the position of the stars noted. Casual, routine work; keeping up the logs. But at any moment, something appears that engages his attention. Thickening of the vapors, white dots moving closer together—some variation from what shows on the chart . . . But our concern with this very evening, this very man, falters. We see how in the natural course of things, the light of all distances is bound to dim. The pictures form; the pictures fade. The circle widens to include the fate of cities, of stars that wax and wane, continue in their courses.

—

The decorated tower stands in the restored city. The bells sound; dark wings cut patterns in the evening air. For all appearances, the city is again as it was. The disaster has been lived through, and lovers once again cross the bridges, race across the polished stones. But there are some who return and cannot find what was here—and as we are among them, I will conclude by saying that while the river may be contained, and the scars on statues and paintings concealed to all but the most expert eye, the soul may not survive, or may leave this chosen home—and go to seek another.

1976

A Little Kitchen Music

. . . Krista in the kitchen. She studies the assembled ingredients—the carrot, the purple onion, the celery. A painter of still lifes, her attention rests there: the colors, textures, the way they are arranged speak to her. She shakes off the momentary reverie: let's get this done, back to work . . . One of the guests wanders in, offers to help. They talk about this and that. She tells the friend, a woman of her own age, that she could use some help—but later. Another comes in, asks for a glass of water. She points to where the glasses are stored, and to the bottled water in the pantry. . . .

—

It is going well. A long time since she has prepared dinner just for friends. A matter of timing. She moves back and forth, eyes the clock on the wall, the pots and pans on the stove. Someone has put on a record; the music reaches her through the fragrances, the sounds, the noise of voices from the other rooms. She recognizes something of what she hears in the music: *A Haydn quartet? Can't be sure. Perhaps one of the lesser known . . .*

—

The windows are beginning to steam up. She turns on the oven fan. The noise takes over. The music disappears. The windows remain smudged. She opens the back door to the pantry. There's enough breeze to make the gas jets flutter. She hesitates, decides to leave the door open. Last time she was frying something in the black iron skillet, and the smoke set off the fire alarm. . . . It doesn't take much to set it off. *I'm doing what I can, as best I can. All this activity for a painter of still lifes. That's what I am now—just that, nothing more. Mother, lover, that is still there—but not like before. Remember: it's your own life, whatever that is, whoever is here, for as long as they stay:* the necessary company.

—

She will know when it is done. Hopefully it all comes out together. They will soon be sitting at the same table. Looking into each other's faces. Listening to each other's voices. As real as they—or rather we—can be. It's not a story, not a movie: we can't be sure how anything, this meal included, will turn out. *Still, I am trying to put this taste in these dishes—the taste that love invites, that friendship furthers. A little sustenance, a little ceremony, and something that makes it seem like an occasion. Did I read that somewhere? Haydn, my dear, sorry you couldn't make it. Better luck next time.*

The Arms/The Wings

1.
A moment of quiet, of respite, but obviously it is not over. That would be too much to hope for. I look around: signs of struggle everywhere. While there is nothing smashed or broken, the evidence is clear enough. *I have done what I could.* What this means, why it should sound now, I cannot tell. It feels, though, like some sort of reassurance—where does it come from, how long will it last?

2.
He is again on the attack: striking a blow here, there, moving quickly, almost invisibly through the air. I have the sensation—as many times before—that the wings have brushed (*slashed?*) the skin. . . . Several times after these close encounters I have touched forehead, cheeks, neck, expecting blood on the fingers. Nothing at all— and yet I feel, at these moments, almost devastated: *how much longer* . . .

3.
She is all over me. I squirm, try to break free, but the hold pinions me. Here at last, as I expected, are the enfolding wings. They form a kind of canopy, a tent, under which the world disappears. Surely we have never been this close before. . . .

4.
It has decided to release me. Sits now in a corner withdrawn into itself. And while I dare not approach, it sulks or mourns—or prepares another attack. (With the features not visible, there is no way to tell.) I wonder whether I had any right to enter here, to have assumed the role of Opponent . . .

5.
They are all around me. Tiny wings beating against the wall, the window, the mirror. The sound they make is quite haunting—the sight of the fragile, iridescent forms that of messengers from another realm. . . .

6.
. . . Lying here close to exhaustion. Yet certain there is no waking, no reassurance that this will fade, move beyond and behind me into a dream. For it is surely day— this day—and I am nowhere else but in this house, this very room. And it is just as certain that outside—just as usual—the streets are filled with people. And wherever they are going, whatever they are doing—*outside the walls*—takes place in a world they, too, are forced to believe in. . . .

Here as It Happens

Here as it happens   in the first place   the awakening:
prepare this day   as if no other   finding a name
to indicate the solemn morning: how it opens here
with white towers in the distance with the sculpted horse
radiant as copper: etched white lines spread
certain as the compass of the known world: Michaelangelo
my dearest friend—and at the same moment   within
the decaying room   light gathers on our shoulders
to define   the weight of passage—before this: so
after: something else. Feeding thus in the dark
we proclaim that we are indeed   the ripest fruit
of legend: no other course to remember—or discover—
except that as light bruises   the soft edge of memory
fire lives within   the core of measured circles—
and waters dance below   beside the mound of sticks & stones:
emblems of the broken & the whole
                         besiege the glittering sand.

Arrow Light. Target Eyes.

Suddenly in the forest   a leaf falls.
Spaces forbidden & spaces we may enter
any hour of any day—consider what Julian Marias
writes about—the forest and the trees—the notion
of the "trajectory" of experience: fear in the
small moment an instant of joy smaller still
we learn that "experiencing" will never hold
the fullest name   salt upon the tongue of Experience . . .

Move then to another part of the forest: *Rashomon*.
Love & death and the glittering silk
dance witnessed by the clicking leaves
stained swords abandoned on the grass: fear
terror & decorum the harsh breathing   dishonored voices
pouring forth: four different versions of the "truth."
We sweat & chill through this   confirms what we know:
how it all must end: "in silence"—the frightened monk
implores the sky   the abandoned child howls. . . .

While the dark, heavy rain   falls out of the film
and into our lives. . . .   sometime later we emerge
to enter the Forest of the City—the enormous
bronze bell continues to toll—we recognize the
flaming arc—here now and . . . gone: the bright, brief
question flickers between the poles of light
more than this we cannot tell   not having followed
the tribes whose footsteps end   beside the river—
can only dream the source: sky that might have been
before there were horizons . . .

On the Recent Unpleasantness at Lake College

Dreaming, they could not be blamed:
nothing in the curriculum about burning—
at the last moment rushed into the library:
nothing under *nightstick*—a reference to *nightwood*
was close but meant something else.

Forgot their own distant fathers
hidden among the shelves and inventories
of last year's goods: buried the flower salesman
and the plumber—suddenly a department head,
guardian of the fire: holding myth in their fingers.

Meanwhile, ducks gathered on the pond.
They quacked: "Tongues are blue, hair is green:
we insist we must be seen." The answer came
with pirouettes of leaden capes:
"Help! My hair is bleeding!"

Again, teachers trained to tell hawks
from handsaws urged attendance in auditoriums
designed for living theater—but the squirt cans
held by failed athletes turned them around
to face the wild morning, the chartered ground . . .

The lake remains invisible: another eye in earth.
Where webbed feet follow, the bread is scattered;
between bayonets and footnotes, another sun is dreaming.

Along These Ways

Along these ways to a place where shadow
performs in tandem with light falling
into a space we have not touched or sculpted—
where the child disappears in the white dust
of summer, where the solemn meadow
is suddenly defiled by the dubious presence of one
who answers to no known image or given name . . .

Along these ways to a small confined room
where the gray cat lies curled in a wicker chair
and the lost child returns with the juice of raspberries
pasted on her cheeks—not where we ever intended to return
that summer when we gathered to watch the trees darken
and someone brought wildflowers inside a silver cup—

We have come this far
                              traveling along a road
that leads to the impasse of silences
                                   somewhere in the distance
                                          inside the city of locked doors.

Reactionary Poem

Must I then to this nonsense
lend attention—passive service of the ear
to whatever mouth is working? Those we grieve
have opinions and are perplexed
by the weight of costumes. I would swear
the light reveals thickening in its fall:
faces of the unfortunate and the less visible,
prepared to learn the catchword, the tone
ripe for the phrase, tongued indifference—

I would make plain then the victim's plight:
those pushed aside toward odd corners
never knowing which theater of disbelief
to enter, or the right color of gems
and earrings—I would bless the bureaucrats
who pound this under-strata into coherence
not from malice or simple afterthought
but with accurate concern for their duties:
to unclog the streets, keep the traffic moving.

Preparing to Leave

1.

. . . Hard to believe we are indeed leaving. That the activity of the past few days is not, as so many times before, a series of wasted motions. I should prefer, of course, to forget those past failures, and for us to go ahead as serious, responsible people, capable of doing what has to be done. This in mind, I have kept any criticism to a minimum, acted in a cheerful manner, offered encouraging words that this time the departure will proceed smoothly and on schedule. . . .

2.

. . . Less than a week to go. So far, just minor difficulties, a few tense discussions about who should be doing what. But our genuine concern for each other has, in each case, proved to be the deciding factor. *How unlike those past experiences, when each setback, no matter how small, brought us close to tears, and even to blows.* I can't help thinking of what a long road it is that we have traveled together—how we have managed to avoid the kind of damage others of our acquaintance have inflicted upon each other—leaving them no alternative but separation, taking the drastic step of ending one part of their lives, trying to look forward to another beginning with someone else. Whatever our own shortcomings, it seems clear that we have at last reached a point where we no longer need to employ the language of blame. . . .

3.

. . . What has happened here? How is it that all of a sudden things have turned around? All I really know is that our voices, our language, our perceptions, are no longer in harmony. But as I come to think of it, there was that moment when she stood in the doorway, holding the folded newspaper, pointing to something—then saying in a quiet voice: "Isn't it obvious? We really do have different destinations." It suddenly struck me then: each time we prepare to leave, to go someplace, there is an undertone I have failed to recognize: that we may be also preparing to leave *each other*. That each departure may be a signal that we might also be departing from each other, rather than with each other . . .

4.

Something has happened to make her change her mind. We are to continue where we left off, making what she now refers to as "the final preparations . . ." The day draws closer; but still we have not acquired the travel schedules, the maps, the compass. I have pointed this out, but she remains unconcerned. Her confidence is rather astounding: as if all these items will appear—place themselves in our hands—at exactly the right time. . . .

5.

. . . I have been sleeping badly the last few nights. Has this any connection with our present destination? Is it the added stress of going where we have never been before—to a place where our faces, our names, would have no meaning to the inhabitants? As I finally fall asleep, my last sight is of the suitcases on the floor. And when I awake in the gray light of morning, that is the first thing I see. Not only a reminder, but a *reproof:* hard evidence that we are never who we think we are . . .

1968/1993

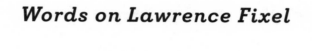

Words on Lawrence Fixel

Peter Johnson

Lawrence Fixel's
"Flight Patterns"

After the literary dust of the last fifty years settles and some academic has the nerve to write the definitive history of the American prose poem from 1965 onward, when trying to canonize the most important poet of that period, that academic will have a long line of fine poets to choose from. But if that definitive history were also to include the parable, I would argue that only one writer stands out above the others and that one collection blows all the others away. That writer is Lawrence Fixel, and that collection is *Truth, War, and the Dream-Game: Selected Prose Poems and Parables,* 1966–1990 (Coffee House Press, 1991).

In his foreword to *Truth, War, and the Dream-Game,* Fixel makes this distinction between the prose poem and the parable:

> [T]he parable is required to be *about something*—something that connects with, even though it conflicts with, our sense of the world. Thus it challenges our assumptions while, paradoxically, it evokes some feeling of universality. The prose poem . . . tends to be lyrical, subjective, impressionistic. Based more on self-expression than the concept of metaphor offered by the parable, it can provide a counterpoint of *possibility* to balance the parable's greater concern with *necessity.*

What Fixel says about the prose poem is true, but I am mostly interested in his parables, which he further discusses in his foreword.

In contrast to the "ancient parable," which sometimes appears as a "riddle or an enigma," Fixel posits the "modern parable." According to him, this parable, exemplified in the works of Kafka and Borges, offers a "devastating illumination of a world split between psyche, spirit, and material concerns." He adds that in this kind of parable, "paradox is a key element, opposing the identity of opposites to any commonsense, linear, or literal world."

Another way of describing this modern parable is to call it an "open parable," a phrase Roy Pascal applies to Kafka's short works. Making a contrast between fables and Kafka's short works, Pascal writes:

Although Kafka invites us to read his parables with the same expectation of a simple moral lesson that will illuminate the meaning of the events related, in fact the reader finds his expectations cheated, for there is no formulated moral and the conclusion of the incident is obscure and ambiguous, leaving the reader baffled and depressed. . . . The essence of the fable or parable is precisely of a clear, defined moral influence or injunction; and here, in Kafka's parables, this essence is absent. . . . The function of fable was to allow us to understand life, to order and label its manifestations, to teach us practical wisdom that will serve to guide our behaviour. But Kafka's fables do not illuminate the mind but terrify and confuse.

I mention the above distinctions because they provide a lens through which we can view and experience Fixel's parables, and we should keep these distinctions in mind when looking at the first parable in *Truth, War, and the Dream-Game*, called "Flight Patterns"—a prose piece that prepares us for all the others that follow.

Flight Patterns

Between the void and the sheer event.
                —Paul Valéry

1.
It is said, of the millions who undertake the journey, that the greatest number are lost somewhere along the way. To prove this, evidence is produced, statistics gathered, witnesses summoned. There are even films of the long, straggling procession, which presumably reveal the fate of the missing. Yet it appears no one—ourselves included—is deterred by this, for it is equally intolerable to remain where we are.

2.
. . . Word continues to arrive from monitors at the highly equipped tracking stations. They report a whole series of unexplained dots and dashes on the flickering screens. Even the most experienced observers—using the most advanced techniques—concede that the habitual flight patterns can no longer be interpreted. . . .

3.
I have seen some of the incoming messages. They bear such strange notations as "missing in action," "dead on arrival," etc. With so many different lan-

guages, from such different worlds, the gap between what is transmitted and received continues to widen.

4.

I have resolved not to be upset by any of this. To limit myself to what can be verified by sensory evidence. One thing is clear: whether we travel the direct route of desire, or detours of illusion, we still miss connection. Something is *there*—ahead of or behind us—and we are drawn in that direction. For a time we seem to have arrived. . . . But as the wind changes, the mist descends, we can no longer tell where we are.

5.

Let us suppose, for instance, that you have been where I have been. We meet one afternoon in a village in a neighboring country. . . . Joining the crowd in the plaza, we observe the stately walk of the costumed women. Moving on, we notice in contrast the immobility of the vendors: the heavy bodies squatting beside the earthen jars.

6.

Is the scene familiar? Then let memory take a further step: to that moment when armed men in gray uniforms appear. . . . Suddenly we feel a sharp intersection of competing gestures, of inviting and disturbing fragrances. Someone drops petals in front of the candle-lit altar; someone else throws poisoned meat to the hungry dogs. . . . Speaking of this later, disturbed by our fragmented impressions, the question arises: What name can we give to this land?

7.

We may of course continue the search, each producing letters, photographs, documents. Or simply recognize that, between any two witnesses, we can expect these differences. Each might then retreat into a private retrospect. . . . But what if we decide to give up these wanderings, returning to this body, this present time? It may then occur to us that what signifies this world is nothing else but the current of our feeling. And as for the flesh that dissolves, disappears, who can say it will not appear again? If not in this form, this familiar image, then perhaps as an *intention* that moves through silence and the quickening wind.

1978/1979

"Flight Patterns"—What a wonderfully ironic title, juxtaposing both the freedom and uncertainty of taking wing with the certainty of a preconceived pattern, which we may choose to follow so we don't get lost. It's an ideal position to be in, but one that, ironically, Fixel's parables always argue against, since no matter how hard his narrator tries to find a fixed location from which to make sense of his surroundings, uncertainty prevails. It's appropriate, then, that "Flight Patterns" begins with this Kafkaesque opening: "It is said, of the millions who undertake the journey, that the greatest number are lost somewhere along the way." Still, the narrator adds, we persist because "it is equally intolerable to remain where we are."

Any physical journey presumes the presence of signposts, which in literary journeys correspond to symbols. But in Fixel's parables, symbols are often difficult, if not impossible, to read because they appear as "sharp intersection[s] of competing gestures." Throughout "Flight Patterns," no course of action is explicitly suggested, and every possible revelation is undercut with qualifiers. Films "*presumably* [italics mine] reveal the fate of the missing"; there are "unexplained dots and dashes on the flickering screens"; and "the most experienced observers—using the most advanced techniques—concede that the habitual flight patterns can no longer be interpreted. . . ." Even the narrator's persistent use of ellipses suggests that just when we are about to ease into a comfortable intellectual or moral position, just when we may have a chance to "give [a name] to this land," our hopes for success unwind in a series of dots, so that the "gap between what is submitted and received continues to widen." Ultimately, all traditional symbols, along with other traditional signifiers, remain untranslatable.

Pretty dismal stuff, except that just as we are about to hang our heads in existential despair, Section Four begins with a surprising and quietly comic assertion: "I have resolved not to be upset by any of this." This is an important moment in "Flight Patterns." In spite of uncertainty, the narrator claims that the "flight" is still worth it, not just in this poem but in all the prose poems and parables that will follow. He also offers to be our guide, while again reminding us that the journey will not be easy, because "whether we travel the direct route of desire, or detours of illusion, we will still miss connection," and just "as the wind changes, the mist descends, we can no longer tell where we are."

I would argue that in Fixel's parables, being situated in this no man's land is not a bad thing. In fact, it's the only thing, and it has its advantages. We should remember Kafka's description of that moment between sleeping and waking, which he calls the "riskiest moment of the day." The narrator of "Flight Patterns" seems to suggest that this risk is necessary, and in the last section of the poem he even gives us a manual of sorts. He admits that we can keep "producing" what we mistakenly believe to be definitive texts, like "letters, photographs, documents," and then "retreat into a private retrospect" to endlessly examine them. But maybe there's a better way. "[W]hat wonder," he writes, "if we decide to give up these [speculative] wanderings, returning to this body, this present time? It may then occur to us that what signifies this world is nothing else but the current of our feeling."

This is where I think Fixel's parables differ from Kafka's. Fixel asserts our strength as individuals, even as he accepts the incomprehensibility that Kafka so intricately praises and damns in "On Parables." Like his fellow WPA poet David Ignatow, Fixel's genes are full of optimism—a guarded optimism perhaps, but one nevertheless. Consequently, we should take heart because, as he suggests in another prose poem/parable called "Above It All": "Even now someone is at work in a garage, a small shed, to find a solution. . . . Some morning soon, a figure will appear on a roof, waiting to lift off. Not an apparition, I assure you, but someone like ourselves . . . "

Someone, of course, like Lawrence Fixel.

PETER JOHNSON is the founder and editor of *The Prose Poem: An International Journal*. Past issues can be found at http://digitalcommons.providence.edu/prosepoem. His own most recent book of prose poems is *Old Man Howling at the Moon*. His earlier book of prose poems, *Miracles & Mortifications*, received the James Laughlin Award from the Academy of American Poets. He also edited the anthology *A Cast-Iron Aeroplane That Can Actually Fly: Commentaries from 80 American Poets on Their Prose Poetry*.

Christina Fisher

Measures & Insistencies:
Days with Lawrence Fixel

What is interesting, I think, is that which one does *say, over
and over, without being really aware of it. For better or for
worse, these insistencies must be the measure of one's acts.*
                                        —Robert Creeley

I first met Lawrence Fixel through Sharon Coleman, a fellow graduate student at San Francisco's New College who needed someone to fill in as his archivist while she went to live on a kibbutz in Israel for the summer. It was the spring of 2000; Sharon and I were at a women's poetry group, and Sharon asked if anyone was interested in helping Larry while she was gone. By nature I'm shy, especially so in those days in the world of poetry; I'm not sure why I said yes, but I did.

The next week we went to Larry and Justine's house on Willard Street and I met him. The first thing that struck me was the color of his eyes: almost black, curious and wise with a childlike innocence, as if he were looking at me from some watery depth. There was also a look of mischief, not lost on me. The next thing that amazed me was his office: a window-surrounded room off the back of their second-story flat with wavy rolled-glass windows, a view of cypress trees, and the sound of parrots squawking. "Those are the parrots of Telegraph Hill," he told me. That was the first of many times the parrots would visit when we'd meet to talk and organize his papers.

Larry loved those birds and said they were a sign of good luck. He was a big believer in luck. That always surprised me, because he was such a realist, but one of his favorite sayings was, "It's important to be lucky." And he meant it. Larry was not one to speak flippantly of things—his gravity showed itself in his language and his presence; his jokes were dark even in their light. I think that a lot of his belief in luck was Justine's doing—she loved Chinese symbolism and Chinese artifacts.

Larry loved that view from the window, and as his appointed archivist, I'm almost embarrassed to admit that we spent more time talking about ideas and readings and poets than we did organizing papers.

Often, we'd talk about Milton's sonnets, the way they roll off the tongue and their political implications, or of his days listening to classical music with Carl

Rakosi, or when he was in the Merchant Marine, at sea for months on end. Usually, he'd come up with a new "Three-Word World," a way of distilling a view of the world that blew our day's conversation wide open. He always treated my ideas and questions as equal to his own.

Looking back, after assisting Jerry Fleming in assembling Larry's work in this book, I can see more clearly that during those days together we were talking about the very bones of Larry's inspirations and inquisitions. His world was a constant series of formulations and questions rolling back on themselves; he found meaning in places that had been abandoned or disregarded by most.

George Oppen was one of Larry's favorite contemporaries and comrades. He loved the fact that Oppen stopped writing "in order to be a political person" when he and his wife went to Mexico, and he told me many times that he would never want his own poems to be sacrificed or labeled as political. In the same way, he took issue with reviews of his work that characterized him as a Jewish poet or a religious writer; he chose instead to take the attention as a compliment and move on. His wife, Justine, had a similar attitude toward her art and her Jungian practice, never wanting to exhibit in women-only shows or to contribute to psychology journals based solely on gender. Both were intensely interested in politics but protected their work from being used for other people's agendas.

In thinking of Oppen, I see Larry as part Objectivist in many ways. Niedecker, Zukofsky, and Rakosi were huge for him, but he never couched his ideas in any school of thought that had already been labeled—who would? There was a purity in his thinking that couldn't be pigeonholed by anyone or anything.

Yes, some reviewers speak of his work as "Jewish work" and of his work as a prose poet (and an awesome one), and still others say he was a philosopher. All of the above is true, yes; but none of the above, too. He would love that ambiguity and might repeat, in that context, that "The gift is also an obligation" or insist, "One at the service of two. In search of three. In pursuit of." It seems to me Larry's mind was never comfortable with an answer. It was the dialectic that he thrived on, almost as a scientist goes from thesis to antithesis to synthesis, but in his case, he often would be unsatisfied with that synthesis and might well push toward thesis/antithesis/new hypothesis, and then find even that new hypothesis ultimately unsatisfying. He moved into ideas the way a spiral expands while constantly keeping its true form. He put galaxies of ideas into motion with words, spoken and written.

My favorite book of his is *The Book of Glimmers*, a journal-like set of musings that includes quotes from Bachelard to the Marx Brothers and beyond. The book, published by the Menard Press, is a sixty-five-page excerpt from over one thousand pages of a Selectric-typed manuscript he was working on until the day he died. The vastness of his scope makes it hard to read a page without stopping to look something up or to write something down or to just sit and stare off into the distance for a while. The horizon—he always talked about the expanding horizon.

His poems move slowly for me, each word chosen exactly as he intended, emblems of the greater meaning he tried to impart. He was not a careerist poet, prose writer, or parable maker—he just wrote because he could, or because he could, or couldn't not.

In one of Larry's favorite books, *Sound and Sense,* Laurence Perrine speaks to the music of poetry:

> An essential element in all music is repetition. In fact, we might say that all art consists of giving structure to two elements: repetition and variation. All things we enjoy greatly and lastingly have these two elements. We enjoy the sea endlessly because it is always the same yet always different. We enjoy a baseball game because it contains the same complex combination of pattern and variation. Our love of art, then, is rooted in human psychology. We like the familiar, we like variety, but we like them combined. If we get too much sameness, the result is monotony and tedium; if we get too much variety, the result is bewilderment and confusion. The composer of music, therefore, repeats certain musical tones; repeats them in certain combinations, or chords; and repeats them in certain patterns or melodies. The poet likewise repeats certain sounds in certain combinations and arrangements, and thus gives organization and structure to verse.

One of many Fixel poems reflects Perrine's words:

By God and By Guess

By brass spokes, circle of the fluid arm,
needle's quiver in the floating bowl,
that worm of light charted in the sky—
Survival hung on precision instruments
sworn to produce that flake of land:
shape darker than any yield of dream
rising to witness what the bells foretold.

I watched the distance dissolve
churning waters wide enough to deceive

the triad of time: birds following
the wake at sunrise, the foam of evening . . .
and there it was: the chartered island
looming above the prow: sheer rock-face
of downgraded farms and salt-filled seasons
brittle acres deserted by the wind—

Departure broke the spell: waters evolved
across the turning wheel of forenoons—
belled into sleep I swam the shifting night
with lost meridians chiming in my ears . . .
Worlds later I navigate the course
that no weave of water ever alters:
here the black arrows of direction,
salt stained on brass, invert the stars—
Those islands shift in streams of time,
but one horizon bowls the numbered glass.

1972

    The beauty of this poem is that it marries sound with sense. There's a protocol
of progression in his sound from the beginning to the end. One letter exchanged for
the next makes all the difference in the elision of his words with the poem's message.
For instance, in the second stanza the *s* becoming the *d* becomes the double conso-
nant *tt* to move the meaning along a trajectory of song and sense. Words fall into
phrases that fall onto the page, making the landscape come to life. The crescendos
at the end of the second stanza, grounding itself from *I watched the distance dissolve
/ churning waters wide enough to deceive / the triad of time* to *sheer rock-face / of down-
graded farms and salt-filled seasons / brittle acres deserted by the wind—* by progressing
from the levity of the *s* to the weight of the *d*, then to be almost broken by the *rat-
a-tat-tat* of the *brittle* double *tt*. Then it's as if the poem changes "acts" in the begin-
ning of the third stanza —*Departure broke the spell: waters evolved*—by enlisting the
w and *o* and *a* to show how *Worlds later I navigate the course / that no weave of water
ever alters*. Here, it seems the weight of the disappointment of reaching a fallen land
in all its disparate shards and pieces is lifted up out of the material *spell* by way of
the woe and the rolling waters, *with lost meridians chiming in my ears . . .*

All the while, the mind of the piece becomes both abstracted and crystalline as the music does in the background—or is it foreground? Maybe both, as it's the horizon here that Larry speaks of, the one that *bowls the numbered glass.*

It seems to me this poem takes place in the opening of the field, as Robert Duncan might say, where the page acts as vessel, holding space for the music rendered in meaning and vice versa. Larry's work always shows a great fondness for the either/or and the both/and, which he addresses deeply in *The Book of Glimmers* and in his voluminous notebooks. It's the *inverted stars* he talks about; they are above and below, surrounding us on all sides, shuttling daydreams of the *rising to witness* into realities like *the chartered island* that then dive back in to swim *the shifting night.* This triad of thesis/antithesis/new hypothesis is an essential quality of Larry's work, a tool for filling the field of inquiry with a poem. I liked to watch him as his mind worked like that.

Lineage/Linkage/Legacy

An admirer of Lorine Niedecker's work, Larry appreciated a poet's efforts to condense grand meaning into its essence. Her "Condensery" was a place he would also go to find the stones hidden among the brush; maybe all his musings left us a trail, rendered a map, showed a way through complexity to clarity. He did love to say that *confusion is our true subject.* And he wasn't one to mince words, rather to examine and shed light on the dedication to the obligation of writing in the hope that a realer truth would reveal itself. His last writings took the form of the Three-Word World: endless jottings in notebooks that occurred to him spontaneously during conversations or while listening to music or watching the news. These three-word worlds distilled anything and everything into just that: three words, constantly unfolding on themselves. One of the most lucid glimmers of this sort in my mind is his Lineage/Linkage/Legacy. When I asked him how he came up with these, or whether there were any parameters for them, he said yes: they use alliteration to connect and are either rising or falling in intensity toward meaning. He knew what he was talking about, and pages and pages of these Three-Word Worlds still exist. They just kept rolling off his pen until the day he died.

Milton's Influence

Another major influence on Larry was the sounding sense of Milton's sonnets. He especially loved to recite Sonnet 18, where the sound of the rolling "O"s (*that roll'd / Mother with Infant down the Rocks. Their moans*) mimics the grief the poem portrays. I can see him now, sitting across the desk from me in the windowed office, his lips forming the *o*'s as if he were singing, his hand making a circular motion in the air, rolling into the sonnet. The poem *seats* in the sort of place you just can't shake. Larry breathed life into Milton's sonnet and emulated his ability to marry sound with sense, feeling with reason, and politics with poetry.

Sonnet 18

On the late Massacre in Piedmont

Avenge, O Lord, thy slaughter'd saints, whose bones

Lie scatter'd on the Alpine mountains cold,

Ev'n them who kept thy truth so pure of old

When all our Fathers worshipp'd Stocks and Stones;

Forget not: in thy book record their groans

Who were thy Sheep and in their ancient fold

Slain by the bloody Piemontese that roll'd

Mother with infant down the rocks. Their moans

The Vales redoubl'd to the hills, and they

To Heav'n. Their martyr'd blood and ashes sow

O're all th' *Italian* fields where still doth sway

The triple Tyrant; that from these may grow

A hundred-fold, who having learnt thy way

Early may fly the *Babylonian woe*.

There's an understanding of the victims of government in this sonnet: the bloodshed, the dying children, the mothers trying to protect them. Larry's wife, Justine, told me she didn't have children because she didn't want to have a boy the government could steal and send to war. (Now we're enlisting women in the racket!) The gravity of this sonnet for Larry was beyond all others.

Larry never pushed his own work into publication; his best friend, Edward Mycue, though, guided him toward journals, books, and readings. Mycue was a pillar and mainstay in Larry's life. A poet/polymath who worked at Stacey's Books on Market Street in downtown San Francisco for years before the bookstore closed, he possesses a grand ability to exist within the details and events of his friends' lives while also creating endless connections among his peers.

One of the last times I attempted to write this essay, I was still living in San Francisco. I couldn't get focused at home, so jumped into the car and asked for some "driving divination" about where to go so that I could enter Larry's world. After wandering across town, thinking, *This café? No. Okay, how about this bar—no—*, I drove all the way from Pacific Heights to the Lower Haight, where I finally parked and walked into a café across the street from a bookstore, and there was Ed Mycue sitting with his partner, Richard, reading the paper over coffee. Divination, most definitely.

    What is Art? Larry Fixel asked in his Glimmers. *Art is the work itself—the tracing that remains—after the hands have done. Art is what is implicit, necessary—even where there are no hands.*

CHRISTINA FISHER earned her MFA in Poetics at the New College of California and now lives in her hometown on the southern Gulf Coast of Florida. Her works have appeared from *Red Ant Press, Auguste Press, Bird & Beckett,* and in various journals. Her latest book is *Honor of Thieves.*

David Lazar

Lawrence Fixel:
Master of the Prose Poem

How delightful and lucky, how extraordinary for me that Lawrence Fixel agreed to send me some prose poems many years ago now for *Hotel Amerika*, the magazine I still edit. I had solicited them because I thought his work was so important—*important* is a lethargic word—so *wonderful*. They delighted me with their Continental verve, playful intellection, and surreal narrative graces. I was astonished and grateful, and we began a correspondence that continued until his death.

He is never as whimsical as Calvino or as outright funny as Galeano, but he has qualities of both, as well as of Kafka, whom he invokes frequently, and the parables/fables of Primo Levi. But there's the hum of Whitman in the urge to speak plainly and urgently about these frequently migratory and inevitably meditative speakers.

Fixel's masterpiece, *Truth, War, and The Dream-Game*, really parts of several previously published works by Fixel, is one of the great books of American prose poetry and parables and belongs on the short list of distinctive works of prose in the late twentieth century.

While reading Lawrence Fixel, I feel as though my own inner conscience, my sanctorum, has been safely invaded by a benign interlocutor. As with all masterful prose writers, Fixel writes with a flexible set of pronouns and doesn't shy away from the first person plural, a dangerous one for anyone who doesn't have our moral, intellectual, emotional or aesthetic allegiance. But Fixel's world, even though frequently allegorical, is very familiar and complex. It's fallen, broken, frequently dark. In "The Situation Room," the war is underway; in "The Trouble with Winds," the weather threatens to leave us bereft of home; in "The Universal Delivery Service," the narrator realizes he's deliverable, as replaceable as a package; in "The Destruction of the Temple"—well, need I extrapolate? Nevertheless, no disaster or intimation of world's dark heart is ever unabashed by the irony of hope. Sometimes, that comes in the form of a recognition that what is happening is just or that the causation is due to our own recognizable calumny. And Fixel will write his narrative response with a neutral acceptance of consequences that borders on the cheerful. See what we've done? Well, so, perhaps we can do better in the future, if there is one.

At other times, Lawrence Fixel seems to combine the harmonic responses of a modern Stoic or a Hinduistic Jew, who sees the trouble we cause ourselves and others by imposing our will, projecting desire, and failing to see the limitless possibilities in the quotidian. In "The Feathers of My Wife," he watches her and himself in memory. He sees her and the setting she is in clearly, but "we seldom walked side by side," he feels. But then, that memory of distance transforms into the distance of memory: "The true distance, I think is in the seeing." The emotional epistemology is the problem, but it is determinant: "What is there to add; what is there to take away? What has escaped me, what has escaped her, that this is not enough?" This is a masterful and inevitable conclusion.

One understands reading these prose poems the full nature of what the form can accomplish, convening narrative, philosophy, and epigram in a page. And the work in *Truth, War, and the Dream-Game* and Fixel's other mature prose poems is so consistently extraordinary that if the prose poem were taken as seriously as it should be, if it were seen as thrilling a form as it is, Fixel would be in the most exclusive canon of modern American writers.

Consider this: "Angel in the Freezer." It's a prose poem by most technical definitions: a one-page piece of prose in concentrated language that has lyrical elements but does not lineate. It begins, rather talky, about a problem with masks, specifically an angel and a devil mask that are worm-infested, moves briskly through the problematic nature of the collector, and ends openly, with a question (many of Fixel's prose poems are like essays in *minima forma*): Should we necessarily preserve even angels and devils who are destined for the trash: "how did we dare to interfere"? Of course, the question bleeds out into so much else. How did we interfere, indeed. There is a stark opulence of philosophical tableau in many of Lawrence Fixel's prose works, of declaration as drama: "the man waiting to be admitted by the Doorkeeper," with keys but missing doors. Or, "It has just occurred to me that I, too, have moved to another country," says the narrator of "The Circus/The Zoo," about his impending change from one employment to another, leaving behind the bearded lady. . . ." In "Limbo," from *Chance Scripts: Selected Prose Poems*, the writer of "another book" realizes that "it is I who have been placed in the hands of strangers." Fixel's grounded sense of the surreal in statement, his gentle severity, which is another way of saying his embrace of paradox, leads us again and again to strange moments—estranged moments—where the disquietingly poised speaker understands the world to be the obverse or inverse of what he thought at first ("I see now what I have retreated from"; "I am wise enough now to know that the story is like all other stories . . . ."; "As for the question I started with . . . that too appears in a different light"). Revelation is usually an ironic or partial dispensation, hinted at elliptically, or bestowed in the margins of insight, not in the full body of comprehension: "And yet when we think of how difficult it has been to have come this far, think of how many of the brightest and the best have fallen along the way. . . ." ("The Fourth Step"). At such moments, Fixel seems to me almost like a kind of Midrashian Beckett, skeptical, perplexed, considering abstruse conundrums, wandering between anxiety and amusement.

There is a distinct Fixel cosmos where ideas, questions, the occasional clown or tree, a telegram or shovel interact to stir the speaker to take us on a foray into a prose disquisition, poetic, distinct, Heraclitian, with a gentle interrogatory that is capable of making us think of things we've never thought before. Whenever I enter his work, it's difficult for me to pry myself away, so enveloping are his worlds, his unexpected pronouns and nouns: "Nothing is more enticing than. . . . that swarm of possibilities" ("The Examination").

DAVID LAZAR edits the literary magazine *Hotel Amerika* and is a professor of nonfiction in the Department of Creative Writing at Columbia College in Chicago. Among his awards is a Guggenheim Fellowship, 2015–16.

Donald L. Soucy

On Lawrence Fixel's
Truth, War, and the Dream-Game

When I first opened Lawrence Fixel's *Truth, War, and The Dream-Game,* I resisted the impulse to start reading at the beginning, to enter, as it were, by way of the front door. Consequently, I went around the *porte-cochère* of the prefatory materials, the opening apothegms, even the table of contents, for what I wanted was to experience the book and the mind behind it as I imagined one would experience the dream-game itself—by playing randomly and learning the rules as I went along. (In another context, doesn't Borges observe that "life and dreams are leaves of the same book: reading them in order is living; skimming through them is dreaming")? I wanted to dream, for unfettered by expectations, I reasoned, I would encounter truth, or rather, truth would come to me unexpectedly, presenting itself with a quiet, "Here I am."

Imagine, then, my surprise and my slight discomfiture when, for no particular reason, I found myself reading the following passage from "Reading Borges":

> For years, I avoided reading him. Then one day, at the urging of friends, I read a few of the parables. . . . I saw at once how one could become intrigued with that intricate vision. . . . there was still the dazzling example of a "world in which somehow we are permitted to enter". . . . [Jean] Perrier's phrase underlies the danger. Especially the word *somehow,* with its suggestion of an "entrance" into another realm—without knowing how we got there, how to manage the passage, the return. . . .

A warning? A clue? Encouragement? Admonition? The speaker is describing the *ficciones* of Borges, but the speaker is also suggesting that any reader entering the world of prose poems and parables is subject to the same dangers, especially that of managing the return. I had broken into the book/world as a thief only to discover that I had been anticipated. The world of Lawrence Fixel, as that of Borges, is a world in which we are *somehow* permitted to enter—a world of Bachelardian spaces and Borgesian labyrinths. I have liked the metaphor of the poem as an interior space ever since I read Robert Bly's wonderful evocation of the farm granaries in his "Warning to the Reader." In that poem, the speaker describes how birds who have entered the empty buildings are tricked by the play of light on the walls and never find their way out again. In this way, the writer of poems is warned against letting the reader out too easily: "Writers, be careful then by showing the sunlight on the walls not to promise the anxious and panicky blackbirds a way out!" The reader, however, is told to beware: "Readers who love poems of light may sit hunched in the corner with nothing in their gizzards for four days, light failing, the eyes glazed . . . / They may end as a mound of feathers and a skull on the open boardwood floor . . ."

The speaker is addressing all who build word structures and all who enter them, but the warning is to the reader. When we read parables, we enter the vaulting spaces of a prose form whose intention is to hook us into staying long enough to see how it comes out. By staying, we are tricked into learning a simple lesson that may indeed be the one we need. With his sly allusion to Borges, Fixel has prepared me, then, to be a reader of parables; he will not hold my hand, certainly, and he will not give me a map out of the labyrinth, but he will beckon, invite, share, perhaps even trap me into staying much longer than I intended.

Fixel, in his own words, uses parables to convey what he calls "the distilled essences of a fragmented world." But which world is he talking about? Borges's world is literary, self-reflexive; Fixel promises us more, I think, for the concreteness of the last image in "Reading Borges," that of a caribou suddenly appearing "in that untouched elsewhere," suggests a reality beyond the "fragrances" of those "endless shelves," a reality that we encounter not in our libraries or in our readings, but paradoxically in our mundane, fragmented lives. This realization, in turn, suggests to me why Fixel chooses the parable form, with its traditions of moral teachings and of the broad implications of the lessons learned. "Therefore speak I to them in parables," Jesus is quoted by Matthew, "because they seeing see not; and hearing they hear not, neither do they understand" (Mt 13:13–15). I wonder if Fixel, by using the parable, points to a reality implicit in all parables —that there are two kinds of listeners: the privileged few and the many nonbelievers. To make sense of the parable, to gather its meaning, the listener must be willing to believe that the parable does contain a truth. This demands a tremendous faith on the part of the reader/listener, as much as it demands a tremendous restraint on the part of the writer/teller. The reader must work at it; the writer must not disclose too readily. I suspect, then, that this restraint is behind the complicated intentions of a long se-lection from the book, "The Choice," which describes a claustrophobic atmosphere of legerdemain, the world of the initiate and master (or of therapist and patient). I detect strains of both, but the ambience here is just right for this contest of wills between the believer and the unbeliever. Says the speaker, "All I can make of this, in terms of choice, is that it seems to exclude retreat." Can this mean that the choices are limited to acceptance or rejection? In just a few lines, then, in a few images,

Fixel has communicated an almost perfect ambiguity—the only way, ultimately, in which truth can be revealed.

In working my way backward and forward in the book, I hear or see a line here or an image there that stuns me with its felicity or freshness. In this way, I snatch at the title "The Loaves/The Fishes." Because it is one of my favorite New Testament stories, I stay to read it. The allusion to the miracle is obvious, and yet what Fixel does here with it is suggest that language and writing are miracles to feed a multitude. The speaker goes on to describe a dream in which he becomes Jesus. The artist as Christ is not a new idea; James Joyce spent his entire life refining and refashioning it until the artist's own flesh and blood become the paper and ink of his own dream book. Here, however, Fixel stays with the fish and the loaves. He conjures up an enormous fish that is fashioned to feed a multitude, in this case one with "carrot slices for eyes . . . cucumber wedges for scales, wavering lines of mayonnaise to represent the sea." Mocks the speaker, "Do we eat the words?" I like this terrific image, for as a chef conjures up fishes and seas with a wave of his pastry tube, so, too, does the poet fashion for us worlds on silver platters, and now the allusion is not so obvious, for the *logos* here, the word *fashioned,* shimmers like an optical illusion. The meaning is there and yet it isn't there. The word creates a reality, and yet the reality is that these are just words. This may be what Gilbert Ryle calls "ideation": "the reader imagines not only the object but "makes present in the image something which is not given." What we have here is the gastronomical certainty of something to eat, but one "can't eat the words." We are given the word, and the word is fish. We are given a fish, and we are not given a fish; even the fish fashioned by the chef is not a fish but something made to look like a fish. We are given, it seems to me, a promise of a reality disguised as art posing as a reality. And yet, I like the conundrum and the subversiveness of it all. Unlike *to construct*, to make, to build, the verb *to fashion* has the right connotations: to influence, but especially to contrive. I am in a labyrinth indeed. And Fixel's enormous joke, "In the beginning there was a loaf, a fish," radiates until I am back on my own and not quite so sure-footed as I was when I first began.

It was at this point, however, that I began to apprehend—though not entirely comprehend—something behind Fixel's narrowing of the distinction between the parable and the prose poem. In Fixel's work, we have both the image-making (I prefer *vates* to *poetas)* that we associate with poetry, and the storytelling of the parable. As poet, Fixel takes words out of their disusages and forces our attention on their myriad possibilities. We also have the terse dramatic structures and resonant voices of a master *raconteur.*

I am struck as well by the enormous seriousness of the play, but I like, too, the wit and the ironies, and the games of the trickster, and never more so than in what has become my favorite selection of the book, "The Poet Digs a Hole." In this delightfully funny and acerbic parable, a poet is described as digging a hole, and not being clear "as to what brought him here." The speaker comments, "Whatever the case, the poet has again undertaken a project involving intense labor, leading to another absurd outcome. And not only the labor, but the purchase of a shovel— when his imagination could have invented one. One that could be lying on the ground next to *the red wheel barrow glazed with rain water, beside the white chickens*."

But in the last paragraph, the speaker notes the theorists and critics who have advice for the poet and adds, "Let us leave it then for some future archaeologist puzzling over a series of holes apparently started and then abandoned—with not a single artifact in sight." The idea of the reader as archaeologist here is tantalizing. As a rule, archaeologists sift through a civilization's ash pit, looking for clues, forming impressions, peering through abandoned intentions and discarded masks. But here, is the poet digging a hole for us to examine, or to fall into? The speaker warns that there are no artifacts. Is the reader, then, the archaeologist digging and sifting with infinite care the site of some disappeared author to gather some insight, some imaginary fancy, to reconstruct a past from the vague impressions left by things? Or are we thieves in the night, letting ourselves in and stealing away furtively, the detritus of a night's work in our satchels? It is a tribute to Fixel and his work that answers to these questions are not forthcoming but that the questions themselves are still worth considering.

DONALD L. SOUCY's essay first appeared in *The Prose Poem*, Volume 2, 1993. Permission granted by Peter Johnson, editor.

Edward Mycue

1. to begin

i am revisioning here, looping backward on some primitive or primal vision quest, the kind that becomes formalized and discussed in cultural studies classes, the phenomenological journey that i will describe here/now as *Journey for a Witness*, the name of the never-published novel lawrence fixel wrote in those rome years (1960–63) that i first read in manuscript in 1971. it is a journey for a witness in a shifting landscape. this is/can be good or/& bad if it is thought of as "dissembling"—something justine jones fixel abhorred: a conscious altering of what happened, depending on your point of view. it can be what propaganda means to us in the worst sense of public lying: a manipulation of truth, not just of facts finally but essentially truth. so there is the disassembly or dis-assembling ("dis" is the lower, underworld, of disharmony, discord, associated with pluto, its god, hades), but it is also a rereading, a re-visioning, a re-framing, new orchestration of old information: information re-viewed, re-seen, re-interpreted, an imagining the event/the speech or/and physical happening from other angles, from other interlocutors, other witnesses. and in this journey it is the nature of witnessing and the recall of the witness. here i part from ludwig wittgenstein, who said you shouldn't speak what can't be clearly expressed: my way is to experience what unfolds and to look at all of it as evidence. so my writing is a swiveling journey of weaving assessment/reassessment. thus i don't retreat from or remove the record of my experience (no such soviet "erasures") however faulty. tomorrow is another re-calling and inch by inch like a snail leaving my trail, the dried goo of it may later appear in a moondream of my youth as a kind of diamond dust just as the glittery broken glass & trash did in that grungy alley behind dartmouth street in boston's southend in 1960 when i went from denton, texas, for more graduate study there. i tell what i remember & as process corrects/re-corrects as each time reconnects, re-braids i could call this memory/meditation "bumps & dimples" the way it recedes & comes forward in the convex & concave—hills & dales, lakes & streams, wells & springs of incidence & coincidence—co-inside/co-outside: the stigmata of mortality that some might consider history yet is but some scattered remains & this a civil testament of it.

2. justine jones fixel

she was from bingham canyon and salt lake city, utah, and she loved the name of her younger cousin jersey justine, justine being the name given to girls all down the generations. her people, mom's and dad's folks, were breakaway mormons. a "justine" said to be the youngest of joseph smith's "six" wives taken in by brigham young to the promised land of utah when smith was murdered in illinois. justine came to san francisco at 21 with a b.a. from the catholic women's college in salt lake city. her dad had a bar in bingham canyon (that city no longer exists because of the copper mines tunneled underneath) and later in salt lake city, and there would be poker games in their salt lake city house late into the night. her brother kendall, ten years older, had come earlier to the university in berkeley. justine went into social work, but i don't recall it that was her first job. when the war began she became a WAC and lived with jean broadbent, winifred lair, cecelia hurwich ("92 stairs," says cecelia, to get to their apt penthouse at 1230B washington st between jones & taylor in "the casbah" on nob hill). farwell taylor (who mingus wrote "farewell, farwell" for) also lived in the casbah and did a painting of justine & cecel, lifetime best pals. bari rolfe also goes back then, & warren anderson who played a beautiful piano and became kendall's lifelong partner. after the war, following an interval of modeling & partying & before getting her master's from the social welfare school at uc berkeley, justine was a social worker, & around that time worked for the canon kip program, still going, of the episcopal church (canon kip was a san francisco hero of 1906 earthquake days). i recall her stories of spending nights with kids rescued, before they were able to be placed, in the loft of the old bldg on 19th avenue and ortega that later became, for decades, the san francisco music conservatory (before its recent move to oak/van ness/market). justine met larry by or in 50s. they'd both been married before. (larry had a daughter and a granddaughter and grandson.) justine & he married 50 some years ago. justine got a fulbright to italy to consult on changing their social work system at university level, etc., and had extensions twice—rare, three years in rome, 1960–63, while larry wrote. they came back a year and headed for mexico for another year (looking for george price, larry's best bud, and to see if they could somehow figure if they could find a way to support/live there). turned out later they'd crossed w/george returning to sf where he became a professor of writing at sf state and perhaps had then met zdena berger. zdena wrote *Tell Me Another Morning*, published 1961, republished in 2007 by paris press as a re-found woman hero writer—about surviving the camps—she was from prague and the only one who survived of her wide family. justine when i first knew her in 1970 was teaching at uc berkeley in the school of social work and practicing as a founding member of the family therapy center in sf (then a pioneering approach).

she had a long, productive life. larry used to complain that justine was a great source of "misinformation" and that amused her because maybe only larry could be teased that way and I heard it as "mixedinformation." in a poem I wrote for my memory of her "fish in a net" (the title's yeatsian) there's influence of dh lawrence (death ship), reference to milton also (the "westering" of his lycidas), influence for mood and the vocabulary of emotions mainly by may swenson (another western girl–utah?), elizabeth bishop, josephine miles ("family," specifically), william carlos williams, ann stanford ("our town"), englishwomen elizabeth jennings, stevie smith, ruth fainlight, and a bit of theodore roethke—these and auden and dylan thomas form a mix when i think of her. probably others. but i take responsibility for this development of a poem i've been writing in my mind and in forty versions to the shade of our west coast "stranger" poet robinson jeffers (and una his wife/muse/doppelganger) because— well, as larry said again and again: *nobody gets out of here alive.*

3. and justine jones fixel

in her practice, justine's "sand tray" therapy, its development and her teaching, its use, all lead back to her work as a painter of oil on canvas, to her incorporations, assemblings, environments with miniature figures, furniture, the natural world & symbols, including her last great achievement "the white house," her venetian paintings, a series of frieze-like sculptures suffused with jungian themes, & household objects combined into a mixed conglomeration arranged into painted autobiography and family history (much of this documented on film by al leveton). memories of justine, of larry, names that drift up, constellate & swim, a history, pantheon, honorable people. I thought of ruth witt-diamant again last night (justine & larry's neighbor and friend who began the poetry center at san francisco state) & thanked her for all her kindnesses; oldest friends george & mary oppen, through whom I met lawrence & justine fixel in 1970; of florence hegi, oldest of the family therapy group of friends & colleagues (al & eva leveton, bob cantor hovering over her to the very end) that justine belonged to: al & eva with ben handleman, the prime founders of the family therapy center, & virginia belfort, sue eldredge, roz parenti, michael geis. neighbors, too, in those early days: lois and roy steinberg & julian, then five, now a photographer; mark citret (ansel adams's last student, then 22—eminent now); of al and minnie (a founding member of the california communist party, related to my sister jane by marriage) and their daughter laura bock down high willard street; judy pollatsek and her kids josh & jessica; the wolfes on farnsworth steps; al palavin; agar & diana jaicks, big democratic people (diana eleanor roosevelt's niece, grew up with E.R.); a nice couple w/kids the goldsworths (he at ucsf & judy) next to ruth witt's; & memories of anaïs nin when she was lodged uphill in a cottage ruth found for her; the then taos-bound dorothy kethler; & in taos, bob eliot, who built, said justine, "the ideal house"; jo lander; florida & angela who worked for the un's fao in rome; bill minshew whom they first met in rome; george hitchcock; cass humble; edouard roditi who often returned from france to stay with them; an old schoolmate of ruth's at uc berkeley in the 30's; james broughton; justine van gundy who taught at sf state; her san diego cousin dianne cawood, a soprano; diane scott her therapist; tom, stephanie, dante sanchez; always cecelia ("cecel," "cese") & b.j., lynn, rudy hurwich; larry's nephew robbie berkelman; & "old jack" (w.w. lyman, jr.) of bayles mill—born there in napa valley 1885–ruth brought me over to meet ("the oldest living poet"). she'd drive up to bring him down to san francisco. i was ruth's gardener & the then-young poet, 35, she wanted lyman to connect with, his wife helen hoyt an esteemed poet who'd been assistant editor to harriet monroe at poetry magazine in chicago, helen dead a decade or more by then (w. w. lyman's three volumes of typed memoir—he lived to 1983, leaving a son, amos hoyt at bayles mill—are in the st. helena, ca public library's locked room); & others who made their entries but whose names now escape me but will possibly come tomorrow; folks we met, knew together—panjandrum press & poetry flash crowds & dennis koran; richard steger; lennart & sonia bruce; shirley kaufman; anthony rudolf; jo-anne rosen; laura beausoleil; david & judy gascoyne; sybil wood/cooper; jack marshall; morton marcus; sharon coleman; gerald fleming; carl rakosi & marilyn kane. many gone before justine & so many more left because this was a woman who knew people & was interested in them: remembering her is to consider friends you make in life, who contributed to who you became, whom you've helped, who've helped you. in the final days, weeks, months, years, close were naomi schwartz, josephine moore, gail lubin, christina fisher, toby damon, andrea rubin, marsha trainer, al & eva leveton, ken meacham & pearl, wendy rosado-berkelman (larry's sister pearl fixel berkelman's daughter), her daughter sunya, tom sanchez, cecilia london (justine's student at uc berkeley who returned to justine in those four years after larry's death as justine's guide/social worker), & always stephanie sanchez, bob cantor, naomi, al & eva, george & zdena, cecel & don—friends, colleagues, confidantes. accretion, attrition. vale.

EDWARD MYCUE was a Lowell Fellow at Boston University, served in the Peace Corps (Ghana), and was a MacDowell Fellow. His books include *Damage Within the Community*, *The Singing Man My Father Gave Me*, *Torn Star*, *Mindwalking*, *Song of San Francisco*, and *I Am a Fact Not a Fiction*. He has published in hundreds of literary magazines, and his archives can be found at Yale's Beinecke Library.

Sharon Coleman

Parable, Parabola, Possible: On Lawrence Fixel

Lawrence Fixel fashioned and inhabited a mental organization of patience. The careful putting into place of elements of the knowable—a puzzle that can be rearranged when new information and, perhaps, knowledge arrives. A syntax of existence that maintains many empty slots for the possible to fill, even tentatively, in the making of meaning. A certain hospitality of thought. A patience for what may or may not come. A slowing down, so when something comes, you recognize it and begin to consider what has arrived.

Parable

He lived in an upper flat on a hill behind UCSF, the medical school. He and Justine moved to Willard Street in the 1950s. I'd ring the bell and wait to be buzzed in, then push the heavy door to look up a tall staircase. Step by step, I'd enter the collected layers of their lives. Justine's paintings lined the stairwell walls; near the top landing, a recent photograph of Lawrence—black and white—him leaning against a circular window and looking straight into the camera lens. In the hallway more photos, paintings, masks. To the right was his office—immaculately organized with file cabinets, bookshelves, every issue of *Parabola* magazine on the top shelf of his closet. A typewriter, desk, whiteboard, scattered notes. Past the office, another room—with an almost empty desk, an old Mac computer given to him by his grandson, which he hardly used, more books, and two walls of windows—a panoramic view of San Francisco, its hills, all the way to the bay. Here is where he sat, thought, and wrote. Here, we spent time talking—because the organizing he hired me for was mostly already organized. He sat facing the windows, and I him, the desk between us. On that desk, a thick needle mounted on wood on which he'd impale his various notes—glimmers, ideas. Here I first witnessed how ink could fade in the light.

Possible

Like an actor leaving the stage for the unstaged world, he emptied the parable of plot, of lesson, of the tight structure of an easy morality. His parables are well situated within the randomness of the daily world, let whatever comes to hand come to mind. His parable approaches the skill of the card players in god's or our dreams, a thinking along the chance shuffle and draw.

Parabola

Among his notes on the needle were collections of three words—Three Word Worlds, he called them, words like *zone, mood, phase* or *imagine, explore, discover.* I'd think of what those words could open and what they'd close. I'd think of what Oppen wrote in one of his Daybooks, that three words are not enough. I'd think of writing thirty poems for three of his words.

Parable

"You're intelligent," he said. He seemed surprised. After a few meetings, he asked me if he could record our conversations. I said no.

Possible

He was mostly self-taught. His first job writing was for the WPA in New York City under the direction of Richard Wright before the war. He tried Hollywood then Los Angeles but moved north. He attended Ruth Witt-Diamant's poetry salon on this hilly street and decided to move in a few doors down.

Parable

His narrator, his "I," enters the words of stories to narrate, dramatize, personalize a quandary. There's never a lesson or a truth but the dream of the pursuit of a truth— and the questioning of the pursuit itself.

Possible

He said he never votes. It's like a vote of no confidence in other countries. Because one is only given the choice of the lesser evil.

Parabola

Together they were Lawrence and Justine—an Italian writer sarcastically joked, he said, at all the parings of their names implied, like law and justice—of course they were Lawrence and Justine, and they weren't.

Possible

The meanings of his parable have not yet arrived and are always yet to come. Meanings become messianic—until we realize they rest with the reader. Our interpretations are what we've waited for and not yet realized.

Parable

I've revisited public tragedies that occurred during my young days—the mass suicide of People's Temple, the assassinations at San Francisco City Hall. Strange tragedies that opened many questions and that I've considered from different perspectives, sometimes from survivors, sometimes from Larry's prose. This revisiting what keeps us unsettled is not at all unlike his many reworkings of poems over the years—most so meticulously dated—and the drafts of each revision he kept in a single file folder in a drawer.

Parabola

From the Greek: "placing side by side" or "to throw beside." His writing often included the physicality of writing—the hands and gestures, the body in a specific place, the environment or even ecology, the writing instruments and paper.

Possible

One night he got up shortly after 1 a.m. and walked through the short hallway to the living room, to the front window then covered by black netting due to construction. In the corner, he collapsed. Justine woke at the noise. His last thoughts? The coroner declared that he died of old age, an experience denied to many.

Parable

When Justine was packing up the house to move on and asked me what I wanted, I requested his wooden file cabinet. She split a matching pair of file cabinets between me and another assistant. In his office with no more books on the shelves, I glimpsed a list of poems on the whiteboard written in my hand years before.

Possible

The parabola represents the epitome of a quest. It is the metaphorical journey to a particular point, and then back home, along a similar path perhaps, but in a different direction, after which the traveler is essentially, irrevocably changed.

—*Parabola* magazine

SHARON COLEMAN writes for *Poetry Flash*, co-curates the reading series Lyrics & Dirges in Berkeley, California, and co-directs the Berkeley Poetry Festival. She is the author of the poetry chapbook *Half Circle* (Finishing Line, 2013) and a book of micro-fiction, *Paris Blinks* (Paper Press, 2016).

Peter Money

"Let's Start Where We Are"
—Lawrence Fixel

What this volume contributes is extraordinary, because Lawrence Fixel is one of the most gifted so-far-underacknowledged writers of the twentieth and twenty-first centuries. Like Pulitzer Prize–winning writer Heinrich Böll's preoccupation with "arrivals and departures," Franz Kafka's "amusement" in absurdity not at all discontinuous from history, and Italo Calvino's recognition and acceptance of enigmatic character, Fixel's lifelong writings are the work of a writer's writer whose posthumously collected humane documents could be a reader's triumph—and timely rescue.

I suppose I ought to set the scene as Larry would.

I was Larry's assistant for a few years toward the end of his life. True to Larry Fixel's studied demeanor and concentrated habits—somewhere between methodical and improvised—the times I spent with him would amount to lessons in trust and patience. I was probably an impulsive young man, even in dawning middle age, and Larry was my opposite. There was never any rush. We worked at whatever pace time and circumstance gave us ("Don't push the river," Larry would say, or, typically, it was a collective "Let's not push the river"—together). As much as he needed my assistance, he was teaching me: I the hurried young man and he the sage. We set our own stage.

I had come to Larry's attention via Carl Rakosi, Larry's friend down the street, as Allen Ginsberg had sent me to Rakosi. As it turned out, Larry needed help, and the "happenstance" of our relationship would seem to characterize much of Larry's personal and writing life. Gale Publishers had requested his autobiography, and at an advanced age, he enlisted me to help him meet the deadline. Our method would be the interview, itself a very "Fixelesque" solution to the need to turn years into pages in fairly short time.

Larry's study, or office, was really two small rooms at the back of the long flat. The flat itself was perched on the edge of Willard Street's primary plateau, not far from the UCSF hospital. Streams of eucalyptus and the peculiar mounds of Twin Peaks, above us to the south, were practically upon the house. The first of the modest office rooms had a central table where an electric typewriter sat. Mostly spare in terms of décor, there were a few shelves for books. On one of these, old *kayak* magazine volumes stood out as having the most aged patina. The end room was really a third-story, three-season porch. We both liked this room because it felt like a tree house, or a tearoom in the hills. Cole Valley's backyards and the tops of trees showed from this room, almost like an ocean. Here, work awaited on a small table and two or three small shelves. Near the floor, Larry's "Italian" novel sat on the lower shelf of a short stand, clean and tidy as a pressed shirt, with its cardboard cover as if waiting for the postman. Years were in this room, even though the overall feeling was "minimal." It was a space where thinking took place, Larry's "glimmers" among them.

In addition to creating an autobiography for Gale, we were preparing Larry's archives for the Bancroft Library at the University of California at Berkeley. Sometimes Larry's partner, Justine, would be in their nearby bedroom or kitchen. Together the two offered a sort of antique reassurance, tranquil and prone to the efficient comment or question. We talked about all manner of things, particularly the state of the world. Their natural joy, an endurance, was measured by disdain for the worst daily news and by the sympathy they expressed for devastating situations around the world. Justine, a Jungian, was an insightful, constant mate to Larry.

Before we began the autobiography sessions, I would sit looking south toward Larry while he faced me looking north toward San Francisco Bay. I envied his position a little. Looking north, he could see the University of San Francisco, where some of his friends taught. But south, there were memories of the many important writers who visited San Francisco State University and its Poetry Center founder, who also lived on Willard Street. Larry would slowly reach for a match, strike it—sometimes two—and light a bowl of tobacco. A ceremony of the moment; I grew to enjoy this moment each time. It was his thinking ritual. His eyes rolled up after two or three quick puffs. "Now, let's begin at the beginning," he might say.

He loved his single-insight aphorisms, which—toward the end of his life—sometimes took all day, even days. Initially, during the time I visited the Fixels regularly, Larry's aphorisms were threefold, then became twofold. He took pride in piecing together profound coincidences from allusions between the weekly news and allegory.

Readers should know that Fixel was erudite but humble, self-belittling but important, in need but perfectly happy. He came from "modest hard-working" immigrant parents, and by all known accounts had a happy and loving childhood. Like many kids, but perhaps in his case as a child of immigrants, his personal trajectory seemed paced by daydream and an individualistic pursuit of what it would mean for him to be both accepted and be a pioneer. As it happened, Fixel was one of the youngest WPA writers involved with the Federal Writers Project (only months before joining the Project, he had worked as a caddy at an exclusive golf course).

Among other things (also a title of one of his works), Larry's studied "silence" printed itself upon the page. Fixel's writing is full of travelers, actors, civil servants, and lovers, each asking multiple questions—as though they were on a quest, as if in addition to their "job" they were compelled not just to find answers but to ask questions. (Let us remember that Kafka's example was important to Larry.) I refer to Larry's Gale Contemporary Authors introduction, in which he wants us to remember: "being Jewish at the time of Nazism and the 'unthinkable' and 'unspeakable' were among the major events." These circumstances shaped him also. As he said, this world view gave him a "different sensitivity" from other American kids in Westchester County and elsewhere. Although I knew him to be always comfortable there on Willard Street, Larry understood he was always an "outsider"—as the Gale interview *[Editor's note: see footnote in Introduction]* bears out.

How ironic, then, is his assertion in "The Conspirators," in which the rather Fixel-like speaker says:

> . . . I seem to be getting it all wrong. Making the familiar mistake of equating the unexplained with a foreboding . . . perhaps I ought to admit that I have little to offer in the way of any genuine "disclosure." . . . Whereas all I can do is suggest what may be taking place in plain sight, but has as yet not been noticed.

Noticed? Haven't we noticed yet? Perhaps his writing got stuck in the problem of our time: Who will publish, who will distribute—as long as wars are fought and stocks are traded? In other words, who hears the bell one person clangs? Yet Larry knew that the events (and indeed the moments) born in "plain sight" revealed plenty. In the piece "In View of This It Begins," Fixel shows no ambiguity in making the writer's choice an act of conscience: "I extend my hand, and it is the right thing." He believed in the "random" fact, and in the notion that a relationship grew—like a sort of wisdom or generosity—from the result of having approached a subject at random.

The writings of Lawrence Fixel remind us that events of our time shape us each day. How do we rise? How do we not turn away? These are questions he'd want to pose. Fixel's work also reminds us that the impermanence of the writer— and any artist, dancer, maker—may be found again, to allude to a tenet of George Oppen (who meant a lot to Larry), in the materials at hand.

The writer's conundrum is real, just as real as it is also the lasting ephemeral angst born from the longing that marks every artist who has struggled but who has given oneself to a society with too little patience to recognize and reward, let alone nurture and cultivate. Larry Fixel's example is, itself, a kind of "Letters to—" (I think both Rilke's *Letters to a Young Poet* and Thomas McGrath's *Letter to an Imaginary Friend* were positive models for him). By chance encounters, Larry met those who would become friendly forces, including the "gracious" Theodore Dreiser and the "disappointed" William Carlos Williams; he would find impetus and material in world wars, fate and injustice, personal freedom, jazz, Charles Mattox, Arshile Gorky, and Clifford Odets.

Fixel's "community of writers" was also subject to flux (his being unaffiliated with any major group and too old for the Beats) except for the stint in the WPA's Federal Writers' Project, and for the friendships formed with writers such as A. T. Rosen, Kenneth Fearing, Tom McGrath, George Hitchcock, Édouard Roditi, Carl Rakosi, Cid Corman, and Ruth Witt-Diamant. More of us came along in later years, and for most, it must be stated emphatically, Lawrence Fixel's steady (if understated) example inscribed its signature in us. It was as if through living a life of writing, beyond any fame or expectation, one could—as Larry writes in "Words Out of Reach"—"locate a source for the clear water of the soul . . ."

The sections of *The Collected Poetry and Prose of Lawrence Fixel*, exceptionally brought together by Gerald Fleming, fit together like landscape of letters *we* once wrote, or should have written, to our own family and friends. Readers will feel they have read the words before, or they have asked themselves the same words while staring into the mirror. "If only there was a voice in the picture—or a picture in the voice," Fixel asks himself before fooling himself into silence. Now the picture is yours, and the voice—whose voice is this you hear?

And addendum. There's always addendum, Larry liked to remind us. On a Menard Press (London) postcard, one side of which bears a poem by Larry from 1996 ("We speak or write of history and memory," the first stanza begins), he wrote to me, "the vision and the voyage—and always asking: 'what comes next?'"

A little more than halfway through this deservedly mammoth *Collected*, Lawrence Fixel's "Glimmers Three: Mining Shadows" is about the closing day of an exhibit of Tan-Han murals. The speaker declares this is "The work of excavation. Of restoration." He is linking the extremes for us, as Fixel himself did, identifying a way of signifying. What gets signified? A clarity, perhaps. A relationship. Words you yourself would have said, had you been in Fixel's shoes.

Lawrence Fixel had several good publishers throughout his life, but never was he properly recognized for the great work that appears here.

I like to think of Larry at his front window, the window open a bit, the breeze from the Pacific streaming in and taking with it his stream of thought, too. A near-perfect life in an imperfect time.

PETER MONEY was Lawrence Fixel's assistant from the late 1990s until 2001. Among his books are co-translations (with Sinan Antoon) of Saadi Youssef's poems, *Nostalgia, My Enemy* (Graywolf Press) and a novel, *Oh When the Saints* (Liberties Press, Dublin). He directs Harbor Mountain Press.

Publication History

Books, in order of appearance:

The Scale of Silence, kayak books, George Hitchcock, editor, Santa Cruz, 1970.

Time to Destroy/to Discover, Panjandrum Press, Dennis Koran, editor, San Francisco, 1972.

Through Deserts of Snow, Capra Press, Noel Young, editor, Santa Barbara,1975.

The Edge of Something, Cloud Marauder Press, Don Cushman, editor, Berkeley, and Menard Press, Anthony Rudolf, editor, London, 1977.

The Book of Glimmers, Cloud Marauder Press, Don Cushman, editor, Berkeley, and Menard Press, Anthony Rudolf, editor, London, 1979.

Truth, War, and the Dream-Game: Selected Prose Poems and Parables, 1966–1990, Coffee House Press, Alan Kornblum, editor, Minneapolis, 1991.

Unlawful Assembly: A Gathering of Poems 1940–1992, Cloudforms, Michael Thorp, editor, Newcastle upon Tyne, 1994.

Lost Subjects, Found Objects, Finders Keepers Press, JoAnne Rosen, editor, San Francisco, 1998.

All This Is Here, Obscure Publications, Paul Rosheim, editor, 2003.

Most of the works in this book first appeared in the following magazines, anthologies, or other publications (included in this category are "uncollected" writings that appeared only in magazines): *Alcatraz, Alea, Antenym, ARTEXT, Ashen Meal, Asylum, Barnabe Mountain Review, Bellevue Press Poetry Broadsides,*

Bottomfish, Caliban, The California Quarterly, City Lights Review, Cloud, Cold-Drill, Crazy Horse, A Curious Architecture: A Selection of Contemporary Prose Poems, Drizzle, Drunken Boat, The Expatriate Review, Exquisite Corpse, First Intensity, Five Fingers Review, 14 Voices, Frank (France), *Furious Fictions, G.P.W.I.T.D., Guabi, Heaven Bone, House Organ, Impasses* (France), *Imperial Messages: One Hundred Modern Parables, KPFA Folio, kayak, Key Satch(el), Madrona, Main Currents in Modern Thought, Margin 5, Meanjin* (Australia), *The Menard Press Mencards* (England), *Minotaur, MX2, New American Writing, The New Commercialist, no:tas, Notus, Panjandrum, Pearl* (Denmark), *Pebble, Pen:umbra, Poetry Flash, Poetry Now, A Poetry Reading for Peace in Vietnam, The Prose Poem (Best of), The Prose Poem, Prosodia, Red Ozier Press Broadsides, Rejection #1, Round Glow of the Family Nest* (England), *Second Aeon* (Wales), *Sky Writing, Soup, Syllogism, Talisman, Unicorn Press Poetry Broadsides,* and *Unscheduled Departures: The Asylum Anthology of Short Fiction.*

Index of First Lines/Phrases

General Index